Dylan Thomas in Print

DYLAN THOMAS IN PRINT

A BIBLIOGRAPHICAL HISTORY

Ralph Maud

Assisted by
Albert Glover

University of Pittsburgh Press

SBN 8229-3201-6
Library of Congress Catalog Card Number 78-101190
Copyright © 1970, University of Pittsburgh Press
All Rights Reserved
Manufactured in the United States of America
Henry M. Snyder & Co., Inc., London

Grateful acknowledgment is made to the National Library of Wales for permission to adapt Ralph Maud's "Dylan Thomas in Welsh Periodicals," first published in *The National Library of Wales Journal*, Vol. XV, Summer 1968.

For permission to reprint a column entitled "An Intimate Look at Dylan Thomas" (appearing here in Section IV, "United States and Canadian Periodicals and News-papers"), grateful acknowledgment is made to its author, Nelson Algren, and to the *Chicago Sun-Times*, where it was published on January 1, 1956.

For permission to reprint material from "A Note on Dylan Thomas" in *Origin*, Vol. XII, Spring 1954 (appearing here in Section IV), grateful acknowledgment is made to the author, Cid Corman.

The cover photograph of Dylan Thomas has been reproduced through the courtesy of The Bettmann Archive, Inc.

This book is dedicated to
MEIRION
and his friends at Rhydypennau School

CONTENTS

Preface
[ix]

Acknowledgments
[xi]

SECTION I
Books, Anthologies, Theses
[3]

SECTION II
Welsh Periodicals and Newspapers
[45]

SECTION III
London, etc., Periodicals and Newspapers
[87]

SECTION IV
United States and Canadian Periodicals and Newspapers
[167]

SECTION V
Foreign-Language Publications
[217]

Index
[229]

PREFACE

This book lists everything by Dylan Thomas published in his lifetime and posthumously. It lists everything written about Thomas that seemed to be of possible interest to the literary historian or the curious general reader.

The first section of this volume lists, under the year in which they appeared, the books by and about Thomas, anthologies containing pieces by him, and academic theses relating to him.

Periodical publications are grouped along geographical lines: (i) Wales; (ii) England and those areas of the world for which London is the literary center; and (iii) the United States and Canada. Periodicals within each section are arranged chronologically according to the date of the first Thomas item appearing in them.

Each section tells its own story. Introducing a shortened version of the Welsh section, published in *The National Library of Wales Journal* (Summer 1968), I said:

> It should be fairly easy to ascertain what segments of the Welsh reading public heard about Thomas and at what stage in his career. The Welsh language press seems to have paid very little attention to him until after his death, and his reputation is still insecure there. Perhaps this state of affairs will be somewhat rectified by the impact of a translation into Welsh of "Under Milk Wood," whose performance is imminent as this bibliography is presented for publication.

This comment produced a response in the *Western Mail*, Cardiff's daily newspaper. At the time of writing, the matter remains an intriguing, unfinished story.

The other sections have their own plots. In England one has to take sides: Holbrook-Grigson-Graves vs. Bayley-Sitwell-Read or some such alignment. Most of the younger dons feel that Leavis said the last word on Thomas by saying nothing, or that Holbrook did: but we have, on the other hand, Empson and Wain to assure us that Thomas has a reputation among the judicious of his own time.

Academic United States is a land of explication where one can get lost among star-maps. The only real story there is the way a number of people have put Thomas to their own use. The more serious question which some Americans have posed for themselves is: "What does it mean to have a poetic genius die on one's hands?" Thomas—as Lawrence almost did—gave the New World his body; it will be interesting to see whether or not American writers can make proper use of that.

There is a final section, foreign-language publications, a tail that wags not by any skill of the compiler but mainly by the good will and international connections of Joseph Gold of Bethesda, Maryland.

The index is full and, I trust, easy to use. It holds the reins on the idiosyncrasy of the rest of the book.

Idiosyncrasy there is, and professional bibliographers will perhaps be disturbed at missing commas. All the unusual features in the format of this bibliography have the aim of avoiding the feeling of dead weight often associated with this kind of book.

The name of Albert Glover appears on the title page because of an intense period of collaboration as teacher and graduate student during 1964 and 1965, with reunions at crucial stages thereafter. His industry allowed the editor to imagine, in the face of some doubts, that the enterprise might one day be completed.

Previous attempts to give a full account of Thomas' published output, and of his reputation as it exists in the writings of others, are almost fifteen years old. The present volume brings the picture up-to-date in a manner which is, I hope, readable and lively.

RALPH MAUD

Buffalo–Aberystwyth–Vancouver
Summer 1964–Summer 1969

ACKNOWLEDGMENTS

We would like to acknowledge the assistance of the staffs of the Lockwood Memorial Library, Buffalo; Erie County Public Library, Buffalo; National Library of Wales, Aberystwyth; University College of Wales Library, Aberystwyth; British Film Institute Information Library, London; BBC Library and Archives, London; Swansea Public Library; New York Public Library; the Academic Center at the University of Texas, Austin; Cambridge University Library; Harvard College Library, Cambridge, Massachusetts; Boston Public Library; Boston University Library; Simon Fraser University Library, Burnaby, British Columbia; University of British Columbia Library, Vancouver; New Directions Publishers, New York; J. M. Dent & Sons, London; Little, Brown and Company, Boston; and the University of Pittsburgh Press. And especially the help of Michael Geare, James Laughlin, Robert MacGregor, Douglas Cleverdon, Aneirin Talfan Davies, John Rolph, Jane MacCormick, Robert Trudell, Stanley Yonge, Donald Tritschler, J. H. Prynne, David Jenkins, Bryn Williams, Cledwyn Vaughan, Janet Croysdale, and Frederick Hetzel. Much work was done on this bibliography while the compiler was the recipient of a John Simon Guggenheim Memorial Fellowship, 1966–1967, of a Canada Council Grant, 1968–1969, and of continuing support from the President's Research Grants Fund of Simon Fraser University.

SECTION I

BOOKS

ANTHOLOGIES

THESES

1934

Dylan Thomas *18 Poems* London: Sunday Referee & Parton Bookshop 1934—an issue of 250 copies "on or within a few days of 18th December 1934."[1] Contents: the first eighteen of the *Collected Poems* (1952). Seven had not been previously published in periodicals: "Before I knocked," "My hero bares his nerves," "When, like a running grave," "In the beginning," "I fellowed sleep," "I dreamed my genesis," "All all and all the dry worlds lever."

ANTHOLOGIES

Denys Kilham Roberts, Gerald Gould, John Lehmann eds. *The Year's Poetry: A Representative Selection* London: John Lane the Bodley Head 1934. Includes "Light breaks where no sun shines" pp. 133–134.

CRITICISM, ETC.

Edith Sitwell *Aspects of Modern Poetry* London: Duckworth 1934 pp. 149–150, on "Our eunuch dreams": "An appalling affair! Metaphysics have not helped here. The idea is really of no importance, and the thick squelching, cloying, muddy substance of the 'which,' 'itch,' 'shapes,' 'starch,' 'welshing rich' verse, and the equally, or almost equally hideous 'kicks,' 'sack,' 'trash,' 'quick,' 'cock,' 'back,' 'smack,' affair—these defeat criticism."

1935

ANTHOLOGIES

Janet Adam Smith ed. *Poems of Tomorrow* London: Chatto & Windus 1935. "Chosen From *The Listener*." Includes "Light breaks where no sun shines" and "Especially when the October wind" pp. 125–128.

Denys Kilham Roberts, Gerald Gould, John Lehmann eds. *The Year's Poetry, 1935* London: John Lane the Bodley Head 1935. Includes "Especially when the October wind" pp. 141–142.

Edward J. O'Brien ed. *The Best Short Stories: 1935* London: Jonathan Cape 1935. Includes "The Visitor" pp. 206–214. U.S. edition—*Best British Short Stories of 1935* Boston: Houghton Mifflin 1935 pp. 193–200.

---

1. J. Alexander Rolph *Dylan Thomas: A Bibliography* London: J. M. Dent; New York: New Directions 1956 p. 40.

1936

Dylan Thomas *18 Poems* London: Sunday Referee & Parton Bookshop 1934—a second issue of 250 copies on 21 February 1936 (Rolph p. 41).

Dylan Thomas *Twenty-five Poems* London: J. M. Dent 1936. First impression 10 September 1936 of 730 copies (Rolph p. 43); further impressions in December 1936, February 1939, and October 1944. Contents: see *Collected Poems* (1952). Five poems had not been previously published in periodicals: "The seed-at-zero," "Shall gods be said to thump the clouds," "Here in this spring," "Out of the sighs," "Now."

ANTHOLOGIES

Denys Kilham Roberts & John Lehmann eds. *The Year's Poetry, 1936* London: John Lane the Bodley Head 1936. Includes "From love's first fever," "Where once the waters of your face," "A grief ago," pp. 118–123.

Michael Roberts ed. *The Faber Book of Modern Verse* London: Faber 1936. Includes "The force that through the green fuse" and "Light breaks where no sun shines" pp. 334–335, with mention in the Introduction.

1937

ANTHOLOGIES

Denys Kilham Roberts & Geoffrey Grigson eds. *The Year's Poetry, 1937* London: John Lane the Bodley Head 1937. Includes "We lying by seasand" and "It is the sinners' dust-tongued bell" pp. 132–134.

Anon. ed. *Welsh Short Stories* London: Faber 1937. Includes "The Orchards" pp. 416–429, which is also included in the 1959 edition, edited with an Introduction by George Ewart Evans.

Elizabeth Bowen ed. *The Faber Book of Short Stories* London: Faber 1937. Includes "The Orchards."

1938

ANTHOLOGIES

Denys Kilham Roberts & Geoffrey Grigson eds. *The Year's Poetry, 1938* London: John Lane the Bodley Head 1938. Includes "In Memory of Ann Jones" pp. 132–133.

Denys Kilham Roberts ed. *The Century's Poetry, 1837–1937* 2 vols. Harmondsworth: Penguin Books 1938. Vol. 2, which became Vol. 5 of *The Centuries' Poetry* (Penguin 1949), includes "The force that through the green fuse" and "Where once the waters of your face."

Anon. ed. *Poems of To-day. Third Series* Published for the English Association by Macmillan 1938. Includes "Especially when the October wind" and "We lying by seasand" pp. 170–172.

CRITICISM, ETC.

Louis MacNeice *Modern Poetry: A Personal Essay* London: Oxford University Press 1938 p. 160: "A good example is Dylan Thomas, who is very obscure and incoherent, but at least more human than the official surrealists; one can sometimes get into touch with him. He is like a drunk man speaking wildly but rhythmically, pouring out a series of nonsense images, the cumulative effect of which is usually vital and sometimes even seems to have a message—this message being adolescence, the discovery of the power and horror of sex and so of all the changes in nature, natura naturans. The statements as statements are nonsense, but it is obvious what his mind is drunkenly running on: [quotes 'Light breaks']."

1939

Dylan Thomas *The Map of Love* London: J. M. Dent 1939. Dedicated "To Caitlin." With portrait by Augustus John. First issue of 1000 copies was on 24 August 1939; the rest of the 2000 sheets printed were issued in three lots between April 1947 and February 1949 (Rolph p. 45). Contents: sixteen poems, see *Collected Poems* (1952), plus seven short stories:

> The Visitor
> The Enemies
> The Tree
> The Map of Love
> The Mouse and the Woman
> The Dress
> The Orchards

The entire contents of the book had previously appeared in periodicals.

Dylan Thomas *The World I Breathe* Norfolk, Connecticut: New Directions 1939. One issue—700 copies—on 20 December 1939 (Rolph p. 46). Contents of this first U.S. collection:

From *18 Poems* (1934)

1 I see the boys of summer in their ruin
2 When once the twilight locks no longer
3 A process in the weather of the heart

4   The force that through the green fuse drives the flower
5   My hero bares his nerves along my wrist
6   Where once the waters of your face
7   If I were tickled by the rub of love
8   Especially when the October wind
9   When, like a running grave, time tracks you down
10 From love's first fever to her plague
11 Light breaks where no sun shines
12 Half of the fellow father as he doubles

From *Twenty-five Poems* (1936)

13 I, in my intricate image, stride on two levels
14 This bread I break was once the oat
15 Incarnate devil in a talking snake
16 To-day, this insect, and the world I breathe
17 Here in this spring, stars float along the void
18 Do you not father me, nor the erected arm
19 Hold hard, these ancient minutes in the cuckoo's month
20 Why east wind chills and south wind cools
21 A grief ago, she who was who I hold
22 Ears in the turrets hear
23 Foster the light nor veil the manshaped moon
24 The hand that signed the paper felled a city
25 Should lanterns shine, the holy face
26 I have longed to move away
27 Grief thief of time crawls off
28 Then was my neophyte
29 Altarwise by owl-light

From *The Map of Love* (1939)

30 I make this in a warring absence when
31 When all my five and country senses see
32 It is the sinners' dust-tongued bell claps me to churches
33 The spire cranes. Its statue is an aviary
34 After the funeral, mule praises, brays
35 Once it was the colour of saying
36 How shall my animal
37 The tombstone told when she died
38 A saint about to fall
39 'If my head hurt a hair's foot'
40 Twenty-four years remind the tears of my eyes

Stories

The Dress
The Visitor

The Map of Love
The Enemies
The Orchards
The Mouse and the Woman
The Holy Six
A Prospect of the Sea
The Burning Baby
Prologue to an Adventure
The School for Witches

ANTHOLOGIES

Thomas Moult ed. *The Best Poems of 1939* London: Jonathan Cape; New York: Harcourt, Brace 1939. Includes "When all my five and country senses see" p. 22, Thomas' only appearance in a series that ran up to 1943.

Gwendolen Murphy. ed. *The Modern Poet* London: Sigwick & Jackson 1939. Includes "The hand that signed the paper" p. 138.

Robert Lynd ed. *Modern Poetry* London: Nelson 1939. Includes "Especially when the October wind" pp. 234–235.

Anon. ed. *A Book of Modern Verse* (Zodiac Books) London: Chatto & Windus 1939. Includes "The force that through the green fuse" p. 62.

CRITICISM, ETC.

Edwin Muir *The Present Age from 1914* London: Cresset Press 1939: New York: McBride 1940 pp. 220–221: "His poetry has in a high degree the 'natural magic' which Arnold attributed to the Celtic genius. It is filled, like Barker's, with images of parturition and death. It contains lines of extraordinary beauty and imaginative force, but the meaning is so obscure, perhaps because of an excessive allusiveness, that I find it difficult to understand."

Saunders Lewis *Is there an Anglo-Welsh Literature?* Caerdydd 1939. Being the Annual Lecture delivered to the Branch (Urdd Graddedigion Prifysgol Cymru Cangen Caerdydd) on December 10th 1938. On pp. 4–5:

Anglo-Welsh then refers not to men or any society, but is a term of literary classification. I take it that it describes a certain group of writings and their writers *qua* writers. Even so, take warning that the term has as yet very small circulation. With rare exceptions English literary critics have never heard that there was, or is, a Welsh literature in a Welsh language, so that when they discuss writers such as Edward Thomas or W. H. Davies they do not call them Anglo-Welsh writers but simply Welsh, and they often add an expression of agreeable surprise that curiously, and at long last, Wales should be producing men who have some gift of literary composition.

It is the less comic and less complacent Welshmen themselves, those who write in English, who use the term Anglo-Welsh to describe their own activities. Let us take it then that an Anglo-Welsh writer is a Welshman who writes of Wales and of Welsh life in the English language. The group would not include Borrow or Theodore Watts-Dunton. Nor would it include living Englishmen who have found themes or "cases" in Wales. It would be well also to exclude from it writers of Welsh birth or living in Wales, who belong otherwise to the English literary tradition, and whose Welsh interests are only incidental or accidental or just social. It would not include, for example, Mr. Richard Hughes in the novel, or Mr. Dylan Thomas in verse. To give an example, here is the first sentence by Mr. Dylan Thomas in that lively little quarterly called *Wales,*—

"As I walked through the wilderness of this world, as I walked through the wilderness, as I walked through the city, with the loud electric faces and the crowded petrols of the wind dazzling and drowning me that winter night before the West died. . . ."

It is a tiptop sentence. But you will recognise that it belongs to the main stream of the English literary tradition. It is not only a deliberate echo of Bunyan, but that way also have gone Ezra Pound and Gertrude Stein, and perhaps the Frenchman, André Breton. Mr. Dylan Thomas is obviously an equipped writer, but there is nothing hyphenated about him. He belongs to the English.

1940

Dylan Thomas   *Portrait of the Artist as a Young Dog*   London: J. M. Dent 1940. The first impression of 1500 copies, published 4 April 1940, went out of print in 1948 (Rolph p. 47). The ten stories in this collection are:

The Peaches
A Visit to Grandpa's
Patricia, Edith and Arnold
The Fight
Extraordinary Little Cough
Just Like Little Dogs
Where Tawe Flows
Who Do You Wish Was With Us?
Old Garbo
One Warm Saturday

The seventh, eighth, and tenth appeared in print for the first time in this volume.

Dylan Thomas   *Portrait of the Artist as a Young Dog*   Norfolk, Connecticut: New Directions 1940. On 24 September 1940 1000 copies were published;

another 2000 were published at the time of Thomas' first visit to the U.S. in 1950 (Rolph p. 48). Contents: same as Dent edition.

ANTHOLOGIES

[J. F. Hendry] ed. *The New Apocalypse* London: Fortune Press [1940]. Includes "The Burning Baby" and "How shall my animal"; and Henry Treece "An Apocalyptic Writer and the Surrealists" pp. 49–58.

Phyllis M. Jones ed. *Modern Verse, 1900–1940* London: Oxford University Press 1940. Includes "Out of the sighs" pp. 187–188. This World's Classics volume was enlarged in 1955 as *Modern Verse, 1900–1950*; "Fern Hill" and "A Refusal to Mourn" were added.

CRITICISM, ETC.

Elizabeth Drew & John L. Sweeney *Directions in Modern Poetry* New York: Norton 1940 especially pp. 110–112.

1941

ANTHOLOGIES

C. Day Lewis & L. A. G. Strong eds. *A New Anthology of Modern Verse, 1920–1940* London: Methuen 1941. Includes "After the funeral," "And death shall have no dominion," "I have longed to move away," "The hand that signed the paper" pp. 187–190.

Gwyn Jones ed. *Welsh Short Stories* Harmondsworth: Penguin Books 1941. Includes "A Prospect of the Sea" pp. 135–142.

Anne Ridler ed. *A Little Book of Modern Verse* London: Faber 1941. Includes three poems by Thomas pp. 150–153.

Oscar Williams ed. *New Poems, 1940* New York: Yardstick Press 1941.[2] Includes "Light breaks," "Altarwise by owl-light," "Twenty-four years," "Into her Lying Down head" pp. 214–224.

Richard Aldington ed. *Viking Book of Poetry of the English Speaking World* New York: Viking Press 1941. Includes "Light breaks" and "The force that

---

2. The first of many anthologies by which Oscar Williams helped to bring Thomas to the attention of a large American audience. He also edited "Poems of the Month" in *The Living Age*, and in the issue of November 1940 included "To Others than You" p. 285, "reprinted from *Seven*."

through the green fuse" pp. 1204–5. The latter poem only appears in Aldington's *Poetry of the English Speaking World* London: Heinemann 1947.

Earl Daniel ed.   *Art of Reading Poetry*   New York: Farrar & Rinehart 1941. Includes "Twenty-four years" p. 419.

CRITICISM, ETC.

Geoffrey Bullough   *The Trend of Modern Poetry*   Edinburgh & London: Oliver & Boyd 1941 especially pp. 163–164. See 1949 edition pp. 217–221.

H. E. Bates   *The Modern Short Story. A Critical Survey*   London: Thomas Nelson 1941 p. 211: Thomas "has brought to the dream-fantasy story a vocabulary of lavish poetic delirium by which the short story makes yet another turn of development."

J. F. Hendry & Henry Treece eds.   *The White Horseman*   London: Routledge 1941 especially G. S. Fraser "Apocalypse in Poetry" pp. 3–31.

1942

Dylan Thomas   *From In Memory of Ann Jones*   Caseg Broadsheet No. 5 Llanllechid, Caernarvonshire: Caseg Press 1942. The names of Alun Lewis, John Petts, and Brenda Chamberlain are associated with this printing venture; Brenda Chamberlain illustrated the broadsheet (Rolph pp. 32, 49).

Dylan Thomas   *18 Poems*   London: Fortune Press [1942]. (Rolph pp. 42–43).

ANTHOLOGIES

M. J. Tambimuttu ed.   *Poetry in War Time*   London: Faber 1942. Includes "Deaths and Entrances" and "On a Wedding Anniversary" pp. 169–171.

Norman Nicholson ed.   *An Anthology of Religious Verse*   Harmondsworth: Penguin Books 1942. Includes "Incarnate devil" p. 35.

Oscar Williams ed.   *New Poems 1942*   Mount Vernon, New York: Peter Pauper Press 1942. Includes "And death shall have no dominion," "Ballad of the Long-legged Bait," "There was a Saviour," "On the Marriage of a Virgin," "The Hunchback in the Park" pp. 227–241.

Louis Untermeyer ed.   *Modern British Poetry*   New York: Harcourt, Brace 1942. Thomas makes an appearance in this 5th edition, with four poems pp. 495–496.

CRITICISM, ETC.

Francis Scarfe   *Auden and After*   London: Routledge 1942 pp. 101–117, a section reprinted from *Horizon* November 1940.

Stanley J. Kunitz & Howard Haycraft   *Twentieth Century Authors*   New York: H. W. Wilson 1942 p. 1397.

1943

Dylan Thomas   *New Poems*   Norfolk, Connecticut: New Directions 1943. "The Poets of the Year" series: 2500 copies issued February 1943 (Rolph p. 49). Seventeen poems:

> There was a Saviour
> Into her lying down head
> And death shall have no dominion
> Among those Killed in the Dawn Raid
> To Others than You
> Love in the Asylum
> The Marriage of a Virgin
> When I woke
> The Hunchback in the Park
> On a Wedding Anniversary
> Unluckily for a death
> Ballad of the Long-legged Bait
> Because the pleasure bird whistles
> Once below a time
> Request to Leda
> Deaths and Entrances
> O make me a mask.

ANTHOLOGIES

Denys Val Baker ed.   *Little Reviews Anthology*   London: George Allen & Unwin 1943. Includes "Deaths and Entrances" pp. 118–119.

Oscar Williams ed.   *New Poems 1943*   New York: Howell, Soskin 1943. Includes "Deaths and Entrances" and "After the funeral" pp. 248–251.

1944

ANTHOLOGIES

Keidrych Rhys ed.   *Modern Welsh Poetry*   London: Faber 1944. Includes seven poems by Thomas.

Oscar Williams ed.   *New Poems 1944*   New York: Howell, Soskin 1944. Includes three poems by Thomas.

1945

ANTHOLOGIES

Oscar Williams ed.   *The War Poets*   New York: John Day 1945. Includes "The hand that signed the paper," "Ceremony After a Fire Raid," "A Refusal to Mourn" pp. 432–435.

Richard Eberhart & Selden Rodman eds.   *War and the Poet*   New York: Devin-Adair 1945. Includes "A Refusal to Mourn" pp. 200–201.

Phoebe Pool ed.   *Poems of Death*   London: Frederick Muller 1945. Includes "And death shall have no dominion" p. 4, with lithograph by Michael Ayrton.

Richard Church & M. M. Bozman eds.   *Poems of Our Time 1900–1942* London: J. M. Dent 1945. Includes two poems by Thomas.

CRITICISM, ETC.

C. L. Boltz   *Crown to Mend. A Letter on Poetry*   London: Hamish Hamilton 1945 pp. 134–135.

Frederick J. Hoffman   *Freudianism and the Literary Mind*   Baton Rouge, Louisiana: Louisiana State University Press 1945 pp. 295–308. New edition —New York: Grove Press; London: Calder 1959 pp. 286–290.

1946

Dylan Thomas   *Deaths and Entrances*   London: J. M. Dent 1946. First impression was 3000 copies on 7 February 1946; still in print after several impressions. Incorporated into the *Collected Poems* (1952) in its entirety, except that "Paper and Sticks" was dropped and "Do not go gentle" substituted, and "Once below a time" was added.

Dylan Thomas   *Selected Writings of Dylan Thomas*   New York: New Directions 1946. Introduction by John L. Sweeney; portrait by Augustus John. Contents: List A was Thomas' selection "very shakily suggested" to James Laughlin of New Directions in February 1945; to these were added list B.

A

I see the boys of summer
The force that through the green fuse
When, like a running grave
I, in my intricate image
A grief ago

Then was my neophyte
Sonnets IX & X
I make this in a warring absence
It is the sinners' dust-tongued bell
The spire cranes
After the funeral
How shall my animal
A saint about to fall
'If my head hurt a hair's foot'
There was a Saviour
Among those Killed in the Dawn Raid
Love in the Asylum
Ballad of the Long-legged Bait
Deaths and Entrances
Ceremony After a Fire Raid
Holy Spring
Vision and Prayer
Poem in October
The Orchards
A Prospect of the Sea
The Peaches
One Warm Saturday

B

When once the twilight locks
Especially when the October wind
From love's first fever to her plague
A process in the weather of the heart
I dreamed my genesis
This bread I break
Hold hard, these ancient minutes
Today, this insect
The hand that signed the paper
Do you not father me
Foster the light
Twenty-four years
When all my five and country senses see
And death shall have no dominion
Once below a time
The Marriage of a Virgin
Fern Hill
The Conversation of Prayers
A Winter's Tale
This Side of the Truth
A Refusal to Mourn
Lie still, sleep becalmed
In my craft or sullen art
The Burning Baby
The Mouse and the Woman

ANTHOLOGIES

Denys Val Baker ed.   *Little Reviews Anthology 1946*   London: Eyre & Spottiswoode 1946. Includes "Poem in October" pp. 89–91.

Oscar Williams ed.   *A Little Treasury of Modern Poetry*   New York: Scribner 1946; London: Routledge 1948. Includes ten poems by Thomas. Some later editions, beginning with 1950, have an appendix of statements by poets, including one by Thomas, "War Can't Produce Poetry" (p. 820), an extract from a letter to Williams.

CRITICISM, ETC.

Stephen Spender   *Poetry Since 1939*   London: Published for the British Council by Longmans, Green 1946. Chapter XII "Dylan Thomas, George Barker, David Gascoyne" quotes "Poem in October" in full.

Henry Treece   *How I See Apocalypse*   London: Lindsay Drummond 1946. Includes "Meaning and John Sparrow" and "Gerard Manley Hopkins and Dylan Thomas" pp. 123–139; the latter is included in his *Dylan Thomas* (1949) and in *Casebook*.[3]

1947

ANTHOLOGIES

A. S. Collins ed.   *Treasury of Modern Poetry*   London: University Tutorial Press 1947. Includes four poems by Thomas.

G. H. Phelps ed.   *Living Writers*   London: The Sylvan Press 1947. Twelve broadcast talks, including Thomas' "Walter de la Mare as a Prose Writer" (BBC Third Programme 30 November 1946) pp. 116–127.

Denys Val Baker ed.   *International Short Stories*   London: W. H. Allen 1947. Includes "A Visit to Grandpa's" pp. 45–51.

Oscar Williams ed.   *A Little Treasury of Great Poetry*   New York: Scribner 1947. Includes "A Refusal to Mourn" p. 128, and "Vision and Prayer" pp. 238–244.

CRITICISM, ETC.

John Hayward   *English Poetry*   A Catalogue of First and Early Editions of Works of the English Poets from Chaucer to the Present Day Exhibited by

---

3. John Malcolm Brinnin ed. *A Casebook on Dylan Thomas* New York: Thomas Y. Crowell 1960. Note: Abbreviated titles are included in their alphabetical place in the index, in boldface type for easy reference.

the National Book League at 7 Albemarle Street, London 1947. Published for the National Book League by the Cambridge University Press 1947. Item on p. 132: *18 Poems* copy lent by Cyril Connolly. See also the 1950 edition p. 148.

C. Day Lewis   *The Poetic Image*   London: Jonathan Cape; New York: Oxford University Press 1947 pp. 122–128.

William Y. Tindall   *Forces in Modern British Literature*   New York: Knopf 1947 especially pp. 351–355. Reprinted in Vintage Books 1956.

THESES

Suzanne Roussillat   "Dylan Thomas"   Sorbonne, Paris 1947.[4]

1948

Dylan Thomas   Prose Introduction to *An Exhibition of Work by Mervyn Levy* Swindon: The Arts Centre 1948.

ANTHOLOGIES

Maurice Wollman ed.   *Poems of the War Years*   London: Macmillan 1948. Includes three poems by Thomas.

John Arlott ed.   *First Time in America: A Selection of Poems Never Before Published in the U.S.A.*   New York: Duell, Sloane & Pearce 1948. Includes "Last night I dived my beggar arm" and "Your breath was shed" pp. 181–182.

CRITICISM, ETC.

Geoffrey Grigson   *The Harp of Aeolus and Other Essays*   London: Routledge 1948. The essay "How Much Me Now Your Acrobatics Amaze" (pp. 151–160), based on his contributions to *Polemic*, is reprinted in both Tedlock and *Casebook*.

[Charles D. Abbott] ed.   *Poets at Work. Essays Based on the Modern Poetry Collection at the Lockwood Memorial Library, University of Buffalo*   New York: Harcourt, Brace 1948. Includes a facsimile of a "Ballad of the Long-legged Bait" worksheet p. 164, with a comment by W. H. Auden pp. 178–179.[5] Also mention of Thomas by Donald A. Stauffer pp. 53–54, 60.

---

4. Perhaps in English; witness her contribution to *Adam* (No. 238) 1953.
5. For similar comment see his "The Dyer's Hand" *Anchor Review* No. 2 (1957) pp. 281–282.

1949

Dylan Thomas   *Portrait of the Artist as a Young Dog*   The 50,000-copy Guild
paperback edition published London: March 1949.

ANTHOLOGIES

Geoffrey Grigson ed.   *Poetry of the Present*   London: Phoenix House 1949.
Includes five poems by Thomas.

Stefan Schimanski & Henry Treece eds.   *A New Romantic Anthology*   London: Grey Walls Press 1949. Includes "Light breaks" in a Welsh section
edited by Glyn Jones. Also mention of Thomas by Alex Comfort in his "An
Exposition of Irresponsibility" p. 33.

Denys Val Baker ed.   *Little Reviews Anthology 1949*   London: Methuen
1949. Includes "In country sleep" pp. 68–71.

Kenneth Rexroth ed.   *The New British Poets*   Norfolk, Connecticut: New
Directions 1949. Eight poems by Thomas pp. 241–250. Also commentary in
the Introduction pp. vii–xxxvii, of which pp. xvii–xx are reprinted in *Casebook*.

Selden Rodman ed.   *100 Modern Poems*   New York: Pellegrini & Cudahy
1949. Two poems by Thomas; also commentary in the Introduction pp.
xxviii–xxx.

CRITICISM, ETC.

Henry Treece   *Dylan Thomas 'Dog Among the Fairies'*   London: Lindsay
Drummond 1949.

George Every   *Poetry and Personal Responsibility*   London: SCM Press 1949.
Chapter III: "The Impact of Joyce especially on George Barker and Dylan
Thomas" pp. 32–40.

Lloyd Frankenberg   *Pleasure Dome: On Reading Modern Poetry*   Boston:
Houghton Mifflin 1949 especially pp. 316–323. Also as Dolphin paperback
Doubleday 1961 pp. 325–331.

THESES

Sol Chaneles   "The Metaphor of Dylan Thomas"   M.A. New York University 1949.

David G. Aivaz   "Image and Theme in the Poetry of Dylan Thomas"   A.B.
Harvard College 1949.

1950

Dylan Thomas *Twenty-six Poems* "This volume of poems by Dylan Thomas was printed in Griffo type by Hans Mardersteig on the hand-press of the Officina Bodoni in Verona for James Laughlin and J. M. Dent & Sons, Ltd. ... December Mcmxxxxix"—actually issued 1950 (Rolph p. 53). A representative collection of poems from previous volumes.

ANTHOLOGIES

Kenneth Allott ed. *The Penguin Book of Contemporary Verse* Harmondsworth: Penguin Books 1950. Includes "A grief ago," "After the funeral," "The Hunchback in the Park," "Poem in October"; discussion of Thomas in the Introduction pp. 11–27 and on pp. 224–226.

Hermann Peschmann ed. *The Voice of Poetry (1930–1950)* London: Evans Bros. 1950. Includes four poems by Thomas.

G. F. Green ed. *First View: Stories of Children* London: Faber 1950. Includes "Extraordinary Little Cough" pp. 236–247.

Cleanth Brooks & Robert Penn Warren eds. *Understanding Poetry* New York: Holt rev. ed. 1950. Includes "The force that through the green fuse" pp. 473–474. The 1960 edition added "A Refusal to Mourn" and commentary.

David Daiches & William Charvat eds. *Poems in English, 1530–1940* New York: Ronald Press 1950. Includes three poems by Thomas, with some commentary on pp. 744–745.

THESES

H. H. Kleinman "The Religious Sonnets of Dylan Thomas" M.A. Columbia University 1950.

1951

ANTHOLOGIES

Michael Roberts ed. with supplement by Anne Ridler *The Faber Book of Modern Verse* London: Faber 1951. Expanded from the 1936 edition. Reprinted as paper-covered edition 1960. Revised edition by Donald Hall in 1965.

Anon. ed.   *Poems of To-day. Fourth Series*   Published for the English Association by Macmillan 1951. Includes four poems by Thomas.

Kimon Friar & John M. Brinnin eds.   *Modern Poetry, American and British*   New York: Appleton-Century-Crofts 1951. Includes eight poems by Thomas pp. 371–384, with commentary on "Vision and Prayer" and "In Memory of Ann Jones" pp. 540–541.

Oscar Williams ed.   *A Little Treasury of British Poetry*   New York: Scribner 1951. Includes fourteen poems by Thomas, with commentary in the Introduction on pp. xv–xix, xxii.

Mark Van Doren ed.   *Introduction to Poetry*   New York: William Sloan Associates 1951. Includes four poems by Thomas.

CRITICISM, ETC.

Vivian De Sola Pinto   *Crisis in English Poetry*   London: Hutchinson's Universal Library 1951 pp. 202–204.

A. S. Collins   *English Literature of the Twentieth Century*   London: University Tutorial Press 1951. Fourth edition, with postscript by Frank Whitehead, 1960.

Josephine Miles   *The Primary Language of Poetry in the 1940's*   University of California Publications in English Vol. 19 No. 3. Berkeley: University of California Press 1951. A word-count analysis pp. 390, 447–448.

1952

Dylan Thomas   *In Country Sleep and Other Poems*   A New Directions Book 1952. Frontispiece photograph by Marion Morehouse. The regular edition, 5000 copies, published 28 February 1952, with a special edition of 100 copies (Rolph p. 54). Contents:

> Over Sir John's hill
> Poem on his Birthday
> Do not go gentle
> Lament
> In the white giant's thigh
> In country sleep

Dylan Thomas   *Collected Poems 1934–1952*   London: J. M. Dent 1952. Dedicated "To Caitlin." Portrait by Augustus John. Published 10 November 1952; still in print after several impressions. Essentially this is a collection of his previously published volumes. An introductory note and a specially written "Author's Prologue" preface the volume. (The numbering below is not Thomas'.)

[*18 Poems*]

1   I see the boys of summer
2   When once the twilight locks no longer
3   A process in the weather of the heart
4   Before I knocked
5   The force that through the green fuse drives the flower
6   My hero bares his nerves
7   Where once the waters of your face
8   If I were tickled by the rub of love
9   Our eunuch dreams
10 Especially when the October wind
11 When, like a running grave
12 From love's first fever to her plague
13 In the beginning
14 Light breaks where no sun shines
15 I fellowed sleep
16 I dreamed my genesis
17 My world is pyramid
18 All all and all the dry worlds lever

[*Twenty-five Poems*]

19 I, in my intricate image
20 This bread I break
21 Incarnate devil
22 To-day, this insect
23 The seed-at-zero
24 Shall gods be said to thump the clouds
25 Here in this spring
26 Do you not father me
27 Out of the sighs
28 Hold hard, these ancient minutes in the cuckoo's month
29 Was there a time
30 Now
31 Why east wind chills
32 A grief ago
33 How soon the servant son
34 Ears in the turrets hear
35 Foster the light
36 The hand that signed the paper
37 Should lanterns shine
38 I have longed to move away
39 Find meat on bones
40 Grief thief of time
41 And death shall have no dominion
42 Then was my neophyte
43 Altarwise by owl-light [sonnets I–X]

[*The Map of Love*]

44   Because the pleasure bird whistles
45   I make this in a warring absence
46   When all my five and country senses see
47   We lying by seasand
48   It is the sinners' dust-tongued bell
49   O make me a mask
50   The spire cranes
51   After the funeral
52   Once it was the colour of saying
53   Not from this anger
54   How shall my animal
55   The tombstone told when she died
56   On no word of words
57   A saint about to fall
58   'If my head hurt a hair's foot'
59   Twenty-four years

[*Deaths and Entrances*
with poem 69 substituted for "Paper and Sticks"; poem 77 added]

60   The Conversation of Prayer
61   A Refusal to Mourn the Death, by Fire, of a Child in London
62   Poem in October
63   This Side of the Truth
64   To Others than You
65   Love in the Asylum
66   Unluckily for a Death
67   The Hunchback in the Park
68   Into her Lying Down Head
69   Do not go gentle into that good night
70   Deaths and Entrances
71   A Winter's Tale
72   On a Wedding Anniversary
73   There was a Saviour
74   On the Marriage of a Virgin
75   In my Craft or Sullen Art
76   Ceremony After a Fire Raid
77   Once below a time
78   When I Woke
79   Dawn Raid
80   Lie Still, Sleep Becalmed
81   Vision and Prayer
82   Ballad of the Long-legged Bait
83   Holy Spring
84   Fern Hill

[*In Country Sleep*
with poem 69 transferred above]

85 In country sleep
86 Over Sir John's hill
87 Poem on his Birthday
88 Lament
89 In the white giant's thigh

Editions after June 1956 include the posthumous "Elegy," constructed by Vernon Watkins.

ANTHOLOGIES

Clifford Dyment, Roy Fuller, Montagu Slater eds. *New Poems 1952* (A P.E.N. Anthology) London: Michael Joseph 1952. Includes "Over Sir John's hill" pp. 149–150.

John Hadfield ed. *A Book of Beauty* London: Hulton Press 1952. Includes "Poem in October" pp. 117–119. Thomas pieces also in his *A Book of Delights* (1954), *A Book of Britain* (1956), *A Book of Love* (1958), and *Love for Life* (1961).

CRITICISM, ETC.

Lawrence Durrell *Key to Modern Poetry* London: Peter Neville 1952 especially Chapter X: "Poetry in the Thirties" pp. 196–208. Published by the University of Oklahoma Press 1952 with the title *A Key to Modern British Poetry*.

Babette Deutsch *Poetry in Our Time* New York: Holt 1952 especially pp. 312–347 (in the second printing, Columbia University Press 1956 pp. 330–347). See also a new edition, Doubleday 1963 pp. 349–388.

Amos N. Wilder *Modern Poetry and the Christian Tradition* New York: Scribner 1952 pp. 100–102: "Man and Nature in Dylan Thomas."

THESES

Max Halperen " 'Moonless Acre': The Poetry of Dylan Thomas" M.A. Florida State University 1952. Included in Kentucky Microcards, Series A.

1953

Dylan Thomas *The Collected Poems of Dylan Thomas* A New Directions Book 1953 (published 31 March). Frontispiece is a photograph by Marion Morehouse. Contents identical with the Dent edition (1952).

Dylan Thomas   *The Doctor and the Devils*   London: J. M. Dent; New York: New Directions 1953. Includes Donald Taylor "The Story of the Film" pp. 135–138. The script itself was written in 1944; the book was in proof in 1947, but its publication delayed (Rolph p. 57). An edition published in the Time Reading Program (1964) has an Introduction by John Ormond [Thomas].

ANTHOLOGIES

John Heath-Stubbs & David Wright eds.   *The Faber Book of Twentieth Century Verse*   London: Faber 1953. "An anthology of verse in Britain, 1900–1950." See Introduction by John Heath-Stubbs, pp. 24–25, 28.

F. McEachran ed.   *Spells*   Oxford: Basil Blackwell 1953. Includes quotations from "The force that through the green fuse" and "The hand that signed the paper" pp. 30–31, 88–89, 196–197.

CRITICISM, ETC.

G. S. Fraser   *The Modern Writer and His World*   London: Derek Verschoyle 1953 pp. 41, 237, 262, 267–269, 273, 275–276, 331, 337. Published in New York by Criterion Books 1955; Penguin edition 1964.

1954

Dylan Thomas   *Under Milk Wood* "A Play for Voices"   London: J. M. Dent; New York: New Directions 1954. Preface by Daniel Jones, with his music for the songs. New Directions edition has a note on the New York performance. Aldine paperback No. 1 1962; New Directions Paperbook No. 73 [1957].

Dylan Thomas   *Quite Early One Morning*   London: J. M. Dent; New York: New Directions 1954. The U.S. edition has the following explanatory "Publisher's Note":

The stories and essays here assembled for the first time were written over a period of some ten years: the latest, "A Visit to America," was read by Dylan Thomas on his last tour of the United States in 1953. Shortly before his sudden illness and death, Thomas sketched out plans for such a volume of prose pieces to be called "Quite Early One Morning." Since so many of the pieces he wanted to include had been commissioned by the British Broadcasting Corporation, his literary executors and the trustees of his estate asked Mr. Aneirin Talfan Davies, Director of the Welsh Region, B.B.C., who had worked closely with Thomas for a number of years, to gather the texts together. The volume Mr. Davies edited for publication in England is made up solely of broadcasts as Dylan Thomas delivered them.

His American publisher, believing that American readers will prefer a broader and more complete collection of Thomas' stories and essays, has preferred to enlarge this edition of *Quite Early One Morning* to include a number of stories and articles published in magazines, and not broadcast. He has also preferred to print here the more finished versions of the broadcast talks, as Thomas revised them for publication.

Although the American edition of *Quite Early One Morning* differs considerably from the English edition, the publisher wishes to acknowledge his large debt to Mr. Davies for his great contribution to the preparation of this volume.

The contents of the New Directions volume is listed below with the differences noted. In addition, the Dent edition has a Preface pp. vii–x, and Notes pp. 171–181 by Aneirin Talfan Davies.

> Reminiscences of Childhood (Dent edition also includes an early version
>   of this script)
> Quite Early One Morning
> A Child's Christmas in Wales (Dent has the shorter "Memories of
>   Christmas")
> Holiday Memory
> A Story (New Directions only)
> The Crumbs of One Man's Year
> Laugharne
> Return Journey
> Our Country (New Directions only)
>
> Welsh Poets (Dent version has more cuts)
> Wilfred Owen
> Sir Philip Sidney
> Artists of Wales (Dent title: "Wales and the Artist")
> Walter de la Mare as a Prose Writer
> A Dearth of Comic Writers
> The English Festival of Spoken Poetry
> On Reading One's Own Poems
> Three Poems (New Directions edition includes only two of them)
> Replies to an Enquiry (New Directions only)
> On Poetry
> How To Be a Poet (New Directions only)
> How To Begin a Story
> The Festival Exhibition, 1951
> The International Eisteddfod
> A Visit to America

The U.S. edition reprinted as New Directions Paperbook No. 90 in 1960.

Dylan Thomas   *Conversation About Christmas*   "Printed at Christmas 1954 for the friends of J. Laughlin and New Directions."

Dylan Thomas   *Two Epigrams of Fealty* and *Galsworthy and Gawsworth* [1954]. Privately printed by John Gawsworth, who has written the following note on them:

These three pieces were written by Dylan Thomas in the Caves de France, Dean Street, Soho—on the bar! I had just been telling him of my escape from winter-bound Stebbing (nr. Dunmow, Essex) where my hostesses' fourteen great Danes were a perpetual pest to me. Dylan's reference to M.P. Shiel, (King Felepe of Redonda, my colleague and predecessor), whose books he had reviewed when a young journalist in Wales, were no more pleasant than his sneers at me—he was in an extremely nasty mood that afternoon. Nonetheless, he had been a boon companion of mine and Philip Lindsay's in London taverns, on and off for some seventeen years and a Duke of Redonda since my Succession in 1947—so I ran off 30 memorial copies to him for the court—though his Fealty was far from respectful!

The manuscript—three verses totalling twelve lines—as I recall (I later provided the titles) was on a lined page torn from Dylan's notebook. I have no idea where it is now, but in the general disintegration of my library, I seem to recall that Elkin Mathews had it.

ANTHOLOGIES

Oscar Williams ed.   *The Pocket Book of Modern Verse; English and American Poetry of the Last Hundred Years from Walt Whitman to Dylan Thomas* New York: Pocket Books 1954. Dedicated to Dylan Thomas.

Charles M. Coffin ed.   *The Major Poets English and American*   New York: Harcourt, Brace 1954. Poems with footnotes pp. 528–539.

CRITICISM, ETC.

Derek Stanford   *Dylan Thomas: A Literary Study*   London: Neville Spearman 1954. Published in New York by Citadel. Revised edition 1964 includes "A Literary Postmortem."

Elder Olson   *The Poetry of Dylan Thomas*   Chicago: University of Chicago Press 1954. Prefaced by a poem by the author, "A Farewell," reprinted in *Garland*. The "Bibliography" by William H. Huff of Northwestern University Library,[6] pp. 102–146, is omitted in the Phoenix paperback edition 1961.

Igor Stravinsky   *In Memoriam Dylan Thomas*   London & New York: Boosey & Hawkes 1954. A setting of "Do not go gentle" with a preface by the composer.

THESES

Allen Wallace Graves   "Difficult Contemporary Short Stories"   Ph.D. University of Washington 1954. *Dissertation Abstracts* XIV No. 11 p. 2067.

David E. Cummings "The Language of Dylan Thomas" M.A. Columbia University 1954.

---

6. Issued there in mimeographed form in May 1953.

1955

Dylan Thomas   *A Prospect of the Sea and Other Stories and Prose Writings*
London: J. M. Dent 1955. Edited by Daniel Jones. Contents:

> A Prospect of the Sea
> The Lemon
> After the Fair
> The Visitor
> The Enemies
> The Tree
> The Map of Love
> The Mouse and the Woman
> The Dress
> The Orchards
> In the Direction of the Beginning
> Conversation about Christmas
> How to be a Poet
> The Followers
> A Story

Reprinted as Aldine Paperback No. 58 1965.

Dylan Thomas   *Adventures in the Skin Trade and Other Stories*   New York:
New Directions 1955. Contents:

> Adventures in the Skin Trade
> After the Fair
> The Enemies
> The Tree
> The Visitor
> The Lemon
> The Burning Baby
> The Orchards
> The Mouse and the Woman
> The Horse's Ha
> A Prospect of the Sea
> The Holy Six
> Prologue to an Adventure
> The Map of Love
> In the Direction of the Beginning
> An Adventure from a Work in Progress
> The School for Witches
> The Dress
> The Vest
> The True Story
> The Followers

Reprinted as a Signet paperback (New American Library) in 1961. The New

Directions Paperbook edition (No. 183) 1964 includes an introduction by Vernon Watkins.

Dylan Thomas   *Adventures in the Skin Trade*   London: Putnam 1955. With a foreword by Vernon Watkins. Reprinted by Ace Books 1961; and as Aldine paperback No. 38 1965.

Dylan Thomas   *A Child's Christmas in Wales*   Norfolk, Connecticut: New Directions [1955]. Separate printing of the essay which had appeared in the New Directions edition of *Quite Early One Morning*. New edition 1959, with woodcuts by Ellen Raskin.

Dylan Thomas   *Portrait of the Artist as a Young Dog*   New Directions Paperbook No. 51, 1955. Dent issued this work as Aldine paperback No. 34 in 1965.

CRITICISM, ETC.

John Malcolm Brinnin   *Dylan Thomas in America: An Intimate Journal*   Boston: Atlantic-Little, Brown 1955. With a statement by Caitlin Thomas. Reprinted as Compass paperback No. 30 1957 and by Avon Books 1966. Dent edition published in 1956. Reprinted in Ace Books 1957 and as Aldine paperback No. 52 in 1965.

Robert Graves   *The Crowning Privilege*   London: Cassell 1955; New York: Doubleday 1956. Reissued in Penguin Books 1959. The pertinent lecture of these Clark Lectures 1954–55 "These Be Your Gods, O Israel!" had appeared in *Essays in Criticism*, and is reprinted in *Casebook*.

John Press   *The Fire and the Fountain: An Essay on Poetry*   London: Methuen; New York: Barnes & Noble 1955 especially pp. 152–154.

Donald Davie   *Articulate Energy: An Inquiry into the Syntax of English Poetry*   London: Routledge 1955. Thomas is presented as one of the few examples in English of "pseudo-syntax" pp. 10, 125–128, 161.[7]

Stanley J. Kunitz ed.   *Twentieth Century Authors: First Supplement*   New York: H. W. Wilson 1955 pp. 990–991.

Louis Untermeyer   *Makers of the Modern World*   New York: Simon & Schuster 1955 pp. 753–757. See also his *Lives of the Poets* (1960) pp. 716–722.

Dorothy W. Goodfellow   "Dylan Thomas 'The Boy of Summer' " in *Lectures on Some Modern Poets*   Carnegie Series in English No. 2 Pittsburgh: Carnegie Institute of Technology 1955 pp. 77–90.

---

7. Davie uses Elizabeth Sewell's mention of Thomas in her *The Structure of Poetry* London: Routledge 1951 p. 128.

THESES

Beatrice E. Bodenstein "Concordance to *18 Poems* by Dylan Thomas" M.A. Columbia University 1955.

Anna P. Ziman "*18 Poems:* With Dylan Thomas's Accent on Death" M.A. Columbia University 1955.

1956

ANTHOLOGIES

Stephen Spender, Elizabeth Jennings, Dannie Abse eds. *New Poems 1956* London: Michael Joseph for P.E.N. 1956. Includes "Elegy" posthumously constructed by Vernon Watkins, with a note.

John Hayward *The Penguin Book of English Verse* Penguin Books 1956. Includes "A Refusal to Mourn" and "Fern Hill." The anthology was republished as *The Faber Book of English Verse* in 1958.

Gwyn Jones ed. *Welsh Short Stories* World's Classics No. 551 London: Oxford University Press 1956. Includes "The Enemies" and "A Visit to Grandpa's."

Lloyd Frankenberg ed. *Invitation to Poetry: A Round of Poems from John Skelton to Dylan Thomas* New York: Doubleday 1956 pp. 99–101.

CRITICISM, ETC.

J. Alexander Rolph *Dylan Thomas: A Bibliography* London: J. M. Dent; New York: New Directions 1956. With a foreword "The Young Dylan Thomas" by Edith Sitwell pp. xiii–xv; facsimile of Thomas letter and other photographs.

Henry Treece *Dylan Thomas: 'Dog Among the Fairies'* 2nd edition London: Ernest Benn; New York: de Graff 1956. A revision of the 1949 edition, with some material omitted and some added.

Giorgio Melchiori *The Tightrope Walkers: Studies of Mannerism in Modern English Literature* London: Routledge 1956. "Dylan Thomas: the Poetry of Vision" pp. 213–242.

Margaret Schlauch *Modern English and American Poetry: Techniques and Ideologies* London: Watts 1956. References throughout.

Robin Skelton *The Poetic Pattern* London: Routledge 1956. References throughout.

THESES

David Clay Jenkins   "Writing in Twentieth Century Wales: A Defense of the Anglo-Welsh"   Ph.D. State University of Iowa 1956. *Dissertation Abstracts* 1956 XVI p. 1906.

May Reifer   "Supernatural Stories of Dylan Thomas"   M.A. Columbia University 1956.

Robert Brady Sennish   "The Early Prose of Dylan Thomas"   M.A. Columbia University 1956.

Nicole Gauchon   "The Theme of Death and its Literary Expression in the Works of Dylan Thomas"   Diplôme d'Études Supérieures, Université de Paris 1956.

Richard L. Faust   "A Study of Dylan Thomas' *Under Milk Wood*"   M.A. Columbia University 1956.

Benjamin W. Jones   "A Study of Four Poems by Dylan Thomas"   M.A. Columbia University 1956.

Elizabeth G. Stevens   "The Symbolic Imagery of Sea, Liquid and Water in the Early Poems of Dylan Thomas"   M.A. Columbia University 1956.

1957

Dylan Thomas   *Letters to Vernon Watkins*   Edited with an introduction by Vernon Watkins. London: J. M. Dent and Faber; New York: New Directions 1957.

ANTHOLOGIES

Anon. ed.   *The Poetry Society's Verse Speaking Anthology 1957*   London: The Poetry Society 1957. For use in the annual poetry reading competition. Includes "And death shall have no dominion." The 1963 edition (William Kean Seymour & John Smith eds.) has "Fern Hill."

Oscar Williams ed.   *The Silver Treasury of Light Verse*   New York: a Mentor book of the New American Library 1957. Includes "The Song of the Mischievous Dog" and also an unpublished limerick p. 198.

CRITICISM, ETC.

G. S. Fraser   *Dylan Thomas*   London: Longmans, Green, for the British Council 1957. This essay is reprinted in his *Vision and Rhetoric* London: Faber 1959 pp. 211–241, and in *Casebook*. Also in *British Writers and Their Work* No. 5 Lincoln: University of Nebraska Press 1965.

Caitlin Thomas   *Leftover Life to Kill*   London: Putnam; Boston: Atlantic-Little, Brown 1957. Grove Press edition [1959]; Ace Books 1959.[8]

Gwyn Jones   *The First Forty Years. Some Notes on Anglo-Welsh Literature*   Cardiff: University of Wales Press 1957. The W. D. Thomas Memorial Lecture, delivered at the University College, Swansea.

John Bayley   *The Romantic Survival: A Study in Poetic Evolution*   London: Constable; New York: Oxford University Press 1957. Chapter X: "Dylan Thomas" pp. 186–227.

Stuart Holroyd   *Emergence From Chaos*   London: Gollanz; Boston: Houghton Mifflin 1957 pp. 77–94, reprinted in *Casebook*.

Anthony Thwaite   *Essays on Contemporary English Poetry*   Tokyo 1957. Revised as *Contemporary English Poetry* London: Heinemann 1959, 2nd edition 1961; also published by Dufours in Philadelphia. Chapter 8: "Dylan Thomas and George Barker."

THESES

James D. O'Hara   "The Religious Poetry of Dylan Thomas"   M.A. Columbia University 1957.

1958

Dylan Thomas   *Under Milk Wood*   (Acting Edition) London: J. M. Dent; New York: New Directions 1958. Edited with an introduction by Daniel Jones.[9]

ANTHOLOGIES

Edith Sitwell ed.   *The Atlantic Book of British and American Poetry*   Boston: Atlantic-Little, Brown 1958; London: Gollanz 1959. Includes six Thomas poems with an introduction pp. 982–984 reprinted in *Casebook*.

David Cecil & Allen Tate eds.   *Modern Verse in English 1900–1950*   New York: Macmillan; London: Eyre & Spottiswoode 1958. Includes seven poems by Thomas, and discussion pp. 34, 36, 40, 641.

---

8. Her second book *Not Quite Posthumous Letters to My Daughter* London: Putnam; Boston: Atlantic-Little, Brown 1963 contains very little direct reference to Thomas. See also Robert Haidukewicz "The Art of Caitlin Thomas" *Artesian* Spring 1958 pp. 22–23.

9. See also the separate publication of Jones' settings, *Songs from Under Milk Wood* London: Keith Prowse Music Publishing Company 1957.

Maurice Wollman M.A. (Perse School, Cambridge) & Kathleen B. Parker (Headmistress Stopsley Girls' School, Luton) eds.   *The Harrap Book of Modern Verse*   London: George Harrap 1958. Includes "The hand that signed the paper" p. 133.

CRITICISM, ETC.

David Daiches   *The Present Age After 1920*   London: Cresset Press 1958 (new Vol. V of "Introductions to English Literature") especially p. 233. Published in Bloomington by the Indiana University Press with the title *The Present Age in British Literature* 1958.

John Press   *The Chequer'd Shade: Reflections on Obscurity in Poetry*   London: Oxford University Press 1958 pp. 1–2, 22, 49, 61, 74, 91, 170, 174–175, 179.

Christine Brooke-Rose   *A Grammar of Metaphor*   London: Secker & Warburg 1958. Examines Thomas' syntax, along with that of fourteen other poets; references throughout.

THESES

Lita R. Hornick   "The Intricate Image: A Study of Dylan Thomas"   Ph.D. Columbia University 1958. *Dissertation Abstracts* XIX No. 2 pp. 327–328.

Ralph Maud   "Language and Meaning in the Poetry of Dylan Thomas" Ph.D. Harvard University 1958.

Charles Sanders   "Poetic Characteristics and Problems of Dylan Thomas" M.A. University of North Carolina 1958.

William Augustine McBrien   "Likeness in the Themes and Prosody of Gerard Manley Hopkins and Dylan Thomas"   Ph.D. St. John's University 1958.

Donald Novick   "The Poetry of Dylan Thomas and His Shaping Conscience" M.A. Columbia University 1958.

1959

CRITICISM, ETC.

Donald McWhinnie   *The Art of Radio*   London: Faber 1959 especially 170–172.

Elizabeth Drew   *Poetry: A Modern Guide*   New York: 1959 pp. 21, 181–183, 215.

THESES

John Ackerman Jones "The Work of Dylan Thomas in Relation to his Welsh Environment" M.A. King's College, London 1959.

Joseph J. Miller "The Grammar of Dylan Thomas in *Collected Poems*" M.A. Columbia University 1959.

Patricia Earle Speyser "The 'Ballad of the Long-legged Bait' Worksheets" M.A. University of Buffalo 1959.

1960

CRITICISM, ETC.

E. W. Tedlock ed. *Dylan Thomas: The Legend and the Poet* London: Heinemann 1960. "A Collection of Biographical and Critical Essays." Reprinted as paperback Mercury Book No. 39 1963.

Rayner Heppenstall *Four Absentees* London: Barrie & Rockcliff 1960.[10]

J. M. Cohen *Poetry of This Age 1908–1958* London: Hutchinson 1960 pp. 170–174.

G. H. Vallins *The Best English* London: Andre Deutsch 1960 pp. 123, 135–136, 185. Published in New York by Oxford University Press 1960. Reprinted in Pan Books 1963.

John Malcolm Brinnin ed. *A Casebook on Dylan Thomas* New York: Thomas Y. Crowell 1960. Previously unpublished items are: John Malcolm Brinnin "Introduction" pp. xi–xiii; Bill Read "A Visit to Laugharne" pp. 266–272; and Howard Moss "Dylan Thomas" pp. 290–292.

Karl Shapiro *In Defense of Ignorance* New York: Random House 1960 pp. 5, 21, 37, 60, 63, 124, 131, 139, 149, 171–186, 268, 309. Also in Vintage paperback.

M. L. Rosenthal *The Modern Poets: A Critical Introduction* New York: Oxford University Press 1960. Chapter 7: "Exquisite Chaos: Thomas and others" especially pp. 203–225. A Galaxy paperback 1965.

James E. Miller Jr., Karl Shapiro, Bernice Slote *Start with the Sun* Lincoln: University of Nebraska Press 1960. Part IV "Whitman and Thomas" pp. 169–190 and other references. Bison Books paperback 1963.

John Gassner *Theatre at the Crossroads* New York: Holt, Rinehart, & Winston 1960 pp. 286–288.

---

10. The reminiscences in this book were anticipated in his *My Bit of Dylan Thomas* "80 copies for private circulation to the friends of T.E.H. [T. E. Hanley]" 1957.

THESES

Joseph F. Vogel "Religious Thought in the Poetry of Dylan Thomas" M.A. University of Miami 1960.

1961

ANTHOLOGIES

A. J. Smith & W. H. Mason eds. *Short Story Study: A Critical Anthology* London: Edward Arnold 1961 pp. 175–190 "The Followers" with commentary.

Alan Durband ed. *New Directions: Five One-Act Plays in the Modern Idiom* London: Hutchinson Educational 1961. Includes "Return Journey" pp. 23–37 with note pp. 14–15.

CRITICISM, ETC.

Boris Ford ed. *The Modern Age* (Pelican Guide to English Literature Vol. VII) Penguin Books 1961. Published in hardcover by Cassell 1964. Notable essays with Thomas references: John Holloway "The Literary Scene" pp. 93–94; David Holbrook "Metaphor and maturity: T. F. Powys and Dylan Thomas" pp. 415–428.

Thomas Blackburn *The Price of an Eye* London: Longmans, Green; New York: Morrow 1961. Chapter 9 "Dylan Thomas" pp. 111–123.

R. C. Churchill "The Age of T. S. Eliot" in George Sampson *The Concise History of English Literature* Cambridge University Press 1961 especially pp. 971–973.

THESES

Katharine Taylor Loesch "Prosodic Patterns in the Poetry of Dylan Thomas" Ph.D. Northwestern University 1961. *Dissertation Abstracts* XXII No. 9 p. 3295.

Suzanne C. Ferguson "The Bellowing Ark: Dylan Thomas's *Ballad of the Long-legged Bait*" M.A. Vanderbilt University 1961.

1962

CRITICISM, ETC.

David Holbrook *Llareggub Revisited: Dylan Thomas and the State of Modern Poetry* London: Bowes & Bowes 1962. Reprinted as *Dylan Thomas and*

Poetic Dissociation Carbondale: University of Southern Illinois Press 1964, with a preface by Harry T. Moore.

Winifred Nowottny *The Language Poets Use* University of London, The Athlone Press; New York: Oxford University Press 1962. Chapter VIII "Symbolism and Obscurity" pp. 174–222, explicates "There was a Saviour" — pertinent sections reprinted in Cox.

Aneirin Talfan Davies "William Barnes, Gerard Manley Hopkins, Dylan Thomas. The Influence of Welsh Prosody on Modern English Poetry" in *Proceedings of the IIIrd Congress of the International Comparative Literature Association* The Hague: Mouton 1962 pp. 90–122.

Claude Rawson "Dylan Thomas" in *Talks to Teachers of English 2* Newcastle upon Tyne: Department of Education, King's College 1962 pp. 30–56.

William York Tindall *A Reader's Guide to Dylan Thomas* New York: Noonday; London: Thames & Hudson 1962.

Clark Emery *The World of Dylan Thomas* Miami: University of Miami Press 1962.

Anon. *An Introduction to the Poetry and Prose of Dylan Thomas* Pennsylvania State University, Center for Continuing Liberal Education 1962.

THESES

William Trumbull Moynihan "The Poetry of Dylan Thomas: A Study of Its Meaning and Unity" Ph.D. Brown University 1962. *Dissertation Abstracts* XXIII No. 7 p. 2531.

Thelma Louise Baughan Murdy "Sound and Meaning in Dylan Thomas's Poetry" Ph.D. University of Florida 1962. *Dissertation Abstracts* XXIII No. 9 pp. 3382–83.

John Cutler Shershow "The Grotesque Imagination of Dylan Thomas" A.B. Harvard College 1962.

1963

Dylan Thomas *The Beach of Falesâ* New York: Stein & Day 1963; London: Jonathan Cape 1964. Film script "based on a story by Robert Louis Stevenson." Also in Ballantine paperback 1965; Panther book 1966.

Dylan Thomas *Miscellany: Poems Stories Broadcasts* London: J. M. Dent 1963. Aldine paperback No. 13. Contents:

Prologue
The force that through the green fuse
Especially when the October wind

From love's first fever to her plague
In the beginning
I fellowed sleep
I dreamed my genesis
I, in my intricate image
Do you not father me
Hold hard, these ancient minutes
The hand that signed the paper
And death shall have no dominion
The Conversation of Prayer
Poem in October
Do not go gentle into that good night
Elegy

The Map of Love
The Mouse and the Woman
The Visitor
The Followers

Reminiscences of Childhood
Memories of Christmas
Return Journey

Ralph Maud & Aneirin Talfan Davies eds.   *The Colour of Saying*   London: J. M. Dent 1963. Aldine paperback No. 42 (1965). "An Anthology of Verse Spoken by Dylan Thomas." Introduction pp. xiii–xxv. Published in New York by New Directions as *Dylan Thomas' Choice* 1964, with a few minor differences in content.

ANTHOLOGIES

R. S. Thomas ed.   *Penguin Book of Religious Verse*   Harmondsworth: Penguin Books 1963. Includes "There was a Saviour" and "Fern Hill," with mention in the Introduction p. 10.

CRITICISM, ETC.

George Firmage ed.   *A Garland for Dylan Thomas*   New York: Clarke & Way 1963; London: Vision Press 1966. Advisory editor: Oscar Williams.
Editor's preface pp. xv–xvi. Includes "In My Craft or Sullen Art" p. 1, and "Notes on the Art of Poetry" (= "Poetic Manifesto") pp. 147–152.

The following poems are stated as having their first printing in this volume:

John Gawsworth "In Memoriam Dylan Thomas"
Elizabeth Lambert "For Dylan Thomas"
Stanley Moss "The Gentle Things"
Oscar Williams "A Poem Is for D.T."

The following poems in this collection are not listed elsewhere in this bibliography:

Helen Bevington "Talk with a Poet." See also her *When Found, Make a Verse Of* New York: Simon & Schuster 1961 pp. 58–61

John W. Clark "Dead Poet" from his *All the Time in the Dark* New York: Clarke & Way 1962

Fred Cogswell "Epistle to Dylan Thomas (re J.M.B.)" from *Pan* Winter 1958

R. R. Cuscaden "Dylan Thomas: An Anniversary"

Carl O. Denham "Words Uttered in Transit (With apologies to Dylan Thomas who chose better)" from *Venture* (Vol. 2 No. 4) 1957–58 p. 14

Allen Curnow "In Memory of Dylan Thomas" from *Landfall* (New Zealand) March 1954 pp. 6–9

Richard Diers "The Hundredth Poem to Dylan Thomas" from his *Singing of Shells* Villefranche-sur-Mer, France 1958

Harold Enrico "'I hold a beast, an angel, and a madman in me . . .'"

Jane Esty "A Refusal to Mourn the Death of Dylan Thomas" from *Mutiny* Winter 1958

Jean Garrigue "A Mourning (for Dylan Thomas)"

Eliot Glassheim "Connections (to Dylan)" from *Wesleyan Poets* 6 April 1960

John Guenther "The Wanderer (for Dylan Thomas)"

Marguerite Harris "Four Poems"

J. D. James "Poem for a Birthday"

T. H. Jones "Swansea" from *The Beast at the Door* London: Hart-Davis 1963

T. James Jones "Dylan" from the program of the Llaregyb Players' production of "Under Milk Wood" 1961

C. Day Lewis "In Memory of Dylan Thomas" from *Chanticleer* Spring 1954

E. L. Mayo "The Prince of Odd and Anger (for Dylan Thomas)" from *Summer Unbound* (University of Minnesota Press 1958)

John Nist "To the Spirit of Dylan Thomas" from *Narceja* (San Paulo, Brazil)

I. R. Orton "The Departure (To the memory of Dylan Thomas)" from *Stand* (no date)

Robert Pack "On the Death of Dylan Thomas" from *Views* (Vol. III No. 2)

Eli Siegel "To Dylan Thomas" from his *Hot Afternoons Have Been in Montana* New York: Definition Press 1957

Felix Stefanile "Christopher Marlowe, Dylan Thomas, Keats" from *Quicksilver* Autumn 1957 p. 8

John Thompson "The Man in the Wind (An Elegy for Dylan Thomas)" from *Michigan's Voices* Spring 1962

Tracy Thompson "The Ghost of Dylan Thomas" from *Beatitude* June 1960 p. 5

Wilfred Watson "An Admiration for Dylan Thomas" from *Fiddlehead* February 1954; "A Contempt for Dylan Thomas" both included in his *Friday's Child* London: Faber; New York: Farrar, Straus 1955

Phyllis Webb "Elegy on the Death of Dylan Thomas" from *CIV/n* No. 4 1954

The poems by Stanley Cooperman and Francis Golffing included in the volume are not, on the testimony of the poets, on Dylan Thomas.[11]

T. H. Jones   *Dylan Thomas*   Edinburgh & London: Oliver & Boyd 1963. Writers & Critics Series. Published in New York by Grove Press 1963; and Barnes & Noble 1966.

Geoffrey Grigson ed.   *The Concise Encyclopedia of Modern World Literature* London: Hutchinson; New York: Hawthorn 1963 pp. 439–440.

Ralph Maud   *Entrances to Dylan Thomas' Poetry*   Pittsburgh: University of Pittsburgh Press; Lowestoft: Scorpion Press 1963.

---

11. The following poems are, for convenience, listed together here since they are not included in *Garland* or mentioned elsewhere in this bibliography:

Raymond Souster "To the Welshman Who Drank with Dylan" *CIV/n* No. 7 (1954) p. 5

Louis Dudek "On the Death of Dylan Thomas" in his *Laughing Stalks* Toronto: Contact Press 1958 p. 93

T. H. Jones "Poem Dedicated to the Memory of Dylan Thomas" in his *The Enemy in the Heart* London: Rupert Hart-Davis 1957 p. 24

Evelyn A. Hardy "Dylan Thomas" in *Poetic Profiles* privately printed 1962

Gil Orlovitz "Art of the Sonnet: XV—To Dylan Thomas" *Climax* Summer 1956 p. 25

Bonnie May Malody "Dylan Thomas" *Epos* Fall 1956 p. 21

Richard Purdum "To Dylan Thomas" *Epos* Fall 1959 p. 22

Leslie Woolf Hedley in *Carleton Miscellany* Fall 1961 p. 53

Robert Scholes "In Memory of Dylan Thomas" in *New Writing from Virginia* Charlottesville 1963 p. 100

Chris Bjerknes "Ballad of the Long-legged Louse" in his *Orpheus Gone to Hell* p. 6

Rachel Graham, poem on *Leftover Life* in *Quicksilver* Spring 1958 pp. 18–19; and in issue of Autumn 1959 "Dylan-Day" p. 12

Telynog Em Morgan "Dylan" (in Welsh) in *English and Welsh Poetry* Ilfracombe, Devon: Arthur H. Stockwell 1962 p. 41

J. D. James "Poem for a Birthday" in Anthony Lodge ed.   *A Selection from Some New Poetry* in *Poetry Book Magazine* Winter 1951 p. 11

William H. Matchett "Visiting Poet" in his *Water Ouzel* Cambridge: Riverside Press 1955 pp. 7–10

Jack Micheline "Night City" (dedicated to Thomas) in his *I Kiss Angels* New York: Interim 1962

Roger Merritt Morrell M.D. "To Dylan Thomas" in his poems New York: Exposition Press 1958 p. 26

Anthony Naumann "Jackal Men (For Dylan Thomas)" in his *If I May Share* London: Collins 1964 p. 25

Natalie S. Robins "In Praise to Dylan" in her *Wild Lace* Denver: Alan Swallow 1960 p. 21

Paul Vesey "Dylan, who is Dead" in *Beyond the Blues* ed. Rosey E. Pool (New Poems by American Negroes) Lympne, Kent: Hand & Flower Press 1962

Robert Chapman "On Hearing of Dylan Thomas's Death" *New Zealand Listener* 4 December 1953 p. 14

Diana Fraser Forbes "Your Voice, Dylan Thomas" *New Ventures* (No. 1) 1954 p. 46

THESES

A. D. Dhall "Dylan Thomas: A Critical Analysis and Re-appraisal of His Earliest Poetry" M.A. Manchester University 1963.

Carolyn Sue Faulk "The Apollonian and Dionysian Modes in Lyric Poetry and Their Development in the Poetry of W. B. Yeats and Dylan Thomas" Ph.D. University of Illinois 1963. *Dissertation Abstracts* XXIV No. 10 pp. 4173–74.

Ralph J. Mills "The Development of Apocalyptic Vision in Five Modern Poets" Ph.D. Northwestern University 1963. *Dissertation Abstracts* XXIV No. 9 p. 3753.

1964

Dylan Thomas *Twenty Years A-Growing* London: J. M. Dent 1964. A film script from the story by Maurice O'Sullivan.

J. S. Dugdale ed. *Dylan Thomas. Under Milk Wood* (Notes on Chosen English Texts) Bath: James Brodie [1964].

ANTHOLOGIES

Robin Skelton ed. *Poetry of the Thirties* Harmondsworth: Penguin Books 1964 Introduction p. 34. Also his *Poetry of the Forties* Penguin 1968.

CRITICISM, ETC.

Sidney Michaels *Dylan: A Play* London: Andre Deutsch; New York: Random House 1964.[12]

Aneirin Talfan Davies *Dylan: Druid of the Broken Body* London: J. M. Dent 1964; New York: Barnes & Noble 1966.

John Ackerman *Dylan Thomas: His Life and Work* London & New York: Oxford University Press 1964.

Bill Read *The Days of Dylan Thomas* New York: McGraw-Hill; London: Weidenfeld & Nicolson 1964. With photographs by Rollie McKenna and others.

H. H. Kleinman *The Religious Sonnets of Dylan Thomas* Berkeley: University of California Press; New York: Cambridge University Press 1964.

Harvey Gross *Sound and Sense in Modern Poetry* Ann Arbor: University of Michigan Press; London: Cresset Press 1964 pp. 128, 265–271.

---

12. Columbia issued a recording of the Alec Guinness performance of this play (1964), with written reminiscences by Goddard Lieberson.

THESES

Robert Kenley Burdette   "Dylan Thomas and the Gnostic Religion"   Ph.D. University of Michigan 1964. *Dissertation Abstracts* XXV No. 12 p. 7262.

1965

Dylan Thomas   *Rebecca's Daughters*   London: Triton; Boston: Little, Brown 1965. Foreword by S. B. [Sidney Box].

Dylan Thomas   *Me and My Bike*   New York: McGraw-Hill 1965; London: Triton 1965. Introduction by Sidney Box; illustrations by Leonora Box.

CRITICISM, ETC.

Constantine FitzGibbon   *The Life of Dylan Thomas*   London: J. M. Dent; Boston: Atlantic-Little, Brown 1965.

Frederick Grubb   *A Vision of Reality: A Study of Liberalism in Twentieth-Century Verse*   London: Chatto & Windus; New York: Barnes & Noble 1965. Chapter IV "Worm's Eye: Dylan Thomas" pp. 179–187.

Jacob Korg   *Dylan Thomas*   New York: Twayne's English Authors Series 1965.

H. Richmond Neuville Jr.   *The Poetry of Dylan Thomas*   New York: Monarch Notes & Study Guides 1965.

Ralph J. Mills   "Dylan Thomas: Poetry and Process" in Nathan A. Scott ed. *Four Ways of Modern Poetry*   Richmond, Virginia: John Knox Press 1965.

THESES

Kent E. Thompson   "Dylan Thomas in Swansea"   Ph.D. University College of Swansea 1965.

Annis Vilas Pratt   "The Early Prose of Dylan Thomas"   Ph.D. Columbia University 1965. *Dissertation Abstracts* Vol. 28 pp. 2260–61 (A).

W. D. Davies   "A Critical Study of the Prose Works of Dylan Thomas, with a Consideration of Uncollected and Unpublished Poems"   B.Litt. Oxford University 1965.

1966

Dylan Thomas   *Collected Poems*   (Everyman Edition) London: J. M. Dent; New York: Dutton 1966.

Dylan Thomas *The Doctor and the Devils and Other Scripts* New York: New Directions 1966. Contents: The Doctor and the Devils; Twenty Years A-Growing: A Film Script; A Dream of Winter; The Londoner (with an introduction by Ralph Maud "The London Model for Dylan Thomas' *Under Milk Wood*").

Dylan Thomas *Miscellany Two* London: J. M. Dent 1966. Aldine paperback No. 49. Contents:

Altarwise by owl-light
After the funeral
Once it was the colour of saying
A Refusal to Mourn
Deaths and Entrances
In my Craft or Sullen Art
Ceremony After a Fire Raid
Ballad of the Long-legged Bait
Fern Hill
Over Sir John's hill
Poem on his Birthday

A Visit to Grandpa's
Extraordinary Little Cough
Where Tawe Flows
Who Do You Wish Was With Us?
A Prospect of the Sea

Quite Early One Morning
A Visit to America

Constantine FitzGibbon ed. *Selected Letters of Dylan Thomas* London: J. M. Dent 1966; New York: New Directions 1967.

CRITICISM, ETC.

Percy Marshall *Masters of English Poetry* London: Dennis Dobson 1966. Chapter 13 pp. 214–228.

Nicolette Devas *Two Flamboyant Fathers* London: Collins 1966; New York: Morrow 1967.

C. B. Cox ed. *Dylan Thomas: A Collection of Critical Essays* Englewood Cliffs, New Jersey: Prentice-Hall 1966. "Twentieth Century Views." Previously unpublished contribution: "Dylan Thomas's Prose" by Annis Pratt pp. 117–129.

William T. Moynihan *The Craft and Art of Dylan Thomas* Ithaca, New York: Cornell University Press; London: Oxford University Press 1966.

Louise Baughan Murdy *Sound and Sense in Dylan Thomas's Poetry* The Hague: Mouton 1966; New York: Humanities Press 1967.

J. Hillis Miller *Poets of Reality. Six Twentieth-Century Writers* Cambridge, Massachusetts: Harvard University Press; London: Oxford University Press 1966. Chapter V "Dylan Thomas" pp. 190–216.

Ruth Z. Temple & Martin Tucker eds. *A Library of Literary Criticism* 3 vols. New York: Frederick Ungar 1966 especially Vol. III pp. 218–224.

THESES

Gretchen Holstein Schoff "The Major Prose of Dylan Thomas" Ph.D. University of Wisconsin 1966. *Dissertation Abstracts* Vol. 28 p. 1086A.

Sue-Jin M. Jo "Dylan Thomas and the Tradition of the Romantic Journey" M.A. Columbia 1966.

1967

Ralph Maud ed. *The Notebooks of Dylan Thomas* New York: New Directions 1967. Published by J. M. Dent in London in 1968 with the title *Poet in the Making*.

Andrew Sinclair *Adventures in the Skin Trade* London: J. M. Dent 1967; New York: New Directions 1968. "A dramatisation of Dylan Thomas's uncompleted novel."[13] Introduced by James Roose-Evans.

CRITICISM, ETC.

Robert Coleman Williams ed. *A Concordance to the Collected Poems of Dylan Thomas* Lincoln: University of Nebraska Press 1967.

Min Lewis *Laugharne and Dylan Thomas* London: Dennis Dobson 1967. Illustrated by Stanley Lewis.

THESES

Martin E. Gingerich "Time and Persona in the Poetry of Dylan Thomas" Ph.D. Ohio University 1967. *Dissertation Abstracts* Vol. 28 p. 2246A.

William Peter Docken "'An enamoured man alone': The Conception of Love in the Poetry of Dylan Thomas" A.B. Harvard College 1967.

---

13. The author writes about his play in the *Camden Journal* February 1966 pp. 115–117.

1968

T. James Jones trans. *Dan Y Wenallt* Llandysul: Gwasg Gomer 1968. *Under Milk Wood* in Welsh. Illustrations by Gaynor Owen.

Dylan Thomas *Two Tales* (*Me and My Bike* and *Rebecca's Daughters*) New York: Sphere 1968, illustrations by Leonora Box.

ANTHOLOGIES

Gerald Morgan ed. *This World of Wales* Cardiff: University of Wales Press 1968. A selection of poems, with an introduction pp. 159–160.

CRITICISM, ETC.

Glyn Jones *The Dragon Has Two Tongues* ("Essays on Anglo-Welsh Writers and Writing") London: J. M. Dent 1968 especially pp. 172–203.

Alphonsus M. Reddington *Dylan Thomas: A Journey from Darkness to Light* New York: Paulist Press 1968.

THESES

Carol Ruth Helmstetter "The Prose Fiction of Dylan Thomas" Ph.D. Northwestern University 1968. *Dissertation Abstracts* Vol. 29 pp. 2262–63(A).

SECTION II

WELSH PERIODICALS AND NEWSPAPERS

SWANSEA GRAMMAR SCHOOL MAGAZINE

The following anonymous tribute ("Mr. D. J. Thomas") to Dylan Thomas' father at the time of his retirement, in the issue of March 1937, gives in an appropriate manner the background information about the school and its magazine:

A glance at the history and development of the School Magazine, the official publication of the School, which, with this issue, reaches its 33rd volume, brings into clear relief, we believe, the invigorating influence, and personality of Mr. D. J. Thomas, Senior English Master, who, to the regret of all, retired at the end of last term.

Mr. Thomas was appointed to this school in 1901, and after a few months spent at Pontypridd County School, became Senior English Master here, where thirty-six years of loyal and effective service gained for him the profound, although perhaps, silent, appreciation of all his pupils and the masters who shared his companionship, and came in consequence to share, imperceptibly, his enthusiasm and scholarship, and to adopt his high values of judgment, and keenness of discrimination. Indeed the school owes to his courtesy and culture a debt which we can best attempt to repay by seeking to emulate.

He was responsible for the first issue of the Magazine in its present form in Xmas Term, 1903, and to those of our readers who are acquainted with its fine tradition of achievement, and high reputation, it is unnecessary to write extensively, but mention should be made of the special issue of July, 1932, which served as a commemoration memoir of the Two Hundred and Fiftieth year of the foundation of the School—a truly worthy production.

The School wishes, in these few words, to express its deep appreciation of the invaluable service given the School, and in particular, this publication, by Mr. Thomas; and extends to him its best wishes in what they hope may be a long and happy retirement.

There is a photograph of the school staff, including D. J. Thomas, in the issue of March 1906, opposite p. 54, and a contribution signed "D.J.T." in the issue of March 1914, a pastiche of Shakespeare quotations under the title "A Portion of 'Twelfth Night.'" Dylan Thomas made his first contribution to the magazine during his first term at the school.

December 1925 (Vol. 22 No. 3) D. M. Thomas 3A "The Song of the Mischievous Dog" p. 74[1]

July 1926   G. M. Gwynn "The Athletic Sports" pp. 52–54: "The event of the afternoon was the winning of the Mile (under 15 years) by D. M. Thomas. Because of his age and size he had a long start; he ran so well however that he was further ahead at the finish than he was at the start."

December 1926   D.M.T. RA. " 'His Repertoire' " p. 76

March 1927   D.M.T. "The Watchers" pp. 16–17

---

1. A facsimile of this—Thomas' first published poem—appears in Read *The Days of Dylan Thomas* (1964) p. 30. Several of Thomas' contributions to the school magazine were reproduced in *Adam* No. 238 and in FitzGibbon *The Life of Dylan Thomas* (1965).

July 1927 D.M.T. "Best of All" p. 64

March 1928 D.M.T. "School Memories (By a very old 'Boy')" p. 14; D.M.T. "Forest Picture" p. 19

July 1928 D.M.T. "Life-belt" p. 42; D.M.T. "Missing" p. 43; D. M. Thomas again first in Mile Handicap (under 15) p. 47

December 1928 D.M.T. "In Dreams" p. 77

March 1929 D.M.T. "Idyll of Unforgetfulness" pp. 15–16

July 1929 (Vol. 26 No. 2) Editors: E. F. McInerny and H. W. V. Thomas. Sub-Editors: P. E. Smart and D. M. Thomas. D.M.T. "A Ballad of Salad" p. 42; Dramatic Society report pp. 48–50, Thomas played Edward Stanton in Drinkwater's "Abraham Lincoln" (he is seen in a photograph of the production); D. M. Thomas listed as first in Quarter Mile (under 15) and One Mile (under 15) p. 54

December 1929 (Vol. 26 No. 3) Editors: P. E. Smart[2] and D. M. Thomas. [D.M.T.][3] "To the Spring-spirit" p. 77; D.M.T. "Desert Idyll. A Play in One Bout" pp. 80–81; D.M.T. "Modern Poetry" pp. 82–84;[4] [D.M.T.] "Triolet" p. 88

April 1930 (Vol. 27 No. 1) Editors: P. E. Smart and D. M. Thomas. Thomas represented the Fifths at the funeral of Marley p. 1; C. B. [Christopher Barrett] Dramatic Society report on Drinkwater's "Oliver Cromwell" with Thomas in the title role pp. 10, 12 with sketches of the main characters on p. 11;[5] D.M.T. "Request to an Obliging Poet" p. 13; D.M.T. "In Borrowed Plumes" pp. 25–26, parodies on the theme of Miss Muffett in the manner of Ella Wheeler Wilcox and W. B. Yeats

July 1930 (Vol. 27 No. 2) Editors: P. E. Smart and D. M. Thomas. D.M.T. "Orpheus" p. 45; D.M.T. "The Films" pp. 54–56; P.E.S. & D.M.T. "Mr. William Shakespeare" pp. 56–58

December 1930 (Vol. 27 No. 3) Editor: D. M. Thomas. Sub-Editor: A. J. Ward. [D.M.T.] "Armistice Day" p. 75; Simple Simon, pseud.[6] "Three

---

2. P.E.S. wrote " 'Under Milk Wood'—and Reminiscence of School Days" in *Spread Eagle* April 1954 p. 134; see unsigned reviews in the same journal (published by Barclay's Bank): June 1953 *Doctor & Devils*; June 1955 *Quite Early*; October 1955 *Prospect*; April 1964 *Colour of Saying*; October 1964 *Druid*; December 1964 *Twenty Years*.

3. Poems designated [D.M.T.] were left unsigned in the pages of the magazine but attributed to D.M.T. in the "Index to Volumes 25 to 27" prepared during Thomas' editorship.

4. This precocious essay is printed in full in FitzGibbon (1965). The same issue of the magazine contains a companion piece, "Tendencies of Modern Music" by D.J.J. [Daniel J. Jones] pp. 72–75.

5. Passages pertinent to Thomas in this and subsequent reviews of his performances are to be found in Ethel Ross "Dylan Thomas and the Amateur Theatre" *The Swan* March 1958 pp. 15–21, quoted in substance by FitzGibbon (1965) pp. 65–69.

6. Swansea Public Library attributes this item to Thomas on the authority of A. Spencer Vaughan Thomas, although the Index does not reveal the pseudonym.

Nursery Rhymes" p. 82; D.M.T. "Children's Hour (or Why the B.B.C. Broke Down)" pp. 87–89; D.M.T. "Captain Bigger's Isle" p. 93; D. M. Thomas listed second in Cross Country, Senior, p. 97; [D.M.T.] "Cento (From the Golden Treasury)" p. 102; [D.M.T.] "O Fickle Sea" p. 109; feature item "Things We Cannot Credit" includes: "That D.M.T. should mispronounce a word" p. 112

April 1931 (Vol. 27 No. 4, misnumbering of Vol. 28 No. 1) Editor: D. M. Thomas. Sub-Editors: A. J. Ward and D. C. McQueen. School Notes include: "The new Reading Circle founded and supervised by Mr. D. J. Davies, D. C. McQueen and D. M. Thomas, is an interesting branch of the Dramatic Society. The first play to be read was Galsworthy's 'Escape' in which 25 boys took part" p. 122; "The 'social' in connection with the Dramatic Society was held at Lovell's cafe early in the term. After a short speech by the Headmaster, D. M. Thomas presented Mr. D. J. Davies with a writing case in appreciation of the great amount of work he has put into the last three productions of the Society" p. 123; also a note that D. M. Thomas took part in the YMCA Players' "The Man of Six" p. 124; C. B. [Christopher Barrett] "Strife"—a report on the Galsworthy play in which Thomas was Roberts, the strike leader pp. 128–130 with photograph facing p. 146; D.M.T. "Brember" pp. 139–140; D.M.T. "Two Images" p. 140; D.M.T. "The Tub" pp. 154–155; D.M.T. Hon. Sec. The Debating Society report: "The first subject chosen was 'That the modern youth is decadent.' D. M. Thomas took the affirmative .... After a very interesting and provocative discussion, Thomas dealing mainly with the aesthetic elements of the subject ... the motion was lost by 34 votes to 4" p. 165[7]

July 1931 (Vol. 28 No. 2) Editor: D. M. Thomas. Sub-Editor: A. J. Ward. D.M.T. "The Terrible Tale of Tom Tipplewhite" pp. 186–187. School Notes: D. M. Thomas and others took part in the YMCA Players' *Captain X* p. 187. D.M.T. "The Callous Stars" p. 190; D.M.T. "The Sincerest Form of Flattery (A Literary Course)" pp. 191–196—parodies; a note, presumably by the Hon. Sec.: "The Debating Society has had no meetings this term. Summer weather, the committee insists, is no time for heated argument. It is, indeed, a time of lethargic agreement, and a debate in which one side yawningly agrees with the other is no stimulant to our intellects" p. 196; D.M.T. "Two Decorations" p. 200[8]

July 1933 D.M.T. (O.B.) "Decline and Fall of Cassius Jones. A Cautionary Poem" pp. 64–65

December 1933 Old Boy,[9] pseud. "Jarley's" pp. 137–139

July 1934 Old Boy, pseud. "In the Garden" pp. 69–70

---

7. In view of Thomas' preoccupation we may assume that the two other feature items dealing with effeminacy are by Thomas (although the Index leaves them anonymous): "The Beauty Department" pp. 152–153, and "? ? ?" pp. 162–163.

8. A short story by Junius, pseud. "The Nightmare" (p. 203) might be by Thomas.

9. This story is attributed to Thomas on the authority of George H. Gwynne, a retired master. The story "In the Garden" of July 1934 has claim, from *internal* evidence, to be considered Thomas'.

March 1937   Anon. "Mr. D. J. Thomas" p. 8; VIA pseud. "Dylan Thomas" pp. 17–19, a general summary

April 1938   W. D. Morgan VIB Arts "Dylan Thomas and Modern Poetry" pp. 15–17

December 1950   I.D.D. [Iolo D. Davies] "Twenty Years On" pp. 10–12, reminiscences

December 1952   R.M. "Jubilee" pp. 20–23, on Thomas' editorship of the school magazine

* * *

December 1953   L.H. [Linton Humphrey] and A.D.E. [A. D. Edwards] (VIA Arts) " 'A Grief Ago' " pp. 6–7, full obituary[10]

Easter 1957   S. Martin Stephens (VIA Arts) on "Under Milk Wood" (Sherek production) in Swansea pp. 12–13

Summer 1963   W.J.B. (VIA Arts) "Epitaph for a Poet" pp. 13–14, on the Jack Howells film of Thomas

Christmas 1963   Dylan Jones VIA Arts "I Remember Dylan Thomas" p. 9:

> (*Dr. Daniel Jones, the distinguished composer, was a life-long friend of Dylan Thomas: the author of this article is the son of Dr. Jones and the godson of the poet.*)

The number of people who claim to have been friendly with or to have known Dylan Thomas is amazing and ever increasing. I, who have a deep abhorrence of the capitalization which prompts so many of these alleged claims, will attempt to add some authentic memories of this great poet to the mass of myth which is accumulating around his name. The main facts of his life, from his birth in Swansea in 1914, through his education at this School and his development into one of the world's most outstanding poets, to his death in New York in November, 1953, are well known; it is not my purpose to reiterate these, but to record some of my personal impressions of him, which will lack continuity and coherence as I was only eight when he died.

In fact, my most vivid memory concerning him was of his death. My parents had been in constant communication with New York during his illness and, when we were informed of his death, the grief which enveloped our house was such that it created an immense impression upon me. Although this, my most vivid memory, is one of sadness, the over-riding impression that I had of him was of kindness and humour.

His visits to our home, which he called his town-house, whereas we referred to the boat-house at Laugharne as our country-residence, were frequent, and remarkable for their unexpectedness and hurried nature. This latter point I well remember because, when he arrived once at our house at seven o'clock in the morning after an unbroken journey from New York, it was I who had to get out of bed to open the door for him. The result of a particularly hurried departure of his serves as a good example of the extent to which his humour coloured his life; for he left all

---

10. See also *Dynevor Secondary School Magazine* (Swansea) December 1953 Old Dy'vorian, pseud. "Defence for Dylan" (poem) p. 15.

his shirts behind in a drawer. On the next day we received the following message by telegram: "For Pete's sake send my shirts, Love, Pete." His bedroom, after each departure, was always littered with apple cores, half-finished packets of liquorice all-sorts, and paper-back detective novels, which he read incessantly. He was ever ready to join in a game, and I remember one particular, back-yard test match, involving myself, my father and Dylan Thomas, in which he broke my bedroom window. I, in fear of being accused of this by my mother, committed the sin of telling on him to her. My general impression was that his visits always heralded a period of laughing and scuffling. One of these sessions of mock fighting resulted in my biting his thumb as hard as I could. Snatching his hand away, he looked at me gravely and said, "Dog does not bite dog."

However, these gifts of humour and frivolity were coupled with an extreme consideration and kindness, many instances of which I can recall. The action that he took when I suffered a disease of the heel is typical of this; for, when he next visited London after I had contracted this condition, he devoted his time, despite the fact that he had very important business to which he had to attend, to inquiring as to the specialists who were best qualified to treat my complaint. In the letter which we then received from him, he listed these specialists and ended by writing: "Of these the last named is the top, Love, Bottom." He was a very welcome guest, and so much a friend of the family, that, when I was born, he became my godfather.

When I think of the man himself, I consider that his outstanding qualities were his generosity, kindness and humour; when I read his prose and, in particular, his poetry, the qualities with which he seems to have been endowed most were his genius for poetical expression, the depth of his sincerity and beliefs, a greatness of intellect, and, again, his gift of humour.

Christmas 1965 "School Notes" p. 3: "Our most famous old-boy, Dylan Thomas, who is fast becoming an institution, has again attracted people to find out all they can about his life. A new biography was published by Constantine FitzGibbon, which seeks to explode 'the myth of Dylan Thomas' but which, inevitably, only adds to it. Unfortunately, the book (now in the school library) contains a number of errors relating to Dylan's schooldays, notably confusion of Mr. J. Morris Williams and Mr. J. Morgan Williams."

SOUTH WALES DAILY POST

Thomas joined the staff of this Swansea daily (with its weekly *Herald of Wales*) when he left school in July 1931. J. D. Williams, the editor (who also wrote "Gossip of the Day" above the pseudonym "The Listener"), was early aware of Thomas' unique talent.

23 June 1926 "Grammar School Sports. Smallest Competitor Wins Mile Race at Swansea" p. 5[11]

---

11. See also the *Cambrian Daily Leader* 23 June 1926 "Grammar School Mile Winner" p. 3, a photograph with the caption: "D. M. Thomas (Mansel), who won the mile race for boys under 15 years of age, at the Swansea Grammar School Sports. He is only 12 years of age." This is the newspaper clipping which, according to John Malcolm Brinnin, Thomas kept in his wallet up to the day of his death. There is a reproduction of it in Read p. 30.

4 May 1929 J.D.H. review of school play "Abraham Lincoln" p. 7—
Thomas not mentioned although he took part

21 February 1930 J.D.H. review of school play "Oliver Cromwell" p. 6

17 December 1930 Anon. review of school play "Strife" p. 7

30 December 1930 The Listener, pseud. mentions Thomas as editor of the
school magazine p. 4

2 June 1931 The Listener, pseud. "A Swansea Publication" p. 4[12]

15 July 1931 [Dylan Thomas][13] "Nellie Wallace's Mimicry" p. 7

10 December 1931 Photo and caption of YMCA play "The Fourth Wall"
p. 7, Thomas included

19 February 1932 J.D.W. review of Little Theatre "Hay Fever" p. 3

On 14 March 1932 the *South Wales Daily Post* changed its name to
SOUTH WALES EVENING POST

22 April 1932 J.D.W. review of Little Theatre "Beaux Strategem" p. 7

7 January 1933 D.M.T. "Genius and Madness Akin in World of Art" p. 7

14 January 1933 " 'Laughing Torso' No Truth in Suggestion That It Was
Banned" p. 1: "On January 7 the 'Evening Post' published an article, from
a contributor, under the heading 'Genius and Madness Akin in World of
Art,' and the following reference was made:— 'Eccentricity is not lacking
among modern artists, a Miss Nina Hammnett, author of the banned book,
"Laughing Torso," is at pains to disclose.' We are informed by Miss
Hammnett that there is no truth in the suggestion that 'Laughing Torso'
has been banned. We are informed by Miss Hammnett it enjoys a very wide
circulation. We offer Miss Hammnett sincere apologies, and regret any
misapprehension the mistake may have caused."

15 February 1933 J.D.W. review of Little Theatre "Merry Wives of Windsor" p. 7, Thomas listed as Host of the Garter

15 March 1933 J.D.W. review of Little Theatre "Peter and Paul" p. 5
(photograph of Thomas as Peter on 14 March 1933 p. 10)

4 July 1933 "Today's Gossip" p. 4, on Swansea "boys": "Dylan Thomas
recently tried his hand at journalism, but his aspirations are for another

---

12. Thomas wanted to edit a magazine to be called *Prose and Verse*. The paragraph
requesting contributions ("their only qualification must be originality of outlook and
expression") is quoted in full in *Colour of Saying* p. xiii.

13. Wynford Vaughan Thomas in *The Listener* 16 January 1958 describes his ac-
companying Thomas to interview the famous comedienne in her dressing room in what
was probably the new reporter's first and perhaps voluntary assignment. We have at this
time no certain information about Thomas' writing in the *Post* between this first piece
and his last, on 7 January 1933.

branch of the craft of writing. He has concluded a novel, which is under consideration by publishers, and last week one of his poems was read over the wireless."

7 December 1933   E.J. review of Little Theatre "Strange Orchestra" p. 5

17 January 1934   J.D.W. review of Little Theatre "Way of the World" p. 6, Thomas listed as Witwoud

15 February 1934   J.D.W. review of Little Theatre "Martine" p. 5: "Miss Goodrich last night had as hard a parcel of luck as any producer can have: her chief male character failed her."

7 March 1934   J.D.W. review of Little Theatre "Richard II" p. 6, Thomas reduced to the King's Groom

19 November 1934   The Listener, pseud. "Our Young Poets" p. 4: "Mr. Dylan Thomas has a volume of verse coming out before Christmas. He is now definitely placed by the critics among our 'coming men.' I hope that the volume will contain the fine lines that he wrote after the performance of the 'Electra' in the garden of Mayor and the late Mrs. Bertie Perkins's home at Sketty. Mr. Thomas has just taken up his quarters in London, where he is doing a lot of book reviewing."

1 January 1935   The Listener, pseud. "Gossip of the Day: Poems of Dylan Thomas" p. 4:

Mr. Dylan Thomas's verse is now published, and those who want to see what the most modern of poetry is like will be able to satisfy their curiosity in the eighteen poems given in the volume.

Mr. Thomas is at the spear-head of the very latest movement. I committed a faux-pas the other day when, mistakenly, I referred to him as of the T. S. Eliot, Ezra Pounds, and Auden school.

"Eliot! Pounds! Auden!" the young man said in derision. "They are back-numbers in the poetical world."

Poetry moves swiftly these days.

5 January 1935   letter from A. E. Trick p. 4: "Are these cultural circles so moribund that they cannot see a new star in the literary firmament?" 10 January 1935 responses from Trevor Hughes, Harrow, and Gwyn I. Lewis, Neath, p. 4; 12 January 1935 reply from A. E. Trick "The New Poetry" p. 4:

Mr. Gwyn Lewis reprimands me for making Dylan Thomas's poems the subject of newspaper controversy, yet displays no lack of haste in joining in it.

Mr. Hughes would have me breathe a benediction and pass on silent feet.

Is poetry then sacrosanct? Something aloof, and beyond the understanding of the masses? There is enough cant in literary fashions without assuming it in our attitude towards literature.

Let us be as clear sighted as the poet himself. His poetry is granite—hard, shed of all romantic illusions. We must adopt the same attitude in our appraisement of them, not treat poetry as though it were a frail spinster, wrapped in blanket cloth, and able to walk abroad only when the sun is at the meridian.

These poems at least are lusty; having the full equipment of young manhood, the courage and strength to walk the macadam roads at all hours, in all weathers, with all sorts. They are of a period other than the inhibited—consumptive—attic period of art.

9 January 1935   The Listener, pseud. "Gossip of the Day: Dylan Thomas's Poems" p. 4:

I was talking at Laugharne at the week-end with Mr. Richard Hughes about the poems of Dylan Thomas—some of which he had seen in the literary weeklies, and much admired—and confessing to him the difficulty of reviewing them adequately.

"You should give the job to a young man of his own period," he said. Which, happily, was exactly the way that had been taken out of the dilemma.

The "18 Poems" will be reviewed in to-morrow's "Herald of Wales" by Mr. A. Spencer Vaughan-Thomas, B.A. Mr. Vaughan-Thomas, who is himself a poet, is English master at Barnet Grammar School, and he has recently been compiling a poetical anthology.

12 January 1935   The Listener, pseud. "Gossip of the Day" p. 4: "Amid all the excitement about the new poetry, do not let us forget the old poets.... E. Howard Harris, for instance, whose recent volume was reviewed in the 'Herald of Wales' some time ago."

4 October 1935   The Listener, pseud. "Swansea Artist" p. 6 report on Alfred Janes' portrait of Thomas

4 November 1935   The Listener, pseud. "Dylan Thomas's New Poems" p. 4: "Dylan Thomas, who was in Swansea over the weekend, told me that his second volume of verse is likely to be appearing shortly. I should imagine that the new poems will cause more discussion than even those in the first volume."

1 September 1936   The Listener, pseud. "Dylan Thomas" p. 4: "Dylan Thomas, the young Swansea poet, has been commissioned to write a book of Welsh travels, with an emphasis on the personal side. It ought to be a lively and provocative piece of work. Augustus John is to contribute a portrait of the author to the book."

10 September 1936   The Listener, pseud.[14] "Dylan Thomas Problems" p. 4

22 January 1937   "Gossip of the Day" p. 4: "After a prolonged stay in London, crowded more than usual with incident and notable chiefly for the long controversy regarding his latest book which spread, finally, to some of the most popular evening newspapers, Mr. Dylan Thomas has returned to Swansea. He is off again shortly, to the Universities of Oxford and Cambridge, where he has consented to address the English Societies."

---

14. This is The Listener's last column. Mr. Williams was killed in a mountain-climbing accident. His last article was on Thomas in the newspaper office; see *Herald of Wales* 19 September 1936. It appears that Charles Fisher, a good friend of Thomas', did some of the subsequent writing of "Gossip of the Day."

13 March 1937 "Gossip of the Day" p. 4: "Mr. Wynford Thomas' persis-
tence has at last been rewarded, and Dylan Thomas is to give a reading of
his own work from the West Regional Transmitter in the near future . . . .
Incidentally his best short story, 'A Prospect of the Sea,' has just been
published. I had the opportunity of reading it in manuscript, and it is an
extraordinary work containing some of the most beautiful images conceiv-
able. The title was chosen as a compliment to 'Mor Olwg,' the musical
work of a Swansea friend, Thomas Warner, broadcast of which, you may
remember, was postponed because of difficulties in rehearsal."

21 April 1937 "Tonight's Wireless" p. 3: "Dylan Thomas, a young Swansea
poet, will read some of his own poems in the Welsh programme at 9.45."

5 July 1937 "Gossip of the Day" p. 4, review of *Wales* magazine; Thomas'
"Prologue to an Adventure" "might best be described as an inverted
Pilgrim's Progress"

21 February 1938 "Gossip of the Day" p. 4: "Dylan Thomas writes to me
from Hampshire that the bulk of his short stories, written over a period
of several years, will be published next month by Europa Press in London
and Paris. During the last few months Mr. Thomas has been working on a
novel which will be published in Paris. He has also been lecturing to
classes at London University, and for these returns to town next week."

28 April 1938 "Gossip of the Day" p. 6, review of the *Swansea Grammar
School Magazine* article on Thomas (April 1938): "unusual of its kind because many of its sentiments are at least defensible. Mr. Thomas has not,
however, 'obviously made a careful study of the French surrealists.' He
told me so yesterday in the plainest manner possible."

18 March 1939 Anon. review of *Wales* No. 6/7: "Dylan Thomas contributes
two poems, each of them bitter, regretful, easier to understand than usual,
and out of the stream of his main creative ability."

27 April 1939 "Gossip of the Day" p. 4: "Staying with Dylan Thomas when I
called at his Laugharne home yesterday was Keidrych Rhys (writes a correspondent), and, of course, a new permanent resident, three months' old
Llewellyn Thomas, whose Godfathers are Richard Hughes and Augustus
John."

26 August 1939 C.F. [Charles Fisher] review of *Map of Love* p. 4

31 August 1939 "Dylan in Discussion on the Air" p. 4, a broadcast with
Keidrych Rhys the following Wednesday

26 April 1940 C.F. review of *Portrait* p. 4

7 July 1941 "Gossip of the Day" p. 3: "Mr. Ernest T. Davies, the well-
known Swansea commercial traveller, has 'broken new ground.' During the
winter he commenced writing a novel, and was much encouraged in his
efforts by Mr. Dylan Thomas and others."

24 January 1942 D.M.R. review of *Folios of New Writing* p. 3, on Thomas'
"A Fine Beginning": "The piece will strike some chords for Swansea

readers in the location of Samuel's house, at least, and in the lines 'Mrs. Mayor's Chain, Madame Cocked Hat, Lady Settee, I am breaking tureens in the cupboard under the stairs.' "

20 February 1943   "Dylan Thomas Broadcast" p. 3, extracts from "Reminiscence of Childhood" (BBC 15 February 1943)

25 September 1944   Dilys Rowe review of *Modern Welsh Poetry* p. 3

 6 April 1945   "New Quay Shooting Charge" p. 3; 23 June 1945 "Army Captain Acquitted" p. 4[15]

 6 April 1946   Dilys Rowe review of *Deaths & Entrances* p. 3

25 July 1947   "Dylan in School" p. 3, reference to "Return Journey" (BBC Wales 20 June 1947); further reference 25 August 1947 p. 3

14 April 1948   "Gossip of the Day" p. 3, on Mervyn Levy's exhibition in Swindon: "Dylan Thomas has written a foreword as an introduction to the drawings which are largely in red chalk, of which the poet says: 'Red chalk glows in his drawings because his passion for the human figure is glowing.' "

13 May 1948   "Gossip of the Day" p. 3, Augustus John's portrait of Thomas attracting attention at the Leicester Galleries

 7 May 1949   Dilys Rowe review of Treece p. 4

25 October 1949   Gwrandawr, pseud. "Wireless in Wales" p. 4, on "Swansea and the Arts" (BBC Wales 24 October 1949)

 8 November 1952   John Ormond Thomas review of *Collected Poems* p. 4

20 January 1953   Gwrandawr, pseud. "Wireless in Wales" p. 4, Thomas read Vernon Watkins' Ballads (BBC Wales 14 January 1953)

16 May 1953   J.O.T. review of *Doctor & Devils* p. 4

27 October 1953   Gwrandawr, pseud. "Wireless in Wales" p. 4, on Daniel Jones' "Barbarous Hexameters" (BBC Wales 20 October 1953) and Thomas' reading

* * *

10 November 1953   News of Thomas' death p. 1; Editorial p. 4. H.D. [Herbert Davies] obituary p. 4: "I last met him some months ago when I mentioned I was looking for some atmospheric music to open a play. 'Ah,' he said, 'what you want is hush-husher music.' "

11 November 1953   "Mayor supports plan to aid Mrs. Dylan Thomas" p. 1[16]

---

15. Several Welsh newspapers reported this incident, in which Thomas' house in New Quay was shot at, unaware that the chief witness was Thomas. See the *Welsh Gazette* (below) for the fullest report.

16. The growth of the Mayor of Swansea's Fund is followed in reports of donations and donors until what appears to be the last mention of the Fund on 6 January 1954 when the total was £813. Though some of the donors were famous people, we have refrained from listing any particular names or sums.

14 November 1953   Report of John Ormond Thomas speaking on Thomas at the University College, Swansea, p. 4

16 November 1953   Letter from Gwen John, Swansea, p. 4

17 November 1953   Letter of tribute from E. Howard Harris p. 4

18 November 1953   "Gossip of the Day" p. 4, quotes letter from a correspondent about Thomas' last reading in New York

19 November 1953   "Council stands in sympathy" p. 3

23 November 1953   "Friends Bear in the Body of Dylan Thomas" p. 1

24 November 1953   Funeral p. 1; 25 November 1953 Herbert Davies, news of funeral with pictures p. 6

28 November 1953   "The Last Portrait" p. 4, Alfred Janes was at work on it when Thomas left for America

11 December 1953   Letter from John Furlong, Niagara Falls, Ontario, p. 6, school memories

14 January 1954   News of Mt. Holyoke students' tribute to Thomas p. 8

28 January 1954   Thomas' name brought into a discussion on Sunday pub opening p. 5

13 February 1954   Lynette Roberts on recent portrait by Ceri Richards p. 4

23 February 1954   "Gossip of the Day" p. 4, reminiscences

24 February 1954   Gwrandawr, pseud. review of "Under Milk Wood" (BBC production 18 February 1954) p. 4

6 March 1954   D.H.I.P. [D. H. I. Powell] review of *Under Milk Wood* p. 4

16 March 1954   Bishop Gore Grammar School tribute p. 5

20 March 1954   David Bell on Ceri Richards "The Painter and the Poet" exhibition p. 4

7 August 1954   E.D.B.P. on Daniel Jones' symphony dedicated to Thomas p. 5

4 November 1954   D.H.I.P. review of *Quite Early* p. 4

13 August 1955   D.H.I.P. review of *Prospect* p. 4

9 November 1955   H.A.R. reminiscence of Thomas reading before the English Society of Cardiff p. 4, also mention of Emlyn Williams' performance at Biship Gore School

28 April 1956   D.H.I.P. review of Brinnin p. 4

7 October 1957   Leslie M. Rees "Dylan on Display" p. 4, on Swansea Public Library exhibition, with reproduction of Mervyn Levy drawings of Thomas in 1936 and 1946

14 November 1957   Froom Tyler review of *Letters to Vernon Watkins* p. 8

10 November 1960   "The Film Makers Come to Dylan Land" p. 6, interview with Jack Howells

19 November 1960   Froom Tyler review of Tedlock p. 4

19 October 1963   Froom Tyler review of *Colour of Saying* p. 4

7 November 1963   Dylan Thomas "The Poets of Swansea" p. 6: to mark the 10th anniversary of Thomas' death, the *Post* reprinted some of the articles on local poets that had appeared in the *Herald of Wales* in 1932. See also 8 November 1963 p. 8, 9 November 1963 p. 4, and 11 November 1963 p. 6

8 November 1963   Alan Road "Portrait of the Poet as a Young Reporter" p. 8

9 November 1963   J. Battenbo "Dylan Thomas" (poem) p. 4

11 November 1963   "Friends of Dylan Mark His Memory" p. 3, Vernon Watkins unveils stone by Ronald Cour in Cwmdonkin Park[17]

14 November 1963   J. R. John "When Dylan was told 'Be intelligible' " p. 8, by a "retired member of Evening Post staff"

16 November 1963   Letter from Keidrych Rhys p. 7, on BBC (Third) programme on Thomas; 20 November 1963 defense by J. Gwyn Griffiths of the University College, Swansea, p. 4: "I was asked to assess his debt to the Welsh literary tradition, that is, the tradition enshrined in the Welsh language. My answer was, and is, that the debt was nil."

19 November 1963   Letter from F. V. Jeffreys p. 6, describing vain efforts to teach Thomas shorthand

11 July 1964   J. Gwyn Griffiths review of *Druid* p. 4

24 October 1964   Froom Tyler review of Ackerman p. 4

16 October 1965   Froom Tyler review of FitzGibbon p. 6

A Saturday newspaper from the same house as the *South Wales Evening Post* and with the same editor, J. D. Williams, was the

HERALD OF WALES

20 December 1930   Photograph of the cast of school play "Strife" p. [8], includes Thomas

21 February 1931   Anon. review of YMCA "Man at Six" p. 9: Thomas as Sir Joseph Pine "provided the required tenseness of atmosphere"; photograph of cast p. 12

2 May 1931   Photograph of the cast of YMCA "Captain X" p. 3

---

17. See Watkins' final elegy "At Cwmrhydyceirw Quarry" in his *Fidelities* London: Faber 1968 pp. 79–80, with a note about the memorial stone.

12 December 1931   Photograph of YMCA "The Fourth Wall" p. 1; Anon. review p. 12, congratulates Thomas as producer[18]—his part "a really sinister blackguard"

 9 January 1932   Dylan Thomas "The Poets of Swansea—Walter Savage Landor to James Chapman Woods" p. 7

23 January 1932   Dylan Thomas "Tragedy of Swansea's Comic Genius—The Story of Llewelyn Prichard" p. 6; [Dylan Thomas][19] " 'Caesar's Wife' At Swansea" p. 12

20 February 1932   Dylan Thomas "Minor Poets of Old Swansea" p. 4

19 March 1932   Dylan Thomas "Minor Poets of Swansea—A Study of Pierre Claire" p. 4

23 April 1932   Dylan Thomas "Verse of James Chapman Woods—A Critical Estimate" p. 4, with a poem "Youth Calls to Age" occasioned by his subject

25 June 1932   Dylan Thomas "A Modern Poet of Gower" p. 8[20]

 5 November 1932   Dylan Thomas "A Baroness Journeys Into Gower" p. 6[21]

15 July 1933   Dylan Thomas "Greek Play In a Garden" p. 1[22]

16 December 1933   Photograph of the Little Theatre "Strange Orchestra" p. 8, with Thomas included

17 February 1934   Photograph of *rehearsal* of Little Theatre "Martine" p. 2, includes Thomas, though the final performance didn't—see 24 February 1934 p. 5

12 January 1935   The Onlooker, pseud. "Classicist and Modernist" p. 5, tells of reaction to Thomas' articles on Swansea poets; A. Spencer Vaughan-

---

18. Thomas succeeded H. E. James as producer for the YMCA Players. A note in the "I Hear" column (9 January 1932 p. 1) indicates that "the YMCA Players, who are always eager to try their hand at something new, are thinking of running a revue this season as well as a full-length play." There appears to be no evidence that either of these plans materialized.

19. Kent E. Thompson in his Swansea thesis (1965) attributes this review to Thomas on the authority of Malcolm Graham, the leading actor in the Little Theatre production.

20. When this essay on E. Howard Harris was reprinted in the *Post* (11 November 1963) it was pointed out that Thomas was 18 and Harris 56 at the time it was written, and that Harris had thought it "a little unkind." But see his tribute to Thomas in the *Post* 17 November 1953.

21. "Lady Barham's Six Chapels. The Story of Paraclete. End of a Great Ministry." A history of the chapel where Thomas' uncle had just retired as minister: "Mumbles, and indeed the whole of Gower, will lose one of its best-known and best-loved inhabitants." A rather strained filial tone in this last of Thomas' professional articles for the *Herald*.

22. "Return Journey" includes in its self-portrait reference to "poems printed in the *Herald of Wales*; there was one about an open-air performance of *Electra* in Mrs. Bertie Perkin's garden in Sketty." The poem is reproduced in the Notes to *Quite Early*.

Thomas B.A. (Oxon) review of *18 Poems* p. 6, with sketch by Harold Morgan

8 June 1935   Dylan Thomas "Poet, 1935" p. 1

19 September 1936   J.D.W. [J. D. Williams] review of *Twenty-five Poems* "The New Poems by Dylan Thomas: Some Of His Joyous Adventures In A Newspaper Office, By J.D.W. (Written Shortly Before His Death.)" pp. 1, 12:

When Dylan Thomas's "Eighteen Poems" was published last year, despairing of ever making anything of poems, none of which brought the least understanding to me, I passed over the task of reviewing the book to a young contemporary of the poet.

He found in it a great treasure; and he said so. I wish he were handy just now, when Dylan Thomas's second volume is hot off the press: "Twenty-Five Poems" (Dent: 2s. 6d.). As he is not, it is my job to say something about them. And as I cannot say much about them, I may say a little about him.

Dylan Thomas is the son of the English master at the Swansea Grammar School. He is in his twenties, the early twenties I should say. I saw him first on the stage, a schoolboy playing in the annual drama show of the Grammar School, Cromwell, I think, in Drinkwater's pageant. It was obvious to the most dense person in the Llewelyn Hall that here was a clean-cut personality. He stood out shoulder high above the rest of the cast: not alone because his part called for it, but because of a certain distinction of voice and bearing.

It was only upon the Grammar School stage that Dylan Thomas then brought credit to the School: I do not believe he sat an examination, and that he left without a certificate!

In the next stage he was a beginner in Swansea journalism, under strict injunctions to learn shorthand within a definite time! It was good discipline, I thought, as I saw him moving about amid the inquests, the police courts, the district council meetings; "making the calls" at those places where newspapers gather their news. But Dylan Thomas never mastered shorthand—did he ever try!—and his career in the reporting room of the "Evening Post" was entertaining, but a sore trial to the chief reporter, who had to see that all the engagements on the "Book" were covered.

I recall a few enlivening incidents. I remember a sub-editor coming to me, with a long face, for assistance in trouble. Mutely, he handed me "copy" written by Dylan Thomas about a chapel concert at ———, the night before. The music was Coleridge-Taylor's setting of parts of Longfellow's "Hiawatha."

As I turned the pages, I said to myself, as a reviewer said long ago: "This will never do." "Cythraul Canu" would have been unleashed in Swansea that night were unexpurgated Dylan Thomas on the music, the poem, and the performance, to have been published. For, as an introduction of some two or three "sticks," Mr. Longfellow was placed in his dustbin, as a gentle prelude to most slighting treatment of composer and singers. And although Longfellow has passed out of fashion, there were too many followers of his poems in Swansea, and indeed too many lovers of the music of "Hiawatha" to have them flouted by a youth whose competency to ride roughshod over the older generations had not been established.

A milder and sedater report of the concert appeared in the "Evening Post" that night. The incident may have its interest in calculating Dylan Thomas's career: it was the first running up of the flag by youth without respect for the achievements of the Victorians!

Dylan Thomas, of course, was not cut out for reporting and shorthand. But the time could not have been wasted; for one thing he wrote, for the "Herald of Wales," week by week until the subject had been exhausted and the Swansea poets all labelled truly, a series upon the verse-writers from Ann of Swansea down to Howard Harris. It was a series that gave me dreadful pangs; it was heart-breaking to give the right of way to an irreverent youth who, week after week, turned in articles in which all that one felt to be established in art was knocked roughly over. Once or twice I persuaded the young iconoclast to moderate a judgment here and there; to be gentler with this and that poet. One of the living Swansea poets felt his hand sorely even after the restraining influence had tempered the wind to the shorn lamb!

James Chapman Woods, however, whose privately-issued poems I had turned over to this dissector, took his medicine like the great gentleman he was; he wrote Dylan Thomas a charming letter of true appreciation. He was the first of the poets to see the new star coming above the horizon.

There was also a short story which the poet submitted for publication in the "Herald of Wales." All that I can recall about it now is that it was sited in a mining valley, and that it ended with a head in the gas stove. This never would have done for the "Herald"; laughingly we agreed that it would not. I see now that, as it stood, it would have had a considerable success in the magazines that cater for the upper intelligence.

Dylan Thomas's press career ended. His shorthand did not become efficient enough to help him at a mothers' meeting. He left us, and presently he embarked upon his London adventure. I think it was just about this time that he wrote for the "Herald of Wales" a poem about the "Electra" in Mrs. Bertie Perkins's garden at Sketty; an exquisitely lovely piece of work (not a bit in his "modern" manner) that gave distinction to one week's issue of this journal.

In London he made phenomenal progress—among the upper intelligences. Poems of his began to appear here and there in the magazines that circulate in Chelsea, and where the high-brows congregate. He began to make the grade. He was in "The Criterion." He was in "The Listener." A story was included in a collection of the year's best short stories. Then "Eighteen Poems" appeared.

I think that I am very successfully circumventing the task of reviewing "Twenty-Five Poems"! Frankly, most of them are outside my range. Consider:

> "Now
> Say nay,
> So star fall,
> So the ball fail.
> So solve the mystic sun, the wife of light,
> The sun that leaps on petals through a nought,
> The come-a-cropper rider of the flower."

Now what am I, child of the Victorian Day, who loves the sweetness and lucidity of Tennyson, who even swims in the enjoyment of Lewis Morris, who still turns to

Wordsworth for sustenance—what am I to make of this! Or:

> "Hold hard, these ancient minutes in the cuckoo's mouth,
> Under the lank, fourth folly on Glamorgan's hill,
> As the green blooms rise upward, to the drive of time;
> Time, in a folly's rider, like a county man,
> Over the vault of ridings with his hound at heel,
> Drives forth my men, my children, from the hanging south."

A line here of splendid imagery: "Here in this spring, stars float along the void"; or "Beginning with doom in the bulb, the spring unravels," can thrill me; but for my sins, for my imprisonment in my own time, I am condemned to read most of these Twenty-Five Poems with uncomprehending heart and eyes. Let it be said for my salvation that I am conscious of my loss. The Poets of "Thirty-Six" have opened a new page. We of the Eighties and Nineties had better stick to our Wordsworth and our Tennyson; even to our Russell Lowell.

A few poems there are in this collection that convey meaning without shedding of blood to such an ancient as I; like: "This bread I break was once the oat, This wine upon a foreign tree Plunged in its fruit." And "Was there a time when dancers with their fiddles, In children's circuses could stay their troubles?" with its last few lines:

> "What's never known is safest in this life.
> Under the skysigns they who have no arms
> Have cleanest hands, and, as the heartless ghost
> Alone's unhurt, so the blind man sees best."

Even a Victorian can be thrilled by that! But what miles away from the robust sanity of the poets who were our Gods!

3 October 1936   E. Howard Harris M.A. "A Comment on J.D.W.'s Last Article—Unrepentent Traditionalist and the Poetry of Dylan Thomas" p. 6

31 July 1937   Charles Fisher, substantial review of *Wales* magazine pp. 1, 12

8 January 1938   Charles Fisher on Thomas Warner p. 1, on his friendship with Daniel Jones, and "impromptu chamber music, in which the 'cello part was sometimes taken by another friend, Dylan Thomas"

5 March 1938   The Onlooker, pseud. paragraph on *Wales* (No. 4) p. 5

12 March 1938   Charles Fisher "Pen Picture of Swansea Grammar School Masters" p. 1, on D. J. Thomas

During the war the *Herald of Wales* apparently had to be content with cultural items repeated from the *Post*: 2 September 1939 C.F. review of *Map of Love* p. 4; 27 April 1940 C.F. review of *Portrait* p. 4; 27 February 1943 repeat of extract from "Reminiscences" p. 4; 13 April 1946 Dilys Rowe review of *Deaths & Entrances* p. 4.

After the war the paper changed its nature altogether, and one finds only a small paragraph at the time of Thomas' death 14 November 1953 p. 4.

WESTERN MAIL

Cardiff morning daily.

14 January 1927 D. M. Thomas, Swansea, "His Requiem" p. 6, one of the daily poems in the "Wales Day by Day" column

10 September 1936 A. T. G. Edwards short review of *Twenty-five Poems* p. 11: the poems merit "serious and thoughtful attention"

30 June 1937 Glyn Roberts "New Literary Vitality in Wales" p. 8, a review of *Wales* magazine; Keidrych Rhys and Thomas called "enfant terribles"

19 July 1939 Dr. T. Gwynn Jones "The Modern Trend in Welsh Poetry" p. 11; this article, which did not specifically mention Thomas, prompted a long exchange of letters which occasionally did: 3 August 1939 from Keidrych Rhys p. 9; 8 August 1939 from Nigel Heseltine p. 9; 10 August 1939 from Davies Aberpennar p. 9; 15 August from Nigel Heseltine p. 9; 17 August from Keidrych Rhys p. 9 (mentions Thomas as "relatively unknown"); 22 August from Davies Aberpennar p. 9; 23 August from Keidrych Rhys p. 9; 24 August from Tom H. Richards p. 9; 26 August from Nigel Heseltine p. 9; 28 August from Keidrych Rhys p. 9; 30 August from Huw Menai p. 9; and 1 September 1939 from Keidrych Rhys p. 9

24 August 1939 A. T. G. Edwards review of *Map of Love* p. 9: "I got on better with the stories"

31 August 1939 Letter from Shinkins Abercwmboi p. 9, scoffs at "Because the pleasure bird whistles"; reply by Keidrych Rhys 11 September 1939 p. 9

28 October 1939 Herbert Read's review of *Map of Love* quoted p. 4

4 April 1940 A. T. G. Edwards review of *Portrait* p. 7

17 January 1945 Letter from Keidrych Rhys p. 3, on the situation of Welshmen writing in English

22 June 1945 News item about the shooting at New Quay p. 3

20 April 1946 Letter from Owen R. Jones p. 3, finds obscure such phrases as "All the moon long" and "Once below a time"

15 May 1946 A. G. Prys-Jones review of *Deaths & Entrances* p. 2

25 November 1946 Idris Davies "Dylan Thomas" (poem) p. 2

13 April 1949 Professor Gwyn Jones M.A. "Dylan Thomas, Poet of Elemental Things" p. 4, the third of a series, "Anglo-Welsh Writers"[23]

10 May 1949 A. G. Prys-Jones review of Treece p. 4

10 November 1952 A. G. Prys-Jones review of *Collected Poems* p. 2

---

23. Another major essay written by Gwyn Jones before Thomas' death is "Language, Style, and the Anglo-Welsh" in *Essays and Studies 1953* London: John Murray 1953 pp. 102–114.

21 January 1953   Photograph of Thomas receiving Foyle prize p. 3

10 June 1953   A. G. Prys-Jones review of *Doctor & Devils* p. 3

*   *   *

10 November 1953   News of Thomas' death pp. 1, 2; Editorial p. 4

11 November 1953   A. G. Prys-Jones, an appreciation p. 6

12 November 1953   *Western Mail* Fund p. 1;[24] Richard Vaughan, obituary p. 1

13 November 1953   Letter from W. A. Rathkey, Cardiff, p. 6, a member of the Victor Neuburg group in 1934

14 November 1953   Letters from A. G. Prys-Jones, Douglas V. Morgan, Pennar Davies p. 6

16 November 1953   Y Tiwniwr, pseud. on "Laugharne" broadcast of 6 November p. 6

23 November 1953   Thomas body arrives on SS United States at Southampton p. 1

25 November 1953   Burial at Laugharne p. 3, with photograph

21 December 1953   News of the Taormina Prize p. 3

24 December 1953   Thomas left an estate of £100 p. 3

 1 January 1954   U.S. National Arts Foundation honors Thomas p. 5

 3 January 1954   A.G.P.-J. review of *Adam* memorial issue p. 3; G.J.P. on *Encounter* Thomas issue p. 3

12 January 1954   Letter from L. W. James, Llandovery, p. 6, complaining that the *Collected Poems* costs too much

23 January 1954   Letter from D. L. Evans p. 6, excluding Thomas from his list of eminent Welshmen. A prolonged correspondence ensued: 30 January 1954 letters from F. Davies, Eliot Crawshay-Williams, W. F. Stevens p. 6; 3 February 1954 letters from Huw Menai, B. F. Phillips p. 6

29 January 1954   Gwyn Thomas speaking on Thomas to Barry Rotarians p. 3

 3 February 1954   Y Tiwniwr, pseud. On "Under Milk Wood" (BBC) p. 3

 8 February 1954   Letters on Thomas' place in poetry and Wales continue: from David Bateman p. 6; 9 February from E. Howard Harris, Hugh

---

24. This fund was established, in the first place, for the return of Thomas' body to Wales. Many distinguished people contributed. The Fund closed on 22 December 1953 at a total of £771, of which £73 was the proceeds of a Memorial Recital by the Cardiff Branch of the British Poetry Association, 7 December 1953, reported in the *Weekly Mail* 12 December 1953 p. 8. Mimi Josephson is photographed presenting the check to the Editor of the *Western Mail* in the *Weekly Mail* 19 December 1953 p. 8. See also her obituary of Thomas, 14 November 1953 *Weekly Mail* p. 8.

Gregor, E. D. J. Lones p. 6; 11 February from Alfred Janes p. 6; 12 February from A. G. Prys-Jones p. 6; 16 February from Huw Menai p. 6; 17 February from D. Glynne Jones p. 8; 18 February from Huw Menai p. 8; 19 February from C. Benson Roberts p. 6

23 February 1954   Wil Ifan "Dylan, the Critics and the People" p. 7

 4 March 1954   Letter from Eliot Crawshay-Williams p. 6, reports on a letter received from the BBC: "We originally used the Welsh pronunciation of the name Dylan, but changed this form in May 1946, to the anglicised form of Dill-an at the request of Mr. Dylan Thomas himself."

 5 March 1954   Letter from I. M. Jones p. 8; 15 March 1954 letter from J. Gareth Jones p. 6

17 March 1954   Gwyn Jones review of *Under Milk Wood* p. 6; George Thomas "Obscurity in Modern Poetry" p. 6

 8 December 1954   Kathleen Freeman review of *Quite Early* p. 4

17 January 1955   H. W. Johns "Tribute from an American" p. 4;[25] letter from Huw Menai p. 8

21 October 1955   "Move to Rebury Dylan Thomas" p. 5—to make the Boat House a shrine

 7 November 1955   Herbert Davies on Emlyn Williams in "A Boy Growing Up"

19 April 1956   Harry Green review of Brinnin p. 8, with photograph of Thomas and friends in a New York bar

21 July 1956   Proposed production of "Under Milk Wood" in Newcastle p. 5

22 August 1956   Anon. on "Under Milk Wood" (Cardiff)

27 August 1956   J. C. Griffith Jones on "Under Milk Wood" (Edinburgh) p. 3

15 May 1957   Letter from Rev. W. Penry Davies on "Under Milk Wood"; 17 May 1957 response from E. D. Davies p. 4; 18 May from M. Davies p. 4; 20 May 1957 letters from Ieuan Lloyd Jones, G. S. Downes, Alice Hall p. 4; 22 May 1957 from Blanche Jones p. 4; 23 May 1957 " 'Milk Wood' and After"—an editorial p. 6, and letters from C. J. Burgess, Brinley Evans p. 6; 24 May 1957 letter from Eva M. Harries p. 4; 27 May from Etienne Raven p. 4; 29 May from Rev. W. Penry Davies, Huw Menai, James Phillips p. 4

15 November 1957   "Cardiff bars 'Under Milk Wood' during Games Week" p. 3—"not truly representative of Welsh life" p. 3; 16 November 1957 Charles Pugh interviews William Griffith and Clifford Evans p. 5; 18 November 1957 further reports on the ban pp. 6–7; 19 November letter from

---

25. Refers to a review of *Quite Early* by Milton Merlin in the *Los Angeles Times* 2 January 1955 pt. 4 p. 12.

Mimi Josephson p. 4; 22 November from C. R. Dennis, Katie Chick p. 6; 26 November from Hubert Evans, Frankie Desmond p. 4

28 November 1957   "London Letter" p. 6: Donald Houston just back from Broadway production of "Under Milk Wood"

5 December 1957   Letters from David Bateman and Huw Menai p. 6

11 December 1957   Crwydryn, pseud. on the Manchester Exhibition p. 6

21 December 1957   Bookman, pseud. mention of *Letters to Vernon Watkins* p. 4

13 February 1958   Andrew Yates on the Reardon Hall tribute p. 3; 18 February letter from Ian Parrott p. 4: first performance of Stravinsky's tribute not at Reardon but at Gregynog 25 June 1955

21 April 1958   Glyn Jones "Dylan Thomas—the Other Man" p. 4—a major memoir, with four further installments: 22 April 1958 p. 4; 23 April p. 6; 24 April p. 6; 25 April p. 6 with letters from Huw Menai and David Bateman

28 April 1958   Various views on Thomas p. 4: from his mother, from Tom Williams, Ivy Williams, Danny Ray of Laugharne, from Ethel Ross, from Morys Williams of the Grammar School; 29 April 1958 further comments p. 4: from Rev. Leon Atkin, Walter Flower, J. Morgan Williams, Ruby G. Graham, W. T. Henry, and Ralph Wishart; 30 April 1958 letters from Caleb Rees, David Bateman, Raymond Hughes p. 4

11 August 1958   Peter Shephard on the preparations for the Laugharne "Under Milk Wood" p. 2; 13 August Harry Green on the Laugharne performance p. 5; 14 August 1958 "Dylan's Walk" dedicated p. 5

18 August 1958   Derrick Harries "Blessing from Mam Dylan as She Dies" p. 5

21 August 1958   "Caitlin Mourns" p. 1: photograph; letter from Laurence Pettigrew p. 6

4 September 1958   Photograph of Llewellyn Thomas in New York p. 1; letter from Huw Menai p. 6

22 April 1959   National Book League Exhibition p. 6: included was MS of "Among Those Burned to Death was a Child Aged a Few Hours"

20 January 1960   Report of talk by William Griffith in London p. 4

30 July 1960   Dylan Thomas "Jack of Christ" p. 5, hitherto unpublished poem from a MS given to Glyn Jones

3 September 1960   Glyn Jones review of Heppenstall p. 5

15 October 1960   Janes portrait of Thomas going to Texas p. 1

26 November 1960   Glyn Jones review of Tedlock p. II

7 January 1961   Count Nicholas Barcynski "Dylan and the Stormy Petrel" p. 5—Thomas' visit to Caradoc Evans

12 August 1961 Graham Samuel on "Under Milk Wood" (Lyric, Hammersmith) p. 5

5 September 1961 Westgate, pseud. on the Times Bookshop MSS of "Under Milk Wood" p. 4; 15 September further report p. 6

12 September 1961 Letter from Islywn Williams on Boat House p. 6; 27 September letter from Min Lewis, Laugharne, p. 6

2 October 1961 Westgate, pseud. p. 6, "Painter's Studio" MSS sold abroad; 6 October letter from Richard Jones p. 6

31 March 1962 Glyn Jones review of Holbrook p. 6

12 June 1962 Interview with Emlyn Davies p. 5

9 July 1962 Westgate, pseud. p. 4, on Thomas MS notebooks

13 July 1962 Westgate, pseud. p. 6, on "Under Milk Wood" in Mexico

19 July 1962 Bust by Hugh Olof de Wet at Swansea p. 1

25 August 1962 Enid Roberts on "Doctor & Devils" (Edinburgh) p. 5

1 November 1962 Westgate, pseud. p. 6, on "Dylan" on Broadway

21 February 1963 Westgate, pseud. p. 6, on award to Jack Howells film

17 April 1963 Joan Hughes mention of T. H. Jones p. 6

1 June 1963 John Carr review of T. H. Jones p. 6

18 September 1963 Tony Austin on the Howells film p. 6

2 November 1963 Robert Nye review of *Colour of Saying* p. 6

8 November 1963 Westgate, pseud. p. 8, on the plaque for Cwmdonkin Drive; 9 November report on 10th anniversary tributes in Swansea p. 4, with photographs of unveiling

15 November 1963 Letter from Phyllis Davies p. 8; 9 December 1963 letter from Mrs. E. Jones p. 6

26 March 1964 Gwyn Thomas "A Welsh Eye" p. 8, extract on Thomas from his forthcoming book[26]

2 April 1964 Letter from John Llewellyn on D. J. Thomas p. 6

6 April 1964 Westgate, pseud. p. 6, interview with Ralph the Books, including transcription of a Thomas letter

15 May 1964 Beata Lipman on "Doctor & Devils" (Cardiff) p. 4

21 May 1964 Photograph of Thomas' death mask presented to the National Library p. 9

11 June 1964 Westgate, pseud. p. 4, on a proposed Laugharne museum

---

26. "A Clutch of Perished Bards" pp. 94–97 in *A Welsh Eye* London: Hutchinson 1964; New York: Greene 1965.

25 June 1964   *Western Mail* award to Jack Howells p. 1, with photographs

 9 July 1964   Saunders Lewis review of *Druid* p. 6

22 July 1964   Letter from Gareth A. Jones p. 6

 1 October 1964   Westgate, pseud. p. 10, on Charles Chaplin's reference to Thomas[27]

29 October 1964   Griffith Williams review of Ackerman p. 10

17 December 1964   Letter from T. H. Williams p. 6, suggesting Thomas is technically Welsh not Anglo-Welsh

24 July 1965   Aneirin Talfan Davies review of Read p. 8

16 October 1965   Griffith Williams review of FitzGibbon p. 8

13 November 1965   Griffith Williams review of *Rebecca's Daughters* p. 8

26 February 1966   Aneirin Talfan Davies "Barddoniaeth Sagrafennol" p. 6, with reference to *Druid*

12 March 1966   MSS of *Under Milk Wood* court judgment p. 4

12 November 1966   Griffith Williams review of Moynihan, *Selected Letters*, *Garland*, and *Prospect* p. 4

19 November 1966   Aneirin Talfan Davies "Mawl pob celfyddyd" p. 4, on the *Selected Letters*

 6 February 1967   "Under Milk Wood" to be staged in Welsh at Laugharne[28]

MUMBLES PRESS

The weekly of the locality of Swansea which housed the Little Theatre in the early thirties.

25 February 1932   J.J. review of "Hay Fever" p. 3: "Equally well done was Simon's part by Mr. D. M. Thomas."

28 April 1932   Anon. review of "Beaux Strategem" p. 2

16 February 1933   Anon. review of "Merry Wives of Windsor" p. 3

16 March 1933   Cor, pseud. review of "Peter and Paul" p. 3

14 December 1933   J.J. review of "Strange Orchestra" p. 3

18 January 1934   Anon. review of "Way of the World" p. 2

15 February 1934   Anon. review of "Martine" p. 3, indicating rather a deterioration in their standard of reviewing, since they say that "other characters were most successfully sustained by ... Mr. Dylan Thomas"—

---

27. See *My Autobiography* London: The Bodley Head; New York: Simon & Schuster 1964 pp. 471–472; also in Penguin Books.

28. On this production, see *Y Cymro* 8 June 1967 p. 3.

whereas, in fact, Thomas left the play at the last minute in a dispute with the director.

8 March 1934   Anon. review of "Richard II" p. 3, Thomas in the cast

3 May 1934   Anon. review of "Hay Fever" at Llewellyn Hall in aid of the Royal Masonic Institution for Boys p. 3

SWANSEA AND WEST WALES GUARDIAN

Swansea editor: John Jennings ("Evan Abertawe"). Regular contributors included A. E. Trick ("20th Century").[29] Founded in January 1934; weekly until 1940.

8 June 1934   Dylan Thomas, letter to the editor: "Telling the Truth to the Public. Expose Humbug and Smug Respectability" p. 10, with poem "Twelve" (= "That the sum sanity might add to nought")

15 June 1934   A. E. Trick, letter to the editor: "Mr. Dylan Thomas. 'Aiming at Wrong Aunt Sally'. Spiritual Need of To-Day" p. 6[30]

---

29. Another independent weekly for the Swansea area, which ran for 81 issues from February 1937 to September 1938, was the *Western Express*. A. E. Trick wrote regularly, and his article on the "Contemporary Scene" on 3 December 1937 gives his view of Thomas at that time. See also R.H.H. [Rod H. Hayes] "About Poetry" *South Wales Sunday News* 26 July 1936 p. 9.

30. Trick's response was part of a concerted effort to create interest. He and Thomas were close collaborators, witness the following poem "For Death Is Not The End" (published 15 June 1934 p. 6) written the previous year in friendly competition with Thomas on a set theme:

> For death is not the end!
> Though soul turns sour
> And faith dry-rots,
> Let maggots feed on flesh
> That once was blossom pink
> And memory sink
> Beneath the dust of falling years,
> Yet death is not the end!
> For death is not the end!
>
> Lungs chewed by poison gas
> Attempt to sing.
> Or woman ript with child
> Comfort the smiling flower,
> And good deeds done
> Bring forth dead fruit.
> Hold fast to hope
> For death is not the end!
>
> For death is not the end!
> Moves a soul in some dark cranny
> Like a fluttering bird
> In upward sweep ascends
> To some high altitude,
> Where breathes a living God.
> Then death is not the end!

6 July 1934   Dylan Thomas, letter to the Editor: "The Real Christ and the False. Peculiar Heavens. Created by Little Orators" p. 6

3 August 1934   Dylan Thomas "A Plea for Intellectual Revolution" p. 11[31]

14 December 1934   Evan Abertawe, pseud. "The Swansea Review" p. 8, a tribute to Thomas, on hearing of acceptance of story by *Adelphi*

11 January 1935   20th Century, pseud. review of *18 Poems* p. 6

25 January 1935   John Jennings "The Swansea Review" p. 8, on *18 Poems*

1 February 1935   Letter from Trevor Hughes p. 8; 8 February 1935 reply from A. E. Trick p. 8; 15 February 1935 reply from Trevor Hughes—with "Last Words" by A. E. Trick on 22 February 1934 p. 8

22 March 1935   Leslie E. Mewis "The New Poetry" p. 8, on *18 Poems*; reply from Another Mother, pseud. [A. E. Trick] on 5 April 1935 p. 8

3 May 1935   The Townsman, pseud. "The Swansea Review" p. 9: "Swansea Author Busy"—expecting a volume of short stories soon

5 July 1935   Evan Abertawe, pseud. "The Swansea Review" p. 9, notes that Thomas is listed as contributor to *Purpose* and *Poems of Tomorrow*

2 August 1935   "Exhibition by a Swansea Artist" p. 9: Thomas' portrait included in the Hampstead Exhibition of Alfred Janes' work; Thomas in West Ireland, returning to London soon

17 January 1936   Dylan Thomas "Books and People. Introducing a Review Column" p. 5

24 January 1936   A. E. Trick "Books and People. A Reply" p. 8: "There is a public ripe for Dylan Thomas and his Book Review. It is up to him to do his stuff."[32]

31 January 1936   Dylan Thomas, review of A. G. MacDonnell *A Visit to America* p. 7

18 September 1936   Don Quixote, pseud. review of *Twenty-five Poems*

CAP AND GOWN

Magazine of the Student's Union Society of the University College of South Wales and Monmouthshire.

---

31. In a letter of 2 August 1934 Thomas told Pamela Hansford Johnson: "I'm doing a new series for the local socialist paper: a series on Intellectual Revolution. I've got some lovely articles to come: on 'Censorship,' 'Sex Ethics,' 'Blood and Force,' 'The Marxian Brothers,' 'State Nurseries,' and 'The Sin of Patriotism.' You should see the letters I'm receiving. I had one from 'Mother of a Boy Scout.'" That letter was apparently not printed, nor did the series continue.

32. Another "reply" to create interest. Thomas apparently did *not* "do his stuff" beyond the short review the following week. The heading "Life Through the Printed Page. Book Reviews: Edited by Dylan Thomas" continues, with John Jennings doing the reviews, until 28 February 1934, when he appends the note: "Dylan Thomas is in London, so, apologizing, I continue with this feature this week."

March 1937 (Vol. XXXIV No. 1) Stanley Jones "A New Name in Poetry" pp. 8–11[33]

THE WELSH NATIONALIST

The official organ of Plaid Cymru; later called *The Welsh Nation.*

April 1937 (Vol. VI No. 4) Aneurin, pseud. "Letter About Our 'Letters'" pp. 8–9, gossip includes reference to Thomas: "And at last, we've got a *Poet.*"

August 1937 Anon. review of *Wales* No. 1, p. 8: dislikes Thomas' *"piéce"*

7 July 1956 Raymond Garlick review of Brinnin p. 2

October 1958 Keidrych Rhys "Colofn Fach" p. 7, on the Dylan "story"

WALES

Founding editor: Keidrych Rhys, Penybont, Llangadog, Sir Gaefyrddin. First series ran eleven issues from summer 1937 until the war.

Summer 1937 (No. 1) Dylan Thomas "Prologue to an Adventure" pp. 1–6 (begins on front cover)

August 1937 (No. 2) H. L. R. Edwards "The Allusionist School of Poetry: A Footnote" pp. 41–45: sees allusion to Masson's etchings in lines from "I, in my intricate image"; Nigel Heseltine review of *Twenty-five Poems* pp. 74–75

Autumn 1937 (No. 3) Dylan Thomas "We lying by seasand" p. 82 and "The Map of Love" pp. 116–123

March 1938 (No. 4) Dylan Thomas "The spire cranes" p. 138 and "In the Direction of the Beginning" pp. 147–148, with a footnote: "Fragment of a work in progress"

Summer 1938 (No. 5) Dylan Thomas "Poem (For Caitlin)" (= "I make this in a warring absence") pp. 179–181; comments quoted from reviews of *Wales* pp. 188–189

March 1939 (Nos. 6/7)[34] Dylan Thomas "On no work of words" and "Once it was the colour of saying" pp. 196

August 1939 (Nos. 8/9) Keidrych Rhys "Ethics of Acknowledgment" p. 241: *"Prologue to an adventure,* a story which appeared in our first number, has

---

33. An exceptional study. The student magazines of the University of Wales seem rather to have ignored Thomas. *The Dragon* (Aberystwyth) Easter 1953 had a review of the *Collected Poems* by B[rian] W[ay] p. 40. *Broadsheet* (Cardiff) had a memorial feature in December 1953 with obituaries by B. J. Morse and R. George Thomas, and poems by D.E.E., H.T., and AUCT. IGN. p. 3. See *Dawn* (Swansea) below.

34. Thomas is listed as coeditor with Keidrych Rhys of this issue, but it is understood that his help was minimal. Nigel Heseltine was nominally the editor of the last three issues.

been reprinted in *Delta* (Paris) without acknowledgement; and *In the direction of the Beginning Wales* No. 4 (also by Dylan Thomas) in *New Directions* (U.S.A.)— again without permission"; Keidrych Rhys "Notes for a New Editor" p. 248, includes comment on *Map of Love*

October 1939 (No. 10)   Dylan Thomas "Just Like Little Dogs" pp. 255–260

Winter 1939–40 (No. 11)   Davies Aberpennar review of *Map of Love* pp. 306–308

The second series of *Wales* ran from July 1943 to October 1949; the editor was at Ty Gwyn, Llanybri, and after 1946 at Carmarthen.

July 1943 (No. 1)   W. Moelwyn Merchant "The Relevance of the Anglo-Welsh" pp. 17–19; Keidrych Rhys on Francis Scarfe's *Auden and After* pp. 89–94

October 1943 (No. 2)   George Ewart Evans "An Emergent National Literature" pp. 50–53; Dylan Thomas "Our Country" pp. 76–78, a Ministry of Information filmscript

January 1944 (No. 3)   Ruthven Todd review of Denys Val Baker's pamphlet *Little Reviews* pp. 101–103: vigorous corrections e.g. "*Caravel* had little to do with bringing Dylan Thomas to the public eye"

Winter 1944/5 (No. 6)   Ivor Lewis on *Modern Welsh Poetry* pp. 92–93

December 1945 (Nos. 8/9 New Series—No. 21 from beginning)   Dilys Rowe "The Significance of Welsh Short Story Writing" pp. 91–100—discussion of Thomas p. 99

Autumn 1946 (No. 23)   [Keidrych Rhys] obituary for Ernest Rhys pp. 7–10; on p. 9: "Dylan Thomas—the Dent connection made him interested in his work—came over by Ferryman to meet him (from Laugharne) at the Castle Hotel ... very much on his best behaviour, amusing despite the threat of impending call-up to the Forces"; Dylan Thomas "Quite Early One Morning" pp. 83–86

Winter 1946 (No. 24)   Dylan Thomas "Memories of Christmas" pp. 10–14

February–March 1948 (No. 28)   Alun Lewis letters pp. 410–431, Thomas mentioned, mainly in connection with Caseg Broadsheet, on pp. 413–419; Dilys Rowe "Thoughts on the Tenth Anniversary of 'Wales' " pp. 442–451

Wales (third series) ran from September 1958 to April 1959.

October 1958 (No. 2)   Huw Menai "The Bilingual Mind" pp. 8–14, on Thomas and Hopkins p. 10

November 1958 (No. 3)   Morris Lane-Jones "As Dylan Thomas might have looked on Criccieth" pp. 65–68; A. F. Tinsley "Some Rare Sportsmen and others" pp. 70–74, on Emlyn Williams as Dylan p. 72

December 1958 (No. 4)   Mervyn Levy "No Time Like the Present" pp. 66–74, Thomas mentioned pp. 66, 73

February 1959 (No. 6)   David Rees on Rhys Davies pp. 70–73: Thomas is Iolo Hancock in Davies' *The Perishable Quality* London: Heinemann 1957

March 1959 (No. 7)   A. F. Churchward-Tinsley on Evan Samuel pp. 27–31, on p. 31 mention of Thomas as watching the London-Welsh rugger games and drinking in the Half Moon Hotel at Herne Hill after the game; Anthony Gower "Laugharne Pilgrimage" pp. 54–56

April 1959 (No. 8)   Letter from J. Idris Jones pp. 74–75; Anon. "How I Nearly Met Dylan Thomas: or Another Story of an Artist as a Young Dog" pp. 82–85

THE WELSH REVIEW

"A Monthly Journal About Wales, its People, and their Activities." Editor: Gwyn Jones. Vol. I No. 1 (February 1939)–Vol. VII (Winter 1948).[35]

October 1939 (Vol. II No. 3)   Glyn Jones review of *Map of Love* pp. 179–180

September 1944 (Vol. III No. 3)   W. D. Thomas on *Modern Welsh Poetry* pp. 220–223, mentions Thomas p. 220

June 1946 (Vol. V No. 2)   S. Beryl Jones review of *Deaths & Entrances* pp. 145–150

Autumn 1946 (Vol. V No. 3)   E. Glyn Lewis "Some Aspects of Anglo-Welsh Literature" pp. 176–186

Winter 1947 (Vol. VI No. 4)   Michael Williams "Welsh Voices in the Short Story" pp. 290–298

Winter 1948 (Vol. VII No. 4)   E. Glyn Lewis "Dylan Thomas" pp. 270–281, reprinted in Tedlock

HEDDIW

Cylchgrawn Misol. Vol. I (1936)–Vol. VII (1942). Golygydd: Aneirin ap Talfan.[36]

Ionawr 1940   A. ap T. review of *Map of Love* pp. 417–420

---

35. See David Clay Jenkins "An Index to *The Welsh Review*" *Journal of the Welsh Bibliographical Society* April 1965 pp. 188–210.

36. Aneirin Talfan Davies, apparently the first, certainly one of the most long-standing, of the few critics who have written about Thomas' poetry in Welsh language papers. It is interesting that Thomas' name gets into Thomas Parry *A History of Welsh Literature* (Oxford 1955) in the translator's (H. Idris Bell) chapter on "The Twentieth Century" when, in talking of Aneirin ap Talfan Davies, he characterizes him as "an admirer of Dylan Thomas, a champion of *vers libre*, and a sympathizer with the advanced school of Welsh poets" p. 471. Thomas is mentioned in several of Aneirin Talfan Davies' books in Welsh, perhaps notably in his county book *Crwydo Sir Gâr* Llandebie: Llyfrau'r Dryw 1955 especially pp. 104–114. See also his article on *Collected Poems* "He Sang of Glory" in *Readers News* (Guild Book Club) October 1954; and "Gyda Gwawr Y Bore" *Llawlyfr Cymdeithas Ceredigion* (1954–55), on the Cardigan associations. His address before the Honorable Society of Cymmrodorion 14 December 1962 was published in the *Transactions* of the society for 1963 pp. 190–222 as "Dylan Thomas—Druid of the Broken Body" and incorporated into his book of the same title (1964).

WELSH GAZETTE

Aberystwyth weekly, covering Cardiganshire as a whole and New Quay where Thomas lived in 1945.

12 April 1945   "Officer and Sten Gun; Attempted Murdur Charge; New Quay Bungalow Incident" p. [6]:

An Army captain who was alleged to have fired a sub-machine gun into a wood and asbestos bungalow where there were five adults and two children, appeared before Aberayron magistrates on Thursday last, charged with being in possession of a machine gun with intent to commit murder. He was William Richard John Killick, aged 28, of Ffynnonfeddyg, Cnwcylili, New Quay, and the charge was preferred by the Director of Public Prosecutions, who was represented by Mr. E. C. Jones, London. Solicitor for the accused was Mr. F. H. Jessop, Aberystwyth.

On the bench were Messrs Simon Davies, Rhys Williams, J. R. Evans and J. P. Davies.

Mr. E. C. Jones said the case arose out of a shooting incident on Mar. 6 at Majoda Bungalow, New Quay. Accused was an Army officer who rented a bungalow, Ffynnonfeddyg, 150 yards away. Living at Majoda were Mr. and Mrs. Dylan Thomas who had been there since last September. On the evening of Mar. 6 Thomas and two friends, Eldridge and a Miss Fisher, left the bungalow at about 6-30 p.m. for New Quay. At about 8-30 they called at the Commercial Hotel and while there the accused came into the bar. There was some conversation and the three persons decided they did not want to continue it, and they went to the Black Lion Hotel, where Eldridge and Miss Fisher were residing. Shortly after, the accused came in. He said something to Miss Fisher and she left him and sat down in another part of the room. At 10 p.m., closing time, Thomas and Miss Fisher went to the passage leading out of the hotel. Killick came out, said something to Miss Fisher and struck her on the face with his hand. Thomas started to fight with Killick and several persons came along to separate them. Thomas went home with Mr. Alastair Graham, of Wern.

Bullets Flying Round

Majoda, said Mr. Jones, was built entirely of wood and asbestos, and the only solid part was the fireplace in the living room. Seated around this fireplace about 10-30 p.m. were a Mrs. Keene, of London; Mr. Dewi Evans, Aberayron; Mrs. Thomas and Mr. Graham, while Mr. Thomas stood with his back to the fire. After about ten minutes they suddenly heard a gun being fired from the back of the bungalow. The next thing they knew was that bullets were flying around the living room. There were two bursts of gunshot, and the people in the bungalow immediately crouched around the fireplace. The door burst open and accused came in looking very wild and wearing dark glasses. There was a sub-machine gun and a grenade in his hands. There were scratches and blood on his face. He was very excited, murmuring to himself and he thoroughly alarmed the occupants of the room. They tried to cool him down and Thomas said "Don't be a fool." Mrs. Thomas told him there were two babies in another room and he then discharged the machine gun into the ceiling and continued to mutter "Hell, hell," stating that six men had held him down and kicked him in the stomach. "If that was so, it was not by any of the persons in the bungalow," said Mr. Jones. He was persuaded to put the gun down but would not leave the room until the gun was handed back to him, threatening that if it were not handed back he would throw the hand grenade and "blow them all up." Mr. Graham persuaded accused to go home to his bungalow. He told Graham he had been "beaten up" by some women. The police were eventually informed, and he told them he was responsible for everything and would make good the damage. He had fired the gun to frighten the people.

"It was an act of Providence," said Mr. Jones, "that several of these people were not killed outright as result of this firing."

Sgt. W. J. Ishmael, Aberystwyth, produced photographs of the bungalow, showing also interior views and indicating marks alleged to have been caused by bullets. Plans of the bungalow were submitted by J. Lewis Evans, architect, Aberystwyth.

Lot of Egoists

Dylan Morlais Thomas, of Majoda Bungalow, New Quay, said he was a writer, and had known Killick off and on for two years. Describing the incident in the bungalow, he said: "There was a noise from the back of the house of glass being smashed and the rattle of a machine gun. Bullets were heard flying through the living room. We crouched down as near the floor as we could. While we were crouching there was another burst. There was silence for a few seconds and we stood up. Then the front door of the living room was burst open and Killick came in with the gun. After being told there were babies in the house, he fired the machine gun to the ceiling and said 'You are nothing but a lot of egoists' and something to the effect that 'You have not seen anything.' "

Fanya Fisher, 9, Hayes Mews, Berkeley-square, London, said that at the Black Lion Killick said something about her not knowing what it was like "out there" (presumably meaning Greece). She had never seen Killick before that night.

John Stuart Eldridge, 3, Devonshire Mews North, London, said on Mar. 6 he was staying at the Black Lion Hotel, New Quay. After the incident in the passage he saw Killick outside the hotel and told him to go home. He then went up the road.

A Bullet Hole

Mary Keene, 1, Selwood-place, London, married woman, said she had been staying at the Black Lion Hotel with her nine months old baby. The evening of Mar. 6 she spent at Majoda with Mrs. Thomas and slept there the night. Describing the shooting incident, Mrs. Keene said she saw a bullet hole appear in the wall. When Killick burst into the room, Mrs. Thomas pleaded with him and said there were people in the house who had no quarrel with him. He became more abusive and truculent and fired another burst into the ceiling. At no time did he give any reason for his behaviour.

Alistair Hugh Graham, Wern, New Quay, lieutenant in the Royal Observer Corps, said when he accompanied Killick from the bungalow after the incident, he was much calmer. Witness attended to his face, which was scratched and bruised. He told him he was in the Army and had been in Greece. He also said he had been beaten up that night by some women. He had fired the shots to give them a fright.

Cartlyn Thomas, wife of Dylan Thomas, having given evidence of what happened at the bungalow, P.C. A. I. Williams, New Quay, said he saw Killick in his bungalow at midnight. He had been drinking but was not drunk. He was wearing dark spectacles and had superficial scratches on the right side of his face. Killick told him "I was beaten up at the Black Lion Hotel, New Quay, earlier in the evening and I fired the shots into the house in order to frighten the people." On the following day he recovered from Majoda 14 empty bullet cases on the gravel near the back door. On the floor of the living room he found five empty bullet cases and three bullet heads.

P.Sgt. Eben Jones, Aberayron, said accused told him the machine guns were his personal weapons. He had brought them home with him from Greece.

Lt.Col. Talbot Rice, of the War Office, gave evidence concerning the regulations permitting the holding of firearms by officers.

Accused was committed for trial to the next Cardiganshire Assizes. He pleaded not guilty and reserved his defence. Bail on his own surety of £50 was allowed.

28 June 1945 "Cardiganshire Assizes. Comando Officer Acquitted" p. [2][37]

12 November 1953 M.E., obituary p. 4

GLAMORGAN COUNTY MAGAZINE

Thomas' county. The magazine apparently ceased publication just before his death.

Summer 1949 (Vol. I No. 4) D.L.E. review of Treece p. 11

[December] 1952 Mimi Josephson "To Dylan Thomas On Reading his 'Collected Poems' " p. 27

DOCK LEAVES

"A National Review in English of Welsh Arts and Letters." Editor: Raymond Garlick.[38]

May 1951 (Vol. 2 No. 5) A. G. Prys-Jones "Anglo-Welsh Poetry" pp. 5–9

Winter 1952 (Vol. 3 No. 9) A. R. Williams "A Dictionary for Dylan Thomas" pp. 30–36

*   *   *

Winter 1953 (Vol. 4 No. 12) Obituary p. 4; statements from Daniel Jones pp. 4–5; and Aneirin Talfan Davies pp. 5–7; announcement of "Dylan Thomas Award" for best poem in tribute p. 16; Anon. review of *Doctor & Devils* pp. 62–63

Spring 1954 (Vol. 5 No. 13) ["A Dylan Thomas Number"][39] Editorial pp. 1–5; Louis MacNeice "A Dylan Thomas Award" pp. 6–7—introduces prize-winning poem, Anthony Conran "For Dylan Thomas (On hearing he was

---

37. The other Aberystwyth weekly, *Cambrian News*, also had the story on 13 April 1945 p. [8]. The *News of the World* (24 June 1945) was, like the jury, on the side of Capt. Killick.

38. For his full-length study of Thomas called "The Endless Breviary," see *Month* March 1954 pp. 143–153.

39. A second issue of this number was reproduced by photo-offset in a small format, and presumably remains in print.

dead)" reprinted in *Garland*;[40] Saunders Lewis "Dylan Thomas" (in Welsh) p. 8 with English translation p. 9; Aneirin Talfan Davies "The Golden Echo" pp. 10–17, on Thomas' broadcast anthologies; Henry Treece "Chalk Sketch for a Genius" pp. 18–23; Glyn Jones "Dylan Thomas and Welsh" pp. 24–25; A. G. Prys-Jones "Death Shall Have No Dominion" pp. 26–29, a tribute paid at the Memorial Recital, Cardiff, 7 December 1953; Peter Preece "On the Death of Dylan Thomas" (poem) p. 29; Roland Mathias "A Merry Manshape (or Dylan Thomas at a distance)" pp. 30–39; R.N.G. review of *Under Milk Wood* and Treece pp. 40–41

Winter 1954 (Vol. 5 No. 15) Pennar Davies "Sober Reflections on Dylan Thomas" pp. 13–17; Sheila Rowlands "The Literary Topography of Laugharne" pp. 38–40

Spring 1955 (Vol. 6 No. 16) R.N.G. review of *Quite Early* and Stanford pp. 48–49

Summer 1955 (Vol. 6 No. 17) Anon. review of *Prospect* pp. 40–41

Winter 1955 (Vol. 6 No. 18) Roland Mathias review of Wilfred Watson's book of poems *Friday's Child* pp. 40–42, with references to Thomas

Winter 1956 (Vol. 7 No. 20) Editorial review of Brinnin p. 8; John Ellis Williams " 'Under Milk Wood' Staged" pp. 51–53

Summer 1957 (Vol. 8 No. 21) Editorial comment on *Leftover Life* p. 6

[1958] (Vol. 8 No. 22) Editorial review of *Letters to Vernon Watkins* pp. 3–5

Dock Leaves became *The Anglo-Welsh Review* in 1959. In 1961, with Vol. 11, Roland Mathias became its editor.

THE ANGLO-WELSH REVIEW

[1959] (Vol. 9 No. 23) Islwyn Jenkins "Idris Davies: Poet of Rhymney" pp. 13–21, letter from Thomas to Davies quoted

[1960] (Vol. 10 No. 26) Anthony Conran "The English Poets in Wales—II. Boys of Summer in their Ruin" pp. 11–21

[1961] (Vol. 11 No. 27) R. George Thomas review of Tedlock pp. 54–56

[1962] (Vol. 12 No. 30) R. George Thomas "Bard on a raised hearth: Dylan Thomas and his Craft" pp. 11–20; Terence Hawkes review of Holbrook pp. 68–71: "The plain fact is that of Dylan Thomas's ninety extant poems, well over half are meaningless, and less than a dozen are worth reading, let alone preserving"[41]

---

40. Also reprinted in a special issue of *Poetry Book Magazine* (Vol. 6 No. 5) 1954 "Poetry from Wales."

41. Terence Hawkes was the editor of a collection of Cardiff poetry with the Dylanesque title *The Lilting House* published by Fortune Press 1955. See also his review of FitzGibbon in *Morgannwg* (Transactions of the Glamorgan Local History Society) Vol. X 1966 pp. 80–83.

[1964] (Vol. 14 No. 33)   Kathleen Raine "Vernon Watkins: Poet of Tradition" pp. 20–38, Thomas mentioned throughout; Kent Thompson "Biographer" (poem) pp. 90–91; Brian Way review of T. H. Jones pp. 119–120

[1965] (Vol. 14 No. 34)   Kent Thompson "An Approach to the Early Poems of Dylan Thomas" pp. 81–89; Kent Thompson review of Ackerman and *Druid* pp. 113–115; Cecil Price review of *Dylan* and the N.Y. performance pp. 116–117

Summer 1966 (Vol. 15 No. 36)   Cecil Price review of Read, FitzGibbon, and *Rebecca's Daughters* pp. 141–142

Spring 1967 (Vol. 16 No. 37)   Ralph Maud review of John Idris Jones' *Way Back to Ruthin* pp. 149–151

Summer 1968 (Vol. 17 No. 39)   Thomas Taig "Swansea Between the Wars" pp. 23–32

Winter 1969 (Vol. 17 No. 40)   Cecil Price review of *Notebooks* pp. 202–203

THE WELSH ANVIL (YR EINION)

Published under the auspices of the Guild of Graduates of the University of Wales. Founding editor: Alwyn D. Rees. Later title is *University of Wales Review.*

1952 (No. IV)   Ioan Bowen Rees "Wales and the Anglo-Welsh" pp. 20–31

1953 (No. V)   Aneirin Talfan Davies "A Question of Language" pp. 19–31, an address on Thomas to the Oxford University Celtic Society

1955 (No. VII)   Bobi Jones "Imitations in Death" pp. 82–86, comment on *Scrutiny*'s criticisms of Thomas

Summer 1965   Raymond Garlick "An Anglo-Welsh Accidence" pp. 18–20

DAWN

Official publication of the Students' Union Council, University College of Swansea.[42]

Summer 1952 (Vol. XXVII No. 2)   Janus, pseud. "Portrait of the Artist" pp. 43–44, oblique satire on the Anglo-Welsh

Ebrill 1954 (Vol. XXIX Rhif. 1)   A. Ross Curtis "The Collected Poems of Dylan Thomas" pp. 13–16; John Summers "Disjointed thoughts on reading in a newspaper that Dylan Thomas IS DEAD" (poem) p. 17

1955 (Vol. XXX Rhif. 1)   G. L. Roberts review of *Under Milk Wood* pp. 27–28; W.L.E. [W. Lindsey Evans] review of *Quite Early* p. 29

1964 (Vol. XXXIX No. 1)   Alan Thornton review of Holbrook pp. 41–43

---

42. The other student publication at Swansea, *Creft* (Vol. XVI No. 8) 25 February 1965 had a survey article on Thomas by J.A.C. pp. 5–7 and a memorial section January 1963 "A Pubber of Genius" with contributions by Ronald Cour, Alfred Janes, Mervyn Levy, Vernon Watkins pp. 102–110.

1966 (Vol. 41 No. 2)   M. J. Emery "An Approach to Dylan Thomas" pp. 32–38

THE WELSHMAN

A weekly newspaper for Carmarthen and District, including weekly local news of Laugharne.

26 December 1952   "Laugharne News" p. 3: D. J. Thomas died Tuesday 16 December at the age of 76, funeral on 19 December at Glyntaff Crematorium, Pontypridd, committal at the Garden of Remembrance, Pontypridd, the mourners "Mr. Dylan Thomas (son) and Mr. Owen, Port Talbot (friend)"

13 November 1953   News and obituary p. 1; Sheila Rowlands, Laugharne "On Hearing of the Death of Dylan Thomas" (poem) p. 1

27 November 1953   funeral p. 1

4 December 1953   Letter of thanks to friends in Laugharne from Caitlin Thomas p. 1[43]

18 December 1953   Laugharne children prepare for the "Under Milk Wood" recordings p. 6; further report on the singing 22 January 1954 p. 6

5 February 1954   "Under Milk Wood" on BBC Third Programme p. 6

23 April 1954   "On Good Friday morning Mrs. Dylan Thomas was admitted to the West Wales Hospital, Carmarthen" p. 6

8 August 1958   Cliff Walk renamed "Dylan's Walk" p. 1

15 August 1958   Performance of "Under Milk Wood";[44] Thomas' only pair of cuff-links on show in Carmarthen County Museum p. 1—presented by John McGrath, who had received them from Thomas in New York p. 1

22 August 1958   Mrs. Thomas dies on day of final performance of "Under Milk Wood" in Laugharne; cremated at Pontypridd p. 1

12 June 1964   "Under Milk Wood" at Laugharne

LLANELLY STAR

Another Carmarthenshire weekly.

27 December 1952   Mention of Thomas' "recent" reading in Llanelly

---

43. The *Carmarthen Journal* published Caitlin Thomas' letter on 11 December 1953, along with a letter of tribute to Thomas from Mab Eryri (Bryn-yr-Ornan, Pembry) p. 5.

44. At the Dragon Theatre, Laugharne, presented by Carmarthen Community Council on 12, 14, 15, 16 August 1958, producer Gwynne D. Evans, with T. H. Evans (as Eli Jenkins) from the London cast supported by an amateur cast including people of Laugharne. The programme contained "A Message from Dylan's Mother" and a "Prologue Note" by Keidrych Rhys, both included in Min Lewis *Laugharne and Dylan Thomas* (1967) pp. 71–72.

23 May 1953   N.H.L. review of *Doctor & Devils* p. 4

21 November 1953   Letter from B. J. Davies on the response to Thomas' death p. 4

 5 December 1953   Letter from Alexander Bowen p. 4

 6 March 1954   Anon. review of *Under Milk Wood* p. 4

13 November 1954   Anon. review of *Quite Early* p. 8

Y DDINAS

The monthly magazine for the Welsh in London.

Chwefror 1953   "Welsh Poet Honoured" report on the Foyle's Luncheon of 20 January ("very few Welshmen" there) p. 9

Rhagfyr 1953   David Raymond "Lament for a Poet" pp. 1–2; Dwynwen James " 'I have longed to move away': An Appreciation of Dylan Thomas" p. 5

Mawrth 1954   Sir Ben Bowen Thomas "From Our President" who has attended two memorial recitals for Thomas p. 1

February 1956   W.G. [William Griffiths] "Memories of Daniel Owen" p. 3, with comparison to Thomas

August 1956   Teifion Griffiths "The Welsh Influence on Modern English Verse" p. 19

In February 1960 with Vol. 15, *Y Ddinas* anglicized its name to read:

LONDON WELSHMAN

January 1961   Keidrych Rhys "Anglo Welsh Verse" p. 18—mentions the "pasticheurs of Dylan" in the collection of Cardiff poetry, *The Lilting House*

May 1961   Keidrych Rhys "Old Hat on Dylan" pp. 9–10, exuberant attack on Tedlock

October 1961   Philip O'Connor[45] "The Englishman in Wales" p. 3: Thomas' "weakness comes very much from his Anglicism, his attempt to peddle charm and spontaneity when he might have in his national setting used his brains—which the English cultural scene encouraged him to liquidate"

June 1962   A. G. Prys-Jones review of Holbrook p. 14

November 1963   Bryn Griffiths on the Jack Howells film of Thomas p. 13

December 1963   Bryn Griffiths "Ten Years After" p. 4, on recent Thomas events, and his Camden Town days

---

45. See his *Living in Croesor* London: Hutchinson 1962 pp. 53, 59–60, 84.

June 1964   Bleddyn Beynon review of *Colour of Saying* (1963) pp. 7–8; Michael O'Halloran and Katherine Reid review of the London Welsh Association Drama Group production of "Under Milk Wood" pp. 12–13, with a letter p. 4

December 1964   A. G. Prys-Jones "Welsh Poets: How it Happened" pp. 11–12 mentions Thomas' first poem in *Western Mail*; Meic Stephens "Where have all the Angloes Gone?" pp. 13–14: includes comment on *Beach of Falesá*, *Twenty Years*, *Dylan*, *Druid*, Ackerman; Bryn Griffiths review of *Druid* pp. 14–15; Jack Raymond Jones review of Ackerman pp. 15–16; Sally Roberts review of *Beach of Falesá* pp. 17–18

January 1965   Letter from Aneirin Talfan Davies p. 18; March 1965 reply by Bryn Griffiths pp. 9–10

December 1965   Editorial mention p. 1; Edward M. Thomas review of Read and FitzGibbon p. 5

April 1966   Bryn Griffiths on "Adventures in the Skin Trade" production p. 15

May 1966   Jack Raymond Jones on "Under Milk Wood" at the Lyric by Swansea University Players p. 12

SOUTH WALES ARGUS

The Newport, Monmouthshire, daily.

21 May 1953   Beatrice M. Worthing review of *Doctor & Devils* p. 2

10 November 1953   News of death p. 4

24 May 1954   T.J.W. review of *Portrait* p. 2

3 January 1955   P.P. review of *Quite Early* p. 2

30 January 1956   F.J.H. review of *Prospect* p. 2

4 June 1956   T.J.W. review of Brinnin p. 2

9 December 1957   T.J.W. review of *Letters to Vernon Watkins* p. 2

9 December 1963   W.J.C. review of *Colour of Saying* p. 4

9 July 1964   Griffith Williams review of *Druid* p. 2

4 December 1964   W.J.C. review of Ackerman and *Twenty Years* p. 6

21 October 1965   Kenneth Loveland review of FitzGibbon p. 2

13 December 1965   Kenneth Loveland review of Brinnin p. 4

TENBY OBSERVER

A Pembrokeshire weekly.

25 September 1953   Announcement of the Tenby and District Arts Club meeting for 2 October, Thomas the speaker p. 2

9 October 1953 Report of his reading of "Under Milk Wood" at Tenby p. 2

13 November 1953 Editorial tribute p. 4

20 November 1953 Letter from Raymond Garlick about the Mayor of Swansea's Fund p. 4

18 December 1953 Note of £7 from Tenby Arts Club to the Fund p. 5

SOUTH WALES ECHO

A Cardiff evening paper.[46]

10 November 1953 "A Village Mourns its Poet" p. 4

27 July 1956 Gareth Bowen "Welsh Premier of 'Under Milk Wood' " (New Theatre, Cardiff)

9 December 1960 A.J.T. review of Tedlock p. 5

22 October 1964 Stroller, pseud. review of Ackerman p. 8

28 October 1965 A.J.T. review of FitzGibbon p. 5

BANER

Baner ac Amserau Cymru. A national newspaper and farmers' journal,[47] published weekly in Denbigh.

11 Tachwedd 1953 "Marw Dylan Thomas" p. 1

18 Tachwedd 1953 Euros Bowen "Dylan Thomas" (poem) p. 8:

> Cynaeafodd frig cynefin y gerdd
> Nes troi'n goch ei ddeufin;
> Gwirionodd ar y grawnwin
> Nes syrthio'n feddw.—Gweddw yw'r gwin.

and H.L. [Haydn Lewis][48] "Bryn Rhedyn" (poem) p. 8:

---

46. Other newspapers in Wales which took notice of Thomas at the time of his death include *South Wales Voice* (Swansea and District) with an editorial tribute 13 November 1953 p. 4, and a poem, "We mourn for you" by Winifred Morgan 11 December 1953 p. 5. *North Wales Times* (Denbigh) had a review of *Quite Early* 25 December 1954 p. 3.

47. Another national Welsh newspaper, *Y Cymro*, contains a tribute from Amanwy, pseud. in the issue of 20 Tachwedd 1953 p. 17: "Rhoed i Gymru dri darllenwr barddoniaeth gwych y ganrif hon, sef Syr John Morris Jones, y Dr. T. H. Parry Williams, a Dylan Thomas." *Y Tyst* for 16 August 1956 has poem "Wrth fedd Dylan Thomas" by E.L.E. p. 8.

48. L. Haydn Lewis won the crown at the Rhos Eisteddfod with a poem incorporating Thomas references and phrases under the subject "Ffoadur" ("Fugitive"). See *Eisteddfod Genedlaethol Frenhinol Cymru* Dyffryn Maelor 1961 pp. 33–66, the poem and discussion by T. H. Parry-Williams, J. M. Edwards, and Euros Bowen. See also his translations of Thomas in his *Cerddi Cyfnod* Caernarfon: Llyfrfa'r Methodistiaid Calfinaidd 1963; and article "Dylan Thomas a'i Feirniaid" *Y Traethodydd* Ebrill 1963 pp. 79–89.

(*Trosiad o dri phennill o gân Dylan Thomas, "Fern Hill"*)

Pan oeddwn ifanc ac esmwyth dan frigau'r afalau
Ogylch y tŷ dyriol mor llon â gwyrddni'r maes,
　　　Y nos uwch y pantle'n sêr,
　　　Amser a roes imi ddringo a galw
　　　Yn euraid yn uchter ei lygaid,
Clodwiw ymhlith cerbydau tywysog oeddwn yn nhrefi'r afalau
Ac unwaith dan amser fel barwn y coed a'r dail
　　　Fe dynnwn flodau a'u cnwd
　　　I lawr hyd afonydd ysgafn afalau'r coed.

Ac fel yr oeddwn wyrdd a diofal, ac enwog ymhlith y tai
Ogylch y buarth llon a'm cân i'r fferm a'm cartrefai,
　　　Yn yr haul nad yw ifanc ond unwaith,
　　　Amser a roes imi chwarae a bod
　　　Yn euraid o fwynder ei foddau,
Gwyrdd ac euraid myfi oeddwn heliwr a hwsmon, a'r lloi
Canent i'm corn, cyfarthai'r llwynogod yn glir ac oer ar y
　　　bryniau,
　　　A'r sabath rhoi gnul yn araf
　　　Yng ngro y ceunentydd sanct.

Dim ni ofidiwn, yn nyddiau gwynder yr ŵyn, yr âi amser â mi
Uchod hyd lofft y wenoliaid a'u llu wrth gysgod fy llaw,
　　　Dan y lloer sydd fyth yn ymgodi,
　　　Na chwaith pan fyddo ar ŵyr
　　　Y clywn ef a'r meysydd uchel ar adain
A deffro a'r fferm am byth ar ffo o'r diblant dir.
O! pan oeddwn ifanc ac esmwyth o fwynder ei foddau,
　　　Amser a'm daliai'n wyrdd a marwol
　　　Er i'm ganu mewn llyffethair fel y môr.

2　Rhagfyr 1953　"Angladd Dylan Thomas" p. 3

5　Ionawr 1955　"Sgyrsiau Dylan Thomas" p. 1, announcement of *Quite Early*

8　Rhagfyr 1966　Aneirin Talfan Davies review of Moynihan

GOWER

The journal of the Gower Society.

1953 (No. 6)　Editorial pp. 2–6, quoting obituaries from the *Times*, *South Wales Evening Post*, and *Western Mail*; Alfred Janes "World's End" p. 6, a short memorial

1964 (No. 16)　J. E. [Ethel] Ross " 'We had Evidence and No Doubt' " pp. 47–50, reminiscences about Thomas' birth and life by his mother and the midwife Mrs. G. Williams

Y DRYCH

The American organ of the Welsh people, published in Utica, New York.

15 December 1953   An Appreciation of Dylan Thomas by the St. David's Society, State of New York, Rev. David R. Evans, President, Robert A. Fowkes, Chairman, Committee on Literature p. 9

15 March 1958   David L. R. Jeffreys "A Welsh Bookshelf" review of Brinnin, *Leftover Life, Letters to Vernon Watkins*, and *Under Milk Wood*

YR ENFYS

"Journal of the Welsh People in Dispersion."

Winter 1954 (No. 22)   J. Roberts Williams "The Year's Events in Wales" pp. 4–5: "Elfed was 93[49]—but Dylan Thomas was only 39. And what can I say of this youthful spirit, except that he must be beloved by the gods.... I hope that the able (and most patient) editor of 'Yr Enfys' will find at least a page for him, and for Elfed. For it is wrong for anyone to dismiss Dylan Thomas in a paragraph"; William Griffiths "Dylan Thomas" pp. 8–9: reminiscences

May 1963 (No. 59)   Aliena, pseud "Teletopics" p. 18: on the Jack Howells film

Y GENHINEN

Cylchgrawn Chwarterol Genedlaethol.

Gwanwyn 1954(Cyf. IV Rhif. II)   J. Oliver Stephens "Dylan Thomas (1914–1953)" pp. 65–73[50]

EMPIRE NEWS

A Kemsley newspaper, which in October 1954 began regional editions: "Wales' Own Sunday Paper. Printed in Wales *for* Wales." Was merged with *News of the World* in October 1950. One of the regular contributors was the Rev. Leon Atkin of Swansea.

6 March 1955   Countess Barcynska "My Life with Caradoc Evans" p. 4 describes Thomas' visit to Caradoc[51]

---

49. Also linking the names of Elfed and Thomas was the editorial by Aneirin Talfan Davies in *Llafar* Gwanwyn 1954 pp. 1–2, which issue contains poems on Elfed and Thomas by Rhydwen Williams p. 3.

50. A translation of this article, by Miss M. G. Williams, is on file in Swansea Public Library. One notes the following personal reminiscence: "Dylan confessed to me that it grieved him that he was unable to read in Welsh, thus the works of Dafydd ap Gwilym were a mystery to him."

51. This episode appears in her *The Miracle Stone of Wales* London: Rider 1957 pp. 14–15; see also pp. 50–55.

20 November 1955   Mrs. Florence Thomas "The Lies they tell about my son" p. 8: interview with David Edmunds[52]

21 October 1956   David Brecon "Humbugs!—lashes at Dylan's phoney 'friends' " p.5

16 February 1958   "Dylan's Friend to American Tycoon: Beware of Fakes" p. 7—aftermath of the Manchester exhibition

20 April 1958   Cadman Rees "Mam Dylan Speaks of Boy We Never Knew" p. 7 another interview with Mrs. Thomas

17 August 1958   "Mam Dylan dies as her son's show ends" p. 1

 9 November 1958   News of Mervyn Levy's *Painting for All* (London: Odhams Press 1958) p. 7

COUNTRY QUEST

"The Magazine for Wales and the Border." Editor: Glyn Griffiths, Wrexham.

Autumn 1960 (Vol. 1 No. 2)   Bert Trick "Dylan—The Eternal Swansea Boy" pp. 26–27[53]

Autumn 1962   Min Lewis "Dylan's Real Shrine is a Painted Wooden Shed" pp. 7–9, sketches of Boat House etc. by S. Lewis

Summer Annual 1965   Min Lewis "Where Dylan met Captain Cat" pp. 21–22: Johnny Thomas, ex-seaman thought to be the "Under Milk Wood" character

BARN

A monthly magazine of opinion, in Welsh.[54]

Awst 1963 (No. 10)   Aneirin Talfan Davies on the Buffalo manuscripts pp. 285–286

Tachwedd 1963 (No. 13)   Aneirin Talfan Davies on Louis MacNeice

Chwefror 1965 (No. 28)   Hugh Bevan review of Ackerman pp. 110–111

Ebrill 1965 (No. 30)   H.L. [Haydn Lewis] "Wedi Dy Fyned" (poem) p. 167 "Atgof drachefn am Dylan Thomas"

Mai 1966 (No. 43)   Euros Bowen "Barddoniaeth Dylan Thomas" p. 191

-----

52. *Everybody's Weekly* (21 April 1956) had a similar interview by Paul Ferris, entitled "Go and Write, Boy" pp. 23, 39.

53. An unsigned article "Dylan Thomas" in the *Wrexham and District National Union of Teachers Association Year Book* (Vol. 7) 1963 pp. 24–26 is attributed to Bert Trick .

54. A similar venture, *Welsh Outlook*, in English, had one mention of Thomas in its few issues, in an article "Profile: David Jones" by Bryn Griffiths in the issue of June 1965 (No. 3) p. 10.

Gorffennaf 1966 (No. 45)   Aneirin Talfan Davies "Ateb I Euros" pp. 240–241

Tachwedd 1966 (No. 49)   Euros Bowen "Barddoniaeth Dylan Thomas" pp. 8, 18

POETRY WALES

Founding editor: Meic Stephens.

Autumn 1965   Colin John Partridge "The Verse of T. H. Jones" pp. 3–7

Spring 1966   John Stuart Williams review of FitzGibbon pp. 37–38

Winter 1968   Meic Stephens "Yr Academi Gymreig and Cymdeithas Cymru Newydd" unnumbered pages, includes extracts from Thomas' letters to Davis Aberpennar; Terence Hawkes review of *Notebooks*

Spring 1969   Anthony Conran "Anglo-Welsh Poetry Today" pp. 11–16; Harri Webb[55] review of Gerald Morgan's anthology *This World of Wales* (1968) pp. 50–53

THE WELSH SECONDARY SCHOOLS REVIEW

Editor: D. Parry Michael.

December 1965   Editorial review of FitzGibbon p. 18

---

55. See his "Two Gunned Gabriel" *Promenade* (Cheltenham) 14 November 1953 pp. 5–6.

SECTION III

LONDON, ETC.,

PERIODICALS AND NEWSPAPERS

BOY'S OWN PAPER

February 1927 (Vol. XLIX Pt. 5)   Dylan Marlais "The Second Best" p. 285.[1]

THE NEW ENGLISH WEEKLY

"A Review of Public Affairs, Literature and the Arts." Vol. I No. 1 was 21 April 1932; ceased publication in September 1949. Edited by A. R. Orage up to his death, 6 November 1934; succeeded by Philip Mairet. See Mairet's biography *A. R. Orage* New Hyde Park, New York: University Books 1966 especially p. 128.

18 May 1933 (Vol. III No. 5)   Dylan Thomas "Death Shall Have..." p. 118[2]

25 January 1934   Dylan Thomas "Out of the Pit" pp. 342–343

15 March 1934   Dylan Thomas "After the Fair" pp. 515–516

22 November 1934   Dylan Thomas "The End of the River" pp. 132–134

23 November 1934   Anon. review of *The Year's Poetry* (1934) p. 117: "It has been left to a newcomer, Dylan Thomas, to make the most exciting contribution to the year's poetry"

3 October 1935   Rayner Heppenstall on Louis MacNeice pp. 416–417: "He's a very good poet indeed.... But, you see, I'm afraid he's in for just such a Hampstead 'ballyoo' as Stephen Spender had and Dylan Thomas. And look what it's done for them"; a reply by Ruthven Todd 10 October 1935 p. 440

16 July 1936   Dylan Thomas "Why east wind chills" and "This bread I break" p. 270

30 July 1936   Dylan Thomas "Before we mothernaked fall" p. 310

3 September 1936   Dylan Thomas "Was there a time" p. 328

1 October 1936   Randall Swingler review of *Twenty-five Poems* pp. 409–410

11 March 1937   A. Desmond Hawkins on Yeats' *Oxford Book of Modern Verse* pp. 431–432: "It is difficult to see why Dylan Thomas is omitted"

28 October 1937   H. W. Treece "The Poetry of Dylan Thomas, An Assessment" pp. 56–57

---

1. In a letter to Trevor Hughes of Christmas 1932 Thomas gave rather the wrong impression in saying that he contributed "now and then funny verses to the *B.O.P.*" It appears that only one poem in the *B.O.P.* is attributable to Thomas, in an issue several years previous to his letter. Elsewhere he wrote "I had a bad poem in the *Everyman*." This appears to refer to the following item in *Everyman* for 10 October 1929 pp. 276–277 giving the competition results (new words for "The Londonderry Air" had been asked for): "There were an unusually large number of isolated stanzas or lines of much beauty in these entries [including] 'dim with arrowy air./ Asleep and slender with the moonslow hour.' DYLAN MARLAIS."

2. This early version of "And death shall have no dominion" is apparently the first poem of Thomas' accepted by a London literary magazine.

10 March 1938   Dylan Thomas "A Visit to Grandpa's" pp. 431–432

17 March 1938   Dylan Thomas "Recent Novels" pp. 454–455: review of Samuel Beckett *Murphy*, and William Carlos Williams *Life Along the Passaic River*

21 April 1938   Dylan Thomas "Recent Novels" pp. 34–35: review of Eric Ambler *Epitaph for a Spy*, and Sheila Radice *Not All Sleep*

19 May 1938   Dylan Thomas "Recent Novels" pp. 115–116: review of A. H. Atkins *Sinister Smith*, C. Daly King *Arrogant Alibi*, John P. Marquand *Haven's End*, and Norah Hurston *Their Eyes Were Watching God*

 1 September 1938   Dylan Thomas "Recent Novels" p. 312: review of Cecil Lewis *The Trumpet Is Mine*, Patrick Kavanagh *The Green Fool*, and Fred Urquhart *Time Will Knit*

22 September 1938   D.T. "Taverns in General" p. 360: review of George N. List *Pub Survey*

13 October 1938   Dylan Thomas "Recent Fiction, Kay Boyle, Mary Butts, and Others" pp. 11–12: reviews of Kay Boyle *Monday Night*, Mary Butts *Last Stories*, F. V. Morley *War Paint*, and Walter Brierley *Dolby Green*

17 November 1938   Dylan Thomas "Recent Fiction" pp. 92–93: reviews of H. G. Wells *Apropos of Dolores*, Rose Wilder Lane *Free Land*, Jane Allen *I Lost My Girlish Laughter*, and Signe Toksvig *Port of Refuge*

 2 February 1939   Dylan Thomas "Dos Passos and Kafka" pp. 256–257: reviews of John Dos Passos *U.S.A.* and Franz Kafka *Amerika*

18 May 1939   Dylan Thomas "Recent Fiction" pp. 79–80: review of Flann O'Brien *At Swim-Two-Birds*, Ruthven Todd *Over the Mountain*, and Erskine Caldwell *Journeyman*

 7 September 1939   Hugh Gordon Porteus "Map of Llareggub" pp. 269–270, review of *Map of Love*, reprinted in Tedlock

14 December 1939   Dylan Thomas "Novels and Novelists" pp. 133–135: reviews of Frederic Prokosch *Night of the Poor*, Dorothy Parker *Here Lies*, and Georg Kaiser *A Villa in Sicily*

13 June 1940   H. B. Mallalieu on Henry Treece p. 98

27 June 1940   Julian Symons review of *Portrait* pp. 121–122

28 May 1942   H. [Hermann] Peschmann on *The White Horsemen* anthology p. 54: "the only well-known poet who can be called an Apocalyptic today is Dylan Thomas"

21 March 1946   Roy Fuller review of *Deaths & Entrances* pp. 225–226

21 April 1949   Howard Sergeant review of Treece pp. 22–23

THE LISTENER

The weekly journal of the BBC.

7 June 1933 "Week by Week" p. 892, poetry competition judged by Edward Marsh[3] and Walter de la Mare, Thomas among the winners[4]

14 March 1934 Dylan Thomas "Light" (= "Light breaks where no sun shines") p. 462[5]

24 October 1934 Dylan Thomas "Poem in October" (= "Especially when the October wind") p. 691

27 December 1934 Anon. review of *The Year's Poetry* p. 1090: Thomas "a poet of promise"

27 February 1935 Anon.[6] review of *18 Poems* p. 381

15 May 1935 Paul Engle and Cecil Day Lewis, discussion on "Modern Poetry" pp. 852–854: Lewis quotes and comments on "Especially when the October wind"

19 October 1939 Anon. review of *Map of Love* pp. 780, 782

25 February 1943 Dylan Thomas "Reminiscences of Childhood"[7] pp. 246–247, with two original sketches by John Petts

6 September 1945 Martin Armstrong "The Spoken Word" p. 276, mention of Thomas "Early One Morning" broadcast

20 December 1945 Dylan Thomas "Memories of Christmas" pp. 734–735; "Contributors" p. 747

---

3. Christopher Hassall describes later contact in his *Edward Marsh* London: Longmans; New York: Harcourt, Brace 1959 pp. 616–619.

4. Thomas' poem "The Romantic Isle" was read by Ian Sinclair Phail on the Daventry National Programme for 28 June 1933, according to the *Radio Times* 23 June 1933 p. 768. See also "Listeners' Poems: Report by the Adjudicators" *Radio Times* 9 June 1933 p. 661. A selection from the prize-winning poems was published in *The Listener* 19 July 1933, but Thomas' was not among them.

5. The publication of this poem while Thomas was still in Swansea produced letters from T. S. Eliot, Geoffrey Grigson, and Stephen Spender, inquiring about his work. A batch of poems typed for submitting to editors is in the British Museum; see K. W. Gransden "Early Poems of Dylan Thomas" *British Museum Quarterly* Vol. XIX No. 3 (1954) pp. 50–51.

6. In a letter to A. E. Trick in February 1935 Thomas says: "My book is selling well. A few complimentary reviews have appeared. And Edwin Muir is to write another in *The Listener* in about a week's or a fortnight's time."

7. Broadcast in the Home Service 15 February 1943. Thomas' broadcasts were, of course, listed in the *Radio Times*. Aneirin Talfan Davies collected Thomas' chief broadcasts into *Quite Early One Morning* (1954). See also FitzGibbon, Appendix I.

9 May 1946   Anon. review of *Deaths & Entrances* pp. 621–622

27 June 1946   Martin Armstrong on Thomas' discussion with James Stephens "On Poetry" p. 860

17 October 1946   Dylan Thomas "How to Begin a Story" p. 508;[8] Martin Armstrong on it p. 536

7 November 1946   Dylan Thomas "Holiday Memory" pp. 634–635

12 December 1946   Martin Armstrong on Thomas' reading of Edith Sitwell's "Shadow of Cain" p. 859

2 January 1947   Dylan Thomas "The Crumbs of One Man's Year" pp. 28–29; Martin Armstrong on it p. 39: "beginning to make a mannerism of a highly personal intonation"

30 January 1947   Letter from Tom Harrisson p. 20, on the Third Programme and the "over-use" of Thomas

20 March 1947   Martin Armstrong on "Poet and Critic" broadcast with T. W. Earp p. 439

18 September 1947   Martin Armstrong on Thomas' reading of Watkins' "Mari Lwyd" p. 499

16 October 1947   Martin Armstrong on Thomas in "The Dog's Colloquy" p. 695

30 October 1947   Martin Armstrong critical of Thomas' reading of Satan in "Paradise Lost" p. 791; also 11 December 1947 p. 1035

15 January 1948   Martin Armstrong praise for Thomas' reading of W. H. Davies' "Autobiography of a Supertramp" p. 115

5 August 1948   Dylan Thomas "The English Festival of Spoken Poetry" p. 205; Martin Armstrong mentions it p. 211

19 May 1949   Anon. review of Treece p. 861

21 December 1950   Martin Armstrong on "Poetic Licence" p. 807, Thomas was Chairman of a discussion with participants George Barker, Roy Campbell, and W. R. Rodgers

24 May 1951   Richard Hughes "Wales Through the Looking Glass" pp. 838–839, mentions Thomas' reputation in Wales

23 August 1951   Martin Armstrong on Thomas' "Festival Exhibition" talk p. 315

6 November 1952   Dylan Thomas "Prologue" p. 773: this "Author's Prologue" to the *Collected Poems* was read on John Lehmann's Third Programme "New Soundings" on 26 October 1952

---

8. John Gawsworth arranged for an edited version ("Starting a Story") to appear in *Literary Digest* Autumn 1948 (Vol. III No. 3) pp. 12–15.

4 December 1952   Raymond Preston review of *Collected Poems* p. 947

5 February 1953   C. Day Lewis "Themes and Subjects in Modern Poetry" pp. 227–229

16 April 1953   Reginald Pound "Television" p. 654, on "Home Town: Swansea" with a photograph of Thomas while on television screen

6 August 1953   Anon. review of *Doctor & Devils* p. 233

17 September 1953   Dylan Thomas "A Story" pp. 458–460, which was BBC-TV broadcast of 10 August 1953 "Speaking Personally"; reviewed by Reginald Pound 20 August 1953 p. 314

* * *

12 November 1953   On Thomas' death, with photograph p. 815[9]

19 November 1953   Huw Menai "Dylan Thomas" (poem) p. 845

26 November 1953   Ken Etheridge "For Dylan" (poem) p. 913

14 January 1954   Dylan Thomas, reprinting of "Especially when the October wind" p. 105

4 February 1954   Martin Armstrong on "Under Milk Wood" p. 236[10]

22 April 1954   Dylan Thomas "A Visit to America" pp. 692–693

27 May 1954   W. R. Rodgers "Dylan Thomas" an appreciation pp. 913–914; Anon. review of *Under Milk Wood* p. 937

24 June 1954   Letter from C. B. Purdom p. 1101 suggesting influence of T. F. Powys on *Under Milk Wood*

20 January 1955   Anon. review of Stanford p. 122

27 January 1955   Reproduction of painting "Under Milk Wood" by Paula Rego p. 162

9 June 1955   Tom Scott "On the Death of Dylan Thomas" (poem) p. 1022 reprinted in *Garland*

25 August 1955   J. MacLaren-Ross review of *Prospect* p. 307

3 May 1956   Anon. review of Brinnin p. 561

7 March 1957   Anon. review of Rolph p. 395

---

9. See also obituary in *Radio Times* 20 November 1953 p. 3, and reminiscences 6 July 1956 p. 12. Also the memorial by Wynford Vaughan Thomas in BBC's *London Calling* 24 December 1953. Further reminiscences of Thomas in the studio in V. C. Clinton-Baddeley "The Written and the Spoken Word" *Essays and Studies 1965* London: John Murray 1965 pp. 73–82.

10. See also Douglas Cleverdon the producer of the radio play, in *Radio Times* 22 January 1954 p. 7 and 28 June 1957 p. 6, and J. C. Trewin "We'll Hear a Play" *The B.B.C. Quarterly* Summer 1954 pp. 85–91; Richard Rowland "The BBC Revisited" *Quarterly of Films, Radio & Television* Spring 1955 pp. 290–291.

16 May 1957   J. C. Trewin on BBC-TV "Under Milk Wood" pp. 802–803, complains of the cutting[11]

 9 January 1958   Anon. review of *Letters to Vernon Watkins* p. 71

16 January 1958   Wynford Vaughan Thomas "Dylan Thomas and Nellie Wallace" p. 94

 6 February 1958   Ralph Pomeroy "In Memory of Dylan Thomas" (poem) p. 234 reprinted in *Garland*

31 July 1958   A. Alvarez "A Library of Poetry" pp. 155–156, on the Lockwood Library, Buffalo

17 December 1959   Ruthven Todd "Dylan Thomas in London" pp. 1065–66

 8 September 1960   P. N. Furbank review of Heppenstall pp. 389–390

17 November 1960   Paul Potts review of Tedlock pp. 904, 907

 4 January 1962   John Davenport "Patterns of Friendship" pp. 26–27, on Thomas, Augustus John, and others

12 April 1962   Raymond Williams review of Holbrook pp. 651–652

26 July 1962   Andrew Davies "A Welshman in London" pp. 137, 140

 3 January 1963   Bernard Bergonzi review of Tindall pp. 37–38; 17 January 1963 letter from Martin Dodsworth p. 127

13 June 1963   Monica Furlong review of *Not Quite Posthumous* p. 1007

14 November 1963   Lois Mitchison "The Spoken Word" p. 806, on "Behind the Dylan Legend" (Third Programme); 21 November 1963 letter from Paul Potts p. 839[12]

 5 December 1963   Letter from Henry Savage p. 932, asking about "Do not go gentle"

12 March 1964   John Russell Taylor on "Under Milk Wood" (TV) p. 445

 2 July 1964   Elizabeth Jennings review of *Beach of Falesá* p. 28

16 July 1964   Bernard Bergonzi review of *Entrances* and *Druid* p. 98

 4 November 1965   George Barker review of FitzGibbon pp. 714–715

16 December 1965   Terence Hawkes "Playboys of the western world" pp. 991–993, on Synge and *Under Milk Wood*

24 November 1966   Ian Hamilton review of *Selected Letters*, *Garland*, Moynihan p. 779

---

11. See also Henry Sherek, the producer of the stage version, in the *Radio Times* 3 May 1957 p. 7; and in his *Not in Front of the Children* London: Heinemann 1959.

12. See also Paul Potts' autobiography *Dante Called You Beatrice* London: Eyre & Spottiswoode 1960.

SUNDAY REFEREE

The editor of this London Sunday newspaper in 1933 was Mark Goulden; the literary editor, Hayter Preston. The "Poet's Corner" directed by Victor Neuburg was begun on 16 April 1933 and ended with reorganization of the newspaper in November 1935.[13]

3 September 1933   Poet's Corner p. 14: Dylan Thomas "That Sanity Be Kept"—with comment by Victor B. Neuburg

17 September 1933   Poet's Corner p. 14: Thomas received a prize for a poem not printed

8 October 1933   Poet's Corner p. 10: "Good poems this week have been received from ... A. E. Trick ... Dylan Thomas ... Pamela H. Johnson."

29 October 1933   Poet's Corner p. 14: Dylan Thomas "The force that through the green fuse drives the flower"—with comment by Victor B. Neuburg

19 November 1933   Poet's Corner p. 10: prize for poem not printed

31 December 1933   Poet's Corner p. 9: "Good poems were received from Dylan Thomas."

7 January 1934   Poet's Corner p. 9: Dylan Thomas "Song" ("Love me, not as the dreaming nurses")—with comment by Victor B. Neuburg

11 February 1934   Poet's Corner p. 10: Dylan Thomas "A process in the weather of the heart"—with comment by Victor B. Neuburg

25 March 1934   Poet's Corner p. 12: Dylan Thomas "Where once the waters of your face"—with comment by V.B.N.

22 April 1934   Poet's Corner p. 12: Thomas awarded "second book-prize"[14]

13 May 1934   Poet's Corner p. 11: Victor Neuburg on "Our Second Book Prize-Winner"

28 October 1934   Poet's Corner p. 6: Dylan Thomas "Foster the light"

25 November 1934   Poet's Corner p. 16: A. E. Trick wins the prize for a criticism of Thomas' "Foster the light," of which the following extracts are quoted: "Modern poetry is roughly divided into two schools: that which

---

13. See Jean Overton Fuller *The Magical Dilemma of Victor Neuburg* London: W. H. Allen 1965, which has many references to Thomas; also for background, Arthur Calder-Marshall *The Magic of My Youth* London: Rupert Hart-Davis 1951 especially pp. 215–225. The correspondence with Pamela Hansford Johnson provides a week by week "diary" on the Poet's Corner. All of Thomas' seven poems in the Poet's Corner, along with Neuburg's comments on them, are reproduced in Runia Sheila Macleod "The Dylan I knew" *Adam* 1953.

14. That is, the *Sunday Referee* would sponsor the publication of a book of poems by the prize-winner. Pamela Hansford Johnson had been the first book prize-winner, and her *Symphony for Full Orchestra* was so sponsored. There were delays with Thomas' book; it was announced again in the Poet's Corner on 6 May 1934 and again on 11 November 1934. *18 Poems* finally appeared just before Christmas 1934.

works towards words, and that which works from words. The latter is abstract and purely intellectual in appeal. Mr. Thomas is its best exponent.... Each line is so impregnated with images, allusion, antitheses, that it becomes a poem with the poem. Words are treated like vials; new meaning being poured into them."

30 December 1934   "Our Literary 'Gangsters'; Young Poet Attacks Modern Writers" p. 3, interview with Thomas on the publication of *18 Poems*, with portrait by 'Julian':

"Most writers to-day move about in gangs. They haven't the strength to stand and fight as individuals. But even as 'gangsters' their machine guns are full, not of bullets, but of dried peas."

So Mr. Dylan Thomas, the young poet whose first volume of collected poems is being produced by the SUNDAY REFEREE, said in an interview yesterday.

About the way life has treated him personally this young poet has no grouses. A normally happy childhood in a normally happy home—a schoolmaster father who encouraged him to express himself in writing. Then two years ago London, and the acceptance of his first poems by the late Mr. A. R. Orage, the discoverer of so many brilliant young writers.

"Not that life is always easy for a poet determined to live for, and by, his work," said Mr. Thomas. "There are times when I'd give much to be a bank clerk in a safe job. I like difficulties—just as I like things that are difficult to write and difficult to understand."

"Do you understand everything you write yourself?" he was asked.

"No poet ever understood everything he wrote himself," replied Mr. Thomas.

19 May 1935   Poet's Corner p. 6: "Wireless Tribute to Dylan Thomas"—C. Day Lewis' broadcast

11 August 1935   Poet's Corner p. 6: Dylan Thomas "Poem for Sunday" ("Incarnate devil")—with comment by Victor B. Neuburg

ADELPHI

A monthly magazine with which John Middleton Murry was still associated in 1933, although Richard Rees was editor. Later a quarterly; ceased publication in 1955.

September 1933 (New Series Vol. 6 No. 6)   Dylan Thomas untitled poem ("No man believes who, when a star falls shot") p. 398

March 1934   Dylan Thomas "The Woman Speaks" pp. 399–400

September 1934   Dylan Thomas review of three poets pp. 418–420: William Soutar *The Solitary Way*, William Montgomerie *Squared Circle*, and Sydney Salt *Thirty Pieces*

December 1934   Dylan Thomas "The Tree" pp. 143–149

January 1935   Dylan Thomas review pp. 255–256: M. K. Gandhi *Songs from Prison*

February 1935   Dylan Thomas review of three poets pp. 312–314: Lyle Donaghy *Into the Light*, John Lehmann *The Noise of History*, and Ruth Pitter *A Mad Lady's Garland*; Rayner Heppenstall review of *18 Poems* pp. 314–315; Dylan Thomas review pp. 317–318: Alfred Hy. Haffenden *Dictator in Freedom*

June 1935   Dylan Thomas review pp. 179–181: Tibble 2 vol. edition of *The Poems of John Clare*

October 1935   Dylan Thomas review pp. 58–59: R. D. Jameson *A Comparison of Literatures*

December 1936   Glyn Jones review of *Twenty-five Poems* pp. 185–186

January–March 1949   Vernon Scannell on Karl Shapiro pp. 157–160

First Quarter 1953   "Editorial" [B. Ifor Evans] pp. 93–94, comment on *Collected Poems*: much in it to "suggest that Dylan Thomas is the outstanding poet of our time"

* * *

First Quarter 1954   "Editorial" pp. 103–104 on Thomas' death; Gwyn Jones "Welsh Dylan" pp. 108–117; Richard Church "Dylan Thomas, the Early Poems" pp. 118–120; John Arlott "Dylan Thomas and Radio" pp. 121–124

Second Quarter 1954   "Editorial" p. 205, many letters received (though none are printed)

Third Quarter 1954   Anon. review of Olson p. 286

Fourth Quarter 1954   Richard Church "The Poet in Contemporary Society" pp. 35–50, pp. 40–41

NEW VERSE

Founding editor: Geoffrey Grigson. No. 1 was January 1933; ceased publication in 1939 after thirty-four issues.

April 1934 (No. 8)   Dylan Thomas "Our eunuch dreams" pp. 11–12

June 1934 (No. 9)   Dylan Thomas "When once the twilight locks no longer" pp. 6–8; "I see the boys of summer in their ruin" pp. 8–9

August 1934 (No. 10)   Dylan Thomas "If I was tickled by the rub of love" pp. 8–9[15]

October 1934 (No. 11)   Dylan Thomas "Answers to an Enquiry" pp. 8–9— (the questions are on p. 2) reprinted in *Casebook*

December 1934 (No. 12)   Dylan Thomas "Half of the fellow father as he doubles" (= "My world is pyramid") pp. 10–12; D.M.T. "Fey, Dollfuss, Vienna" pp. 19–20, review of Spender's *Vienna*

---

15. Included in Geoffrey Grigson ed. *New Verse: An Anthology* London: Faber 1939 pp. 145–148.

February 1935 (No. 13)   Anon. review of *18 Poems* pp. 21–22

August–September 1935 (No. 16)   Dylan Thomas "A Poem in Three Parts" (= "I, in my intricate image") pp. 2–5

December 1935 (No. 18)   Dylan Thomas "The hand that signed the paper" pp. 15–16; "Should lanterns shine" p. 16; "I have longed to move away" p. 17

Xmas 1936 (No. 23)   C.B.S. [Bernard Spencer] review of *Twenty-five Poems* pp. 19–21

May 1937 (No. 25)   George Barker "Epistle to D.T." (poem) pp. 2–3, reprinted in *Garland*

November 1937 (Nos. 26–27 "Auden Double Number")   Dylan Thomas, one of "Sixteen Comments on Auden" p. 25

JOHN O'LONDON'S WEEKLY

Absorbed into *Time and Tide* in 1963.

5 May 1934 (Vol. XXXI No. 786)   Dylan Thomas "Dare I?" (= "Ears in the turrets hear") p. 149[16]

18 December 1936   Auda, pseud. "What I hear" p. 521, comment on the Edith Sitwell letters to the *Sunday Times*; Gerald Bullett on *The Year's Poetry, 1936* quotes Thomas p. 526

19 April 1940   Lilian Arnold review of *Portrait* p. 90

8 March 1946   Margaret Willy review of *Deaths & Entrances* p. 230

26 December 1952   Richard Church review of *Collected Poems* p. 1198

22 May 1953   Richard Church review of *Doctor & Devils* p. 453

7 August 1953   Mimi Josephson "Poet in the Boat House" pp. 701–702

* * *

20 November 1953   Sara Jackson "To Dylan Thomas" (poem) p. 1038; Colophon, pseud. "A Bookman's Diary" p. 1040: "from the moment Edith Sitwell discovered him, at the age of twenty-two, he never lacked admirers"

27 November 1953   Letters from Derek Parker (tribute from a young poet) and Mimi Josephson p. 1097

1 January 1954   Richard Church, reminiscences p. 12; J. A. Lindon "Dylan Thomas" (poem) p. 12[17]

---

16. Among a selection of poems from *John O'London's*, this poem was included in Frank Whitaker & W. T. Williams eds. *Saturday to Monday* London: Newnes 1938 pp. 12–13.

17. His parody of "Poem in October" entitled "Poem in Tubwater" appeared in *The Guinness Book of Poetry 1958/59* London: Putnam 1960.

12 March 1954   Richard Church review of *Under Milk Wood* p. 251

24 March 1960   Bill Hopkins "Dylan Thomas recorded" p. 335, a survey of Thomas on records

15 September 1960   Elizabeth Hamilton review of Heppenstall p. 319

22 September 1960   Letter from Geoffrey K. Roberts on "Fern Hill" p. 364

1 December 1960   Perry Madoc "True Thomas" pp. 704–705, on Edward, Dylan, and R. S. Thomas

22 December 1960   John Barrows review of Tedlock p. 799

24 August 1961   Alan Dent on Caedmon records p. 234

29 November 1962   Mervyn Levy "A womb with a view" pp. 484–485, reminiscences, with drawings on cover; a letter from Roydon Victor 13 December 1962 p. 543 asks who did the drawings

NEW STORIES

Founded in early 1934 by H. E. Bates, Arthur Calder-Marshall, Hamish Miles, Edward J. O'Brien, L. A. Pavey, and Geoffrey West. Eight issues were published by Basil Blackwell in the following two years.

June–July 1934 (Vol. 1 No. 3)   Dylan Thomas "The Enemies" pp. 194–198

CRITERION

Editor: T. S. Eliot. Founded 1922; ceased publication 1939.

October 1934   Dylan Thomas "From love's first fever to her plague" pp. 27–28

January 1935   Dylan Thomas "The Visitor" pp. 251–259

April 1935   Michael Roberts review of *18 Poems* pp. 496–499

July 1936   Dylan Thomas "The Orchards" pp. 614–622

October 1938   Dylan Thomas "How shall my animal" pp. 29–30

THE BOOKMAN

Thomas contributed to the last two issues of *The Bookman* before its incorporation in the *London Mercury* in January 1935.

November 1934 (Vol. LXXXVII No. 518)   Dylan Thomas "Mr. Pudney's Second Volume" p. 132, a review of John Pudney *Open to the Sky*

Christmas 1934   Geoffrey Grigson "The Year's Poetry" pp. 150–151 comments on Thomas' poems in *New Verse*; Dylon Thomas "Individual and Collective" p. 12, a review of Ruth Pitter *A Mad Lady's Garland*, Wilfred Gibson *Fuel*, John Lehmann *The Noise of History*, and Thomas Moult ed. *The Best Poems of 1934*

MORNING POST

London daily newspaper. "Books of the Day"—under which heading Thomas' many reviews of thrillers appeared—was nominally edited by E. B. Osborn. Geoffrey Grigson was responsible for Thomas' being adopted as reviewer; see his autobiography *The Crest on the Silver* London: Cressett Press 1950 pp. 172–174.

1 January 1935 Anon. review of *18 Poems* p. 17

5 April 1935 D.T. "Death on All Sides" p. 19: review of John Dickson Carr *Death-Watch*, H. C. Bailey *Mr. Fortune Objects*, Angus MacVicar *The Screaming Gull*, Robin Forsythe *The Ginger Cat Mystery*, and Herbert Corey *Crime at Cobb's House*

12 April 1935 D.T. "Five Thrillers a la Mode" p. 17: review of Ellery Queen *The Spanish Cape Mystery*, Francis D. Grierson *Murder in Black*, Lord Gorell *Red Lilac*, George Goodchild & Bechhofer Roberts *The Dear Old Gentleman*, and Nigel Burnaby *The Clue of the Green-Eyed Girl*

7 May 1935 D.T. "Too Many Pigs on the Wing" p. 5: review of Carleton Kendrake *The Clue of the Forgotten Murder*, Q. Patrick *Darker Grows the Valley*, Means Davies *Murder Without Weapon*, M. Doriel Hay *Death on the Cherwell*, and Cecil Freeman *The Ten Black Pearls*

14 May 1935 D.T. "Post-morticians" p. 17: review of C. St. John Sprigg *Death of a Queen*, Roger East *Twenty-Five Sanitary Inspectors*, Freeman Wills Croft *Crime at Guildford*, and G. D. H. & M. Cole *Dr. Tancred Begins*

24 May 1935 D.T. "By Hooks and By Crooks" p. 17: review of John Creasey *Death Round the Corner*, E. R. Punshon *Death of a Beauty Queen*, Anthony Weymouth *The Doctors Are Doubtful*, and Eimar O'Duffy *Head of a Girl*

21 June 1935 D.T. "A Few Corpses and Puzzles" p. 17: review of Augustus Muir *Raphael M.D.*, Moray Dalton *The Belgrave Manor Crime*, Willoughby Sharp *Murder in Bermuda*, and Elaine Hamilton *Tragedy in the Dark*

28 June 1935 D.T. "Blood Without Thunder" p. 16: review of Cornelius Cafyn *The Death Riders*, Phoebe Atwood Taylor *The Mystery of the Cape Cod Tavern*, Florence Leighton *As Strange a Maze*, John Rhode *Hendon's First Case*, and Rose & Dudley Lambert *The Mystery of the Golden Wings*

5 July 1935 D.T. "A. E. W. Mason: King Thriller" p. 16: review of A. E. W. Mason *They Wouldn't Be Chessmen*

9 July 1935 D.T. "Two Thrillers" p. 16: review of R. Philmore *Riot Act* and Leonard R. Gribble *Mystery at Tudor Arches*

24 September 1935 D.T. "New Thrillers" p. 14: review of M. G. Eberhart *The House on the Roof*, Donald Macpherson *Go Home, Unicorn*, Jean Lilly *Death in B Minor*, and Robert Curtis *The Children of Light*

4 October 1935 D.T. "Queer Things in Mexico" p. 17: review of Todd Downing *The Cat Screams*, David Hume *Call in the Yard*, R. C. Woodthorpe *The Shadow on the Downs*, and John Bude *The Lake District Murder*

11 October 1935   D.T. "Frequent, Gory and Grotesque" p. 15: review of John Dickson Carr *The Hollow Man*, John Rhode *Mystery at Olympia*, J. Y. Dane *Murder in College*, and Mary M. Atwater *Murder in Midsummer*

15 October 1935   D.T. "Revolver, Sandbag, Handgrenade" p. 16: review of Douglas G. Browne *The Stolen Boat-Train*, Grierson Dickson *Gun Business*, Miles Burton *The Milk Churn Murder*, and Kathleen Moore Knight *Death Blew Out the Match*

25 October 1935   D.T. "A Choice of New Thrillers" p. 15: review of Rex Stout *The League of Frightened Men*, Francis D. Grierson *Death on Deposit*, and Arthur Somers Roche *The Case Against Mrs. Ames*

1 November 1935   D.T. "Two Thrillers" p. 14: review of Dorothea Brande *Beauty Vanishes* and John Newton Chance *Murder in Oils*

5 November 1935   D.T. "Grand Goose Flesh Parade" p. 16: review of Denis Wheatley ed. *A Century of Horror*, and *50 Years of Ghost Stories*

15 November 1935   D.T. "Three New Thrillers" p. 6: review of Cecil Freeman Gregg *Danger at Cliff House*, Mignon G. Eberhart *The Cases of Susan Dare*, and William Gore *Death in the Wheelbarrow*

22 November 1935   D.T. "Lord Peter Does Another Job" p. 14: review of Dorothy L. Sayers *Gaudy Night*, Carter Dickson *The Red Widow Murders*, Henry Wade *Heir Presumptive*, and Carroll John Daly *Death's Juggler*

29 November 1935   D.T. "He Was Framed with a False Eye" p. 16: review of Erle Stanley Gardner *The Case of the Counterfeit Eye*, Bruce Graeme *Not Proven*, S. S. Van Dine *The Garden Murder Case*, and Gavin Holt *The Emerald Spider*

7 January 1936   D.T. "Murders for the New Year" p. 15: review of Agatha Christie *The ABC Murders*, Miles Burton *Death in the Tunnel*, and Peter Drax *Murder by Chance*

17 January 1936   D.T. "Dead Bodies, Live Villains" p. 14: review of Todd Downing *Vultures in the Sky*, Richard Hull *Murder Isn't Easy*, Colin Davy *Agents of the League*, and Gordon Valk *Cliffs of Sark*

31 January 1936   D.T. "Murder from Inside" p. 14: review of Baroness von Hutten *Cowardly Custard*, Ngaio Marsh & H. Jellett *The Nursing Home Murder*, Moray Dalton *The Strange Case of Harriet Hall*, and David Hume *Meet the Dragon*

7 February 1936   D.T. "Patient Detection" p. 20: review of Freeman Wills Croft *The Loss of the Jane Vosper*, Phoebe Atwood Taylor *Sandbar Sinister*, and Hugh Austin *It Couldn't Be Murder*

11 February 1936   D.T. "The Week's Blood and Fun" p. 16: review of R. Philmore *The Good Books*, Stuart Palmer *The Puzzle of the Briar Pipe*, F. J. Whaley *Reduction of Staff*, and Sutherland Scott *Murder Without Mourners*

27 March 1936   D.T. "Death and Fun" p. 16: review of Milward Kennedy *Sic Transit Gloria*, D. H. Landels *His Lordship the Judge*, James Street *Death in an Armchair*, and Cecil M. Wills *Defeat of a Detective*

28 August 1936   D.T. "Four Thrillers" p. 4: review of Erle Stanley Gardner *The Case of the Sleepwalker's Niece*, Seldon Truss *Rooksmiths*, Lee Thayer *Murder in the Mirror*, and H. H. Stanners *Murder at Markendon Court*

11 September 1936   D.T. "Mysteries" p. 14: review of Mary Fitt *Murder Mars the Tour*, Charman Edwards *Fear Haunts the Roses*, Guy Morton *Mystery at Hardacres*, and Ruth Burr Sanborn *Murder on the Aphrodite*

EUROPEAN QUARTERLY

February 1935   Anon.[18] review of *18 Poems* p. 274: "It is one of the most remarkable books of poetry which have appeared for several years."

TIME AND TIDE

Independent non-party weekly.

9 February 1935 (Vol. XVI No. 6)   Desmond Hawkins review of *18 Poems* pp. 204, 206:

A verse-critic may review 500 books in a decade. He will be fortunate if, in the same period, he discovers ten considerable poets . . . .

Mr. Auden is already a landmark. His own poetry stands clear above fashion. But the Audenesque convention is nearly ended; and I credit Dylan Thomas with being the first considerable poet to break through fashionable limitation and speak an unborrowed language, without excluding anything that has preceded him. Barker and others have promised this, but Dylan Thomas goes much further towards realization. For a first book this is remarkably mature.

Thomas's poetry is personal or universal, but not social. He is thereby purer than the fashionable. He is a grateful heir to Eliot's magical sense of the macabre and to Auden's textural firmness, but by inheritance rather than by imitation. A full digestive stage intervenes . . . .

Appreciation of new poetry cannot be adequately rationalized until we have lived with it for a time. It is at first a matter of excited recognition. Mr. Thomas's poems are not easily swallowed, but their quality proclaims itself at a touch. He is at present obsessed with the vocabulary of physiology in its more sinister aspect, and he is apt to repeat certain block-phrases of a private code of thought. These are minor faults, however, and they vanish in the achievement of fusing metaphysical poetry into sensuous terms. None of his contemporaries has such central

---

18. Presumably written by Edwin Muir, one of the editors of this short-lived journal of international affairs. Muir was one of the earliest figures of established reputation to notice Thomas in print. See his *An Autobiography* London: Hogarth Press; New York: William Sloan 1954 pp. 232, 237. His review of *Twenty-five Poems* appeared in *Scotland* Autumn 1936 pp. 66–67.

clarity of thought as a poetic experience. This is not merely a book of unusual promise; it is more probably the sort of bomb that bursts not more than once in three years.

24 October 1936   Hugh Gordon Porteus review of *Twenty-five Poems* p. 1483

9 October 1937   Dylan Thomas "The Amherst Poet" p. 1328—a review of *Poems of Emily Dickinson* and Edna St. Vincent Millay's *Conversation at Midnight*

7 October 1939   Clifford Dyment review of *Map of Love* p. 1308

4 May 1940   Desmond Hawkins review of *Portrait* pp. 487–488

23 February 1946   Walter Allen review of *Deaths & Entrances* p. 182

15 November 1952   Alan Ross review of *Collected Poems* pp. 1337–38

* * *

14 November 1953   "Diary" p. 1476, on Thomas' death

12 December 1953   Raymond Garlick "Poem for Dylan" (poem) p. 1643

24 April 1954   Geoffrey Taylor review of *Under Milk Wood* p. 550

17 September 1955   James Kirkup review of *Prospect* and *Adventures* p. 1205

21 April 1956   David Wright review of Brinnin pp. 453–454

13 October 1956   Burns Singer review of Rolph p. 1242

8 June 1957   Dannie Abse review of *Leftover Life* pp. 719–720

14 December 1957   Hugh Gordon Porteus review of *Letters to Vernon Watkins* pp. 1596–97

26 November 1960   Paul Potts review of Tedlock p. 1446

12–18 March 1964   Duncan Roberts "The transfer of 'Milk Wood' to television" p. 39

TIMES LITERARY SUPPLEMENT

14 March 1935   Anon. review of *18 Poems* p. 163

19 September 1936   Anon. review of *Twenty-five Poems* p. 750

4 September 1937   Anon. review of *Wales* (No. 1) p. 643: "wasting his strength to achieve obscurity"

26 August 1939   Anon. review of *Map of Love* p. 499

6 April 1940   Anon. review of *Portrait* p. 173

9 March 1946   Anon. review of *Deaths & Entrances* p. 116

22 July 1949   Anon. review of Treece p. 476

24 August 1951   Dylan Thomas "Over Sir John's hill" p. xxi (supplement)

7 December 1951   Dylan Thomas "In the white giant's thigh" p. 786

28 November 1952   Anon. "Salute to a Poet" p. 776—review of *Collected Poems*

29 May 1953   Anon. review of *Doctor & Devils* p. 351

* * *

27 November 1953   "Dylan Thomas Memorial Fund" p. 762: letter of appeal signed by T. S. Eliot, Peggy Ashcroft, Kenneth Clark, Walter de la Mare, Graham Greene, Augustus John, Louis MacNeice, Edwin Muir, Goronwy Rees, Edith Sitwell, Osbert Sitwell, Vernon Watkins, Emlyn Williams

15 January 1954   Letter from Derek Stanford p. 41—writing a commissioned book on Thomas, requesting personal recollections

5 March 1954   Anon. review of *Under Milk Wood* p. 148

6 August 1954   Stephen Spender "Greatness of Aim" p. vi (supplement)[19]

10 September 1954   Letter from T. A. Sinclair p. 573—noting misprint in "This bread I break"

19 November 1954   Anon. review of *Quite Early* p. 731; 17 December 1954 Letter from Aneirin Talfan Davies p. 821

7 January 1955   Anon. review of Stanford and Olson p. 10

5 August 1955   Anon. review of *Prospect* p. 446; Anon. "The Two Literatures of Wales" p. xii (supplement)

30 September 1955   Anon. review of *Adventures* p. 569

11 May 1956   Anon. review of Brinnin p. 284

18 May 1956   Letter from Boris Watson (proprietor, Mandrake Club)[20] p. 297

1 June 1956   Anon. "Anglo-Welsh Attitudes" p. 328

6 July 1956   Letter from Trustees of the Dylan Thomas Estate (Stuart Thomas, Wynford Vaughan Thomas, David Higham) p. 409, requesting Thomas' correspondence for forthcoming edition

---

19. Reprinted in his *The Making of a Poem* London: Hamish Hamilton 1955 pp. 35–44.

20. Roy C. Moose in reviewing Brinnin in *Carolina Quarterly* Winter–Spring 1956 pp. 45–47 gives a first-hand account: "In London, Thomas frequented a Bohemian cellar dive called the Mandrake Club in Meard Street, where I got to know him since it was a gathering place for Oxford students. There Thomas would come nightly with John Heath Stubbs and the other younger poets for a binge of drinking and talking. Always amid the chatter of students, artists, prostitutes, and pimps and the sounds of Spanish guitars, singers, and screams, there always would be the resonant musical voice of Dylan Thomas, not once faltering to betray the eating away, like Prometheus, of his liver—a condition that was to lead to a slow agonized death."

27 July 1956   Anon. review of Rolph p. 451

10 August 1956   Anon. review of Treece, 2nd edition, p. 479

17 August 1956   Anon. "Experiment in Verse" p. iii (supplement) Thomas contrasted with Donald Davie

31 May 1957   Anon. review of *Leftover Life* p. 336

 8 November 1957   Burns Singer "The Least of Elegies" (poem) p. 670 reprinted in *Garland*

15 November 1957   Anon. review of *Letters to Vernon Watkins* p. 691

24 October 1958   Anon. mention of *Under Milk Wood* (acting version) p. 64

 2 September 1960   Anon. review of Heppenstall p. 555

23 December 1960   Anon. review of Tedlock and Sanesi p. 826

14 July 1961   Anon. review of "Homage to Dylan Thomas" record p. 434

13 April 1962   Anon. review of Holbrook p. 250; 4 May 1962 letter from Holbrook p. 309, with rejoinder by the reviewer

27 April 1962   Letter from E. M. W. Tillyard p. 281 describing young Dylan drunk at Cambridge; 11 May 1962 correction by E. M. W. Tillyard p. 339

21 December 1962   Anon. review of Tindall p. 987

28 June 1963   Anon. review of *Not Quite Posthumous* p. 475; letter from Constantine FitzGibbon p. 477

12 July 1963   Anon. mention of T. H. Jones p. 511

13 September 1963   Southeby's sell inscribed *18 Poems* for £78 p. 696

16 January 1964   Letter from Keidrych Rhys p. 53 re *Colour of Saying*

 5 March 1964   Anon. [G. S. Fraser] "The Legend and the Puzzle" pp. 185–186: lead article on *Garland, Colour of Saying*, Kleinman, *Entrances*

19 March 1964   Letter from J. H. Martin p. 235—lengthy reminiscences of Thomas in Cornwall; 26 March 1964 letter from Keidrych Rhys p. 255; 2 April 1964 letters from Constantine FitzGibbon, Raymond Garlick, David Rees p. 273; 16 April 1964 letter from Eithne Wilkins p. 311

30 July 1964   Anon. review of *Beach of Falesá* p. 670

22 October 1964   Anon. review of *Dylan, Druid*, Ackerman, and *Twenty Years* p. 960

21 October 1965   Anon. review of Read and FitzGibbon p. 940

26 May 1966   Anon. review of *Collected Poems* p. 477

 2 March 1967   Anon. [Geoffrey Grigson] review of *Selected Letters*, Moynihan, Murdy, *Garland* p. 157

 2 May 1968   Anon. [Walford Davies] review of *Notebooks* p. 460

THE SPECTATOR

26 April 1935   I. M. Parsons review of *18 Poems* p. 704

11 December 1936   Desmond Hawkins review of *Twenty-five Poems* p. 1058

25 August 1939   Desmond Hawkins review of *Map of Love* pp. 300–301

 5 April 1940   Derek Verschoyle review of *Portrait* p. 496

 9 April 1943   Edgar Anstey review of film *These Are the Men* p. 338

23 June 1944   Edgar Anstey on film *Conquest of a Germ* p. 570

29 June 1945   Edgar Anstey on film *Our Country* p. 594

 8 February 1946   W. J. Turner review of *Deaths & Entrances* pp. 148, 150:

> Thus I make just my own personal declaration that in this new book of twenty-four poems Mr. Dylan Thomas shows himself to be the authentic, magical thing, a true poet—original and traditional, imperfect but outstanding, with the unmistakeable fire and power of genius. If anyone is looking for new contemporary poetry worthy of our great—and, I would add, world-supreme—English tradition, here it is. For I do not find such wealth of poetry elsewhere among the poems of most of our deservedly known and genuinely gifted writers. A fine, thin-worn Georgian coin of gold is tossed up here and there by one of our finer craftsmen; but here we are in an ocean of poetry and there is a spate of immense long rollers, huge-shouldered, transparent-green with magic light and foaming into billows of the purest snow of creation with the energy of an earlier age.
>
> I think that this is all that is really necessary to be said, for anything else can be but of minor importance. And if I add that, for good or ill, Mr. Thomas is not an intellectual poet, I only mean that he does not obtrude his intellectual processes upon us. That there are a powerful mind and a great driving force behind this remarkable poet is implied when I am ready to declare that not only is Mr. Thomas a truly creative writer, but that this book alone, in my opinion, ranks him as a major poet.

20 June 1947   L. C. Lloyd "On the Air" p. 717—on "Return Journey" broadcast

16 April 1948   Virginia Graham on film *Three Weird Sisters* p. 465—"dialogue has a pleasantly civilized sound"

29 October 1948   Virginia Graham on film *No Room at the Inn* p. 558

 5 December 1952   Stephen Spender review of *Collected Poems* pp. 780–781

12 June 1953   Bonamy Dobrée review of *Doctor & Devils* pp. 763–764

* * *

13 November 1953   John Arlott, obituary p. 534

20 November 1953   Letters from Rosamond Lehmann and Geoffrey Tillotson p. 574; 27 November 1953 letters from Mark Goulden (of the *Sunday Referee*), David Wright, and John Arlott p. 632

9 April 1954   John Arlott review of *Under Milk Wood* pp. 441–442

20 August 1954   Charles Tomlinson review of Olson pp. 235–236

12 November 1954   Anthony Thwaite review of *Quite Early* p. 586

12 August 1955   Kingsley Amis "Thomas the Rhymer" pp. 227–228, review article on *Prospect*[21]

19 August 1955   Letter from John Davenport p. 250; 26 August 1955 letter from Thomas Archer p. 277; 2 September 1955 letter from John Davenport p. 304

7 October 1955   Elizabeth Jennings review of *Adventures* pp. 462–463

27 April 1956   John Arlott review of Brinnin pp. 387–388

4 May 1956   Letter from Alan Hunter p. 617; 11 May 1956 letter from John Arlott p. 654; 18 May 1956 letter from Alan Hunter p. 687

7 June 1957   Isabel Quigly review of *Leftover Life* p. 754

15 November 1957   John Davenport review of *Letters to Vernon Watkins* p. 651

29 November 1957   Kingsley Amis "An Evening with Dylan Thomas" p. 737 —recalling Thomas' visit to the University College at Swansea[22]

6 December 1957   Letter from Robert Boothby p. 789: "Sir—After all the mush one has had to wade through about Dylan Thomas during the past two years, Kingsley Amis's article came as a refreshing draught of cool, clear water; and I, for one, would like to express my gratitude."

2 September 1960   Hugh Gordon Porteus "Nights Out in the Thirties" pp. 342, 344—review article on Heppenstall, with personal reminiscences

9 September 1960   Letter from Rayner Heppenstall p. 369; 16 September 1960 letter from Hugh Gordon Porteus p. 400

21 October 1960   D. J. Enright "Once Below a Time" pp. 607–608—review article on Tedlock[23]

11 November 1960   Letter from Brian Way p. 730; 18 November 1960 letter from Richard Eberhart p. 775—on the loaned raincoat

6 April 1962   Bernard Bergonzi review of Holbrook p. 452

20 April 1962   Letter from Adrian Bell p. 508; 27 April 1962 letter from Paul Potts p. 538

---

21. This review gained the approval of Lord Holborn in the *Baptist Times* 18 August 1955 p. 3.

22. See also the satirical portrait in Kingsley Amis' *That Uncertain Feeling* London: Gollanz 1955.

23. Included in his *Conspirators and Poets* London: Chatto & Windus 1966 pp. 42–47.

31 August 1962   Clifford Hawley on "Doctors & Devils" (Edinburgh) p. 305

28 June 1963   Simon Raven reviews *Not Quite Posthumous* pp. 843–844

13 December 1963   Keidrych Rhys review of *Colour of Saying* pp. 796, 798

14 February 1964   Caryl Brahms on "Dylan" in New York p. 213—Alec Guinness "miscast"

13 March 1964   Quoodle, pseud. "Homage to DMT" p. 339—sarcastic

21 August 1964   David Rees "Windy Boy and a Bit" pp. 246–247, review article on Kleinman, *Beach of Falesá*, *Entrances*, and *Druid*

28 August 1964   Letter from Keidrych Rhys p. 272; 4 September 1964 letter from Bryn Griffiths p. 308; 11 September 1964 letter from John Tripp p. 337; 25 September 1964 letters from Vernon Watkins, Bryn Griffiths, W. M. J. Alves p. 399; 2 October 1964 letter from John Tripp pp. 433–434

27 November 1964   Constantine FitzGibbon "The Posthumous Life of Dylan Thomas" pp. 704, 707, review article on Ackerman, with comment on *Druid*

11 December 1964   Letter from Aneirin Talfan Davies p. 812; 18 December 1964 letter from Constantine FitzGibbon p. 842; 25 December 1964 letter from James Dale p. 870

25 June 1965   John Davenport review of Read pp. 826–827

 2 July 1965   Letter from Keidrych Rhys p. 12; 9 July 1965 letter from John Davenport p. 39; 13 August 1965 letter from Bill Read p. 204

15 October 1965   John Davenport review of FitzGibbon pp. 487–488

18 March 1966   Hilary Spurling on "Adventures in the Skin Trade" (Hampstead) p. 327

 4 November 1966   Anthony Burgess "The Writer as Drunk" p. 588, on Behan and Thomas

25 November 1966   Anthony Burgess review of *Selected Letters*, Moynihan, *Garland* pp. 69–70

SCOTTISH BOOKMAN

A literary review, edited by David Cleghorn Thomson. Six issues 1935–36.

October 1935 (Vol. I No. 2)   Dylan Thomas "Do you not father me" p. 78

PROGRAMME

An Oxford review, 1935–1937.

23 October 1935 (No. 9)   Dylan Thomas "How soon the servant sun" pp. [2–3]; "A grief ago" pp. [10–12]

LIFE AND LETTERS TO-DAY

With volume 13 *Life and Letters* "modernised its title," and gained a new editor, Robert Herring. The quarterly became a monthly with volume 19; ceased publication with volume 65 (1950).

December 1935   Edith Sitwell and Robert Herring "A Correspondence on the Young English Poets" pp. 16–24; Dylan Thomas "Poems for a Poem" (= sonnets I–VII) pp. 73–75; Notes on Contributors p. 232: "Dylan Thomas is the young Welsh poet whose first book, *Eighteen Poems* (Sunday Referee and Parton Bookshop) created such a favorable impression last year. He is shortly publishing another. A history attaches to the publication of the present poem. We had previously accepted another, but when this appeared in a small paper which had been thought to have ceased, we wrote to the author for another. He favoured us with this, which is part of a work in progress, hoping we would 'like it, despite its obscurity and incompleteness. It's the first passage of what's going to be a very long poem indeed.' We are glad to print it and shall be following it in March with a story by him."

Spring 1936   Dylan Thomas "The Lemon" pp. 129–132

Winter 1936   C. Day Lewis "Autumn Verse" pp. 37–41, includes review of *Twenty-five Poems* p. 40

Spring 1937   Dylan Thomas "A Prospect of the Sea" pp. 65–70

Summer 1938   Dylan Thomas "In Memory of Ann Jones" p. 45; Julian Symons review of *Wales* (No. 4) pp. 191–194

September 1938   Dylan Thomas "O make me a mask" pp. 59–60

October 1938   Dylan Thomas "Peaches" pp. 76–95

December 1938   Dylan Thomas "Birthday Poem" (= "Twenty-four years") p. 42

July 1939   Dylan Thomas "Old Garbo" pp. 66–80

September 1939   Dylan Thomas "Extraordinary Little Cough" pp. 415–425

October 1939   Dylan Thomas "Poem (To Caitlin)" (= "Unluckily for a death") pp. 66–68

November 1939   Vernon Watkins "Portrait of a Friend" (poem) pp. 195–197 reprinted in *Garland*; Charles Williams review of *Map of Love* pp. 237–239

December 1939   Dylan Thomas "The Fight" pp. 326–339

March 1940 ["Welsh Number"]   Dylan Thomas "Once below a time" pp. 274–275; Rhys Davies review of *Portrait* pp. 336, 338

November 1940   Dylan Thomas "Into her lying down head" pp. 124–126

August 1941   Dylan Thomas "Among Those Killed in the Dawn Raid was a Man Aged One Hundred" p. 116

October 1941   Dylan Thomas "The Hunchback in the Park" pp. 41–42; "The Marriage of a Virgin" pp. 42–43

March 1943   Gwyn Jones "Note on the Welsh Short Story Writers" pp. 156–163

September 1944   Gordon Bottomly review of Keidrych Rhys ed. *Modern Welsh Poetry* pp. 179–181

June 1945   Dylan Thomas "Lie Still, Sleep Becalmed" p. 155

July 1945   Dylan Thomas "This Side of the Truth" pp. 28–29; "The Con ersation of Prayers" p. 29

October 1945   Dylan Thomas "In My Craft or Sullen Art" p. 31

April 1946   Editorial comment on *Deaths & Entrances* pp. 1–4

November 1946   Denis Botterill "Among the Younger Poets" pp. 93–99, *Deaths & Entrances* reviewed pp. 93–94

COMMENT

"Incorporating Poets' Corner." Edited by Sheila MacLeod and Victor B. Neuburg. Started after the Poets' Corner was dropped from the *Sunday Referee*. Ran weekly from 7 December 1935 to 30 January 1937.

4 January 1936 (Vol. I No. 5)   Dylan Thomas "The Dress" pp. 34–35

1 February 1936   Dylan Thomas "Grief thief of time" p. 66[24]

15 February 1936   G. N. Oborn "St. Valentine's Day: February, 1936" p. 82: Thomas gets eight lines in this Valentine poem

21 March 1936   Victor B. Neuburg "A Note on Helminthology" p. 126: "The distinguished poet and fictionist, Dylan Thomas, whom we are proud to have as a contributor, did a doubtful service to contemporary verse by making worms popular. Many poets think, apparently, that the mention of worms transforms an otherwise mediocre lyric into a poem of surpassing beauty. I do not share this view; and I hope that the Vermicular School will not continue to run their worms to death: a word to wise poets."

12 September 1936   Richard Byrde review of *Twenty-five Poems* p. 80

19 September 1936   Benji, pseud. "After a Poem in (?on) Progress by Thomas Dillon" p. 95, a parody

JANUS

Founding editors: Reginald Hutchings and John Royston Morley. Apparently there were two issues, published from a London address.

---

24. This poem was included in *First 'Comment' Treasury* London: Comment Press 1937.

January 1936   John Mair on *The Year's Poetry 1935* p. 29, quotes Thomas

May 1936   Dylan Thomas "The Horse's Ha" pp. 4–6, 8–9

LONDON MERCURY

In October 1934 R. A. Scott-James replaced J. C. Squire[25] as editor. Absorbed into *Life and Letters To-day* in April 1939.

February 1936   (Vol. XXXIII No. 196)   Edith Sitwell "Four New Poets" pp. 383–390, reviews *18 Poems* and "A grief ago"

September 1936   "Forthcoming Books" p. 476: "*Poems in Sequence* by Dylan Thomas will be published by Messrs. Dent."

October 1936   Michael Roberts review of *Twenty-five Poems* p. 555

CARAVEL

Five issues 1934–1936, published in Majorca.

March 1936 (Vol. 2 No. 5)   Dylan Thomas "Hold hard, these ancient minutes" p. [15]

PURPOSE

A London quarterly, edited by W. T. Symons. Desmond Hawkins became literary editor with Vol. VIII.

April–June 1936   (Vol. VIII No. 2)   Dylan Thomas "Fine meat on bones that soon have none" pp. 102–103 (misprint for "Find meat on bones")

October–December 1936   Dylan Thomas "Then was my neophyte" pp. 230–231; "To-day, this insect" pp. 231–232

April–June 1937   Michael F. Cullis "Mr. Thomas and Mr. Auden" pp. 101–104, reviewing *Twenty-five Poems*

October–December 1939   Edwin Muir review of *Map of Love* pp. 241–243

April–June 1940   Elizabeth Bowen review of *Portrait* pp. 92–95

POINTS

6 May 1936   A.H. [Alan Hodge] review of *18 Poems* pp. [11–12]

---

25. In a letter to Trevor Hughes (Christmas 1932) Thomas mentioned that Squire had accepted a story called "The Diarists" for publication in the *London Mercury*. In his next letter (January 1933) he says: "The *London Mercury* has not yet printed my story. Neither have I received a cheque for it."

CONTEMPORARY POETRY AND PROSE

Editor: Roger Roughton; ten issues 1936–1937.

May 1936 (No. 1)   Dylan Thomas "This was the crucifixion on the mountain" (= sonnet VIII) p. 2; "Foster the light, nor veil the manshaped moon" pp. 2–3; "The Burning Baby" pp. 10–14

July 1936 (No. 3)   Dylan Thomas "Two Poems Towards a Poem"   (= sonnets IX and X) p. 53

August–September 1936 (Nos. 4/5)   Dylan Thomas "The School for Witches" pp. 95–100

Spring 1937 (No. 9)   Dylan Thomas "The Holy Six" pp. 18–26

TRANSITION

A quarterly review, edited by Eugene Jolas, Paris.

Fall 1936 (No. 25)   Dylan Thomas "Then was my neophyte" pp. 20–21; "The Mouse and the Woman" pp. 43–58[26]

LIVERPOOL DAILY POST

16 September 1936   Announcement of *Twenty-five Poems* and a photograph

30 August 1939   O.E. review of *Map of Love* p. 5

6 March 1946   A., pseud. review of *Deaths & Entrances* p. 2

18 November 1952   Sydney Jeffery review of *Collected Poems* p. 3

10 November 1953   John Morgan "Poet with an aura of Bohemianism" p. 6, obituary

9 March 1954   Sydney Jeffery review of *Under Milk Wood* p. 3: "As philosophy 'Under Milk Wood' is disappointing. As sardonic literature it is magnificent"

19 November 1954   E.H. review of *Quite Early* p. 8

9 August 1955   Sydney Jeffery review of *Prospect*

24 April 1956   Conrad Howe review of Brinnin p. 8

2 May 1956   Letter from Mark Bourne, Machynlleth, p. 4

10 July 1956   Sydney Jeffery review of Rolph p. 6

15 November 1963   Cymro, pseud. "Why is his work so popular?" p. 10

16 September 1964   Sydney Jeffery review of *Druid* p. 9

28 October 1965   Robin Oakley review of FitzGibbon p. 6

---

26. Included in *transition workshop* New York: Vanguard Press 1949.

CATHOLIC HERALD

2 October 1936   J. Alban Evans review of *Twenty-five Poems*

1 September 1939   Review of *Map of Love*

5 July 1946   Review of *Deaths & Entrances*

16 April 1954   Derek Stanford review of *Under Milk Wood*

20 December 1957   Derek Stanford review of *Letters to Vernon Watkins*

3 September 1965   Michael Geare review of FitzGibbon

NEW STATESMAN

3 October 1936   G. W. Stonier review of *18 Poems* and *Twenty-five Poems* p. 482

16 September 1939   Cyril Connolly review of *Map of Love* p. 404

20 April 1940   Anthony West review of *Portrait* p. 542

2 March 1946   G. W. Stonier review of *Deaths & Entrances* pp. 160–161

18 June 1949   Stephen Spender review of Treece pp. 650–652

29 November 1952   G. S. Fraser review of *Collected Poems* pp. 640, 642

7 February 1953   Martin Shuttleworth "Without Apologies" pp. 144–145: an account of the Foyle's luncheon, reprinted in *Casebook*

27 June 1953   Anon. review of *Doctor & Devils* p. 786

* * *

14 November 1953   Kathleen Raine, tribute p. 594; 21 November 1953 letter from Pamela Hansford Johnson p. 637; 28 November 1953 letter from Mark Goulden p. 675 concerning *Sunday Referee*

28 November 1953   Gavin Ewart "On the Death of Dylan Thomas" (poem) p. 692 reprinted in *Garland*

23 January 1954   George Reavey "The Child of Summer" (poem) p. 102 reprinted in *Garland*

6 February 1954   William Salter on "Under Milk Wood" (BBC) pp. 159–160

15 May 1954   William Empson "Books in General" pp. 635–636: on *Collected Poems* and *Under Milk Wood*, reprinted in *Casebook* and Cox

18 September 1954   G. S. Fraser review of Olson p. 330

6 November 1954   Walter Allen review of *Quite Early* p. 586[27]

---

27. Allen uses Thomas' parody of T. F. Powys in his *Tradition and Dream* London: Phoenix House 1964 pp. 46–47 (in New York *The Modern Novel*).

13 November 1954   Letter from John Holdsworth p. 614 on *Under Milk Wood* and T. F. Powys; 27 November 1954 letter from C. Benson Roberts p. 697: "I once asked Dylan which of the three Powys writers he considered the greatest artist and he replied 'T.F.' "; letter from Graham T. Ackroyd p. 697; 4 December 1954 letter from John Levitt p. 743; 11 December 1954 reply from Albert Hunt p. 789; 18 December 1954 further reply from Donald Hatwell pp. 828–829; also letter from H. Coombes p. 829[28]

15 January 1955   Anon. review of Stanford p. 82

11 June 1955   G. S. Fraser "Artist as Young Dog" p. 812: on Emlyn Williams' performance, reprinted in Tedlock; letter from Caitlin Thomas on same, p. 815

20 August 1955   Anon. review of *Prospect* pp. 223–224

10 September 1955   Michael Crampton "New Novels" pp. 305–306 reviews *Adventures* p. 306

21 April 1956   Louis MacNeice review of Brinnin pp. 423–424

 1 September 1956   William Salter on "Under Milk Wood" (TV) pp. 241–242

29 September 1956   John Raymond on "Under Milk Wood" (New Theatre) p. 372

 8 June 1957   Louis MacNeice review of *Leftover Life* p. 741

 3 September 1960   John Mander review of Heppenstall pp. 316–317

19 November 1960   Walter Allen review of Tedlock p. 800

18 August 1961   Roger Gellert on "Under Milk Wood" (Lyric, Hammersmith) p. 226

 2 February 1962   Philip Larkin on the recordings pp. 170–171

30 March 1962   D. J. Enright review of Holbrook pp. 453, 456

 4 May 1962   Letter from Lawrence L. Lee p. 635, on the Utah visit

21 June 1963   Stevie Smith review of *Not Quite Posthumous* p. 941

26 June 1964   Stephen Hugh-Jones review of *Beach of Falesá* pp. 999–1000

18 December 1964   Geoffrey Grigson "Dylan and the Dragon" pp. 968–969, review of Tindall, Ackerman, *Druid*, Emery

18 June 1965   Geoffrey Grigson review of Read and *Me & My Bike* pp. 963, 966

29 October 1965   William Empson review of FitzGibbon pp. 647–648

25 November 1966   Ted Hughes view of *Selected Letters* p. 783

---

28. See also H. Coombes *T. F. Powys* London: Barrie & Rockliff 1960 p. 18.

MANCHESTER GUARDIAN

6 October 1936   C.P. review of *Twenty-five Poems* p. 6[29]

8 September 1939   Charles Powell review of *Map of Love* p. 3

5 April 1940   J. D. Beresford review of *Portrait* p. 3

16 December 1943   M.C. review of *Wales* (No. 2) p. 6

5 June 1946   Charles Powell review of *Deaths & Entrances* p. 3: "the vision remains dark and the prayer inarticulate"

14 November 1952   L. F. Duchene review of *Collected Poems* p. 4

16 June 1953   G.F. review of *Doctor & Devils* p. 4

* * *

10 November 1953   Anon. obituary p. 3

2 March 1954   Philip Hope-Wallace on "Under Milk Wood" (Old Vic reading) p. 5

2 April 1954   L. F. Duchene review of *Under Milk Wood* p. 4

24 August 1954   Column on "Under Milk Wood" (recordings) p. 6

8 November 1954   Radio Critic, pseud. review of *Quite Early* p. 3

2 August 1955   Douglas Hewitt review of *Prospect* p. 2

13 September 1955   Norman Shrapnel review of *Adventures* p. 4

24 April 1956   Maurice Cranston review of Brinnin p. 4

6 July 1956   Anon. review of Rolph p. 5

5 July 1957   Norman Shrapnel review of *Leftover Life* p. 7

28 November 1957   News of Thomas exhibition at the University p. 5

3 December 1957   Roy Perrott review of *Letters to Vernon Watkins* p. 4

13 April 1962   Malcolm Bradbury review of Holbrook; 16 April 1962 response from Keidrych Rhys

11 May 1963   John Horder "Poetry with Profit" p. 4: article on J. A. Rolph

15 October 1965   Geoffrey Grigson review of FitzGibbon p. 8

MANCHESTER GUARDIAN WEEKLY

13 October 1960   Stephen Hugh-Jones review of Heppenstall p. 10

---

29. Other provincial newspapers reviewing this volume include *Northern Echo* (Darlington) 16 September 1936 and *Shetland Times* 7 November 1936.

1 December 1960   Malcolm Bradbury review of Tedlock p. 11

27 December 1962   W. J. Weatherby "Guinness for Dylan" p. 14

GRANTA

Cambridge University student magazine.

21 October 1936   G.B.E. review of *Twenty-five Poems*[30]

8 March 1946   Review of *Deaths & Entrances*

8 June 1957   Dennis Levy review of *Leftover Life* p. 26

5 May 1962   Barbara Everett review of Holbrook pp. 24–25

11 May 1963   Terry Eagleton review of T. H. Jones and *Miscellany* pp. 30–31

THE SUNDAY TIMES

15 November 1936   Edith Sitwell "A New Poet" p. 9, review of *Twenty-five Poems* (reprinted in Treece as Appendix I, with Thomas' response in a letter to Treece)

22 November 1936   Letters from Kenneth Hare, W.P., Edward Vandermere Fleming p. 9; 29 November 1936 replies from Edith Sitwell, Pamela Hansford Johnson, A. Warren Dow, T.J.W. Morgan, Trevor Hughes p. 9; 13 December 1936 further letter p. 18; 20 December 1936 further letter p. 10; 27 December 1936 letters from Edith Sitwell, Francis W. Hacquoil p. 6; 3 January 1937 letters from Beatrice Eve, Edward Vandermere Fleming, S. T. Starr, G. H. Fry, editor of *Poetry Review* p. 12; 10 January 1937 letters from Edith Sitwell, W.K. Scudamore, A.P., Robert Varnbury p. 7[31]

10 February 1946   Anon. mention of *Deaths & Entrances*

9 November 1952   Cyril Connolly review of *Collected Poems*

24 May 1953   J. W. Lambert review of *Doctor & Devils*

* * *

15 November 1953   Cyril Connolly, obituary

3 January 1954   Announcement of Globe Theatre tribute p. 1[32]

---

30. Another early notice of this volume in a student periodical is by "N.J.D." in the Liverpool *Sphinx* November 1936 pp. 26–27.

31. "Dylan himself never wrote; but after one particularly insulting letter from a member of the Athenaeum Club, he asked me whether the paper would print a letter asking the member to meet him on the steps of the Athenaeum so that he could hit him"—*Letters to Vernon Watkins*, Introduction p. 16.

32. *Homage to Dylan Thomas.* Sponsored by the Sunday Times, the Group Theatre in association with the Institute of Contemporary Arts. A Programme of Poetry, Drama & Music, devised by Louis MacNeice, Rupert Doone, and Vera Lindsay. Personal tribute written by Dr. Edith Sitwell and Requiem Canto by Louis MacNeice.

31 January 1954   Letter from Henry Moore p. 6, congratulating Group Theatre on the program of tribute, with editor's note that £1,169 was sent to the Fund; K.P. on "Under Milk Wood" (BBC)

21 February 1954   Letter from John Davenport p. 2: "Dylan Thomas, for instance, owed a great deal to Pound. At least, it was a debt I frequently heard him acknowledge."

7 March 1954   Richard Hughes review of *Under Milk Wood* p. 5, reminiscences;[33] 14 March 1954 response from Allan Ross Macdougall p. 2; 21 March 1954 reply by Richard Hughes

14 November 1954   Richard Church review of *Quite Early* p. 5

19 June 1955   News of performance of Stravinsky's "In Memoriam Dylan Thomas"

31 July 1955   J. W. Lambert review of *Prospect* p. 3

11 September 1955   Richard Hughes review of *Adventures*

25 December 1955   John Betjeman includes *Prospect* in his "Books of the Year" p. 4

22 April 1956   Edith Sitwell review of Brinnin p. 5; 29 April 1956 letter from James Norbury p. 8

27 May 1956   "Do not go gentle" reprinted in the Poetic Heritage series p. 8

22 July 1956   Anon. mention of Rolph p. 5

26 August 1956   Harold Hobson on "Under Milk Wood" (Edinburgh) p. 4

23 September 1956   Harold Hobson on "Under Milk Wood" (London) p. 13

26 May 1957   Cyril Connolly review of *Leftover Life* p. 7

17 November 1957   Penelope Mortimer "Don't Tell Me of Dylan" p. 8, an imaginary dialogue purporting to be a review of *Letters to Vernon Watkins*[34]

28 September 1958   Augustus John "Dylan Thomas and Company" p. 17 reprinted in *Casebook*[35]

Decor by Ceri Richards. Staged by John Moody. The Globe Theatre, Sunday 24 January 1954 at 8 p.m. The printed program includes "A Message from W. H. Auden, New York, January 1954" and "A Grief Ago"—reminiscences by Cyril Connolly. Those taking part included Richard Burton, Hugh Griffiths, Edith Evans, Emlyn Williams, and Louis MacNeice. A recording was made of the programme; see a review by B.T. *The Gramophone* November 1954 p. 267.

33. Supplementary reminiscences are found in Lance Sieveking's *The Eye of the Beholder* London: Hulton Press 1957 pp. 178–179.

34. Rather more successful skits of this kind are Miles Kington "So I Said to Dylan" *Town* (London) December 1964 p. 116 and Anon. "The Dylan Thomas I knew by the late Walter McFarg" *Private Eye* 5 November 1965.

35. See his *Finishing Touches* London: Jonathan Cape 1964. Augustus John has another section on Thomas in his *Charioscuro* London: Cape; New York: Pellegrini & Cudahy 1952. Also see references in W. K. Rose ed. *Letters of Wyndham Lewis* London: Methuen; New York: New Directions 1963.

5 October 1958   Letter from Peter Davies p. 4, on Thomas' extensive reading; 12 October response from Augustus John p. 4

13 November 1960   Cyril Connolly review of Tedlock p. 25[36]

1 April 1962   George MacBeth review of Holbrook p. 30

8 September 1963   E. F. Bozman "Publishers' Autumn Pick" p. 32, chooses *Colour of Saying*

20 October 1963   P.D. review of *Colour of Saying* p. 36

10 November 1963   David Leitch "Dylan Thomas is Big Business" p. 7[37]

12 January 1964   John Press review of Kleinman p. 37

24 May 1964   Nicholas Tomalin "Relic" p. 31, on Thomas' old caravan in Camden Town

13 September 1964   Jeremy Rundall review of *Dylan* p. 34

4 April 1965   Edith Sitwell "Old Friends and Others" p. 22, memoirs[38]

6 June 1965   Anon. review of Read p. 42

13 June 1965   " 'Under Milk Wood' widow sues" p. 4

17 October 1965   W. R. Rodgers review of FitzGibbon p. 53

21 November 1965   Montague Haltrecht review of *Rebecca's Daughters* p. 33

29 May 1966   "Mrs. Dylan Thomas sues for £9,000" p. 4

5 June 1966   Robert Troop on real estate p. 52, "Fern Hill" to be sold

13 November 1966   Cyril Connolly review of *Selected Letters* and *Garland* p. 28; 20 November 1966 letters from Francis Kelly and Margaret Duncan p. 14, with comment by Cyril Connolly

The color supplement to *The Sunday Times* was started in 1962 under the title

SUNDAY TIMES MAGAZINE

30 June 1963   John Press review of *Miscellany* p. 27

12 September 1965   Christopher Ricks review of *Portrait* and *Adventures* (Aldine paperbacks) p. 46

28 November 1965   Peter Dunn "Swansea: Still-life with Wagnerian butcher" pp. 16–17, 19, 21

20 March 1966   Christopher Ricks review of Brinnin (paperback) p. 62

---

36. Included in his *Previous Convictions* London: Hamish Hamilton 1963 pp. 324–327.
37. The widely circulated *Coming Events in Britain* had an article "The Last Home of Dylan Thomas" by Susan Lester in the issue of January 1957 pp. 30–31.
38. See her *Taken Care Of: An Autobiography* London: Hutchinson; New York: Atheneum 1965 pp. 166–173.

29 January 1967   Geoffrey Nicholson "Dylan Thomas" p. 17, retrospective biography

NEWS CHRONICLE

London daily; absorbed into *Daily Mail* 1960.

21 November 1936   Quiz question on *Twenty-five Poems*

23 November 1936   Timothy Shy, pseud. on the *Sunday Times* controversy

18 February 1950   Alan Dent "Dead Loss" p. 2: reviewer walked out of the production of the Picasso play in which Thomas took part

14 May 1953   Frederick Laws review of *Doctor & Devils*

* * *

10 November 1953   Frederick Laws, obituary p. 3

25 November 1953   Anthony Davies "Bohemian Funeral for Poet" p. 5

19 February 1954   Alan Dent review of *Under Milk Wood* p. 6

15 September 1955   G.B. review of *Adventures*

19 April 1956   G.B. [Gerald Barry] review of Brinnin p. 8

21 September 1956   David Holloway on "Under Milk Wood" (stage)

27 May 1957   Tom Baistow review of *Leftover Life*

POETRY REVIEW

Official publication of the Poetry Society.

November–December 1936   J.H.E. "Analysis of Poetry" pp. 486–488, mention of *Twenty-five Poems* p. 486

January–February 1940   Edward Vandermere Fleming "The Old and the New" pp. 38–43—review of *Map of Love* pp. 38–40: "At the risk of incurring the contempt of posterity I will say, with that ancient Quarterly Reviewer, 'This will never do.'"

April–May 1946   Anon.[39] "Poets and Pretenders" pp. 126–140, review of *Deaths & Entrances* pp. 128–129

April–May 1948   Aneurin Rhys "Dylan Thomas: A Further Estimate" pp. 214–216, unfavorable comments in the form of a letter to the editor

April–June 1953   John Graddon & Geoffrey Johnson "Dylan Thomas Yes and No: Two Reviews of One Book" pp. 338–343, on *Collected Poems*

---

39. Identified in *Casebook* as William Kean Seymour. He has several pieces on Thomas including a review of *Letters to Vernon Watkins* in *St. Martin's Review* February 1958 pp. 55–56.

(reprinted in Tedlock); July–September 1953 responses from T. E. Van den Bergh, Stanton A. Coblentz, Madge Hales, C. B. Toosey, John Hoffman, Eve Wilson, Jane, W. R. Drake pp. 393–396; October–December 1953 responses from John Glossop, Elsie M. Banister, D. G. Davies, I. Zuidema, J.F.R.

January–March 1954   Stuart Holroyd "The Celtic Genius in Modern Poetry" pp. 21–26, tribute to Thomas pp. 25–26

July–September 1954   Michael Ayrton's drawing reproduced p. 135, with editorial comment p. 134; Stephen Pike & Stuart Holroyd " 'Under Milk Wood' Yes and No" pp. 164–167

October–December 1954   Letter from Dallas Kenmare p. 230, on the portrait

January–March 1955   John Graddon "Book of the Year" p. 39, he chooses *Under Milk Wood*; Anon. mention of Olson p. 49

July–September 1955   Malcolm H. Tattersall "Did he once see Dylan plain?" (poem) p. 161

January–March 1956   D. S. Thomas "Elegy on a Poet's Death (For D.T.)" p. 15 reprinted in *Garland*

July–September 1956   Tony Van den Bergh review of Brinnin pp. 165–166

October–December 1956   Kathleen Valmai Richardson review of Treece (2nd edition) and Rolph pp. 240–241

October–December 1957   Stephen Graham review of *Leftover Life* pp. 222–223

April–June 1961   Kathleen Valmai Richardson review of Tedlock pp. 101–102

Summer 1962   William Kean Seymour review of Holbrook pp. 184, 186–187

Winter 1963/64   Rosalind Wade "The Parton Street Poets" pp. 290–297, a substantial memoir; Gilbert Thomas review of Jones pp. 326, 328

Spring 1964   Letter from Jean Overton Fuller p. 39 with reply by Rosalind Wade

DAILY WORKER

London Communist Party daily.

2 December 1936   Stephen Spender review of *Twenty-five Poems*

1 May 1940   Review of *Portrait*

14 May 1953   Alison MacLeod review of *Doctor & Devils*

11 March 1954   John Bridger review of *Under Milk Wood*

4 November 1954   Alison MacLeod review of *Quite Early*[40]

---

40. Reprinted in *People's World* (U.S.) 31 December 1954.

25 August 1955   Alison MacLeod review of *Prospect*

15 September 1955   B.J. review of *Adventures*

19 April 1956   James Fielding review of Brinnin[41]

29 December 1960   Jack Lindsay review of Tedlock

19 July 1962   Roland Hackett review of *Under Milk Wood* (paperback) and Holbrook

22 October 1964   Review of Ackerman

14 October 1965   Jack Lindsay review of FitzGibbon

THE OBSERVER

London weekly newspaper.

13 December 1936   Mention of *Twenty-five Poems*

 3 January 1937   Charles Powell mention of *Twenty-five Poems*

 7 April 1940   Frank Swinnerton review of *Portrait* p. 6

 5 May 1946   V. Sackville-West review of *Deaths & Entrances*

16 December 1951   Dylan Thomas "Flamboyants All the Way" p. 7: review of Roy Campbell's *Light on a Dark Horse*

 6 July 1952   Dylan Thomas "Blithe Spirits" p. 7: review of Amos Tutuola's *The Palm-Wine Drinkard*

 9 November 1952   Philip Toynbee review of *Collected Poems*

17 May 1953   John Davenport review of *Doctor & Devils*

* * *

15 November 1953   Edwin Muir, obituary p. 10

31 January 1954   Lionel Hale on "Under Milk Wood" (BBC) p. 11

 7 February 1954   Dylan Thomas "Under Milk Wood" pp. 10–11, continued on 14 February 1954 pp. 10–11, with drawings by John Minton

21 February 1954   Letters on "Under Milk Wood" from J. McLaughlin and Graham Lewis p. 2; 28 February 1954 responses from John Davenport and P. E. Dunn p. 2

12 December 1954   Philip Toynbee review of Stanford and *Quite Early* p. 9

 2 January 1955   Letter from Geoffrey Grigson p. 2, on Thomas' debt to Francis Thompson; 9 January reply from William Empson p. 2: "The ideas of Mr. Geoffrey Grigson about verse have long seemed to me very odd"; 16 January reply from Geoffrey Grigson p. 2: "I think Dylan Thomas's poetry

---

41. Reprinted in *People's World* 18 May 1956.

is bad because of the huddle of badly manipulated images, which are often frigid, false and sentimental; I think it is bad for the bad ear it reveals, for bad lines faltering from cliché rhythms into flatness, for cheapness, and profundity which is not profound; above all, for lack of a grown-up and masterly execution"; 23 January 1955 reply from William Empson p. 2

11 September 1955   John Davenport review of *Adventures* and *Prospect* p. 10

22 April 1956   Philip Toynbee review of Brinnin p. 12

26 August 1956   Kenneth Tynan on "Under Milk Wood" (Edinburgh) p. 10; 23 September, on London production p. 11[42]

23 December 1956   Kenneth Tynan on his choice for 1956 p. 6, picks Brinnin, "that terrible footnote to literary history"

12 May 1957   Maurice Richardson on "Under Milk Wood" (BBC) p. 15

26 May 1957   Caitlin Thomas "Life with Dylan" p. 3, extracts from *Leftover Life*; continued 2 June p. 12, and 9 June p. 3, with photographs by John Deakin

 2 June 1957   Letters from Mary Sheridan and Sven Berlin p. 3; 9 June 1957 letter from Agnes Kemmis p. 17

16 June 1957   Naomi Lewis review of *Leftover Life* p. 18

 6 October 1957   "A Letter from Dylan Thomas" p. 12; 13 October 1957 Watkins comments that the original letter had three paragraphs, not seven as printed

24 November 1957   Stephen Spender review of *Letters to Vernon Watkins* p. 18; 1 December 1957 letter from Vernon Watkins p. 6, on Thomas' borrowing; 8 December 1957 reply from Stephen Spender p. 6; 15 December 1957 further letter from Vernon Watkins p. 6

 6 September 1959   John Wain "Thomas the Voice" p. 21, on the recordings

 4 September 1960   Philip Toynbee review of Heppenstall p. 27

13 November 1960   Philip Toynbee review of Tedlock p. 29; 20 November 1960 letter from Geoffrey Grigson p. 22, saying that his essay in Tedlock was included "without my permission, which I should have refused"; 27 November 1960 letter from George Barker p. 22 on Thomas' drinking, with reply by Philip Toynbee

20 November 1960   Edith Sitwell "Dylan the Impeccable" p. 24, in the series "Personal Encounters"

20 December 1964   Ian Nairn "Storm Clouds Over Laugharne" p. 18

17 October 1965   Philip Toynbee review of FitzGibbon p. 26

23 October 1966   "The private voice of Dylan Thomas" p. 21, extracts from the *Selected Letters*; continued 30 October 1966 p. 21

---

42. See Kenneth Tynan *Curtains* London: Longmans; New York: Atheneum 1961.

13 November 1966   Philip Toynbee review of *Selected Letters* p. 26

1 October 1967   Alan Road "The Ghost under Milk Wood" pp. 28–30 (Supplement)

21 April 1968   Anon. review of *Notebooks* p. 29

TWENTIETH CENTURY VERSE

Eighteen issues, 1937–1939; editor: Julian Symons. See his *The Thirties* London: Cresset Press 1960 p. 144.

January 1937 (No. 1)   Dylan Thomas "Poem, Part 1" (= "It is the sinners' dust-tongued bell") p. [3]; Julian Symons review of *Twenty-five Poems* pp. [17–19]

January/February 1938 (No. 8)   Dylan Thomas "Poem (For Caitlin)" (= "I make this in a warring absence") pp. [3–4]

December 1938 (No. 14)   Editorial "Ethics of Acknowledgement" p. 142: "Dylan Thomas's poem 'To Caitlin' appeared in TWENTIETH CENTURY VERSE in January 1938. Since then it has been reprinted, without acknowledgement, in *Delta* and *Wales*. Latterly it has been reprinted again, by *New Directions*, with acknowledgements—to *Delta*"

February 1939 (Nos. 15–16)   Dylan Thomas "January 1939" (= "Because the pleasure bird whistles") p. 149

ENGLISH REVIEW

February 1937   Gilbert Armitage review of *Twenty-five Poems* pp. 254–256

June 1937   Pamela Hansford Johnson "Altarwise By Owl-light" pp. 720–732, a story whose title and epigram come from Thomas' poem

THE NATIONAL AND ENGLISH REVIEW

New title of *English Review*, 1937.

December 1952   Eric Gillett short review of *Collected Poems* p. 369

April 1954   Eric Gillett "Books New and Old" pp. 235–236, reviews *Under Milk Wood*

January 1955   Eric Gillett review of *Quite Early* pp. 45–46, with some personal reminiscences

August 1955   Eric Gillett review of *Prospect* p. 109

May 1956   Eric Gillett review of Brinnin pp. 281–282

January 1958   Eric Gillett review of *Letters to Vernon Watkins* pp. 30–31

FORTNIGHTLY

February 1937   C. Henry Warren review of *Twenty-five Poems* pp. 248–289

July 1940   H. E. Bates review of *Portrait* pp. 111–112

June 1950   Norman Nicholson review of Howard Sergeant's *The Cumberland Wordsworth* pp. 419–420, Thomas discussed

October 1950   Patric Dickinson review of F. R. Leavis's *New Bearings in English Poetry* p. 281

October 1951   Herbert Palmer "English Poetry: 1938–1950"—Thomas mentioned p. 697

December 1952   B. Evan Owen review of *Collected Poems* pp. 419–420

December 1953   B. Evan Owen "For Dylan Thomas" (poem) p. 409, reprinted in *Garland*

July 1954   Norman Nicholson[43] on "Under Milk Wood" (BBC) pp. 48–49

December 1954   Grace Banyard review of *Quite Early* p. 431

Fortnightly was then absorbed by

CONTEMPORARY REVIEW

September 1955   Grace Banyard review of *Prospect* pp. 214–215

June 1956   Grace Banyard review of Brinnin p. 380

September 1957   Joan Harding "Dylan Thomas and Edward Thomas" pp. 150–154

July 1958   Carl Bode review of Alvarez's *The Shaping Spirit* p. 52, noting the omission of Thomas

July 1962   William Kean Seymour review of Holbrook p. 53

May 1963   Anon. review of T. H. Jones p. 278

January 1966   William Kean Seymour review of FitzGibbon pp. 49–50

April 1967   William Kean Seymour review of *Selected Letters* p. 221

LIGHT AND DARK

Oxford, January 1937–February 1938.

March 1937 (Vol. I No. 2)   Dylan Thomas, review of Djuna Barnes' *Nightwood* pp. 27, 29

---

43. He reviewed FitzGibbon in *Church Times* 19 November 1965 p. viii (supplement).

DELTA

Successor to *The Booster*, "erstwhile house organ of the American Country Club of Paris," which did not contain items by Thomas in its four numbers put out under the direction of Henry Miller. See Bern Porter *Henry Miller: Chronology and Bibliography* Baltimore: Waverly Press 1945 p. 33, and George Wickes ed. *Lawrence Durrell Henry Miller: A Private Correspondence* New York: Dutton 1963 pp. 119, 199.

Durrell, as editor of *Delta*, asked Thomas for contributions and published something by him in all three issues of the magazine. See "Letters to Lawrence Durrell" in *Two Cities* 15 May 1960 pp. 1–5; and Harry T. Moore *The World of Lawrence Durrell* Carbondale: Southern Illinois University Press 1962 pp. 237–238.

April 1938   Dylan Thomas "Poem for Caitlin" (= "I make this in a warring absence") pp. 6–7

Xmas 1938   Dylan Thomas "Prologue to an Adventure" pp. 7–12

Easter 1939   Dylan Thomas "January 1939" (= "Because the pleasure bird whistles")

SEVEN

Founding editors: John Goodland and Nicholas Moore. Eight issues from Summer 1938 to Spring 1940.

Winter 1938 (No. 3)   Dylan Thomas "I, the first named" p. 17; "Her tombstone told when she died" p. 17; Henry Treece "Dylan Thomas and the Surrealists" pp. 27–30

Spring 1939 (No. 4)   Parker Tyler "The Poetic Athlete" pp. 20–25, a rejoinder to Treece's article; Dylan Thomas "An Adventure from A Work in Progress" pp. 45–48

Autumn 1939 (No. 6)   Dylan Thomas "To Others Than You," "Paper and Sticks," "When I Woke" pp. 5–6; Herbert Read review of *Map of Love* pp. 19–20:

With this volume Mr. Thomas quells any reasonable doubts about the quality of his poetic genius. In his early work there was a certain monotony that might have developed into mannerism: and a surfeit of imagery that dulled the reader's appetite. But these immaturities have now entirely disappeared. The diction has gained clarity and strength; and there is a variety of rhythm or measure which shows the completest mastery of technical means. There are only sixteen poems in the volume, but every one is solidly shaped, vital in the sinew, and brilliant in the word. Some of the poems will need a dozen readings before they yield their meaning or intention; others are comparatively simple, tempered to pathos, humble before the elemental tragedy of life. How simple his expression can be is seen in some of the prose pieces, and it was an excellent idea to print these with the poems—both gain by the juxtaposition. "One day I may have no limbs to walk with, no hands to touch with. No heart under my breast." Between this utmost prose simplicity and the complexity of the verse there is a contrast of moods, but poetic identity.

The verse-form seems sometimes to cramp the syntax, and the punctuation of the verse is often so arbitrary that it would be clearer with none.

It is mainly a poetry of the elemental physical experience: birth, copulation, death. But not entirely: there are poems, such as No. 7, "The spire cranes," which are quite abstract, or arabesque, in their beauty. The birth and death poems are not less absolute in their beauty, but they have reverberations in sentiment which add another dimension. I know of no poem since Hopkins which has the pathetic intensity of the elegy "In memory of Ann Jones" . . . .

These poems cannot be reviewed; they can only be acclaimed . . . . *The Map of Love* is a unique book. I do not wish to qualify the achievement of it in any way. It contains the most absolute poetry that has been written in our time, and one can only pray that this poet will not be forced in any way to surrender the subtle course of his genius.

Christmas 1939 (No. 7)   Dylan Thomas "Patricia, Edith, and Arnold" pp. 4–11

Spring 1940 (No. 8)   G. S. Fraser review of *The New Apocalypse* pp. 27–31, Thomas mentioned p. 30, and also in the editorial p. 32

VOICE OF SCOTLAND

A quarterly magazine of Scottish arts and affairs, edited by Hugh MacDiarmid, Dunfermline, Scotland. See his *The Company I've Kept* London: Hutchinson 1966 pp. 216–217; also his poem "On the Death of Dylan Thomas" in *Lines Review* January 1954 pp. 30–31, which appears as "In Memoriam Dylan Thomas" in *In Memoriam James Joyce* William Maclellan 1955 and in his *Collected Poems* 1962. Publication was discontinued during the war years.

December 1938–February 1939 (Vol. 1 No. 3) ["Celtic Front Number"] Dylan Thomas "The tombstone told me when she died" p. 12

June–August 1939 (Vol. 2 No. 1)   Editorial[44] "The English Literary Left" pp. 1–6: "Dylan Thomas alone is worth a dozen Audens or Spenders or Day Lewises any day; and *Wales* was a far more wholesome and promising affair than all the organs of the London Literary Left together"; Henry Treece "Some Notes on Poetry Now" pp. 7–10, includes a defence of Thomas

December 1948   "Tributes to Hugh MacDiarmid" at a "disjune . . . given in the Scotia Hotel, Edinburgh, on 28th August under the auspices of the Makars Club"—pp. 22–24 contains an "address given by Dylan Thomas to the Scottish P.E.N. Centre, on Saturday, 4th September, 1948, at the Scotia Hotel, Edinburgh"; includes a "lallans" poem presumably by Thomas

July 1955   Jack Lindsay "Last Words With Dylan Thomas" (poem) pp. 10–13, reprinted in *Garland*

---

44. Appears in Chapter III "The Kind of Poetry I Want" in Hugh MacDiarmid's *Lucky Poet* London: Methuen 1943.

POETRY (London)

Founding editor: Tambimuttu. No. 1 (February 1939) to No. 23 (Winter 1951). Issues after September 1949 edited by Richard March and Nicholas Moore.

February 1939 (No. 1)   Tambimuttu "First Letter" pp. [3–6], comment on Dylan Thomas' "A saint about to fall," which is printed pp. [26–27]

April 1939 (No. 2)   Dylan Thomas " 'If my head hurt a hair's foot' " p. [23]; a letter from Thomas p. [31]: "I congratulate you a lot on the handsomest 'intelligent' poetry magazine I know of, and on the courage of your un-fashionable introduction . . . . *Poetry*—it's needed alright, verse magazines in England are very sad—grow into something extremely entertaining and popular. Poetry editors are mostly vicious climbers, with their fingers in many pies, their ears at many keyholes and . . . *you've* shown, in your intro-duction, how much you believe in the good of poetry and in the mischief of cliques, rackets, scandal schools, menagerie menages, amateur classes of novitiate plagiarists, etc. More subscribers and power to you."[45]

January–February 1941 (No. 4)   Dylan Thomas "On a Wedding Anniversary" p. 91

May–June 1941 (No. 6)   Dylan Thomas "Love in the Asylum" pp. 186–187; Henry Treece "Cockscrew or Footrule? Some Notes on the Poetry of Dylan Thomas" pp. 196–199[46]

[April] 1944 (No. 9)   Dylan Thomas "Last night I dived my beggar arm" and "Your breath was shed." p. 34

December 1944 (No. 10)   Editorial "Tenth Letter" pp. 1–9, Thomas men-tioned on p. 1

September–October 1947 (No. 11)   Editorial "Eleventh Letter" pp. 5–8, de-fends Thomas against Geoffrey Grigson's attack in *Polemic* No. 7; Ceri Richards illustrates "The force that through the green fuse" in a four-page lithograph between pp. 36 and 37[47]

June–July 1948 (No. 13)   Letter from Geoffrey Grigson, with Tambimuttu's rejoinder pp. 46–47

Tambimuttu[48] also edited *Poetry London–New York*, based in New York, a continuation of *Poetry (London)*.

---

45. These extracts may be compared with the full letter in *Selected Letters* pp. 187–188. To another correspondent, he indicated that his words were not meant for publication.
46. Further comments on Thomas are found in his "Considerations on Revolt" in *New Road* for 1943 p. 143; see also "Are Poets Doing Their Duty?" by Kathleen Raine pp. 12–13 in that annual.
47. Ceri Richards' "Do not go gentle" is reproduced in the E. & A. Silberman Gal-leries *An Exhibition of Contemporary British Art* 1956.
48. See also his "Letter from New York" in *Nimrod* Winter 1954 p. 29.

POETRY LONDON–NEW YORK

March–April 1956 (Vol. 1 No. 1)   Letters from Lawrence Durrell and Roy Campbell pp. 34–36, reminiscences; Dylan Thomas' two poems from the April 1944 issue are reprinted p. 12;[49] Tambimuttu review of Brinnin pp. 42–48

YELLOWJACKET

Edited by Constantine FitzGibbon.

March 1939 (Vol. 1 No. 1)   Dylan Thomas "The Enemies" pp. 32–37

May 1939 (Vol. 1 No. 2)   Dylan Thomas "The True Story" pp. 60–63; "The Vest" pp. 64–67

THE RIGHT REVIEW

Published and largely written by Count Potocki of Montalk. Other contributors included D. S. Savage, Nigel Heseltine, and Roy Campbell.

April 1939   "Social Climbers in Bloomsbury"[50]—a general satire of the social scene; Thomas appears as Andyl Motsah and, apparently, Divine Thomas, with parodies of his style

DAILY EXPRESS

24 August 1939   James Agate "Mr. Agate takes a chip off some verbal sculpture" p. 12, an attack on *Map of Love* with special attention to "If a pleasure bird whistles"[51]

14 October 1965   Peter Grosvenor review of FitzGibbon p. 16

SUNDAY EXPRESS

8 July 1956   Robert Pitman, an interview with Caitlin Thomas in Naples[52]

---

49. "Your breath was shed" was included in *Best Poems of 1956* "Borestone Mountain Poetry Awards" Stanford University Press 1957 p. 92.

50. The whole series published by Count Potocki of Montalk as *Social Climbers in Bloomsbury* London: The Right Review 1939.

51. See his *Ego 4* London: Harrap 1940 p. 151; also *Ego 6* London: Harrap 1944 p. 24: "Diary for 1 September 1942: 'Met Keidrych Rhys at the Cafe Royal. A large, shock-haired, intelligent, and witty soldier. The Traddles sort. Haversack full of Welsh poems. He said about another of the unintelligible brood: "My dear sir, like all the others, he is merely a leak from Dylan Thomas's petrol-tank." ' "

52. Other week-end newspaper interviews with Caitlin Thomas can be found in the *Sunday Graphic* 19 February 1956 pp. 6–7 and 26 February 1956 p. 6. See also the obituary by Maurice Wiggin in the issue of 22 November 1953. The Sunday *People* has several reports by Keidrych Rhys on 17 July 1955, 26 May 1957, 11 May 1958 etc.; also in the issue of 26 May 1957 Patrick Kent "How long should a woman grieve for the poet she loved?" p. 8, a review of *Leftover Life*.

5 February 1967   Graham Lord "The tormented widow of Dylan Thomas" p. 3, an interview with Caitlin Thomas in Rome

13 November 1966   Robin Douglas-Home "Would you allow your love letters to be published?" p. 3—interview with Pamela Hansford Johnson

REYNOLDS NEWS

The Sunday newspaper of the Cooperative Movement.

27 August 1939   H.F. review of *Map of Love*

2 January 1944   David Raymond on *Wales* magazine

3 March 1946   David Martin review of *Deaths & Entrances*

13 September 1955   Howard Culpin review of *Adventures*

12 January 1958   Mary Morgan "Laugharne Replies to Caitlin" p. 8, local residents react to *Leftover Life*

IRISH PRESS

Dublin daily.[53]

29 August 1939   F.MacM. review of *Map of Love*

23 May 1946   F.MacM. review of *Deaths & Entrances*

6 June 1953   Charles Allen review of *Doctor & Devils*

13 March 1954   Gabriel Fallon on "Under Milk Wood" and death

22 October 1955   Benedict Kiely review of *Adventures*

21 April 1956   Francis MacManus review of Brinnin

30 November 1957   Francis MacManus review of *Letters to Vernon Watkins*

3 December 1960   Pearse Hutchinson review of Tedlock

14 November 1964   Review of Ackerman

TRIBUNE

The weekly of the Labour party left wing.

1 September 1939   Patrick Redmond review of *Map of Love* p. 10

---

53. In another Dublin daily, *Irish Times*, Valentin Iremonger reviewed *Deaths & Entrances* 13 April 1946; Austin Clarke reviewed *Doctor & Devils* 13 June 1953, *Under Milk Wood* 27 March 1954, *Prospect* and *Adventures* 19 November 1955; P.MacA. reviewed Brinnin 21 April 1956; Maurice Kennedy reviewed *Leftover Life* 1 June 1957; Terence de Vere White reviewed FitzGibbon 16 October 1965. The *Cork Examiner* reviewed Brinnin 26 April 1956; R. O'D. reviewed *Colour of Saying* 13 February 1964, and *Twenty Years* 7 January 1965. Dylan Thomas' script *Twenty Years A-Growing* was reprinted by the Eire Tourist Office in *Ireland of the Welcomes* January–February 1966 pp. 15–21 with photographs.

5 July 1940   John Lehmann review of *Portrait* pp. 18–19

8 February 1946   Norman Cameron review of *Deaths & Entrances* p. 19:
"In short, Mr. Thomas has become, as a poet, more mature"

5 December 1952   John Berger review of *Collected Poems* p. 7

26 June 1953   R.F. review of *Doctor & Devils* p. 7

26 November 1954   Review of *Quite Early*

29 July 1955   Bruce Bain review of *Prospect* p. 7

27 April 1956   Bruce Bain review of Brinnin

31 May 1957   Jack Beeching review of *Leftover Life* p. 15, outspoken personal reminiscences

13 December 1957   Raymond Fletcher review of *Letters to Vernon Watkins* p. 14, recommends the "voluntary liquidation of the 'Dylan Thomas industry' "[54]

6 January 1961   Paul Potts review of Tedlock p. 11

8 November 1963   Robert Nye review of *Colour of Saying* p. 12

23 October 1964   David Arthur review of Ackerman, *Beach of Falesá*, and *Twenty Years*

5 November 1965   Philip Callow review of FitzGibbon p. 14, with photograph

25 November 1966   Glenda Leemig review of *Selected Letters* and Moynihan p. 13

BIRMINGHAM POST

26 September 1939   Review of *Map of Love*

23 April 1940   Review of *Portrait*

2 April 1946   E. E. Duncan Jones review of *Deaths & Entrances*

23 December 1952   B. Ifor Evans review of *Collected Poems*

23 March 1954   B. Ifor Evans review of *Under Milk Wood*

30 November 1954   Review of *Quite Early*

7 January 1955   John Moore "Milk Wood in Soho"—reminiscences

9 August 1955   G.B. review of *Prospect*

13 September 1955   Geoffrey Bullough review of *Adventures*

---

54. The Independent Labour party weekly, *Socialist Leader,* had a similar article by "Plain Speaker" in the issue of 20 February 1954 p. 4, where the "pother" at Thomas' death is contrasted with Maxwell Bodenheim's funeral in New York.

24 April 1956 Reginald Reynolds review of Brinnin[55]

19 November 1957 Review of *Letters to Vernon Watkins*

27 March 1962 Keith Brace "A Hwyl of Protest" review of Holbrook

9 November 1963 Keith Brace "The Dylan Legend"

24 October 1964 Robert Nye review of Ackerman, *Druid* and *Twenty Years*

23 October 1965 Gareth Lloyd Evans[56] review of FitzGibbon

8 November 1965 W. E. Hall review of FitzGibbon

HORIZON

Founded by Cyril Connolly, Peter Watson, and Stephen Spender in January 1940.

January 1940 Geoffrey Grigson review of *Map of Love* pp. 57–61

May 1940 Dylan Thomas "There was a Saviour" pp. 318–319

June 1940 Editorial "Comment" on Thomas and others pp. 389–393

November 1940 Francis Scarfe "The Poetry of Dylan Thomas" pp. 226–239, included in Tedlock and *Casebook* as well as in his *Auden and After* (1942)

January 1941 Dylan Thomas "Deaths and Entrances" pp. 12–13

July 1941 Dylan Thomas "Ballad of the Long-legged Bait" pp. 9–12

July 1942 Dylan Thomas "Request to Leda: Homage to William Empson" p. 6; Norman Cameron "The Dirty Little Accuser" (poem) p. 7, included in *Garland*

January 1945 Dylan Thomas "Vision and Prayer" pp. 8–13; "Holy Spring" p. 14

February 1945 Dylan Thomas "Poem in October" pp. 82–83

October 1945 Dylan Thomas "Fern Hill" pp. 221–222; "A Refusal to Mourn the Death, By Fire, of a Child in London" p. 223

January 1946 "Comment" p. 7: "The HORIZON prize for 1945 is awarded to Dylan Thomas for his poems in the January, February, October, and the French numbers"[57]

---

55. The *Birmingham Gazette*, now incorporated into the *Post*, had a review of Brinnin by John Hood on 19 April 1956.

56. See also his "Dylan Thomas and Under Milk Wood" *Experiment* Winter 1957 pp. 180–186; and his review of Kleinman, Ackerman, and Tellier in *Modern Language Review* October 1965 pp. 608–609.

57. Cyril Connolly has supplied the following information about this French issue: " 'La Littérature Anglaise depuis la guerre' [London: Éditions 'Horizon' 1945] was entirely distributed in France by the Ministry of Information who took 10,000—only contributors copies went off in this country." It contained Thomas' "A Winter's Tale"— possibly its first appearance pp. 11–14.

April 1946   Stephen Spender "Poetry for Poetry's Sake and Poetry Beyond Poetry" pp. 221–238, review of *Deaths & Entrances* pp. 233–234

September 1946   Dylan Thomas, answers to "Questionnaire: the Cost of Letters" pp. 173–175 (the questions are on p. 140)[58]

December 1947   Dylan Thomas "In country sleep" pp. 302–305

THE TIMES

The Index to the *Times* will provide references to some minor news items not included here.

 6 April 1940   Anon. review of *Portrait* p. 11

16 May 1953   Anon. review of *Doctor & Devils* p. 5

* * *

10 November 1953   [Vernon Watkins] obituary p. 11

24 December 1953   Thomas' will p. 8, an estate of £100 recorded

26 January 1954   On "Under Milk Wood" (BBC) p. 6

 6 March 1954   Anon. review of *Under Milk Wood* p. 8

13 March 1954   Photograph of portrait and bust by Augustus John p. 12

20 August 1954   On "Under Milk Wood" (recording) p. 2

19 May 1955   On Emlyn Williams "A Boy Growing Up" p. 3; also 1 June 1955 p. 2

 2 August 1955   Letter from Vernon Watkins p. 9: "Do not go gentle" was not written *in memory* of Thomas' father; 6 September 1955 response from J. Michinton p. 11

15 September 1955   Anon. review of *Adventures* p. 13

21 October 1955   On the application for Thomas' reinterment in the Boat House p. 5

22 August 1956   On "Under Milk Wood" (Lyceum Theatre, Edinburgh) p. 4 with photograph

12 December 1957   Anon. review of *Letters to Vernon Watkins* p. 13

 6 February 1959   Emlyn Williams performs "The Fight" on BBC-TV p. 5

23 May 1959   Lecture by Bonamy Dobrée at Gresham College, London p. 10

24 December 1959   Michael Ayrton's charcoal portrait of Thomas bought by the National Portrait Gallery p. 2

 7 October 1960   Anon. review of Heppenstall p. 18

---

58. Reprinted in Cyril Connolly *Ideas and Places* London: Weidenfeld & Nicolson 1953.

25 October 1960   Portrait by Alfred Janes sold to Texas despite Swansea's wish to buy it p. 5

14 February 1961   On "Doctor & Devils" (Vanbrugh Theatre) p. 6

21 June 1961   MS of "Under Milk Wood" bought by Times Bookshop p. 8[59]

9 August 1961   On "Under Milk Wood" (Lyric, Hammersmith) p. 11

22 August 1962   On "Doctor & Devils" (Edinburgh) p. 5

6 January 1964   On Toronto production of "Dylan" p. 6

20 May 1964   National Museum of Wales buys bust from death mask made by David Slivka and Ibran Lassaw p. 14

25 June 1964   Anon. review of *Beach of Falesá* p. 13

17 September 1964   On "Doctor & Devils" (Queen's Theatre, Hornchurch) p. 15

4 February 1965   On "Return Journey" (Embassy Theatre) p. 16

15 June 1965   MS of "Prologue" acquired by British Museum p. 6

14 October 1965   Anon. review of FitzGibbon p. 15

8 March 1966   Anon. review of "Adventures in Skin Trade" (Hampstead Club) p. 15

9 March 1966   MS of "Under Milk Wood" court case p. 5; also 10 March p. 6; 11 March p. 8; 12 March p. 12; and 19 March p. 5

17 October 1966   Anon. "Dylan" (Gaiety Theatre, Dublin) p. 6

10 November 1966   Anon. review of *Selected Letters* and Moynihan p. 14

8 December 1966   On broadcast of "In Country Heaven" p. 18

23 January 1968   Boat House for sale p. 2

28 September 1968   "Adventures in the Skin Trade" being filmed p. 19

THE BYSTANDER

Weekly society paper. Later *Tatler and Bystander.*

24 April 1940   V. S. Pritchett review of *Portrait* p. 116

3 June 1953   E. V. Knox review of *Doctor & Devils* p. 550

19 June 1957   Elizabeth Bowen review of *Leftover Life*

GLASGOW HERALD

25 April 1940   Anon. review of *Portrait*

---

59. The editor of the *Literary Repository*, J. Stevens Cox, describes this manuscript passing through his hands in issue No. 2/1961 and No. 1/1967.

15 September 1955   Anon. review of *Adventures*

19 April 1956   Anon. review of Brinnin

23 August 1956   Anon. review of Rolph

18 May 1962   Walter Allen review of Holbrook

30 November 1963   Philip Drew review of *Colour of Saying*

19 December 1964   Stanley Jones review of Ackerman, *Druid*, and *Twenty Years*

16 October 1965   Stanley Jones review of FitzGibbon[60]

4 December 1965   Leo Beharrel review of *Rebecca's Daughters*

12 November 1966   Stanley Jones review of Moynihan and *Selected Letters*

DAILY TELEGRAPH

11 May 1940   Review of *Portrait*

16 February 1954   G. R. on the Royal Festival Hall Recital

1 March 1954   W. A. Darlington on "Under Milk Wood" (BBC)

9 June 1954   Letter from Graham T. Ackroyd

8 September 1954   On "Under Milk Wood" (BBC)

5 August 1955   John Betjeman review of *Prospect*

16 September 1955   John Betjeman review of *Adventures*

20 April 1956   H. D. Ziman review of Brinnin

10 August 1956   H. D. Ziman review of Rolph

21 September 1956   W. A. Darlington on "Under Milk Wood"

31 May 1957   Kenneth Young review of *Leftover Life*

15 November 1957   Kenneth Young review of *Letters to Vernon Watkins* p. 13

9 December 1960   Derek Stanford review of Tedlock

3 December 1964   David D. Galloway review of Ackerman and *Twenty Years*

14 October 1965   Anthony Powell review of FitzGibbon

---

60. Jack House reviews this with reminiscences in *Glasgow Evening Times* 21 October 1965. See Robert Nye in *Scotsman* 16 October 1965; also his review of *Selected Letters* and Moynihan in the issue of 12 November 1966.

10 November 1966   H. D. Ziman review of *Selected Letters* and Moynihan
p. 21

THE WEEKEND TELEGRAPH

18 November 1962   Caitlin Thomas "Letter to my Daughter" p. 10

10 November 1963   Stephen Potter review of *Colour of Saying*

12 April 1964   "New Boom for Dylan"

22 August 1964   Francis King review of Peter de Vries *Reuben Reuben*, which contains a fictional representation of Thomas

24 October 1965   John Lehmann review of FitzGibbon

16 December 1966   Douglas Cleverdon "Dylan Thomas—An Unpublished Poem" p. 13, presenting "In Country Heaven"

SUNDAY TELEGRAPH

13 November 1966   Nigel Dennis review of *Selected Letters* p. 14

PALESTINE POST

26 May 1940   Douglas Goldring review of *Portrait*

25 February 1949   Paul Potts restrospective review up to *Deaths & Entrances*

MELBOURNE AGE

Australian daily.[61]

1 June 1940   Anon. review of *Portrait*

27 April 1946   Anon. review of *Deaths & Entrances*

20 March 1954   "Under Milk Wood" (London production)

19 May 1956   I.M. review of Brinnin

18 January 1958   Stephen Spender review of *Letters to Vernon Watkins*

25 January 1964   W. A. P. Phillips review of *Colour of Saying*

11 December 1965   Dennis Douglas review of FitzGibbon p. 24

------

61. *Melbourne Herald* had a review of *Collected Poems* by A. L. Phillips 31 January 1953 and a review of FitzGibbon by Noel Hawken 23 November 1965.

SYDNEY MORNING HERALD

Australian daily.[62]

1 June 1940 Anon. review of *Portrait*

11 September 1954 James McAuley review of *Under Milk Wood*

1 October 1955 Charles Higham review of *Prospect*

7 January 1956 C.H. review of *Adventures*

2 June 1956 J. M. D. Pringle review of Brinnin

3 August 1957 Charles Higham review of *Leftover Life*

4 April 1964 Clement Semmler review of *Colour of Saying*

16 January 1965 Gustav Cross review of *Druid*

SCRUTINY

Edited by F. R. Leavis and others, Cambridge, England. Vol. 1 (1932)–Vol. 19 (1953); index in Vol. 20.[63]

June 1940 (Vol. IX No. 1) W. H. Mellors "The Bard and the Prep School" pp. 76–80: *Portrait* reviewed with Spender's *The Backward Son*

Spring 1943 (Vol. XI No. 3) F.R.L. "The Liberation of Poetry" pp. 212–215, a refusal to review Francis Scarfe's *Auden and After*

Summer 1946 (Vol. XIV No. 1) Wolf Mankowitz review of *Deaths & Entrances* pp. 62–67

September 1949 (Vol. XVI No. 3) R. G. Cox review of Treece pp. 247–250

Winter 1949 (Vol. XVI No. 4) F. R. Leavis review of George Every's *Poetry and Personal Responsibility* pp. 339–344

Winter 1952–53 (Vol. XIX No. 2) Robin Mayhead review of *Collected Poems* pp. 142–147

---

62. *Sydney Bulletin* had Anon. review of *Deaths & Entrances* 21 January 1948; review of Brinnin by R.McC. 22 August 1956; review of FitzGibbon by Vivian Smith 8 January 1966.

63. The index item for Thomas:

THOMAS, DYLAN
  bardic element, IX, 77, 79
  confusion in his attempts at complexity, XIV, 65–6
  cult of Dylan Thomas in 1950's, XIX, 142–3; repudiated by critics with high standards, XVI, 249–50
  decorative conceits, XIX, 145–6
  failure to mature, IX, 78–9; XVI, 248–9; XIX, 147

  incantations, XIV, 63, 66–7
  mythology dismissed, XIV, 63
  religious writing an 'indulgence,' XIV, 65; XIX, 143, 146
  rhetorical exaggeration, IX, 76–7; XIX, 145
  rhythmic flaccidity, XIX, 144–5
  sexual fantasies, XIV, 63–4
  Shelleyan qualities, XIX, 143–4, 147

CAMBRIDGE FRONT

Summer 1940   (No. 1) Dylan Thomas "The Countryman's Return" pp. 8–9

THE PENGUIN NEW WRITING

Edited by John Lehmann, whose reminiscences of Thomas' relationship with the magazine can be found in his autobiographical *I Am My Brother* New York: Reynal; London: Longmans, Green 1960 pp. 86–88. Also edited by John Lehmann was *Folios of New Writing*, where appeared in No. IV (Autumn 1941) Dylan Thomas "A fine beginning" pp. 19–27, the first part of "Adventures in the Skin Trade."

May 1941 (No. 6)   Reprints "A Visit to Grandpa's" pp. 97–103

July 1941 (No. 8)   Reprints "The Peaches" pp. 17–35

November 1941 (No. 11)   Reprints "Extraordinary Little Cough" pp. 74–83

1948 (No. 35)   Linden Huddlestone "An Approach to Dylan Thomas" pp. 123–160

LILLIPUT

Monthly magazine of light entertainment and photographs.

December 1941   "Young Poets of Democracy" Thomas included p. 479 with photograph by Bill Brandt

January 1942 (Vol. 10 No. 1)   Dylan Thomas "A Dream of Winter" pp. [65–72], eight three-line stanzas as captions for photographs of winter scenes

DOCUMENTARY NEWS LETTER

Publication concerned with documentary films.

May 1942 (Vol. 3 No. 5)   Anon. review of *This is Colour* p. 71:

> **This is Colour.** *Production:* Strand Films for Imperial Chemical Industries. *Producer:* Basil Wright. *Location Direction:* Jack Ellitt. *Camera:* Jack Cardiff. *Sound Track:* Richard Addinsell, Dylan Thomas, Marjorie Fielding, Joseph MacLeod, Valentine Dyall. Made in Technicolor.
>
> *Subject:* The history, production and use of British dyes.
>
> *Treatment:* This film is a sight for sore eyes. In a world which war is making drabber every day, with its camouflage, its khaki and its rationing of paint and wrappings, *This is Colour* gives us seventeen minutes of pure visual pleasure. The treatment fortunately is academic, thus coordinating what might have easily turned out to be a colour riot. It first discusses colour in general terms of landscape, of prisms, of sunlight and of a red rose in the moonlight. The discovery of new dyeing methods leads us on to experiments with dyes and then to their manufacture. In a superbly mysterious sequence, with the camera moving slowly across the dark paraphernalia of the dye factory with its flamboyant splashes

of colour, we see the dyes being prepared and applied. The rollers turn, placing colour upon pattern and colour upon colour, reeling out yards of gaiety. So far the film has swung along, now it stops. A gabbling voice endeavours to review, in too neat poetry, the uses of colour in the world to-day. Scarlet tooth-brush is followed by green hot-water bottle, book-jackets by window curtains. This sequence is not only jarring, it also shows up one of the great deficiencies of the use of colour in film. The coloured image lingers in the eye for much longer than the black and white, and quick cutting produces an irritating blur.

But as if aware of this coloured hiccough, the film makes up for it by ending superbly. A voice says: "Now let all the colours dance," and the last sequence is a beautifully conceived movement of colour in abstract shapes. Poetry, movement and colour combine to enchant the eye and ear.

Propaganda Value: Perhaps exports are not of such vital importance nowadays. If this is so, the march of events have left the vital propaganda message of this film behind. But it still remains a good film and does its job superbly well.

June 1942 (Vol. 3 No. 6)   Anon. review of *New Towns for Old* p. 90:

New Towns for Old. Strand Films. *Direction:* John Eldridge. *Camera:* Jo Jago. *Script:* Dylan Thomas. *Production:* Alexander Shaw. M.O.I. Five minutes.

Subject: The re-planning of British towns after the war.

Treatment: The film confines itself to one industrial town in the North of England. It shows what has so far been done—both good and bad—and details the essential problems which must be solved in the period of reconstruction after the war. Sensibly enough, the film aims not at the detailing of expert opinion but rather at making the citizenry conscious of their own responsibility as regards planning as well as of the difficulties involved. The style adopted is very pleasant. It consists of a dialogue between two men as they walk through the various areas of "Smoke-dale" and discuss the things they see. One of the men takes the lead and is virtually the commentator; as he has a particularly attractive Yorkshire accent, everything he says gets home with a punch—notably at the end of the film, when he turns abruptly to the audience and points out that the realisation of the ideas of the planners rests entirely in our own hands.

Propaganda Value: Very good for the Home Front, particularly since the film makes it clear that plans for the future are bound up with the war effort which we are all engaged in here and now.

July 1942 (Vol. 3 No. 7)   Anon. review of *Balloon Site 568* p. 100:

Balloon Site 568. *Production:* Strand Film Company. *Producer:* Alexander Shaw. *Direction:* Ivan Moffat. *Camera:* Jo Jago. *Script:* Dylan Thomas and Ivan Moffat.

Subject: W.A.A.F.'s take over a barrage balloon site.

Treatment: A dress shop assistant (blonde sex-appeal), a domestic servant (practical-Scottish), and an office secretary (feminine-efficient), attracted by posters or by friends already in the Service, apply to join the Balloon Service. A pleasant interviewer warns them the job is tough; but they accept it, want to do something more productive than they found their civilian jobs. After some weeks of training— splicing wire cable is tough on the hands, but has got to be learnt just the same— the girls go off to "a place in the country," recognisable to those who saw *Squadron 992.* They get familiar with their floppy elephantine charges. The weird flock of balloons going in to bed makes a striking picture, suggests a whole world of new interests. The girls get along happily with new friends and new jobs. The cheery domestic servant takes to driving a winch; our blonde shop assistant, at a canteen dance, turns down a date—the group is going off to its balloon site next day. It's not an inviting place, in an industrial town, with winter slush underfoot. But they know they are doing important work.

These stages in a balloon girl's training are shown as short episodes; the story flows naturally, usually by a dialogue reference to the next stage. This snappy exposition, and the good technical quality keep interest alert right through. There is a pleasant sound opening of the girls singing one of their choruses.

Propaganda Value: A job, which the film admits must at times be hard, even depressing, is shown to be an inviting one. Burdensome military discipline is not to be seen—but the girls drop their sing-song in the recreation hut quickly enough when an operational order comes through. The film should bring in recruits to the Service.

There is an important wider issue. Women are ready to don uniform and get down to a job which can be tough. We have moved a little since *Squadron 992* so pleasantly mirrored our then conception of total war.

September 1942 (Vol. 3 No. 9)   Anon. review of *C.E.M.A.* p. 125:

C.E.M.A. Strand Film Co. *Producer:* Alex Shaw. *Directors:* John Banting, Dylan Thomas, Charles de Lautour, Alan Osbiston, Peter Scott, Desmond Dickenson. *Camera:* Charles Marlborough. Two reels. M.O.I.

If this were not a non-theatrical film one would feel justified in complaining about the tedious and unattractive introduction in which Richard Butler, President of the Board of Education, outlines the purposes of the Council for the Encouragement of Music and Art. Otherwise the film is rich in picture and sound. It takes one to rehearsals, to concerts, plays and recitals, and succeeds in giving the impression that the workers of Britain are getting entertainment of a high standard in their spare time. What it omits to tell is how much of this entertainment is given and how widespread it is. It does show the use being made of available buildings, churches, canteens, etc.

In this film an experiment in production was made by utilising different directors for different episodes. As the film that follows Mr. Butler's introduction is impressionist and not explanatory, the experiment would seem to have succeeded in giving added colour and vitality.

February 1943 (Vol. 4 No. 2)   Dylan Thomas "These Are the Men" pp. 174–175—extracts from the film script

March 1943 (Vol. 4 No. 3)   Anon. review of *These Are the Men* pp. 195–196:

These Are the Men. *Into Battle No. 4.* Strand. *Production:* Donald Taylor. *Devised and compiled* by Alan Osbiston and Dylan Thomas. *Commentators:* J. McKechnie and Brian Herbert. M.O.I. 12 mins.

Subject: These Are the Men takes an abbreviated version of Leni Reifenstahl's *Triumph of the Will* and superimposes upon the Nuremberg speeches of the Nazi leaders a set of orations in English in which Hitler, Goebbels, Göering, Streicher and Hess report their sins and mistakes as frankly as if they were victims of one of those notorious "confession drugs."

Treatment: The commentary and speeches are in verse by Dylan Thomas (published in the last issue of *D.N.L.*). The film opens with scenes of ordinary decent men going about their day-to-day work. These are "the makers, the workers, the bakers." In a superimposition sequence we see these peaceful men plunged into the horrors of war. A voice cries out to know who was responsible for this crime.

The scene changes to the long Nüremburg vista of brown-shirts and banners. Three tiny figures approach the rostrum. The shot is held so that the suspense becomes almost intolerable. Then they move up to the microphones and Hitler begins the speeches. "We are the men," he shouts.

He describes his early frustrated life, his hatred of Jews and socialists, his belief in the power of blood. The other leaders follow, each to profess his sadistic faith. The speeches are punctuated by the regimented cries of the crowd and rhythmical screams of "Sieg Heil!" The mass shouting and the picture is untouched and remains exactly as it was in the original film; only the superimposed English voices have been brought up to date and now carry the fully matured horror of the pre-war Nazi festival. Now we know for certain where it was all leading.

At the end of the film, the narrator says that many of the eager young Germans whom we see worshipping their Führer may in time be purged and cured and become capable of serving mankind. But their leaders, the narrator shouts, "Can never, never be forgiven."

Alan Osbiston's editing is brilliant. He has used suspense in a masterly way and has brought in the animal Nazi war cries at just those moments when they will give a sharp point of horror, irony, even of bitter comedy to the whole fantastic pageant. Dylan Thomas's verse frequently cuts like a knife into the pompously bestial affectations of this race of supermen. The verse which accompanies the ordinary peaceful citizens of the world is, however, less effective, perhaps because the poet has too often found himself obliged to fall back upon an over-conventional democratic line. His democrats are over-passive in spirit to the point of becoming puny in moral stature.

Propaganda Value: Excellent. Less sophisticated audiences will, however, need to have their wits about them. They have to cope simultaneously with sensational pictures, English voices speaking verse, and faint German voices emanating from speakers whose neuroticisms frequently distract all attention from the sound. Yet audiences will make the effort and find it repaid. In its insistence on the essential anti-semitic and anti-socialist character of German leadership, the film strikes a blow for clear thinking about the true nature of the war—and strikes a blow, therefore, for clear thinking about what must be the nature of our war aims, if the sacrifice of blood is to be worth while. The high level of intense feeling is maintained until almost the very end, but the last few feet fall a little flat. The shouting voice affirming that the Nazi leaders can never be forgiven (shouting with a suspicion of hysteria rather than with confident determination) fails to strike the right finishing note. Most ordinary people have no intention of forgiving Hitler, Goebbels, Göering, Streicher or Hess, and they will be somewhat bewildered to find the Government regarding it as a matter worth announcing so excitedly.

1944 (Vol. 5 No. 4)   Anon. "Two Views on *Our Country*" p. 46:

Our Country. *Production:* Strand for M.O.I. *Direction:* John Eldridge. *Photography:* Jo Jago. *Music:* William Alwyn. Specialised commercial. 50 minutes.

Subject: A lyrical look at the face of war-time Britain.

Treatment: This film wanders gracefully, if somewhat nebulously, from the ships of Liverpool, through the bombed streets of London, the apple orchards, hopfields and airfields of Kent, the mining valleys of South Wales and the steelworks of Sheffield, up to the West Indian lumber camps in Scotland, to finish round a bottle of rum in the cabin of a trawler tied up at Point Law, Aberdeen. The different sections are held loosely together by a merchant seaman (David Sime), who travels from one place to the other on his tour of inspection on foot, by lorry, by car, by train, with his kitbag slung over his shoulder and a ready welcome waiting for him everywhere. He joins the apple and hop-pickers in Kent, gets an invitation to a harvest supper, watches the Welsh miners sing, picks up a girl in Sheffield, rides on a train with the engine driver, jitterbugs with the lads from Honduras and boozes with the trawlermen of Aberdeen, all in an atmosphere of almost painfully perfect friendliness. The whole film is exquisitely shot and, in particular, beautifully photographed—not so much the conventional over-filtered landscapes and cloud effects as the natural, effective low-key scenes as the seaman wanders around St. Paul's or the railway station. And there are many pleasant incidents—the tough dame in the hopfields darning his socks, the vicious-looking Welsh school-master with his temporarily unterrorised class, and, best of all, the firm masculine ring and bite of the Welsh miners singing. But of its very nature and approach the film suffers from vagueness and woolliness. It has one of those "poetic" com-mentaries (the style of the whole film is impressionistic) which pound[s] on and on with very little relation to what the picture's doing—like somebody determined to finish a funny story in spite of the fact that all the company is busily engaged on something else—and which I'd sincerely hoped we'd seen the last of; and, for once, Bill Alwyn's music is disappointing. The director has, I think, concentrated on trying to give an impression of good looks, and of a natural unforced "Christian" friendliness, which no doubt he finds the most pleasant characteristic of British life, and in that he has in a large measure succeeded. It is a pity that this air of well-meaning friendliness should carry, like the vicar's fixed smile at the village fete, such an effect of coldness and gutlessness. I should have thought the warmth and strength of those Welsh miners or the toughness of that Welsh schoolmaster were the British qualities to-day more in need of exploration for our-selves and of presentation for the world. But that is not to deny that this is a very good-looking and well-made film.

Propaganda Value: Good prestige among the artistically inclined.

* * *

The stress and urgencies of war do not make for experiments in technique. For the past five years documentary has been developing the various shapes and formulae which were evolved during the Thirties, and which were, in 1939, so diverse that they formed first-class foundations for the period of rapid expansion which has since taken place. Documentary has in no sense been marking time. But new methods have, in general, been forced to await a period of somewhat different atmosphere. It is a likely guess that such a period, whose prerequisite is not so much leisure as a definite mood which war usually damps, is about to open.

Highly significant therefore is *Our Country*, which is, as far as I know, the sole and successful experimental film of the war period. It says important things in a new way. And because this new way involves poetry, impressionism, and in general a lyrical approach, the film may, perhaps, be a source of controversy and perhaps heart-searching amongst documentary workers who have so long had their noses pressed against the war-time grindstone.

Now it would be absurd to urge everyone in documentary to make films like *Our Country*. In the first place John Eldridge is the only person who can; and in the second place it is a film which is important in itself, for what it is; and that is the sort of film which documentary ought to produce at least once in every five years.

Our Country says a great deal about Britain, and says it with deep emotion. It uses film-continuity in a specially exciting manner, and one which it has always been difficult to bring off; for it involves an absolute logic arising not from a definite story, but from a flow of visuals and sounds (Alwyn's score is his best so far) which achieve logicality because they are purely and simply film. You can't translate the plot of *Our Country* on to paper; it doesn't belong on paper, only on celluloid. You can do no more than say that the film is about a sailor who comes ashore in wartime and participates, as a visitor from another world, in the lives and work, fears and happinesses of men and women and children everywhere in these Islands. You may add, if you like, that there is a prologue by an American soldier; add to that there is a girl who is there because she is your girl or mine (and therefore in this film, the sailor's—watch please the lovely reversed continuity by which Eldridge gets this point across, thus achieving universality without making a dreary "symbolic woman" at the same time).

For fifty minutes this waking dream, or rather this live vision of the inwardness of our daily life, evokes both thoughts and emotions which you cannot find other than valid. By rights it should be noticeably episodic, but it is not; indeed it is so much the reverse that after it is over you feel that everything has been superimposed on everything—and yet every single facet is in itself as clear as crystal.

It would be idiotic to claim perfection. There are things wrong in the film—patches of commentary which are a mere combination of hurriedly spoken words, and which stand out all the more alarmingly amongst the long stretches in which Dylan Thomas succeeds for the first time in wedding (and subordinating) his style to the needs of the medium. There are some unnecessary repetitions of mood, and, thereby, of type-visuals.

But in general the film achieves a genuine integrity, of aesthetic and sentiment (in the proper use of that misused word); and it is an object lesson in inspired shooting. Eldridge has developed his technique slowly, and obviously with much pain and grief, but here he comes out on top, with an ability to portray the most trivial gestures and sights of our daily life with an insight and affection which move us because they are not tricks, but truth. What he does next will be of prime interest to documentary. He cannot repeat himself, because *Our Country* is of itself, and inimitable; but his personal approach to our medium is bound to bring documentary something it needs.

1944 (Vol. 5)   Dylan Thomas "Our Country" p. 96—"Excerpts from the commentary, written by Dylan Thomas, and reproduced by courtesy of the Ministry of Information."

MONTHLY FILM BULLETIN

British Film Institute.

31 July 1942 (No. 103)   On *New Towns for Old* p. 92

31 March 1943 (No. 111) On *These Are the Men* p. 32, issued between February 21 and March 20, 1943

31 August 1944 (No. 128) On *Conquest of a Germ* p. 93, produced by Verity for the Ministry of Information, dealing with the discovery of the drugs prontosil and penicillin

31 March 1945 (No. 135) On *Wales—Green Mountain, Black Mountain* p. 42

31 July 1945 (No. 139) A.R.M. review of *Our Country* p. 84

30 November 1945 (No. 143) Review of *C.E.M.A.* p. 142

[1948] (No. 171) On *Three Weird Sisters* p. 30

[1948] (No. 178) On *No Room at the Inn* p. 138

OUR TIME

Incorporating *Poetry and the People.*

May 1944 Dylan Thomas "Ceremony After a Fire Raid" p. 10, included in a "May Day supplement" compiled by Paul Potts and Jack Lindsay; June 1944 letter from Arthur G. Sier p. 8

October 1945 Arthur Martin review of *Our Country* pp. 52–53: Thomas' script "pretentious"

April 1946 Edith Sitwell review of *Deaths & Entrances* pp. 198–199 [64]

THE BRITISH ANNUAL OF LITERATURE

Published by the British Authors' Press.

1946 (Vol. III) Keidrych Rhys "Contemporary Welsh Literature (ii)" pp. 17–22: Thomas essentially urban

1949 (Vol. VI) Noel A. Jones "Dylan Thomas as a Pattern" pp. 12–16: Thomas a "literary oddity"; Anon. review of Treece p. 89

ISIS

Oxford student magazine. [65]

13 February 1946 Miles Vaughan Williams review of *Deaths & Entrances* p. 24

28 April 1948 Kenneth Hopkins on *Deaths & Entrances* in relation to *Twenty-five Poems* p. 10

---

64. Reprinted in *Angry Penguins Broadsheet* (New Zealand) July 1946 with D. S. Savage's review from *New Republic*, responded to by Kenrick Smythyman "Thomas and the Sycophant" pp. 10–11.

65. An Oxford student weekly, *Cherwell*, includes a review by James Gordon of *Miscellany* 9 February 1966.

27 April 1949   J. D. James review of Treece p. 12

26 November 1952   Donald Hall review of *Collected Poems* p. 31

16 February 1955   Gordon Snell review of *Quite Early* p. 18

30 November 1955   D.J.W. review of *Prospect* and *Adventures* p. 23

29 May 1957   David Cocks review of *Leftover Life* pp. 19, 29

EVENING STANDARD

London.[66]

14 February 1946   Anon. review of *Deaths & Entrances*

19 January 1953   George Malcolm Thomson review of *Collected Poems*

10 March 1954   George Malcolm Thomson review of *Under Milk Wood*

24 April 1956   George Malcolm Thomson review of Brinnin

28 May 1957   George Malcolm Thomson review of *Leftover Life*

19 October 1965   Arthur Calder-Marshall review of FitzGibbon

 8 March 1966   Milton Shulman on "Adventures in the Skin Trade" (Hampstead)

DAILY HERALD

27 February 1946   John Betjeman "A Great Poet" p. 2, a review of *Deaths & Entrances*

 5 March 1954   Sydney Tremayne review of *Under Milk Wood* p. 6

19 April 1956   Allen Andrews review of Brinnin p. 4

27 May 1957   Trevor Williams review of *Leftover Life*

14 November 1960   Bernard Wall review of Tedlock p. 3

THE SUN

New title of the *Daily Herald*, September 1964.

14 October 1965   Arthur Pottersman review of FitzGibbon[67]

20 October 1965   Letter from Alan Smithies

---

66. Of the other London evening papers the *Star* 19 April 1956 has a review of Brinnin by Joseph Taggart p. 14; and the *Evening News* has the following: 10 March 1954 John Connell on *Under Milk Wood*, 21 April 1956 Ernest Reoch review of Brinnin p. 8, and 15 October 1965 Leslie Thomas review of FitzGibbon.

67. Other reviews of this book in London dailies: *Daily Sketch* 14 October 1965 by Robert Ottaway; *Daily Mirror* 16 October 1965 by Alexander Muir.

YORKSHIRE POST

Leeds daily.[68]

5 March 1946   Anon. review of *Deaths & Entrances*

5 December 1952   Leonard Clark review of *Collected Poems*

19 May 1953   Brian Beedham review of *Doctor & Devils*

19 March 1954   Leonard Clark review of *Under Milk Wood*

24 November 1954   K.Y. review of *Quite Early*

12 August 1955   Lettice Cooper review of *Prospect*

9 September 1955   Lettice Cooper review of *Adventures*

20 April 1956   Denis Botterill review of Brinnin

13 September 1956   Denis Botterill review of Treece (2nd. edn)

30 May 1957   Denis Botterill review of *Leftover Life*

21 November 1957   Denis Botterill review of *Letters to Vernon Watkins*

17 November 1960   Denis Botterill review of Tedlock

29 March 1962   Peter Green review of Holbrook

20 June 1963   W. Price Turner review of *Not Quite Posthumous*

3 December 1964   Robert Nye review of Ackerman

21 October 1965   Denis Botterill review of FitzGibbon

13 November 1965   Denis Botterill review of *Rebecca's Daughters*

POETRY QUARTERLY

Editor after Spring 1940: Wrey Gardiner.

Spring 1946   Paul Potts review of *Deaths & Entrances* pp. 29–31

Winter 1948–49   Nicholas Moore "The Poetry of Dylan Thomas" pp. 229–236

Summer 1949   Aneurin Rhys review of Treece pp. 119–120

Winter 1952–53   R. H. Bowden review of *Collected Poems* pp. 126–128

POLEMIC

Editor: Humphrey Slater. Eight issues, 1945–1947.

---

68. The *Yorkshire Observer* (Bradford) had a review of *Collected Poems* by Kenneth Grose 6 January 1953; a review of *Prospect* by K.G. 21 September 1955; and an editorial on Brinnin 21 April 1956. The *Yorkshire Evening Press* (York) had a review of *Under Milk Wood* by J. H. B. Peel 8 March 1954; a review of FitzGibbon by S. S. Stewart 21 October 1965.

May 1946 (No. 3)   Geoffrey Grigson "How Much Me Now Your Acrobatics Amaze" pp. 8–13[69]

March 1947 (No. 7)   John Parry "Scrutiny and Re-scrutiny" pp. 44–50, a reply to Wolf Mankowitz in *Scrutiny* Summer 1946; Geoffrey Grigson "On a Present Kind of Poem" pp. 52–64, with a reprinting of Thomas' "On the Marriage of a Virgin" and "When I Woke"

ADAM

"An International Review," edited by Miron Grindea, London.

May 1946 (No. 158)   Alex Comfort review of *Deaths & Entrances* p. 19

1953 (Nos. 235, 237)   "O Weep for Adonais!": Memorials by Roy Campbell p. 3; Elisabeth Lutyens p. 3; John Lehmann p. 4, included in Tedlock; Emanuel Litvinoff (poem) p. 4, reprinted in *Garland*; and Stephen Spender pp. 4–5.

1953 (No. 238)   "Our Dylan Thomas Memorial Number": "A Telegram from Edith Sitwell" and message from Igor Stravinsky[70] p. ii; "For Dylan"— Editorial pp. ii–7, includes a printing of poems from the *Swansea Grammar School Magazine:* "The Song of the Mischievous Dog," "His Repertoire," "Best of All," "Forest Picture," and comments from Frank Atkinson and Professor Raymond Las Vergnas; letter to the editor from Igor Stravinsky p. 8; Augustus John "The Monogamous Bohemian" pp. 9–10, reprinted in Tedlock

"Three First Memoirs" by Phillip Lindsay p. 11, David Daiches p. 12 (in Tedlock), and Glyn Jones pp. 12–13; "Une Larme pour Adonais"—a translation into French of the previous memorials by Roy Campbell, Elisabeth Lutyens, John Lehmann, Stephen Spender, and Emanuel Litvinoff pp. 13–14; George Barker "A Swansong at Laugharne" (poem) pp. 15–16, in *Garland*; Pierre Emmanuel "In Memoriam Dylan" p. 16 (poem); photograph by John Dickin opposite p. 16; Runia Sheila Macleod "The Dylan I Knew" pp. 17–23, includes a reprinting of several poems from the *Sunday Referee*

"Seventeen Further Memoirs": Pamela Hansford Johnson[71] pp. 24–25, in Tedlock and *Casebook*; Mario Luzi p. 25, in Tedlock; Derek Patmore pp. 25–26; John Davenport pp. 26–27; his publisher[72] pp. 27–28; Hugo Manning p. 29; Clifford Dyment p. 29; William Griffiths p. 30; Robert Pocock pp. 30–31; R. B. Marriott pp. 31–32; Michael Ayrton p. 32 with charcoal drawing; Leslie Rees p. 33; Ralph Wishart pp. 33–34, in Tedlock; Hugh MacDiarmid

---

69. This article does not mention Thomas, but forms the first part of the essay of that title appearing in his *The Harp of Aeolus* (1948), the second part being the essay in No. 7; see Tedlock and *Casebook*.

70. See his book written with Robert Craft *Conversations with Stravinsky* London: Faber; New York: Doubleday 1959; and Eric Walter White *Stravinsky, The Composer and his Works* London: Faber 1966 pp. 436–440.

71. See her Introduction to the 1961 edition of *This Bed Thy Centre*.

72. E. F. Bozman of J. M. Dent and Sons wrote a further memoir in *Books, the Journal of the National Book League* No. 282, December 1953 pp. 114–115.

p. 35; Phillip Burton pp. 36–37, in Tedlock; Cecil Price pp. 37–39, in Tedlock; Griffith Williams p. 39

Georges-Albert Astre "Victoire de la Poesie" pp. 40–42; Jean Wahl translation of "Out of the sighs" p. 42; Claude Delmas translation of "In Memory of Ann Jones" p. 43; Linden Huddlestone "To Take to Give is All" pp. 44–47; passages from "Adventures in the Skin Trade" pp. 48–65; Suzanne Roussillat "His Work and Background" pp. 66–72, in Tedlock; W. S. Merwin "The Religious Poet" pp. 73–78, in *Casebook* and Tedlock; Ronald Bottrall "The Sea (for Dylan Thomas)" (poem) p. 78, in *Garland*; Ken Etheridge "Dylan Marlais Thomas: In Memoriam" pp. 79–80, in *Garland*; reproduction of portrait by Alfred Janes opposite p. 80

1956 (No. 257) Raymond Garlick "The Interpreted Evening" pp. 10–15 a study of "Vision and Prayer"

BRITAIN TODAY

May 1946   Review of *Deaths & Entrances*

January 1953   Edwin Muir review of *Collected Poems* pp. 41–42

May 1953   Philip Henderson review of *Doctor & Devils*

January 1954   Stephen Spender "Dylan Thomas" pp. 15–18

May 1954   Philip Henderson review of *Under Milk Wood*

December 1954   Stevie Smith review of *Quite Early*

OXFORD MAIL

Daily.[73]

30 May 1946   S.P.B. Mais review of *Deaths & Entrances*

4 December 1952   S.P.B. Mais review of *Collected Poems*

4 August 1955   Maida Stanier review of *Prospect*

15 September 1955   M.S. review of *Adventures*

19 April 1956   B. Evan Owen review of Brinnin

16 July 1964   B. Evan Owen review of *Druid*

14 October 1965   B.E.O. review of FitzGibbon

WORLD REVIEW

Monthly, incorporating *Review of Reviews*; ceased publication 1953.

June 1946   David Wright review of *Deaths & Entrances* p. 69

April 1947   Alan Ross "Poetry: The Contemporary Landscape" pp. 55–59

---

73. *The Oxford Times*, the weekly from the same house, had a review of Tedlock by E.E. on 2 December 1960.

July 1951   Henry Treece "Apocalypse Revisited" pp. 22–28

October 1951 (New Series 32)   Dylan Thomas "Poem on his Birthday" pp. 66–67, a version shorter than the one in *Collected Poems*

October 1952 (New Series 44)   Dylan Thomas "The Followers" pp. 41–45

AUKLAND STAR

New Zealand paper.[74]

20 September 1946   C.T. review of *Deaths & Entrances*

11 August 1956   G.W. review of Brinnin

THE WIND AND THE RAIN

Autumn 1946   Anon. review of *Deaths & Entrances* pp. 159–162[75]

PROSPECT

Winter 1946–47   Phil Harmon review of *Deaths & Entrances* pp. 9–10

Christmas 1949   J. C. H. Goodwin "Interpretations—I. The Poetry of Dylan Thomas" pp. 4–6

OUTPOSTS

1947 (No. 7)   Hardiman Scott "From Death to Entrance" pp. 12–14; Elliobe Collins "Imagery and the Poet" pp. 15–16

Spring 1949   Evan Owen "Poetry and Painting" pp. 18–21; Charles Orwell "Labour by Singing Light" pp. 26–28

Winter 1949   Lionel Montieth review of Treece pp. 33–34

May 1953 (No. 23)   Hardiman Scott review of *Collected Poems* pp. 13–14

1954 (No. 25)   Lawrence Lipton "Death of a Poet" (poem) reprinted in *Garland*

1955 (No. 28)   Howard Sergeant review of Stanford pp. 18–20

Summer 1957 (No. 33)   Eric A. Pfeiffer "For Dylan Thomas" (poem) p. 11

---

74. The *New Zealand Herald* had a review of *Doctor & Devils* by John Davenport 16 July 1953; *New Zealand Listener* had article by Owen Jensen 6 May 1966; and *New Zealand Truth* anon. review of Brinnin 14 December 1955 pp. 21, 24.

75. Another anonymous but interesting review of this book, also from a theological slant, is to be found in *The Decachord* July–August 1946. See also John Heath-Stubbs "Both Sides of the Herring-Pond" in *London Forum* Winter 1946 pp. 86–87; and Kathleen Raine's review in *New English Review* May 1946 pp. 484–485.

Winter 1957–58 (No. 35) Leslie Norris "At the Grave of Dylan Thomas" (poem) pp. 14–15 reprinted in *Garland*

STRAND

January 1947 "Thirty Books of the Year" p. 77, a small notice of *Deaths & Entrances*

March 1947 "To Understand a Modern Poem" pp. 60–64: "A Refusal to Mourn" and "The Explanation" by William Empson; illustration by Michael Ayrton; also comment p. 112

Under the title "I-n-s-u-l-t-s" p. 65: "One should tolerate the Labour Government because running down Labour eventually brings you alongside the Conservatives, which is the last place you want to be."—Dylan Thomas (3 guineas paid to the sender of each "insult" printed)

July 1948 John Betjeman "The English Poets" pp 28–37: Thomas photograph with caption p. 34, and quotation from "Fern Hill" p. 37

THE CRITIC

Editors: Wolf Mankowitz, Clifford Collins, Raymond Williams. Continued as *Politics and Letters* after Autumn 1947.

Spring 1947 (Vol. 1 No. 1) D. J. Enright "The Significance of 'Poetry London'" pp. 3–10

Autumn 1947 (Vol. 1 No. 2) "Two Poems"—a response to Thomas' "We lying by seasand" and "A Refusal to Mourn": (1) Edith Sitwell "Comment on Dylan Thomas" pp. 17–18; (2) Henry Gibson "A Comment" pp. 19–20 both reprinted in *Casebook*

Winter–Spring 1947 Letter from J. T. Brockway pp. 94–95, on the debate in the Autumn 1947 *Critic*

ENGLISH

Quarterly periodical of the English Association.[76]

Summer 1947 Association Notes p. 269

Spring 1953 B. L. review of *Collected Poems* pp. 149–150

Spring 1954 Margaret Willy "Dylan Thomas: 1914–53" (poem) pp. 12–13

---

76. *Literature and Life* (Second Series), published by George G. Harrap for the English Association (1951), includes the address of 30 September 1950 "English Poetry of Today" by the Right Hon. Viscount Samuel G.C.B., G.B.E., D.C.L., LL.D. pp. 46–59, in which he disparages Thomas' "A grief ago." An account of what appears to be this Association meeting is given by Rose Macaulay in her *Letters to a Sister* London: Collins; New York: Atheneum 1964 p. 173, and mention is made by Sheila Kaye-Smith in *All the Books of My Life* New York: Harper 1956 p. 191.

Autumn 1954   Hermann Peschmann "A Critical Appreciation" pp. 84–87

Spring 1957   "Theatre Notes" on "Under Milk Wood" (New Theatre) pp. 146–148

Spring 1960   Paul West "Poetic Form Today" pp. 8–12; letter from Robin Atthill on "Fern Hill" p. 35

Summer 1961   Hermann Peschmann review of Tedlock and Heppenstall pp. 198–199

Summer 1962   Timothy Rogers review of Holbrook and Nowottny pp. 67–68.

Spring 1963   R. George Thomas "Dylan Thomas: a Poet of Wales?" pp. 140–145

Summer 1964   Hermann Peschmann review of Kleinman pp. 67–68

Spring 1965   Timothy Rogers review of Ackerman, *Druid*, and *Twenty Years* pp. 148–149

Spring 1968   Howard Sergeant review of Moynihan pp. 28–31

ENGLISH STUDIES

A journal of English letters and philology, edited from Groningen, Holland, by R. W. Zandvoort.

June 1947   Frederick T. Wood "Current Literature, 1946"—includes review of *Deaths & Entrances* pp. 91–92

June 1953   Frederick T. Wood "Current Literature, 1952"—includes paragraph on *Collected Poems* p. 187

February 1960   Ralph Maud "Obsolete and Dialect Words as Serious Puns in Dylan Thomas" pp. 28–30

December 1961   Frederick T. Wood review of Tedlock p. 407

June 1962   Richard Morton "Notes on the Imagery of Dylan Thomas" pp. 155–164

February 1964   Richard L. Drain review of Nowottny pp. 76–78

December 1965   Frederick T. Wood review of Tellier and Ackerman p. 522

December 1966   Frederick T. Wood review of FitzGibbon p. 472

October 1968   David Ormerod "The Central Image in Dylan Thomas' 'Over Sir John's Hill' " pp. 449–450

PICTURE POST

Popular London weekly.

27 December 1947   Dylan Thomas "Conversation About Christmas" p. 26

4 March 1950 "Pablo Picasso—Playwright" pp. 20–21, photograph and caption: "Dylan Thomas Acts as the Stage Manager who Gives the Clues"[77]

28 November 1953 John Pudney[78] "Wales Loses a Great Poet" p. 25: a tribute with a reprinting of "In my Craft or Sullen Art"

5 December 1953 Letter from J. Ormond [Thomas] about the Appeal, with personal reminiscences

BLACKFRIARS

A monthly review edited for St. Dominic's Priory.

March 1948 Illtud Evans "Words from Wales" pp. 148–151: Thomas mentioned

March 1955 David Lloyd James review of *Quite Early* pp. 102–103

December 1957 Saunders Lewis review of *Leftover Life* p. 539

July–August 1962 Raymond Garlick review of Holbrook p. 354

EXE

Publication of the University of Exeter Literary Society.[79]

Spring 1948 Gwyn Oliver Jenkins "Some Notes on Anglo-Welsh Poetry" pp. 39–43

BAND WAGON

October 1948 C. Gordon Glover "Poet in a Pub" pp. 37–39, article based on an interview with Thomas during the time he was living near Oxford

---

77. The Institute of Contemporary Art presented Picasso's "Desire Caught by the Tail" (Translated by Roland Penrose) on 16 February 1950 at the Rudolf Steiner Hall, London, produced by Eric Capon. As a second item, Blake's "An Island in the Moon" was read, with Thomas as Mr. Obtuse Angle.

78. Thomas is mentioned in John Pudney's autobiography *Home and Away* London: Michael Joseph 1960 pp. 47, 86, 168.

79. Other publications in students magazines include David Humphreys "The Poetic Method of Dylan Thomas" *Imprint* (Cambridge) November 1949 (No. 2) pp. 20–25; Ian Roy review of *Collected Poems* in *Blast* (St. Andrews University) March 1953 pp. 20–22; review of *Deaths & Entrances* by C. H. in *Student Forward* May 1946 pp. 33–34; Michael Srigley "The Myth of Dylan Thomas" *Icarus* (Trinity College, Dublin) October 1954 pp. 51–57; review of *Quite Early* in *Trinity College Dublin Magazine* 12 November 1954; Josiah Turner review of *Quite Early* in *Zebra* (Bristol) December 1954 pp. 25–27; Timothy Brownlow review of *Druid* in *The Dubliner* (Trinity College) Winter 1964 pp. 75–77.

BOTTEGHE OSCURE

An international journal published from Rome "a cura di Marguerite Caetani"—see biographical sketch by Iris Origo in *The Atlantic* February 1965 pp. 81–88.

[December] 1949 (IV)   Dylan Thomas "Over Sir John's hill" pp. 397–399

[November] 1950 (VI)   Dylan Thomas "In the white giant's thigh" pp. 335–338, with "Note" about "In Country Heaven"

[November] 1951 (VIII)   Dylan Thomas "Do not go gentle into that good night"; "Lament" pp. 208–210

[April] 1952 (IX)   Dylan Thomas "Llareggub, A Piece for Radio Perhaps" pp. 134–153, with an explanatory "From a Letter" pp. 154–155

[April] 1954 (XIII)   Dylan Thomas "Three Letters" pp. 93–102, with a note by M.C.; Vernon Watkins "Elegy for the Latest Dead (for Dylan Thomas)" (poem) pp. 103–105, reprinted in *Garland*

Autumn 1956 (XVIII)   José Garcia Villa "Death and Dylan Thomas" (poem) pp. 352–353, reprinted in *Garland*

NINE

Editor: Peter Russell; eleven numbers 1949–1956.

Winter 1949–1950   G. S. Fraser "Editorial" pp. 7–8; Anon. "*Nine* Salutes Some Passing Figures" pp. 64–65

Summer 1950   Bernard Bergonzi "Stopping the Rot" pp. 201–202

Autumn 1950   Letter from Emanuel Litvinoff pp. 356–357

Spring 1952   John Heath-Stubbs "Triumph of the Muse" (poem)—some references to Thomas p. 237

CIRCUS

"The Pocket Review of Our Time."

April 1950 (No. 1)   Dylan Thomas "How to Be a Poet (I)" pp. 7–12, "a worldly lecture in two parts"—illustrated by Ronald Searle

May 1950 (No. 2)   Dylan Thomas "How to Be a Poet (2)" pp. 5–8[80]

RANN

An Ulster quarterly of poetry; twenty issues 1948–1953.

December 1951 (No. 14)   W. R. Rodgers "Balloons and Maggots" pp. 8–13 quotes Thomas in conversation: "A writer's *will* must be stronger than his talents"

---

80. The two pieces were reprinted in *Now* (London) 1954 (Vol. I No. 2) pp. 5–11.

March 1953 (No. 18)   Arthur Terry review of *Collected Poems* pp. 20–22

April 1953 (No. 19)   Glyn Jones "Three Anglo-Welsh Prose Writers" pp. 1–5, Thomas considered with Caradoc Evans and Gwyn Thomas; A. G. Prys-Jones review of *Collected Poems* pp. 21–23

POETRY AND POVERTY

[1952] (No. 1)   Horace Gregory "The 'Romantic' Heritage in the Writings of Dylan Thomas" pp. 22–30

1953 (No. 4)   Editorial pp. 4–5; Vernon Scannell "Elegy for a Dead Toper" (poem) p. 12 reprinted in *Garland*; Anon. review of *Collected Poems* pp. 39–40

1954 (No. 6)   Dannie Abse "Elegy for Dylan Thomas" (poem) pp. 5–6 reprinted in *Garland*

1954 (No. 7)   John Heath-Stubbs "Mors Poetarum" (poem) pp. 6–9, stanza on Thomas; George Woodcock "Notes on the Poetry No. 2 (Dylan Thomas and the Welsh Scene)" pp. 20–25[81]

TABLET

Weekly.

6 December 1952   Gerard Slevin review of *Collected Poems* p. 460

4 July 1953   Ursula Branston review of *Doctor & Devils* p. 16

13 March 1954   Illtud Evans review of *Under Milk Wood* p. 253

4 December 1954   Maryvonne Butcher review of *Quite Early* p. 550

5 February 1955   Anthony Bertram review of Olson pp. 134–135

3 September 1955   David Ballard-Thomas review of *Prospect* pp. 229–230

28 April 1956   David Ballard-Thomas review of Brinnin p. 402

5 January 1957   David Jones review of Gwyn Williams' *The Burning Tree* Faber 1956[82]

17 December 1960   Illtud Evans review of Heppenstall pp. 846–847

28 April 1962   Benet Weatherhead O.P. review of Holbrook p. 402

16 October 1965   Illtud Evans review of FitzGibbon pp. 1152–53

BRITISH BOOK NEWS

February 1953   Anon. review of *Collected Poems*

July 1953   Anon. review of *Doctor & Devils*

---

81. See also his *British Poetry Today* Vancouver: University of British Columbia 1950.
82. Jones' review, which mentions "Under Milk Wood," is included in his *Epoch and Artist* London: Faber 1959 pp. 56–65.

May 1954   Anon. review of *Under Milk Wood*

January 1955   Anon. review of *Quite Early*

October 1955   Anon. review of *Prospect*

February 1956   Anon. review of *Adventures*

January 1958   Anon. review of *Letters to Vernon Watkins*

March 1959   Anon. review of *Under Milk Wood* (acting edition)

May 1962   Anon. review of Holbrook

January 1964   Anon. review of *Colour of Saying*

September 1964   Anon. review of *Druid*

December 1964   Anon. review of *Twenty Years*

December 1965   Anon. review of FitzGibbon

TWENTIETH CENTURY

Formerly *Nineteenth Century and After;* editor: Michael Goodwin.

February 1953   John Davenport review of *Collected Poems* pp. 142–146[83]

December 1953   John Davenport an appreciation pp. 475–477

June 1956   John Davenport review of Brinnin pp. 608–610

October 1956   W. John Morgan "Evans, Thomas and Lewis" pp. 322–329

March 1958   Christine Brooke-Rose review of *Letters to Vernon Watkins* and Fraser pp. 280–281

September 1958   W. John Morgan " 'Under Milk Wood' under Milk Wood" pp. 275–276, on the production at Laugharne

January 1961   Jack Common review of Heppenstall pp. 93–94

Summer 1965   Brian Higgins "Now a thirst is not enough" pp. 37–39

TRUTH

London weekly.

29 May 1953   B. Ifor Evans review of *Doctor & Devils* p. 657

2 April 1954   Edwin Birch review of *Under Milk Wood* p. 439

28 January 1955   R. C. Scriven review of *Quite Early* and Stanford pp. 110–111

12 August 1955   Philip Oakes review of *Prospect* p. 1020

---

83. Other periodicals giving attention to Thomas for the first time with reviews of *Collected Poems* include *Apollo* John Gibbins March 1953 p. 101; *London Quarterly and Holborn Review* T. B. Shepherd October 1953 pp. 290–294.

16 September 1955   Kay Collier review of *Adventures* p. 1162

27 April 1956   James Hanley review of Brinnin p. 483

21 June 1957   Oswell Blakestone[84] review of *Leftover Life*

15 November 1957   Richard Church review of *Letters to Vernon Watkins* p. 1295

PUNCH

17 June 1953   R.C.S. [R. C. Scriven] review of *Doctor & Devils* p. 725

18 November 1953   Stephen Spender "Dylan Thomas: November 1953" (poem) p. 618 reprinted in *Garland*

3 March 1954   J. B. Boothroyd "No Telly-Belly for Larry Gibb" pp. 282–283 "A dual commemoration of Dylan Thomas's 'Under Milk Wood' and the Ideal Home Exhibition"

2 May 1956   Anthony Powell review of Brinnin pp. 532–533

29 August 1956   Eric Keown on "Under Milk Wood" (Edinburgh) pp. 257–258

24 July 1957   R.G.G.P.[85] review of *Leftover Life*

2 November 1960   R. G. G. Price review of Heppenstall p. 649

29 August 1962   Eric Keown on "Doctor & Devils" (Edinburgh) pp. 317–318

18 November 1964   John Press review of Ackerman p. 783

10 November 1965   Julian Symons review of FitzGibbon p. 705

23 November 1966   Julian Symons review of *Selected Letters* p. 787

15 February 1967   Patrick Ryan "Wales, Wales" pp. 220–222

17 April 1968   Julian Symons review of *Notebooks* p. 584

DAILY MAIL

12 August 1953   Report on "Speaking Personally" on BBC-TV

10 November 1953   Obituary[86]

---

84. His review of FitzGibbon appeared in *Freethinker* 12 November 1965 p. 367: "This book, some four hundred readable pages, is called a definite biography; but now, I suppose, we will have a spate of books with such titles as *What Constantine FitzGibbon Left Out*. Someone will surely want to talk about Emily Holmes-Coleman, Max Chapman, Humphrey Searle, and a host of others who are definitely "part of the story" but do not appear in the 400 pages." See "Letters to Oswell Blakestone" (some not included in *Selected Letters*) *Ambit* (No. 27) 1966 pp. 10–12.

85. R. G. G. Price reviewed *Twenty-five Poems* in *Sunday at Home* March 1937 pp. xxix–xxx.

86. See obituary in *Daily Mirror* 10 November 1953, and "Cassandra's" column "The Genius of the Year" 18 December 1953.

12 August 1955   Peter Quennell[87] review of *Prospect*

30 January 1956   John Marshall—a series on Thomas which continues each day for the next four days, on p. 4

19 April 1956   Peter Quennell review of Brinnin p. 4

28 May 1957   George Murray "Don't Count Me Among the Dylan Thomas Worshippers"

26 April 1962   Kenneth Allsop[88] "Q: Why Was Dylan like Brigitte?" incorporating a review of Holbrook

14 October 1965   Julian Holland review of FitzGibbon p. 8

MEANJIN

A Melbourne, Australia, quarterly.[89]

Summer 1953   Dylan Thomas "Give London a Chance" pp. 373–382 part of "Adventures in the Skin Trade"; Gavin Ewart "On the Death of Dylan Thomas" p. 382 reprinted in *Garland*

Spring 1955   William Fleming "How to Write Poetry" pp. 379–389, includes a discussion of "Ceremony after a Fire Raid"

Winter 1955   Arthur Phillips "Poetry and Radio" pp. 218–223

March 1956   Letter from Noel Stock, with reply by Arthur Phillips pp. 99–100

April 1959   D. C. Muecke "Come Back! Come Back!—A Theme in Dylan Thomas's Prose" pp. 67–76

Autumn 1966   Jack Lindsay "Memories of Dylan Thomas" pp. 48–75[90]; references in Edith Sitwell "Letters to Jack Lindsay" pp. 76–80

MANDRAKE

Literary quarterly, edited by Arthur Boyers, London.

Summer–Autumn 1953   John Wain review of *Collected Poems* pp. 261–263[91]

Autumn–Winter 1954–55   John Wain review of *Under Milk Wood* p. 354

---

87. See his reminiscences *The Sign of the Fish* London: Collins; New York: Viking Press 1960 pp. 41–44.

88. See his *The Angry Decade* London: Peter Owen 1958.

89. Another Melbourne periodical, *Twentieth Century*, has a review by Evan Jones in the volume for 1961 pp. 32–45.

90. Reprinted in his *Meetings with Poets* London: Frederick Muller 1968 pp. 3–48.

91. Included in his *Preliminary Essays* London: Macmillan; New York: St. Martin's Press 1957 pp. 180–185, and in *Casebook* and Cox. See also Wain's Introduction to *Anthology of Modern Poetry* London: Hutchinson 1963 especially pp. 26–34.

BRITISH WEEKLY

"A Christian Journal of News and Comment," edited by Shaun Heron.

8 October 1953   Shaun Heron review of *Doctor & Devils* p. 2

2 December 1954   S.H. review of *Quite Early* p. 17

6 January 1955   R.G.S. [R. G. Smith] review of Stanford p. 2

17 May 1962   Erik Routley review of Holbrook

THOUGHT
Delhi, India.

24 October 1953   Manjeet Lal Singh review of *Doctor & Devils*

28 November 1953   R. L. Bartholomew, obituary article

9 January 1954   Jag Mohan obituary[92]

11 September 1954   T. K. Thomas review of *Under Milk Wood*

7 July 1956   Shankar Raj, article on *Deaths & Entrances*

14 July 1956   Krishna N. Sinha review of Brinnin

4 August 1956   Ahab, pseud. review of Brinnin

6 July 1957   P. C. Chatterji on Brinnin

26 October 1957   P. C. Chatterji review of *Leftover Life*

TIMES EDUCATIONAL SUPPLEMENT

13 November 1953   Obituary p. 956

12 October 1956   Anon. account of "Under Milk Wood" (London production) p. 1217

18 November 1960   Anon. review of Tedlock

3 December 1965   Anon. review of FitzGibbon p. 1229

THE ILLUSTRATED LONDON NEWS

21 November 1953   Obituary p. 816

19 March 1955   On "Under Milk Wood" (Vanbrugh Theatre) p. 520

---

92. A Bombay periodical, *Freedom First*, had a substantial obituary of Thomas by Rex Berry in the February 1954 issue. See also February 1954 issue of *Indian Review* for "The Poetry of Dylan Thomas" by B. N. Chaturvedi pp. 63–64. Dom Moraes has an article in the *Times of India* 23 November 1965. *Siddha* (Bombay) has in No. 3 (1968) Frank D'Souza "The Gay Wild Dog from Wales" pp. 39–42, and Jagdish Shivpuri "Peter Pan: Sticking the Shadow" pp. 43–48. See also Joseph Minattur "Dylan Thomas: Cherubic Lover and Magic Poet" *Modern Review* (Calcutta) November 1954 pp. 396–397.

17 December 1960   E. D. O'Brien review of Tedlock p. 1119

15 September 1962   J. C. Trewin on "Doctor & Devils" at Edinburgh p. 414

FILM FORUM

December 1953   Crawford Robb review of *Doctor & Devils*[93]

ENCOUNTER

Vol. I No. 1 was published October 1953; founding editors: Stephen Spender and Irving Kristol.

December 1953   Reprinting of "Do not go gentle" with a note pp. 3–4

January 1954   "Dylan Thomas: Memories and Appreciations": I. Daniel Jones pp. 9–10 reprinted in *Casebook*; II. Theodore Roethke p. 11; III. Louis MacNeice pp. 12–13;[94] IV. Marjorie Adix pp. 13–16 reprinted in *Casebook*;[95] V. George Barker pp. 16–17 (all five memoirs are included in Tedlock)

July 1954   Dylan Thomas "Reminiscences of Childhood" pp. 3–7 with drawings by Mervyn Peake (a note on p. 80 states that this is its first publication)

November 1954   Dylan Thomas, James Stephens, Gerald Bullett "On Poetry: A Discussion" pp. 23–26, a more complete version than that in *Quite Early*

January 1955   Herbert Read "The Drift of Modern Poetry" pp. 3–10[96]

May 1955   Karl Shapiro on Louis MacNeice's *Autumn Sequel* pp. 87–88

February 1956   Dylan Thomas "Elegy" pp. 30–31,[97] the unfinished poem edited with a note by Vernon Watkins

May 1956   Hillary Corke[98] review of Brinnin pp. 89–90

---

93. This was reviewed in *Film News* (Vol. XIV No. 1) by George L. George p. 17; in *Films in Review* for March 1954 by Robert Downing pp. 150–151; and in *Newsreel* for September 1953 by Allan Borshell. *Cine-Technician* for January 1954 had an obituary p. 15.

94. See also his "I Remember Dylan Thomas" in *Ingot* (Steel Company of Wales) December 1954 pp. 28–30.

95. In the April 1954 issue there is a note p. 88 indicating that this report of Thomas' discussion session at Utah had previously appeared in *Poetry and Audience* (Leeds) No. 1 (1954). Reprinted in *Explorations* No. 4 (Toronto) February 1955 pp. 34–39.

96. The Francis Bergen Lecture at Yale; see his *The True Voice of Feeling* London: Faber 1955 p. 86.

97. Included in *New Poems 1956* (edited for P.E.N. by Stephen Spender, Elizabeth Jennings, Dannie Abse) London: Michael Joseph 1956 pp. 60–62. A note on the manuscript of the "Elegy" appears in the *Fifth Annual Report to the Fellows of the Pierpont Morgan Library* edited by Frederick B. Adams Jr. New York (November 1954) pp. 57–58.

98. His review of Tedlock appeared in *Weekly Post* (Uxbridge) 15 October 1960.

June 1956   Vernon Watkins "Comment" pp. 78–79, a long letter to the editor on Brinnin

August 1957   Phillip O'Connor review of *Leftover Life* p. 87

December 1957   Lawrence Durrell "The Shades of Dylan Thomas" pp. 56–59 a memoir, included in Tedlock; also December 1959 Kenneth Young "A Dialogue with Durrell" pp. 61–68

March 1961   John Wain review of Tedlock pp. 81–82

July 1962   Stephen Spender review of A. Alvarez *The New Poetry* pp. 73–75; September 1962 letter from Ruthven Todd p. 94

August 1968   David Holbrook "R. D. Laing and the Death Circuit" pp. 35–45

LONDON MAGAZINE

Vol. 1 No. 1 was dated February 1954. Founded by John Lehmann: see his *The Ample Proposition: Autobiography III* London: Eyre & Spottiswoode 1966 pp. 94, 96, 155, 201, 257–258, 262.

February 1954   Louis MacNeice "Canto in Memoriam Dylan Thomas" (poem) pp. 17–21 (with Note p. 104) included in *Garland*; Harvey Breit "Letter from New York" pp. 71–76; letter to the Editor from James Michie pp. 77–79

March 1954   George Barker "At the Wake of Dylan Thomas" (poem) pp. 32–34 reprinted in *Garland*; letter from Donald Davie pp. 74–75

April 1954   Response to Donald Davie from R. G. Bentall p. 73; Louis MacNeice review of *Under Milk Wood* and *Doctor & Devils* pp. 74–77

August 1954   Dylan Thomas "Artists of Wales" pp. 62–63

December 1954   Vernon Watkins "A True Picture Restored: Memories of Dylan Thomas" (poem) pp. 40–43 reprinted in *Garland*

January 1955   L. D. Lerner "The Life and Death of *Scrutiny*" pp. 68–77

May 1955   Louis MacNeice review of *Quite Early*, Olson, and Stanford pp. 106–109; August 1955 letter from Robert Greacen[99] p. 65, with MacNeice's reply p. 66

January 1956   George Barker "Coming to London—IV" pp. 49–54;[100] James Michie review of *Adventures* and *Prospect* pp. 81–83

April 1956   J. I. M. Stewart review of Melchiori pp. 71–73

---

99. He reviewed Treece in *Poetry Commonwealth* Summer 1949 pp. 13–14.
100. See also William Sansom's contribution to the same series in the issue of December 1956 pp. 29–37. Both included in John Lehmann ed. *Coming to London* London: Phoenix House 1957.

June 1956   John Lehmann "Foreword" pp. 9, 11—on Brinnin; August 1956 rejoinder by Tom Scott pp. 56–57

September 1956   Dylan Thomas "I Am Going to Read Aloud" pp. 13–17

July 1957   John Lehmann "Foreword" pp. 9–11—on *Leftover Life*

September 1957   Dylan Thomas "A Letter to Vernon Watkins" pp. 36–38; Geoffrey Grigson "Recollections of Dylan Thomas" pp. 39–45 reprinted in *Casebook*; Thom Gunn[101] review of Bayley pp. 76–79

April 1958   Anthony Thwaite review of *Letters to Vernon Watkins* pp. 61–63

August 1960   Alex Comfort "Dylan Thomas on a Gramophone Record" (poem) pp. 33–34 reprinted in *Garland*

December 1960   Richard Rees review of Heppenstall pp. 60–62

London Magazine New Series begins April 1961; editor: Alan Ross.

November 1964   J. MacLaren Ross "The Polestar Neighbour" pp. 102–112[102]

December 1965   Anthony Dickins "Tambimuttu and Poetry London" pp. 53–57; Gavin Ewart "Tambi the Great" pp. 57–60

PLAYS AND PLAYERS

London monthly, incorporating *Theatre World*.[103]

August 1954   Anon. review of *Under Milk Wood*

October 1956   Iain Crawford on "Under Milk Wood" (Lyceum) p. 1 with photographs pp. 3, 18–19

November 1956   Caryl Brahms on "Under Milk Wood" (New Theatre) p. 15

February 1957   Dylan Thomas "Under Milk Wood" pp. 23–29—text and production photographs; continued March 1957 pp. 25–29

December 1957   Saul Colin on "A Boy Growing Up" p. 30

February 1958   Saul Colin on "Under Milk Wood" (New York) p. 32

October 1958   Caryl Brahms on "A Boy Growing Up" p. 23

March 1959   Frank Granville Barker "Eavesdropping on Milk Wood" p. 8

December 1959   Horst Koegler on "Doctor & Devils" (Germany) p. 33

September 1961   Peter Roberts on "Under Milk Wood" (RADA production) pp. 13, 15

November 1961   Peter Hamilton on "Doctor & Devils" (Glasgow) p. 36; on the Edinburgh production, October 1962 p. 18

---

101. See his review of *Collected Poems* in the *Cambridge Review* 22 November 1952 pp. 159–160.
102. Included in expanded form in his *Memoirs of the Forties* London: Alan Ross 1965.
103. See also *Stage* 11 February 1954 and *Amateur Stage* February 1959.

ESSAYS IN CRITICISM

Founding editor: F. W. Bateson,[104] Oxford.

October 1954   Ralph Maud "Dylan Thomas's Poetry" pp. 411–420[105]

April 1955   Robert Graves "These Be Your Gods, O Israel!" pp. 129–150;[106] Ralph Maud review of Olson pp. 164–168; S. W. Dawson "Mr. Maud on Dylan Thomas" pp. 187–189

October 1955   John Holloway "The New and the Newer Critics" pp. 365–381, discusses Olson on Thomas pp. 377–378

January 1958   A. D. S. Fowler review of Davie pp. 79–87

January 1963   Ralph Maud review of Holbrook pp. 86–88; April 1963 response from William Empson pp. 205–207

July 1964   Walford D. Davies review of Kleinman pp. 318–323

January 1968   Ralph Maud "A Clark Lecture Revisited" pp. 60–62

July 1968   Walford Davies "Imitation and Invention: The Use of Borrowed Material in Dylan Thomas's Prose" pp. 275–295

THE EUROPEAN

"The Journal of Opposition," edited by Alan Neame.

October 1954   Ivor Powell review of *Under Milk Wood* pp. 40–41

February 1956   A.J.N. review of *Adventures* p. 44

July 1957   D.M. review of *Leftover Life* pp. 312–313

March 1958   Roy MacGregor-Hastie[107] "Obscurity in Modern Poetry" pp. 36–44

LUCIFER

The magazine of King's College, London University.[108]

March 1955 (Vol. 53 No. 3)   John A. [Ackerman] Jones "Dylan Thomas: The new Romanticism and its Significance to Life" pp. 30–34

---

104. See his *A Guide to English Literature* New York: Anchor *Books* 1965 p. 197.

105. A version of this article previously appeared in *Poetry & Audience* (Leeds) 21 January 1954 and 12 February 1954.

106. One of the Clark Lectures 1954–55 included in his *The Crowning Privilege* London: Cassell 1955—in part reprinted in *Casebook*. See also comment by Douglas Day in *Swifter Than Reason* Chapel Hill: University of North Carolina Press 1963 p. 195 and comment by Anthony Cronin in *Nimbus* Summer 1956 p. 33.

107. See also his "Ricordo di Dylan Thomas" in *Ausonia* (Siena) January–February 1959 pp. 61–64, reminiscences translated into Italian by Emanuele Mandarà; also article in German in *Die Kultur* 6 January 1958 p. 10.

108. Another University of London student publication, *Sennet*, has a review of Brinnin by Elizabeth Murray 22 May 1956 and of *Letters to Vernon Watkins* by Michael Hanson 26 November 1957. *The London Review* (#3) Spring 1968 Brian Finney "Further Remarks on a Poem by Dylan Thomas" pp. 65–67—discusses an early version of "I have longed to move away."

PLAN

Journal of the Progressive League.

July 1955   Alec Craig review of *Collected Poems*, Treece, Olson, and Stanford pp. 74–75

August 1956   Alec Craig review of Brinnin and Rolph

ENGLISH MISCELLANY

"A Symposium of History, Literature and the Arts," edited by Mario Praz, published for the British Council, Rome.

1955 (No. 6)   Oliver Evans[109] "The Making of a Poem: Dylan Thomas' 'Do not go gentle into that good night' " pp. 163–173 with eight plates of the MS

1956 (No. 7)   Oliver Evans "The Making of a Poem (II): Dylan Thomas' 'Lament' " pp. 244–249, with four plates of the MS; Glauco Cambon[110] "Two Crazy Boats: Dylan Thomas and Rimbaud" pp. 251–259, with specific reference to "Ballad of the Long-legged Bait"

BOOKS AND BOOKMEN

London book review and feature magazine.

October 1955   Derek Stanford review of *Prospect*

November 1955   Gordon Wharton review of *Adventures*

June 1956   W. R. Rodgers review of Brinnin p. 6; Caitlin Thomas reply to Brinnin p. 7

June 1957   [James Gordon, editor] review of *Leftover Life* p. 26, with extracts

January 1958   Derek Stanford review of *Letters to Vernon Watkins* p. 23

October 1960   William Kean Seymour review of Heppenstall p. 19

November 1960   Pamela Hansford Johnson "Tradition in Retreat" pp. 14–16, with treatment of Thomas on p. 15

February 1961   William Kean Seymour review of Tedlock p. 25

January 1963   Caroline Scott review of Tindall p. 24

April 1963   Richard Whittington-Egan review of Tedlock p. 29

March 1964   Kenneth Hopkins review of Kleinman p. 19

July 1964   William Saroyan "The Wild Boy" pp. 5–7[111]

---

109. See also his "Dylan Thomas' Birthday Poems" in *Studies in Honor of John C. Hodges and Alwin Thaler* Nashville: University of Tennessee Press 1961 pp. 131–139.

110. See also his "After the First Death There is No Other" in *Aut-Aut* November 1953 pp. 540–544.

111. This reminiscence had previously appeared in the U.S. in the *Saturday Evening Post* 25 January 1964 pp. 34, 36.

August 1964   Richard Whittington-Egan review of *Druid* p. 18

December 1964   Richard Whittington-Egan review of *Twenty Years* p. 34

July 1965   Bill Read "Dylan Thomas with love to Pamela Hansford Johnson" pp. 12–15, 49–50

December 1965   Richard Whittington-Egan review of FitzGibbon; Alex Hamilton review of Brinnin (Aldine paperback)

January 1966   Richard Whittington-Egan review of *Rebecca's Daughters* p. 34

August 1966   Richard Whittington-Egan review of *Beach of Falesá* p. 64

November 1966   Richard Whittington-Egan "The Tosspot" pp. 24–25, 100— on drink and writers

February 1967   Richard Whittington-Egan review of *Selected Letters* pp. 55–56

April 1967   Michael Baldwin review of *Garland* pp. 51–52

LIBRARY REVIEW

A Glasgow quarterly for librarians.[112]

Summer 1956   Anon. review of Brinnin p. 361

Spring 1961   Anon. review of Tedlock

Winter 1964   Anon. review of *Twenty Years* p. 610

Spring 1966   Anon. review of FitzGibbon pp. 358–359

THE BOOK COLLECTOR

Autumn 1956   Cecil Woolf review of Rolph pp. 287, 289, 291

Spring 1957   William B. Todd "Note 81. The Bibliography of Dylan Thomas" pp. 71–73; James Campbell "Note 82. Issues of Dylan Thomas's *The Map of Love*" pp. 73–74

Autumn 1964   Timothy d'Arch Smith "Note 227. The Second Edition of Dylan Thomas's *18 Poems*" pp. 351–352, the Fortune Press edition

ECONOMIST

8 June 1957   Anon. review of *Leftover Life* p. 880

4 December 1965   Anon. review of FitzGibbon p. 1084[113]

---

112. The *School Librarian* had a review of *Prospect* by Norman Culpan December 1955 p. 415.

113. Peter Duval Smith reviews FitzGibbon in the *Financial Times* 14 October 1965 and Anthony Hartley in *New Society* 21 October 1965.

12 November 1966   Anon. review of *Selected Letters* and Moynihan p. 687

27 April 1968   Anon. review of *Notebooks* p. 57

NOTES AND QUERIES

June 1958   M. E. Grenander on sonnet V p. 263

March 1961   Howard L. McCord "Dylan Thomas and Bhartrihari" p. 110

April 1963   Chris Longcore "A Possible Echo of Jonathan Swift in Dylan Thomas" p. 153

July 1965   Terence Hawkes "Some 'sources' of 'Under Milk Wood' " pp. 273–275; Paul C. Ray "Dylan Thomas and the Surrealists" p. 275

February 1968   Walford Davies "An Allusion to Hardy's 'A Broken Appointment' in Dylan Thomas's 'In country sleep' " pp. 61–62; C. J. Rawson "Some Sources or Parallels to Poems by Ted Hughes" pp. 62–63, mention of the hawk in "Over Sir John's hill"

CRITICAL QUARTERLY

Spring 1959   Raymond Williams "Dylan Thomas's Play for Voices" pp. 18–26, reprinted in Cox

Summer 1959   C. B. Cox "Dylan Thomas's 'Fern Hill' " pp. 134–138[114]

Spring 1962   A. J. Smith "Ambiguity as Poetic Shift" pp. 68–74, on "Our eunuch dreams" and the early poems as Empsonian[115]

ADULT EDUCATION

Spring 1960   Brian Way "Anglo-Welsh Writing" pp. 290–293

January 1964   P. Le Brun review of *Colour of Saying* pp. 281–282

November 1964   T. F. Evans review of *Druid* p. 224

UNICORN

Bath, Somerset; editor: Norman Harvey.

Spring 1961   Norman Harvey "Standards of Criticism" pp. 33–34, includes a discussion of "Fern Hill"

Spring 1962   David Holbrook[116] "Poem on the Table" pp. 26–28; poetic reply by John Wilkie Summer 1962 p. 21

---

114. Reprinted in C. B. Cox & A. E. Dyson eds. *Modern Poetry: Studies in Practical Criticism* London: Edward Arnold 1963 pp. 122–127; see also the Introduction pp. 28–30.

115. See also his "The Art of the Intricate Image" in *Letterature Moderne* November–December 1958 pp. 697–703.

116. See his review of Tedlock in *Cambridge Review* 27 May 1961 pp. 563, 565.

Autumn 1962   Maurice Carpenter[117] review of Holbrook pp. 12–17; Winter 1962 reply by David Holbrook p. 41; Spring 1963 letters from Frances Bellerby and Maurice Carpenter pp. 37–38, and from Geoffrey Grigson p. 40

Spring 1963   Alasdair Aston[118] "Friends Beyond" (poem) p. 11

Summer 1963   Letters from David Holbrook and Vernon Watkins pp. 39–40

RECORDED SOUND

Journal of the British Institute of Recorded Sound.

Summer 1961 (Vol. I No. 3)   Marie Slocombe & Patrick Saul "Dylan Thomas Discography" pp. 80–95:[119]

This list of Dylan Thomas records is divided into the following sections:
1. Numerical catalogue, with full details of each record, in order of make and of maker's catalogue prefix and number;
2. Index of works, other than his own, recorded by Dylan Thomas as speaker or actor;
3. Index of works by Dylan Thomas on records;
4. Index of speakers who have taken part in recordings of works by Dylan Thomas;
5. Supplementary index of names of people and organisations concerned in recordings relating to Dylan Thomas and his works;
6. Records of translations and of musical settings of works by Dylan Thomas.

REVIEW OF ENGLISH LITERATURE

Editor: Professor Jeffares, University of Leeds.

April 1962   Howard Sergeant "The Religious Development of Dylan Thomas" pp. 59–67[120]

April 1965   Geoffrey Leech " 'This bread I break'—Language and Interpretation" pp. 66–75

---

117. He has a poem "for Dylan Thomas" entitled "Vision of the Triumph of Anarchy" included in his *Gentle Exercise* London: Fore Publications 1950 pp. 15–18.

118. See his review of *Portrait*, *Adventures*, and *Beach of Falesá* in *Kolokon* Summer 1966.

119. See also Helen Roach *Spoken Records* New York: Scarecrow Press 1963 pp. 41–45; and Edward Sackville-West & Desmond Shawe-Taylor *The Record Guide* rev. ed. London: Collins 1955 p. 725.

120. See his "Religion in Modern British Poetry: The Ambiguities of Dylan Thomas" *Aryan Path* August 1966 pp. 354–360. Other articles discussing this question include: Frederic Vanson "The Parables of Sunlight: Dylan Thomas as a Religious Poet" *Methodist Magazine* January 1958 pp. 22–24; H. J. Hammerton "Christian Love in Dylan Thomas" *Theology* (London) February 1966 pp. 72–77; Robert S. Phillips "Death and Resurrection: Tradition in Thomas's 'After the Funeral' " *McNeese Review* 1964 (Vol. XV) pp. 3–10; Gilbert Thomas review of *Druid* in *Methodist Recorder* 13 August 1964 p. 8; Frank Edmead review of *Under Milk Wood* in *The Friend* 18 June 1954 p. 581, and of *Quite Early* on 12 August 1955 p. 800; Richard Austin "Dylan Thomas: A Religious Poet" *The Bell* (Dublin) April 1954 pp. 47–50.

LITERARY HALF-YEARLY

Bangalore Central College, India.

July 1962   M. Bryn Davies[121] "Dylan Thomas—An Appraisal" pp. 53–56

January 1964   Geoffrey Johnson "Louis MacNeice, 1907–1963" pp. 15–17;
M. Bryn Davies "A Few Thoughts About Milk Wood" pp. 41–44

THE TEACHER

Weekly journal of the National Union of Teachers.

1 November 1963   Jack Raymond Jones "The Death of a Poet" p. 14

15 January 1965   Shirley Toulson review of *Druid* p. 22

SOUTHERN REVIEW

An Australian journal of literary studies.

1964 (Vol. 1 No. 2)   Arieh Sachs "Sexual Dialectic in the Early Poetry of Dylan Thomas" pp. 43–47

1965 (Vol. 1 No. 4)   Norman Talbot "Polly's Milk Wood and Abraham's Bosom" pp. 33–43; Arieh Sachs review of Ackerman pp. 86–87

ENGLISH STUDIES IN AFRICA

1965 (Vol. 8 No. 2)   Theodore R. Robinson "Dylan Thomas's 'On the Marriage of a Virgin' " pp. 157–165

LETTERS FROM ENGLAND

Edited by Robert Brittain in London, for use in American high schools.

May 1966 (No. 9 Series II)   Emrys Evans on Laugharne and Thomas' poetry

---

121. See also his review of Ackerman and *Druid* in *AUMLA* November 1965 pp. 310–314.

SECTION IV

UNITED STATES AND CANADIAN
PERIODICALS AND NEWSPAPERS

POETRY

"A Magazine of Verse." Founded 1912 by Harriet Monroe in Chicago. Morton Dawen Zabel became editor in 1936; he was followed by George Dillon, Peter De Vries, Hayden Carruth, Karl Shapiro, and Henry Rago.

May 1936   Letters from Geoffrey Grigson and William Empson pp. 115–116

November 1936   Geoffrey Grigson "A Letter from England" pp. 101–103— on *New Verse:* "Some of its lions have shrunk to mice. . . . My opinion of Mr. Dylan Thomas's new *Twenty-five Poems*, for example, must be honest— that twenty-four twenty-fifths of them are psychopathological nonsense put down with a remarkable ineptitude in technique; but that does not mean that I would damn Mr. Thomas, who is a very tough creature, or that I would write off every failure in precosity."

January 1937 [English number edited by W. H. Auden & Michael Roberts] Dylan Thomas "We lying by seasand" p. 183; Michael Roberts "Aspects of English Poetry 1932–37" pp. 210–217; William Empson "A London Letter" pp. 218–222, including the following paragraph (on Thomas?):

I was shocked recently by a Welsh poet who turned up in Kleinfeldt's saying he needed money and had had an offer as checker-in at a Welsh mine; this was very absurd, and he had a much more cozy plan to become a grocer. What with the Welsh nationalism, the vague and balanced but strong political interests of this man, the taste for violence in his writing, and the way he was already obviously exhausting his vein of poetry about events which involved the universe but happened inside his skin, it seemed to me that being a checker-in was just what he wanted; and I shouted at him for some time, against two talkers I should otherwise have been eager to hear, to tell him that he was wasting his opportunities as a Welshman and ought to make full use of a country in which he could nip across the classes. I still think that something like that ought to happen to him, but no doubt he was right in saying that that plan was no good. The English no less than the Americans cling to a touching belief that social distinctions in modern England are more bitter than elsewhere.

February 1938   D. S. Savage "London Letter" pp. 277–288—"Thomas outstanding among the younger poets"

August 1938   Dylan Thomas "When all my five and country senses see," "O make me a mask," "Not from this anger" and "The spire cranes" pp. 247–249; notes on contributors p. 304 (the first two poems were reprinted in the issue of November 1938 at the announcement of the award of the Oscar Blumenthal Prize p. 102)

January 1939   D. S. Savage "Poetry Politics in London" pp. 200–208— Thomas and George Barker praised; William FitzGerald on *New Directions, 1938* pp. 209–214 mentions Thomas

April 1939   Letters from Geoffrey Grigson, Julian Symons, and H. B. Mallalieu pp. 52–55

July 1939   H. R. Hays "Surrealist Influence in Contemporary English and American Poetry" pp. 202–209—Thomas mentioned on p. 204

November 1939   Dylan Thomas "Her tombstone told when she died" pp. 66–67 (title given on the cover as "A Winding Film")

June 1940   Conrad Aiken review of *World I Breathe* pp. 159–161[1]

August 1940   "News Notes" p. 289: Thomas "now serving with an anti-aircraft unit somewhere along the channel coast"

July 1941   Leon Edel on Oscar Williams ed. *New Poems, 1940* (1941) pp. 215–219, Thomas praised p. 219

December 1941   Harvey Breit on George Barker's *Selected Poems* pp. 159–162 —on p. 160: "Thomas seems imprisoned in his morbidity"

June 1943   David Daiches "Contemporary Poetry in Britain" pp. 150–164— Thomas discussed as apocalyptic pp. 158–160; August 1943 letters from William Van O'Connor[2] and Daiches pp. 291–292

October 1943   Edouard Roditi[3] review of *New Poems* pp. 48–50

February 1945   Dylan Thomas "Poem in October" pp. 257–259; notes on contributors p. 287

July 1945   Dylan Thomas "A Winter's Tale" pp. 175–180; notes on contributors p. 231 (in the issue of November 1945 it was announced that Thomas had won the Levinson Prize of $100 p. 111)

October 1946   "News Notes" p. 58—plans for a Dylan Thomas issue of Harvard *Wake* (apparently never materialized)

March 1947   Horace Gregory "Romantic Heritage in the Writings of Dylan Thomas" pp. 326–336, a response to *Selected Writings*[4]

March 1949   Patrick Anderson "For Dylan Thomas" (poem) pp. 323–324 reprinted in *Garland*

March 1950   Bernard Baum review of Treece pp. 357–360

February 1952   G. D. Bridson "Broadcast Poetry in Britain" pp. 301–304— Thomas mentioned on p. 303

December 1952   Winterset Rothberg[5] "One Ring-tailed Roarer to Another" pp. 184–186, a review of *In Country Sleep*

---

1. Included in his *A Reviewer's ABC* New York: Meridian Books 1958 pp. 370–371.
2. See his review of Kleinman in *South Atlantic Quarterly* Summer 1964 pp. 414–417.
3. See his reminiscences "London Reunion" *Literary Review* Spring 1960 pp. 425–429.
4. See also his answer to a "Questionnaire" on Thomas' influence on "Modern American Poetry" in *Focus Five* (1950); the question was also answered by Marianne Moore, Robert Penn Warren, Wallace Stevens, Allen Tate, James Laughlin, and William Carlos Williams.
5. Pseudonym for Theodore Roethke. Reprinted in Tedlock pp. 211–213, where a note says that it was "written at Thomas's request."

January 1954   Elder Olson review of *Collected Poems* pp. 213–220, reprinted in Tedlock; tribute by the editors pp. 224–245

August 1954 to March 1955: In the issues after Thomas' death the "Poetry Chronicle" contained several items of news about memorial issues of periodicals etc.

November 1955 [special issue]   Edith Sitwell "Elegy for Dylan Thomas" (poem) pp. 63–67 reprinted in *Garland*; Dylan Thomas "Five Early Poems" pp. 84–90 transcribed from the Buffalo notebooks; photograph taken in Chicago April 1952 p. 91; facsimile reproductions of worksheets of "Poem on his Birthday" pp. 92–99;[6] Karl Shapiro "Dylan Thomas" pp. 100–110, a substantial essay, reprinted in *Casebook*, Tedlock, and Cox; Roy Campbell "Memories of Dylan Thomas at the B.B.C." pp. 111–114; David Lougee review of *Quite Early* and *Adventures* pp. 114–115; Parker Tyler review of *Doctor & Devils* pp. 116–118; Brewster Ghiselin review of Olson pp. 118–119; Gene Baro review of *Under Milk Wood* pp. 119–122; note on the special issue pp. 128–129

August 1956   Ruthven Todd "Laugharne Churchyard in 1954" (poem) pp. 293–294 reprinted in *Garland*

August 1958   Karl Shapiro vs. David C. Mearns on the question of libraries collecting the manuscripts of living writers pp. 330–332 Thomas used as an example[7]

January 1959   Umashankar Joshi "The Death of a Poet. In Memoriam Dylan Thomas" (poem) p. 230

May 1959   David Lougee review of *Letters to Vernon Watkins* pp. 114–117; Jean Garrigue "Dark Is a Way and Light Is a Place" pp. 111–114, a review of *Collected Poems* (augmented edition)

May 1961   Vernon Watkins "Exegesis" (poem) p. 125 reprinted in *Garland;* Vernon Watkins review of Tedlock pp. 124–125: "It is difficult to explain to anyone who did not know Dylan Thomas why any study of him must remain totally inadequate."

July 1964   Harry Strickhausen "Recent Criticism" pp. 264–267—review of Kleinman p. 266

September 1965   William Stafford—review of eight books including *Choice* p. 432

April 1966   Frank Lentricchia, Jr. review of Holbrook pp. 65–67

---

6. The gift to Harvard by Isabella Gardner of these worksheets is noted in *Houghton Library 1961–62* "Report of Accessions" p. 50. See also the facsimile of the Harvard worksheets of "Prologue" in Herman W. Liebert ed. *Authors at Work* New York: The Grolier Club 1957 item 71.

7. Karl Shapiro writes further on this subject in "No Patronage" *Arts in Society* Fall–Winter 1962–63 p. 21.

NEW DIRECTIONS IN POETRY AND PROSE

Edited by James Laughlin, who became Thomas' publisher with *World I Breathe* (1939).

1938   Dylan Thomas "The Orchards," "In the Direction of the Beginning," "In Memory of Ann Jones," "How shall my animal," "I make this in a warring absence" pp. [256–272]

1939   Dylan Thomas "The Burning Baby," "The School for Witches," "Her tombstone told when she died," "Poem in the Ninth Month" (= "A Saint about to Fall"), "January 1939" (= "Because the pleasure-bird whistles"), "If my head hurt a hair's foot" pp. 79–98

PARTISAN REVIEW

Fall 1938   Dylan Thomas "It is the sinner's dust-tongued bell" p. 230[8]

March–April 1942   Dylan Thomas "Ballad of the Long-legged Bait" pp. 137–150

Spring 1944   Andrews Wanning[9] review of *New Poems* pp. 210–215

January–February 1947   John Berryman "Lowell, Thomas, etc." pp. 71–85

January–February 1952   Dylan Thomas "Do not go gentle" and "Lament" pp. 7–9

September–October 1953   Hayden Carruth review of *Collected Poems* pp. 576–580

Spring 1956   Elizabeth Hardwick "America and Dylan Thomas" pp. 258–264, a review article on Brinnin, reprinted in *Casebook*[10]

KENYON REVIEW

Founding editor: John Crowe Ransom, Kenyon College, Gambier, Ohio.

Winter 1939 (Vol. 1 No. 1)   Philip Blair Rice on *New Directions 1938* pp. 109–111, considers at some length "I make this in a warring absence"

Summer 1939   Dylan Thomas "If my head hurt a hair's foot" pp. 283–284

Autumn 1939   Herbert Read "The Present State of Poetry: I. In England" pp. 359–369: Thomas considered with George Barker pp. 367–368

Winter 1940   Julian Symons "Obscurity and Dylan Thomas" pp. 61–71, an article from England, apparently written without benefit of *Map of Love*[11]

---

8. Included in William Phillips & Philip Rahv eds. *The Partisan Reader* New York: Dial Press 1946 p. 230.

9. He had reviewed *World I Breathe* in the *Southern Review* Spring 1941 pp. 806–809.

10. Also reprinted in *The Partisan Review Anthology* New York: 1962 pp. 179–184, and in her *A View of My Own* New York: Farrar, Straus, & Cudahy 1962.

11. Similarly his comments in "Of Crisis and Dismay" especially pp. 107–108 of *Focus One* London: Dennis Dobson 1945.

Autumn 1940   John Berryman review of *World I Breathe* pp. 481–485, a tribute to Thomas, with a rejoinder to Symons' "very bad article published some time ago in these pages"[12]

Spring 1945   Robert Horan "In Defense of Dylan Thomas" pp. 304–310, an article in the form of a letter to the editor in response to a comment on Thomas as "baroque" by Arthur Mizener in the issue of Winter 1944; utilizes *New Poems*; reprinted in Tedlock

Spring 1947   Howard Moss "Ten Poets" pp. 290–298, beginning with *Selected Writings*

Summer 1951   John Crowe Ransom "The Poetry of 1900–1950" pp. 444–454:[13] Thomas hard to classify as major or minor pp. 452–453

Summer 1953   Howard Nemerov "The Generation of Violence" pp. 477–483, a review article on *Collected Poems*, but dwelling mainly on "Hold hard, these ancient minutes" and other early poems

Spring 1955   Dannie Abse "Elegy for Dylan Thomas" pp. 256–257 reprinted in *Garland*; Geoffrey Moore "Dylan Thomas" pp. 258–277[14] article reprinted in Tedlock

Winter 1957   Richard Ellmann[15] "Wallace Stevens' Ice Cream" pp. 89–105: Thomas used for comparison pp. 97, 101

Spring 1961   George Steiner "The Retreat from Word" Thomas mentioned on p. 207

FANTASY

Editor: Stanley D. Mayer, Pittsburgh.

1939 (No. 2)   Dylan Thomas "Here in this spring," "Poison or Grapes" (= "Ears in the turrets hear"), and "Incarnate devil" pp. 28–30

1940 (No. 4)   Parker Tyler review of *World I Breathe* pp. 71–73[16]

1941 (No. 1)   Arthur E. DuBois review of *Portrait* pp. 75–76

THE NEW YORKER

27 January 1940   Louise Bogan review of *World I Breathe* p. 60–62[17]

26 October 1940   Anon. mention of *Portrait* p. 86

---

12. Robert Lowell also answered Symons in a review of *World I Breathe* in the student magazine *HIKA* March 1940 pp. 19–22.

13. He has a similar article in *ELH* June 1951, Thomas mentioned p. 161.

14. See also his British Council pamphlet *Poetry Today* London: Longmans, Green 1958 especially pp. 29–33.

15. See his contribution on Thomas in *The World Book Encyclopedia* Vol. 18 (1969) p. 200.

16. See also his "Eros at Home" *Compass* February 1940 pp. 65–69.

17. Reprinted in her *Selected Criticism* New York: Noonday 1955.

21 December 1946   Anon. review of *Selected Writings* p. 99

 2 August 1952   Louise Bogan review of *In Country Sleep* p. 65

10 October 1953   Anon. review of *Collected Poems* p. 160

*   *   *

 6 February 1954   Mollie Panter-Downes on "Homage to Dylan Thomas" pp. 67–68

 6 March 1954   Anon. review of *Doctor & Devils* p. 120

29 May 1954   Anon. review of *Under Milk Wood* p. 104

22 January 1955   Anthony West review of *Quite Early* pp. 106–108

11 June 1955   Anon. review of *Adventures* p. 138

13 July 1957   Mollie Panter-Downes mention of *Leftover Life* pp. 52–56

12 October 1957   Louise Bogan review of *Leftover Life* pp. 193, 195, 197

26 October 1957   Wolcott Gibbs on "Under Milk Wood" (Henry Miller Theatre) pp. 87–88

12 April 1958   Anon. review of *Letters to Vernon Watkins* pp. 163–164

13 June 1959   Whitney Balliett review of Muriel Spark's *Momento Mori* dwelling on a passage about Thomas pp. 119, 120

 5 November 1960   Patricia Collinge "Once More Unto the Breach" pp. 48–49—a parody

 8 April 1961   Whitney Balliett on "Under Milk Wood" (Circle Theatre) pp. 132, 134

15 December 1962   Edith Oliver on "Under Milk Wood" (Circle in the Square) pp. 130, 132

 5 October 1963   Anon. review of *Beach of Falesá* p. 191

22 January 1966   Naomi Bliven review of FitzGibbon pp. 100–102

 7 October 1967   Howard Moss review of *Selected Letters* pp. 185–189

PROVIDENCE JOURNAL

Rhode Island.

11 February 1940   W.T.S. review of *World I Breathe*[18]

11 November 1940   W.T.S. review of *Portrait*

10 January 1954   W.T.S. review of *Doctor & Devils*

---

18. Other newspaper reviews of *World I Breathe* include *Brooklyn Eagle* 9 February 1940 (Anon.); *Argonaut* 19 July 1940 (Anon.); *Boston Transcript* 20 March 1940 (by John Holmes); *Hartford Connecticut Times* 18 January 1941 (by M.L.S.); *Santa Barbara News-Press* 23 June 1940 (by Maurice Swan).

16 May 1954   Charles Philbrick review of *Under Milk Wood*

16 January 1955   Charles Philbrick review of *Quite Early*

5 June 1955   Charles Philbrick review of *Adventures*

27 November 1955   Eleanor M. Scott review of Brinnin p. vi

13 October 1957   Winfield Townley Scott review of *Leftover Life* p. vi–6

31 October 1965   Charles Philbrick review of FitzGibbon

14 May 1967   Lawrence Goldstein review of *Selected Letters*

NEW YORK HERALD TRIBUNE BOOK REVIEW

25 February 1940   Kerker Quinn review of *World I Breathe* p. 14

17 November 1940   Paul Rosenfeld review of *Portrait* p. 26

15 December 1946   Anon. review of *Selected Writings* p. 20

23 March 1952   Babette Deutsch review of *In Country Sleep* p. 4

10 May 1953   Edith Sitwell review of *Collected Poems* pp. 1, 14

29 November 1953   W. T. Scott review of *Doctor & Devils* p. 16

23 May 1954   W. T. Scott review of *Under Milk Wood* and Olson p. 4

19 December 1954   Gene Baro review of *Quite Early* p. 3

12 June 1955   Gene Baro review of *Adventures* p. 4

20 November 1955   W. T. Scott review of Brinnin p. 1

13 October 1957   Gene Baro review of *Leftover Life* p. 4

26 January 1958   Babette Deutsch review of *Letters to Vernon Watkins* p. 3

3 November 1963   John Malcolm Brinnin review of *Beach of Falesá* and *Not Quite Posthumous* pp. 5, 23

BOOK WEEK

Formerly *New York Herald Tribune Book Review.*

24 October 1965   Richard Burton review of FitzGibbon pp. 1, 43

18 June 1967   Alan Pryce-Jones review of *Selected Letters* pp. 8, 11 with Eli Siegel poem

THE NATION

New York weekly. Edited in 1940 by Freda Kirchwey; literary editor: Margaret Marshall; present editor: Carey McWilliams.

23 March 1940   Paul Rosenfeld "Decadence and Dylan Thomas" review of *World I Breathe* pp. 399–400

23 November 1940   Anon. review of *Portrait* p. 512

18 September 1943   Anon. review of *New Poems* p. 332: " 'Ballad of the Long-legged Bait' . . . stems straight from Swinburne"

15 December 1945   Margaret Marshall "Notes by the Way" pp. 664–665 prints whole of "Fern Hill" with comment

10 August 1946   Arthur Mizener "Poets" compares Thomas and Treece pp. 160–161

22 February 1947   William Empson review of *Selected Writings* pp. 214–216

19 April 1952   Rolfe Humphries review of *In Country Sleep* pp. 389–390

2 May 1953   Thomas Riggs Jr. review of *Collected Poems* pp. 376–378

14 November 1953   Jacob Korg review of *Doctor & Devils* p. 413

5 December 1953   Letter from Elizabeth Toohy p. 456 on *Doctor & Devils*

24 April 1954   Jacob Korg review of *Under Milk Wood* and Olson p. 360

25 December 1954   Jacob Korg review of *Quite Early* pp. 552–553

29 January 1955   Kay Boyle "A Declaration for 1955" pp. 102–104, an account of meeting Thomas

19 March 1955   Jacob Korg review of Stanford p. 245

30 July 1955   Jacob Korg review of *Adventures* p. 102

17 December 1955   M. L. Rosenthal review of Brinnin p. 539; Anon. review of *Child's Christmas* p. 540

2 November 1957   M. L. Rosenthal review of *Leftover Life* p. 308; Harold Clurman on "Under Milk Wood" pp. 309–310

26 April 1958   Vivian Mercer review of *Letters to Vernon Watkins* pp. 369–370

1 September 1962   Ralph Maud "Letter from Wales" pp. 98–100

FURIOSO

"A magazine of verse," New Haven, Connecticut.

Spring 1940 (No. 1)   Dylan Thomas "When I Woke" and "To Others than You" pp. 18–19

Spring 1947   Robert Griffiths "New Verse" pp. 80–81, *Selected Writings* discussed

THE VIRGINIA QUARTERLY REVIEW

Spring 1940   Theodore Maynard "The New Artificiality" review of *World I Breathe* pp. 311–314

Spring 1951   Babette Deutsch "Orient Wheat" pp. 221–236 uses *Selected Writings* throughout

Summer 1954   Richard Eberhart "Time and Dylan Thomas" review of Olson pp. 475–478

Winter 1955   Anon. review of *Under Milk Wood* p. xvi

Autumn 1955   Anon. review of *Adventures* p. ci

Spring 1956   Anon. review of Brinnin p. l

Winter 1958   Anon. review of *Leftover Life* p. xxv

Summer 1963   Oscar Mandel "Artists without Masters" pp. 401–419 mention of Thomas p. 404

Spring 1964   Anon. review of *Beach of Falesá* p. lxi, and of Kleinman and *Entrances* p. lxv

Winter 1966   Anon. review of *Me & My Bike* p. xvii

Autumn 1966   Anon. review of *Doctor & Devils and Other Scripts* p. clxiv

VOICES

Spring 1940   Clark Mills "Aspects of Surrealism" pp. 47–51

Winter 1947   William Porter Gram review of *Selected Writings* pp. 47–49

September–December 1954   Thomas Cole review of *Collected Poems* pp. 46–50

September–December 1954   Robert E. Stauffer review of *Under Milk Wood* pp. 40–43

September–December 1955   Barbara Avirett "Dylan Thomas" (poem) p. 33 reprinted in *Garland*

January–April 1957   Witter Bynner "Dylan Thomas" (poem) p. 4 reprinted in *Garland*

May–August 1959   Francis C. Rosenberger review of *Letters to Vernon Watkins* pp. 52–59

September–December 1961   Lewis Turco review of *Casebook* pp. 39–43

THE NEW REPUBLIC

1 April 1940   Dunstan Thompson review of *World I Breathe* pp. 447–448

22 April 1940   Conrad Aiken "Poetry: 1940 Model" pp. 540–541 [19]

30 December 1940   F. W. Dupee review of *Portrait* p. 906

3 January 1944   Conrad Aiken review of *New Poems* pp. 26–27 [19]

14 May 1945   Dylan Thomas "A Refusal to Mourn" p. 675

2 July 1945   Dylan Thomas "This Side of the Truth" p. 20

---

19. Included in his *A Reviewer's ABC* New York: Meridian Books 1958.

16 July 1945 Dylan Thomas "The Conversation of Prayers" p. 76

29 April 1946 D. S. Savage "Poetry of Dylan Thomas" pp. 619–622: article from England after *Deaths & Entrances*, reprinted in Tedlock

2 December 1946 G.M. mention of *Selected Writings* p. 742

17 March 1952 John L. Sweeney review of *In Country Sleep* pp. 18, 22–23

6 April 1953 John L. Sweeney review of *Collected Poems* pp. 24–28

25 January 1954 John Malcolm Brinnin review of *Doctor & Devils* p. 19

11 July 1955 Hans Meyerhoff review of *Adventures* pp. 17–19

12 September 1955 Theodore Roethke "Elegy" (poem) p. 19 reprinted in *Garland*

27 February 1956 Robert Graves "These Be Thy Gods, O Israel" pp. 16–17; continued 5 March 1956 pp. 17–18; replies 19 March 1956 from Delmore Schwartz, W. M. Laetsch, Henry M. Pachter, Jack Lindeman, Ridgely Cummings, pp. 20–22; 2 April 1956 letter from Karl Shapiro pp. 2, 23

28 October 1957 Robert Graves "And the Children's Teeth Are Set on Edge" review of *Leftover Life* pp. 15–18[20]

10 June 1967 Stanley Moss review of FitzGibbon and *Selected Letters* pp. 19–20

THE SATURDAY REVIEW

New York weekly. Norman Cousins: editor; John Ciardi: poetry editor.

11 May 1940 D.F. [Dudley Fitts] review of *World I Breathe* p. 20

28 August 1943 Dudley Fitts review of *New Poems* pp. 8–9

16 October 1943 William Rose Benét "The Season's Poetry"—*New Poems* reviewed p. 24

21 June 1952 Gerard Previn Meyer review of *In Country Sleep* pp. 17–18

29 November 1952 Irwin Edman "The Spoken Word" pp. 68–69, on Caedmon recordings

11 April 1953 W. T. Scott review of *Collected Poems* pp. 29–30

6 June 1953 Henry Hewes review of "Under Milk Wood" pp. 24–25

* * *

5 December 1953 Letter concerning the Fund from W. H. Auden, E. E. Cummings, Arthur Miller, Marianne Moore, Wallace Stevens, Tennessee Williams, and Thornton Wilder

16 January 1954 Melville Cane "Are Poets Returning to Lyricism?" pp. 8–10

---

20. Reprinted in his *Steps* London: Cassell 1958.

20 February 1954   Raymond Walters Jr. "Trade Winds" pp. 6, 8 on different versions of *Under Milk Wood*

6 March 1954   Robert Halsband review of *Doctor & Devils* p. 38

13 March 1954   H.S. [Harrison Smith] "Whose Is the Guilt?" on Thomas in the U.S. p. 24; 3 April 1954 letters from Atlantis Hallam, Mark Pape, Irma Lange pp. 24–25

1 May 1954   Dudley Fitts review of Olson p. 30

3 July 1954   I.L. Solomon review of *Under Milk Wood* p. 18

8 January 1955   W.T. Scott review of *Quite Early* pp. 17–18

2 July 1955   William Peden review of *Adventures* p. 18

19 November 1955   Edith Hamilton "Words, Words, Words: the Modern School of Verse" pp. 15–16; Louis Untermeyer review of Brinnin pp. 16–18; Henry Hewes biographical sketch of Brinnin p. 17

10 December 1955   Letters from Richard E. Madtes, Charles C. Rand, J. N. Wood, W. I. Price, Robert W. Shields, James L. Rosenberg p. 23; 17 December 1955 letter from Shirley W. Hentzell p. 23

6 October 1956   Henry Hewes on "Under Milk Wood" (Edinburgh production) p. 39

15 December 1956   John Ciardi "A Thousandth Poem for Dylan Thomas" p. 21 reprinted in *Garland*

12 October 1957   William Bittner review of *Leftover Life* pp. 22–23

19 October 1957   Henry Hewes on Emlyn Williams p. 53

16 November 1957   John G. Fuller "Trade Winds" pp. 8, 10, 12—on Thomas and the White Horse Tavern

1 March 1958   John Ciardi review of *Letters to Vernon Watkins* pp. 18, 31

15 November 1958   John Ciardi "Six Hours of Dylan Thomas" the Caedmon recordings p. 50

4 June 1960   Henry Hewes on "Under Milk Wood" (Dallas, Texas) p. 30

13 May 1961   John Ciardi "Discs for the Library" p. 58

3 August 1963   Haskel Frankel review of *Beach of Falesá* p. 18

30 November 1963   Gloria Vanderbilt review of *Not Quite Posthumous* pp. 42–43

5 December 1964   Haskel Frankel review of *Choice* p. 37

30 January 1965   Anon. review of Read p. 33

30 October 1965   William Bittner review of FitzGibbon pp. 44–45

22 July 1967   Bill Read review of *Selected Letters* p. 39

30 December 1967   M. L. Rosenthal review of *Notebooks* p. 24

TRAMP

Published in Anacortes, Washington, Summer 1939–Winter 1941.

Spring–Summer 1940   Harry Roskolenko[21] review of *World I Breathe* pp. 13–14

Fall 1940   Henry Treece "Myself Sitting Down" pp. 13–15

THE ATLANTIC

Editor Edward Weeks mentions Thomas in relation to the magazine in his autobiographies, *The Open Heart* Boston: Atlantic–Little, Brown 1955 and *Breaking Into Print* Boston: The Writer 1962.

August 1940   Conrad Aiken "Back to Poetry" pp. 217–223, mention of *World I Breathe* p. 222

December 1947   Dylan Thomas "In Country Sleep" pp. 83–85

July 1951   Dylan Thomas "How to Be a Poet" pp. 46–49

September 1951   Dylan Thomas "In the White Giant's Thigh" and "Note" pp. 31–32; November 1951   letters from Eric Barker, Mildred C. Tallant, Ernest Bradley, Gene Baro, Florence B. Cobb and a note by the editors pp. 22–23

March 1952   Dylan Thomas "Poem on his Birthday" pp. 62–64

January 1953   Dylan Thomas "Prologue" p. 46

May 1953   Phoebe Adams review of *Collected Poems* pp. 79–80

November 1953   Charles J. Rolo review of *Doctor & Devils* pp. 110–111

* * *

February 1954   Edith Sitwell "Dylan Thomas" obituary pp. 42–45

June 1954   Letter from Joan Lee Corbin p. 17, and a note on the Fund

July 1954   Charles J. Rolo on *Under Milk Wood* pp. 82–83

August 1954   Dylan Thomas "August Bank Holiday" pp. 28–30

November 1954   Dylan Thomas "The Welshman as Poet" pp. 76–84

December 1954   Kenneth Tynan "Prose and the Playwright" pp. 72, 74, 76, on *Under Milk Wood*

January 1955   Edward Weeks on *Quite Early* p. 78

February 1955   Eric Barker[22] "In Memory of Dylan Thomas" (poem) p. 60 reprinted in *Garland*

---

21. See also his review of *Collected Poems* in *Chicago Jewish Forum* Summer 1957 pp. 253–254; and of *Letters to Vernon Watkins* in *Socialist Call* April 1958 p. 23.

22. See also his "Dylan Thomas is Dead" *Simbolica* (#10) 1953 pp. 1–3.

July 1955   Charles J. Rolo on *Adventures* p. 81

October 1955   John Malcolm Brinnin "Dylan Thomas in Wales" pp. 37–44; Caitlin Thomas' statement p. 44

November 1955   John Malcolm Brinnin "Cockles, Brambles and Fern Hill" pp. 50–55; December 1955 letters on Brinnin from Mrs. Emerson W. Peterson, Lorne Coutts, and Olive Eckerson p. 29

January 1956   Charles J. Rolo on Brinnin p. 84

June 1956   Vernon Watkins presents Dylan Thomas' "Elegy" pp. 42–43

June 1957   Caitlin Thomas "This Was Dylan" pp. 33–38

October 1957   Alfred Kazin "The Posthumous Life of Dylan Thomas"[23] pp. 164–168, dealing with Brinnin and *Leftover Life*

June 1959   Alfred Kazin "The Causes Go, the Rebels Remain" pp. 65–67, on Thomas and Brendan Behan

October 1965   Constantine FitzGibbon "Young Dylan Thomas" pp. 63–70; continued November 1965, pp. 66–72

December 1965   Phoebe Adams review of *Me & My Bike* p. 162

May 1966   Phoebe Adams review of *Rebecca's Daughters* p. 132

July 1967   Phoebe Adams review of *Selected Letters* p. 114

SEATTLE POST-INTELLIGENCER

4 November 1940   J.G.L. review of *Portrait*[24]

THE CHRISTIAN SCIENCE MONITOR

23 November 1940   John Ritchey review of *Portrait* p. 12

6 May 1954   Francis Russell review of *Under Milk Wood* and Olson p. 7

10 October 1957   Earl W. Foell review of *Leftover Life* p. 11

30 January 1958   Eric Forbes-Boyd review of *Letters to Vernon Watkins* p. 5

9 December 1965   Colin Campbell review of FitzGibbon

18 May 1967   Melvin Maddocks review of *Selected Letters* p. 11

---

23. Reprinted in his *Contemporaries* Boston: Atlantic-Little, Brown 1962 pp. 192–202.
24. Other reviews of *Portrait* include the *Glen Ridge Paper* 29 November 1940 (by William Francis Jr.); *Experimental Review* November 1940 p. 82 (Anon.); *Writers' Markets and Methods* November 1940 p. 18 (Anon.); *Harvard Advocate* November 1940 p. 24 (by M.B. [Marvin Barrett]); *New Haven Journal-Courier* 11 November 1940 (by D.L.U.); *Salt Lake Tribune* 2 March 1941 (Anon.); *Cincinnati Times-Star* 13 January 1941 (by E.L.); *Los Angeles Times* 2 March 1941 (by Milton Merlin); *Memphis Commercial Appeal* 16 March 1941 (by T. C. Holpfner).

NEW YORK TIMES BOOK REVIEW

29 December 1940   Marianne Hauser review of *Portrait* pp. 4, 14

25 July 1943   Horace Gregory review of *New Poems* p. 19

 8 December 1946   John Malcolm Brinnin review of *Selected Writings* p. 24

14 May 1950   Harvey Breit "Talk with Dylan Thomas" p. 19 reprinted in *Casebook*

17 February 1952   Harvey Breit "Talk with Dylan Thomas" p. 18 reprinted in *Casebook*[25]

 6 April 1952   Lloyd Frankenberg review of *In Country Sleep* p. 4

 5 April 1953   Louis MacNeice review of *Collected Poems* pp. 1, 17

* * *

22 November 1953   Dylan Thomas "I have longed to move away" and "This side of the truth" p. 2; Harvey Breit "Farewell and Hail" p. 8

 6 December 1953   James Agee review of *Doctor & Devils* p. 38

10 January 1954   Stephen Spender "A Literary Letter from London" p. 14

 7 March 1954   J. Donald Adams weekly column p. 2

18 April 1954   Harvey Breit "Dylan Report" p. 8 on the Fund

 9 May 1954   Richard Eberhart review of *Under Milk Wood* p. 5

19 December 1954   Louis MacNeice review of *Quite Early* p. 1

22 May 1955   Delmore Schwartz review of *Adventures* pp. 4, 20

20 November 1955   Katherine Anne Porter review of Brinnin p. 5

18 December 1955   Harvey Breit review of *Child's Christmas* p. 8

16 December 1956   Horace Gregory review of Treece pp. 4–5

16 June 1957   Harvey Breit mention of *Leftover Life* p. 8

13 October 1957   Katherine Anne Porter review of *Leftover Life* pp. 3, 32; 24 November 1957 letter from Sarah Stewart

20 October 1957   J.H.B. Peel "The Echoes of the Booming Voice" pp. 40–41 compares Thomas and G.M. Hopkins; 10 November 1957 letters from Lloyd Frankenberg, Barbara Leggett, Morton N. Felix, W.B. Lee, Kenneth J. Schmidt, David Coldoff, Caroline Hogue, Thomas E. Connors, Thane Guhl

 2 February 1958   Katherine Anne Porter review of *Letters to Vernon Watkins* p. 4; cartoon, p. 2

23 March 1958   Letters from A. I. Vaughan-Thomas and G.K. Davies on D.J. Thomas p. 40

---

25. Both interviews are reprinted in his *The Writer Observed* Cleveland: World 1956; London: Alvin Redman 1957.

3 November 1963 William T. Moynihan "Boily Boy and Bard" pp. 6, 48; Anon. "The Thomas Legacy" p. 6

24 November 1963 Elizabeth Janeway review of *Not Quite Posthumous* p. 66

21 June 1964 Denise Levertov review of *Garland* pp. 10, 12

31 October 1965 Stanley Kunitz review of FitzGibbon pp. 1, 86

28 November 1965 Walter Allen "London Letter"

25 June 1967 Horace Gregory review of *Selected Letters* pp. 5, 26, 28

25 February 1968 Anon. review of *Notebooks* p. 16

NEW YORK TIMES MAGAZINE

13 October 1946 Stanton A. Coblentz "What Are They, Poems or Puzzles?" pp. 24, 50–51, 53; 3 November 1946 Harvey Breit reply to Coblentz pp. 20, 58, 60–61[26]

6 October 1957 Harvey Breit "Haunting Drama of Dylan Thomas" pp. 22, 24, 26

COMMONWEAL

New York weekly review of literature and public affairs since 1924.

10 January 1941 Barry Byrne review of *Portrait* p. 307

15 May 1953 Dachine Rainer review of *Collected Poems* pp. 159–161

26 June 1953 Richard Hayes review of YMHA "Under Milk Wood" pp. 297–298

6 November 1953 Nicholas Joost review of *Doctor & Devils* p. 243

4 December 1953 Patrick F. Quinn review of *Doctor & Devils* p. 243

18 December 1953 Anne Fremantle "Death of a Poet" pp. 285–286, includes poem by John Logan "Lines for the Death of Dylan Thomas (November 9, 1953)" included in *Garland*

26 March 1954 Sam Hynes "Dylan Thomas: Everybody's Adonais" pp. 628–629

14 May 1954 Nicholas Joost review of Olson p. 151

3 December 1954 Dylan Thomas "Morning in Wales" pp. 243–245, a reprinting of "Quite Early One Morning"

7 January 1955 Nicholas Joost review of *Quite Early* p. 387

10 June 1955 Chandler Brossard review of *Adventures* pp. 262–263

---

26. This dialogue, or at least Coblentz's side of it, was prolonged by Albert Ralph Korn in his privately printed pamphlet *The Case for Clarity in Poetry* (1947), and revived in Stanton A. Coblentz *The Generation that Forgot to Sing* Mill Valley California: Wings Press 1962 pp. 15–16, 20, 40.

 2 December 1955   J. N. Moody review of *Adventures* p. 242

25 October 1957   Bette Richart review of *Leftover Life* pp. 94–95

 8 November 1957   Richard Hayes on Emlyn Williams and "Under Milk Wood" p. 151

12 January 1962   Katharine Jo Privett "The Death of Dylan Thomas" (poem) p. 415 reprinted in *Garland*

23 February 1962   Bruce A. Cook review of Heppenstall pp. 560–562

 8 November 1963   Anon. mention of *Beach of Falesá* p. 200

 6 December 1963   Jean Holzhauer review of *Not Quite Posthumous* pp. 330–331

21 February 1964   J. S. Rubenstein review of Kleinman and Emery pp. 642–643

14 May 1965   Irving D. Suss review of Ackerman pp. 262–264

17 December 1965   Irving D. Suss review of FitzGibbon pp. 350–351

VICE VERSA

Edited by Harry Brown and Dunstan Thompson in New York 1940–1942.

January–February 1941 (No. 2)   Dylan Thomas "Into her lying down head" pp. 8–10

DECISION

New York monthly; Klaus Mann, editor.

September 1941   Dylan Thomas "Deaths and Entrances" p. 66

NEW MASSES

New York Communist monthly; Samuel Sillen, editor.

14 September 1943   Samuel Sillen "Mr. Sillen Comments" pp. 24–25

MASSES AND MAINSTREAM

New title of *New Masses*. Later called *Mainstream*.

April 1952   Jack Lindsay "British Writers for Peace" p. 61 mentions Thomas

September 1954   Charles Humboldt "The Tragedy of Dylan Thomas" pp. 53–56, review of Olson

February 1955   Jack Lindsay "Last Words with Dylan Thomas" (poem) pp. 43–45 reprinted in *Garland*

October 1956   Thomas McGrath on Graves on Thomas p. 55

March 1957   George Hitchcock "Intact Vision" review of *Collected Poems* of Edna St. Vincent Millay, Thomas mentioned p. 55

CANADIAN FORUM

Toronto monthly news and political opinion magazine.

September 1943   Margaret Avison review of *New Poems* p. 143

September 1954   Alan Brown review of Olson p. 140

November 1954   Marshall Maclure pp. 179, 181; Millar Maclure on *Under Milk Wood* p. 191

November 1955   Millar Maclure[27] review of *Prospect* p. 188

October 1956   Millar Maclure review of Treece p. 165

March 1957   Clara Lander "The Macabre in Dylan Thomas" pp. 274–275, 278

THE YALE REVIEW

Yale University quarterly.[28]

Winter 1944   Louis Untermeyer "Eight Poets" pp. 348–351, *New Poems* discussed p. 351

Summer 1953   David Daiches review of *Collected Poems* p. 625

Winter 1954   Paul Pickrel review of *Doctor & Devils* pp. xx–xxiv

Winter 1955   Louis L. Martz "New Poetry" pp. 301–309, discusses *Under Milk Wood* p. 302

Spring 1957   Reed Whittemore "The 'Modern Idiom' of Poetry, and All That" pp. 357–371

Spring 1966   Helen Hennessy Vendler review of FitzGibbon pp. 439–442

THE ROCKY MOUNTAIN REVIEW

Murray, Utah; quarterly from 1938–1946; editor: Ray B. West.

Spring 1944   Brewster Ghiselin "Use of a Mango" review of *New Poems* pp. 111–112

Spring 1945   B.G. [Brewster Ghiselin] review of Oscar Williams ed. *New Poems 1944* pp. 152–153

---

27. See also his "Tower of Words" *Explorations* (No. 4) February 1955 pp. 40–51.

28. The *Yale Poetry Review* had a review of *Deaths & Entrances* by R. F. [Rolf Fjelde] Summer 1946 p. 26.

WESTERN REVIEW

State University of Iowa; new title of *The Rocky Mountain Review*, 1946

Winter 1947   Leslie A. Fiedler "The Latest Dylan Thomas" pp. 103–106, review of *Selected Writings*

Spring 1954   Brewster Ghiselin review of *Collected Poems* pp. 245–249

Winter 1955   Brewster Ghiselin review of Olson pp. 145–147

Spring 1956   V. R. Cassill "The Trial of Two Poets" pp. 241–245, review of Brinnin

SEWANEE REVIEW

Published quarterly in Sewanee, Tennessee, since 1892.

July–September 1944   Marshall W. Stearns "Unisex the Skeleton: Notes on the Poetry of Dylan Thomas" pp. 424–440, reprinted in Tedlock[29]

October–December 1944   Horace Gregory mention of *New Poems* p. 588

Spring 1945   Dylan Thomas "Holy Spring" p. 259

Summer 1945   Dylan Thomas "Vision and Prayer" pp. 413–424

Summer 1947   Robert Lowell "Thomas, Bishop, and Williams" pp. 493–503 includes review of *Selected Writings* pp. 493–496

Autumn 1955   Robert Phelps "In Country Dylan" pp. 681–687, mainly on *Doctor & Devils*, *Under Milk Wood*, and *Quite Early*

Summer 1957   John Wain "English Poetry: the Immediate Situation" pp. 353–374, Thomas mentioned especially pp. 357–358; Autumn 1958 John Lehmann "The Wain-Larkin Myth: A Reply to John Wain" pp. 578–587

Summer 1968   Gene Montague "Dylan Thomas and *Nightwood*" pp. 420–434

ACCENT

Urbana, Illinois, quarterly; Kerker Quinn, editor.

Winter 1945   Dylan Thomas "Ceremony After a Fire Raid" pp. 69–71

Winter 1953   Cid Corman "Dylan Thomas: Rhetorician in Mid-Career" pp. 56–59 review of *Collected Poems* reprinted in Tedlock

Winter 1957   Jacob Korg[30] "Imagery and Universe in Dylan Thomas' 'Eighteen Poems'" pp. 3–15

---

29. Was earlier reprinted in Stefan Shimanski & Henry Treece eds. *Transformation Three* London: Lindsay Drummond 1945 pp. 145–158.

30. See his "The Short Stories of Dylan Thomas" *Perspective* (Kentucky) Spring 1948 pp. 184–191; and his review of Ackerman, *Poets of Reality*, FitzGibbon, and Moynihan in *Antioch Review* Summer 1966 pp. 281–288.

Spring 1960   Ralph J. Mills "Dylan Thomas: the Endless Monologue" pp. 114–136[31]

THE EXPLICATOR

May 1945   Marshall W. Stearns "After the funeral" #52

June 1950   G. Giovannini "The force that through the green fuse" #59; S. F. Johnson "The force that through the green fuse" #60

December 1950   Sam Hynes "From love's first fever" #18

February 1952   S. F. Johnson "The force that through the green fuse" #26; "The hunchback in the park" and "The marriage of a virgin" #27

December 1953   Phyllis Bartlett "Among those killed in the dawn raid" #21[32]

February 1954   D. R. Howard "In my craft or sullen art" #22

June 1954   Elmer L. Brooks "Among those Killed in the Dawn Raid" #49

October 1955   Sister M. Laurentia "Fern Hill" #1

December 1955   Ralph Maud [sonnet I] #16

February 1956   Thomas E. Connolly "And death shall have no dominion" #33

November 1956   Ihab H. Hassan "The tombstone told when she died" #11

December 1956   Bernard Kneiger [sonnet I] #18

February 1957   Bernard Kneiger "Light breaks where no sun shines" #32

December 1957   Mary Ellen Rickey "The Conversation of Prayer" #15

February 1958   William T. Moynihan "Light breaks where no sun shines" #28

March 1958   Richard A. Condon "Ballad of the Long-legged Bait" #37

June 1958   Erhardt H. Essig [sonnet I] #53

November 1958   R. J. Stonesifer [*Adventures*] #10

December 1958   John A. Clair "A Refusal to Mourn" #25

March 1959   Bill Casey "To-day, this insect" #43

April 1959   Robert C. Jones "Conversation of Prayer" #49

May 1959   William T. Moynihan "In the white giant's thigh" #59

November 1959   Bernard Kneiger [sonnet II] #14

December 1959   Patricia Meyer Spacks "In my Craft or Sullen Art" #21

---

31. See also his "Theodore Roethke" in *Poets in Progress* Northwestern University Press 1962 p. 4; and his *Theodore Roethke* University of Minnesota Press 1963 pp. 7, 14, 18. Further comparisons with Roethke will be found in Allan Seager *The Glass House* New York: McGraw-Hill 1968 pp. 153, 178, 192–193, 199–200, 203–205, 213–214, 217, 220, 226, 228, 234, 275.
32. See her *Poems in Progress* New York: Oxford University Press 1951 p. 151.

January 1960   Bernard Kneiger [sonnet III] #25

October 1960   Marlene Chambers "In the white giant's thigh" #1

November 1960   James Zigerell "When all my five and country senses see" #11

December 1960   Gene Montague "To-day, this insect" #15

March 1961   Marlene Chambers "In the white giant's thigh" #39

May 1961   Bernard Kneiger "On the Marriage of a Virgin" #61

June 1961   L. P. query on "The hand that signed the paper"

September 1961   Bernard Kneiger "Twenty-four years" #4

October 1961   Bernard Kneiger "Love in the Asylum" #13

January 1962   Laurence Perrine "Hunchback in the park" #45

September 1962   Laurence Perrine "Especially when the October wind" #1

November 1962   Max Halperen "If I were tickled by the rub of love" #25[33]

May 1964   David Ormerod "Twenty-four years" #71

February 1965   H. Richmond Neuville Jr. and Lee J. Richmond both on "Ballad of the Long-legged Bait" #43

April 1965   Max Halperen "How soon the servant sun" #65

October 1967   Olga DeHart Harvill "O make me a mask" #12

TIME

2 December 1946   Anon. review of *Selected Writings* p. 112

6 April 1953   Anon. "Welsh Rare One" review of *Collected Poems* p. 112 with pen drawing, and stanzas from "Vision and Prayer" and "Fern Hill"

5 October 1953   Anon. review of *Doctor & Devils* p. 110

16 November 1953   Obituary p. 93

21 December 1953   Short note on *Collected Poems* p. 99

17 May 1954   Dylan Thomas "The Lecturer's Spring" pp. 32–33—passages from "A Visit to America"

27 December 1954   Anon. review of *Quite Early* pp. 68–69

2 May 1955   "The Spoken Word" p. 104—on the Caedmon recordings

30 May 1955   Anon. review of *Adventures* pp. 90, 92, 95, a biographical account in keeping with the title "The Legend of Dylan Thomas"

---

33. See also his "Dylan Thomas: A Soliloquy" in *Florida State University Studies* #11 1953 pp. 117–141; and his review of *Quite Early* in the *Miami Herald-Leader* 6 February 1955.

13 June 1955   Letters from John K. MacKenzie, Harmon Tyler, Margo M. Gildea, Donald Dougherty pp. 10, 12; 27 June 1955 letters from Donald C. Ream and Gertrude Goebel p. 8

14 October 1957   Anon. review of *Leftover Life* p. 122

21 October 1957   On Emlyn Williams p. 56

28 October 1957   On "Under Milk Wood" p. 93

 2 December 1957   Kenneth Rexroth poem on Dylan Thomas p. 71 in article entitled "The Cool Cool Bards"

25 August 1958   "People" p. 34—Caitlin Thomas and Guiseppe Fazio

 9 March 1962   Anon. "Poetry in English 1945–1962" pp. 92–95

27 September 1963   Anon. review of *Beach of Falesá* p. 47

29 October 1965   Anon. review of FitzGibbon pp. 102, 104

18 March 1966   Photo of Caitlin and children at "Under Milk Wood" script court case p. 58

30 June 1967   Anon. review of *Selected Letters* pp. 74–76

22 December 1967   Anon. review of *Notebooks* pp. 82–83

NEW QUARTERLY OF POETRY

Winter 1946–47   Peter J. Stephens "Dylan Thomas: Giant among Moderns" pp. 7–11 [34]—response to *Selected Writings*

BARD REVIEW

Published quarterly at Annandale-on-Hudson, New York, by Bard College from 1946–1950.

Spring 1947   Roger Hecht review of *Selected Writings* pp. 57–58

VOGUE

New York fashion magazine since 1892. [35]

15 July 1947   Dylan Thomas "Holiday Memory" pp. 37, 76 with photo by Lee Miller

---

34. Reprinted in *Poetry Book Magazine* Winter 1950 pp. 16–20; where see also his "Poetry from Wales," reminiscences in an address before the N.Y. Branch of the Women's Welsh Clubs, in the Winter 1955 issue pp. 8–15.

35. The British edition apparently has independent literary editorship. It included the following: November 1954 Dylan Thomas "Return Journey" pp. 106–107; December 1954 Siriol Hugh Jones review of *Quite Early*; August 1955 John Davenport biographical sketch pp. 47, 99, 101 reprinted in Tedlock; June 1957 Caitlin Thomas, passages from *Leftover Life* pp. 84–85, 135–136; December 1957 Penelope Gilliatt review of *Leftover Life*; February 1966 Polly Devlin review of FitzGibbon.

March 1954   Photo by John Deakin and notice of death

September 1954   Dylan Thomas "Visit to America" pp. 194, 220, 222

15 March 1960   Gilbert Highet "The Great Welsh Poet: Dylan Thomas" pp. 110–111, 152–154[36]

THE NEW MEXICO QUARTERLY

Summer 1947   Robert Bunker review of *Selected Writings* pp. 385–386

Spring 1954   Myron Ochshorn "The Love Song of Dylan Thomas" pp. 46–65

SPIRIT

Published monthly in New York since 1934 by the Catholic Poetry Society of America.

November 1947   John Duffy "Perhaps Potential Poetry" pp. 145–148 review of *Selected Writings*

November 1949   Robert Resor review of Kenneth Rexroth's *The New British Poets* (1949) pp. 157–159

September 1954   R. J. Schoeck review of *Collected Poems* pp. 120–122

September 1955   Sister Maura "No Dirge for Dylan Thomas" (poem) p. 16

January 1965   M. Whitcomb Hess review of Holbrook pp. 178–179

THE AMERICAN SCHOLAR

Quarterly journal of Phi Beta Kappa.

Autumn 1948   William York Tindall "The Poetry of Dylan Thomas" pp. 431–439; Spring 1949 letter from L. L. Rice pp. 254–255

Autumn 1953   William York Tindall[37] "Burning and Crested Song" review of *Collected Poems* pp. 486–490

Spring 1955   Rosemary Thomas "Dylan Thomas 1914–1953" (poem) pp. 180–181

Spring 1957   John Hall Wheelock "A View of Contemporary Poetry" pp. 335–341, Thomas mentioned p. 339

Summer 1959   Robert Langbaum "The New Nature Poetry" pp. 323–340, Thomas mentioned p. 324

Autumn 1959   Letter from J. Donald Adams p. 536 in reference to a column of Randall Jarrell in the previous issue

---

36. From his *The Powers of Poetry* New York: Oxford University Press 1960 pp. 151–157; see also his broadcast talk on Brinnin "Death of a Poet" in his *Talents and Geniuses* New York: Oxford University Press 1957 pp. 84–91.

37. See also his *The Literary Symbol* New York: Columbia University Press 1955; and his contribution to *Collier's Encyclopedia* New York 1964 Vol. 22 p. 288.

Winter 1960–1961   Frank A. Butler "On the Beat Nature of Beat" pp. 79–92, Thomas mentioned pp. 83–84

NEW YORK HERALD TRIBUNE

26 December 1949   Joe Pihodna on the film *No Room at the Inn*

10 November 1953   Obituary p. 20

15 December 1954   John K. Hutchens review of *Quite Early* p. 23

15 November 1955   Lewis Gannett review of Brinnin p. 25

14 December 1957   Maurice Dolbier review of *Letters to Vernon Watkins* p. 10

30 November 1960   Edith Sitwell "The Dylan Thomas I Knew"

 3 December 1963   Alan Pryce-Jones review of *Not Quite Posthumous*

20 January 1964   Walter Kerr on "Dylan" p. 10[38]

23 August 1964   Charles Portis "An American on Dylan's Trail" pp. 11, 13

28 October 1965   Alan Pryce-Jones "Dylan: A Knowing Fondness" p. 23, review of FitzGibbon

NEW YORK HERALD TRIBUNE MAGAZINE

12 January 1964   Barbara Holdridge "Dylan as He Was" pp. 31, 65

19 July 1964   Sidney Michaels "Wearing the Other Fellow's Skin" p. 17

COLLEGE ENGLISH

February 1950   Richard R. Werry "Poetry of Dylan Thomas" pp. 250–256

December 1953   Anon. review of *Doctor & Devils* p. 194

April 1954   Anon. review of Olson p. 421

May 1954   Henry W. Wells "Voice and Verse in Dylan Thomas's Play" pp. 438–444

October 1954   David Daiches "Poetry of Dylan Thomas" pp. 1–8[39]

January 1955   Anon. review of Treece p. 260

March 1960   Sister M. Maura "After a Class in Poetry" (poem) p. 347 reprinted in *Garland*; Monroe C. Beardsley and Sam Hynes "Misunderstanding Poetry: Notes on some Readings of Dylan Thomas" pp. 315–322; Terence Hawkes "Dylan Thomas's Welsh" pp. 345–347

---

38. See also his *The Theatre in Spite of Itself* New York: Simon & Schuster 1963 pp. 78–82.

39. Reprinted in a pamphlet "For the friends of T. E. Hanley" 1958. It was also reprinted in *College English* November 1960; in his *Literary Essays* London: Oliver & Boyd 1956 pp. 50–61; and in Cox.

May 1962   Bernard Kneiger "The Christianity of the 'Altarwise by Owl-light' Sequence" pp. 623–628

April 1964   J. Rea "A Topographical Guide to 'Under Milk Wood'" pp. 535–542

October 1964   Clifford A. Nault Jr. review of Kleinman p. 65

January 1966   Richard Ohmann[40] "Literature as Sentences" pp. 261–267

CONTEMPORARY VERSE

Victoria, British Columbia, quarterly; Alan Crawley, editor.

Spring 1950   Floris McLaren "Dylan Thomas in Vancouver" pp. 26–27[41]

THE HUDSON REVIEW

New York quarterly. Editors: William Arrowsmith, Joseph Bennett, Frederick Morgan.

Autumn 1950   Dylan Thomas "Over Sir John's Hill" pp. 380–381; David Aivaz "The Poetry of Dylan Thomas" pp. 382–404 reprinted in Tedlock

Winter 1954   William Arrowsmith "The Wisdom of Poetry" pp. 589–604, *Collected Poems* reviewed pp. 597–600 reprinted in *Casebook*

Summer 1954   Patrick Cruttwell "Letter from England" pp. 272–275; William Arrowsmith "Menander and Milk Wood" pp. 291–296, Thomas' play compared with Eliot's *The Confidential Clerk*

Spring 1955   Robert Martin Adams "Taste and Bad Taste in Metaphysical Poetry: Richard Crashaw and Dylan Thomas" pp. 61–77[42]

Summer 1964   John Simon "Theatre Chronicle" pp. 232–242, "Dylan" reviewed pp. 233–234[43]

Winter 1964–1965   Hayden Carruth comment on *Garland* p. 157

HARPER'S BAZAAR

December 1950   Dylan Thomas "A Child's Memories of Christmas in Wales" pp. 86–87, 186, 188[44]

---

40. See Harold C. Martin & Richard M. Ohmann eds. *Inquiry and Expression* New York: Rinehart 1958 p. 475, on "A Refusal to Mourn."

41. On Thomas' Vancouver visit, see also Les Wedman review of *Prospect* in *Vancouver Province* December 1955.

42. Included in his *Strains of Discord* Ithaca, New York: Cornell University Press 1958, and adapted for inclusion in Cox.

43. Included in his *Acid Test* New York: Stein & Day 1963, references to Thomas on pp. 68, 86, 101, 140, 228, 233.

44. This version, used in the U.S. edition of *Quite Early*, was reprinted in *London Calling* 20 December 1956.

December 1953   Dylan Thomas "A Story" pp. 100, 152, 158–159, 161–162, 165

February 1954   Edwin Muir "Dylan Thomas" obituary p. 128 with photo by Bill Brandt

August 1959   Dylan Thomas "Beach of Falesá" pp. 76–79, 132–144

June 1962   John Davenport "Black Sheep" pp. 88–89, 97, includes reminiscences of Thomas

June 1963   Dylan Thomas "Dylan Thomas on Edgar Lee Masters" radio talk on *Spoon River Anthology*[45] with introduction by Ralph Maud pp. 68–69, 115

THEATRE ARTS

February 1952   Henry Popkin "Poets as Performers" pp. 27, 74

December 1956   Anon. review of Treece p. 12

May 1957   Margaret Webster on "Under Milk Wood" (London) pp. 32, 92–93

December 1957   Anon. review of *Under Milk Wood* pp. 22–23;[46] Anon. review of Emlyn Williams pp. 27, 82

TALISMAN

Denver, Colorado, quarterly.

Winter 1952   James L. Rosenberg review of *In Country Sleep* pp. 51–52

SAN FRANCISCO CHRONICLE

9 March 1952   Lawrence Ferling review of *In Country Sleep* p. 23[47]

12 April 1953   Lawrence Ferling review of *Collected Poems* p. 9

7 March 1954   L.G.O. review of *Doctor & Devils* p. 20

13 June 1954   Lawrence Ferling review of Olson p. 21

19 December 1954   D. M. Stocking review of *Quite Early* p. 16

27 November 1955   Jere Witter review of Brinnin p. 12

10 October 1957   William Hogan review of *Leftover Life* p. 21

27 April 1958   N.K.D. review of *Letters to Vernon Watkins* p. 28

31 December 1961   N.K.D. review of *Casebook*

15 May 1966   James Schevill review of FitzGibbon p. 38

---

45. May Swenson's introduction to the 1962 edition of *Spoon River Anthology* published by Collier mentioned *Under Milk Wood* p. 11.

46. See also review in *Dramatics* by Willard Friederich December 1954.

47. See also "Side View of a Poet" *Counterpoint* (San Francisco) June 1952, for Lawrence Ferlinghetti on Thomas' reading in San Francisco.

LIBRARY JOURNAL

15 March 1952   Gerald D. McDonald review of *In Country Sleep* p. 533

15 August 1953   Gerald D. McDonald review of *Collected Poems* p. 1334

15 December 1953   Gerald D. McDonald review of *Doctor & Devils* p. 2214

15 June 1954   Gerald D. McDonald review of *Under Milk Wood* p. 1232

15 November 1954   Gerald D. McDonald review of *Quite Early* p. 2208

15 February 1955   Gerald D. McDonald review of Stanford pp. 458–459

July 1955   Eli M. Oboler review of *Adventures* p. 1594

15 October 1955   Gerald D. McDonald review of Brinnin p. 2232

1 October 1957   Dorothy Nyren review of *Leftover Life* p. 2450

15 February 1958   Herbert Cahoon review of *Letters to Vernon Watkins* p. 601

1 January 1962   Burton A. Robie review of *Casebook* p. 98–99

15 March 1962   Burton A. Robie review of Tindall p. 1137

1 March 1963   Ben W. Fuson review of Emery p. 1014

15 October 1963   Dorothy Nyren review of *Not Quite Posthumous* p. 3847

1 December 1963   Dorothy Nyren review of *Beach of Falesá* pp. 4659–60

1 February 1964   Ray Smith review of Kleinman p. 632

1 March 1964   Ray Smith review of *Garland* p. 1095

15 January 1965   Anon. review of *Choice* p. 402

1 April 1965   John R. Willingham review of Ackerman p. 1720

1 December 1965   Gerald D. McDonald review of FitzGibbon p. 5262

1 May 1966   Ben W. Fuson review of *Druid* p. 2344

15 May 1966   Gerald D. McDonald review of Cox p. 2495

1 June 1966   Gerald D. McDonald review of *Rebecca's Daughters* p. 2870

August 1966   Gerald D. McDonald review of *Doctor & Devils and Other Scripts* p. 3732

SHENANDOAH

Washington and Lee University quarterly; James Boatwright, editor.

Spring 1952   Thomas H. Carter review of *In Country Sleep* pp. 24–26

Spring 1954   John L. Sweeney "The Gardener and the Prince" pp. 20–23; Roy Campbell "Dylan Thomas—the War Years" pp. 26–27; Vernon Watkins

"Portrait of a Friend" (poem) pp. 24–25 reprinted in *Garland;* John Montague "A First Response" pp. 28–31

OCCIDENT

Twice yearly; Associated Students of the University of California.[48]

Spring 1952 "Interview with Dylan Thomas" pp. 5–6

NEW WORLD WRITING

Mentor Books (New American Library); Warren French, editor.[49]

April 1952 (First selection) Thomas Merton "Sports without Blood. A Letter to Dylan Thomas" (poem) pp. 74–77 reprinted in *Garland;*[50] John Malcolm Brinnin "Carmarthen Bar" (poem) p. 159 reprinted in *Garland*

November 1952 (Second selection) Dylan Thomas "Adventures in the Skin Trade" pp. 158–189; May 1953 (Third selection) "Four Lost Souls" (continuation) pp. 192–207

* * *

April 1954 (Fifth selection) Dylan Thomas "The Followers" pp. 291–298; reprint of [Vernon Watkins] *Times* obituary pp. 298–301

April 1955 (Seventh selection) Dorian Cooke "In Memory of Dylan Thomas" (poem) pp. 109–110, reprinted in *Garland;* Dylan Thomas "Seven letters to Oscar Williams (1945–1953)" pp. 128–140; Dylan Thomas "After the Fair" and "The True Story" pp. 141–147; Charles Fenton "The Writer as Professor" pp. 163–170, Thomas mentioned p. 170

November 1956 (Tenth selection) Michel Manoll "A Sea Chant for Dylan Thomas" translated by Wallace Fowlie pp. 95–96

May 1957 (#11) Kenneth Rexroth "Disengagement: the Art of the Beat Generation" pp. 28–41;[51] Gerald Weales "The Poet as Player" pp. 231–243, Thomas pp. 233–234

---

48. Other student publications with reports of Thomas' readings include *Duke Chronicle* 1 May 1953 and 8 May 1953; *Vassar Chronicle* 13 May 1950 Iona Horowitz "Thomas Reads Modern Poetry By Well Known Contemporaries" pp. 2–3; *Vassar Miscellany News* Obituary by Barbara Swain 18 November 1953 p. 2.

49. Warren French "Six Years of *New World Writing*" *Twentieth Century Literature* January 1958 p. 190.

50. Previously printed in his *Selected Poems* London: Hollis & Carter, 1950; see also *The Secular Journal of Thomas Merton* New York: Farrar, Straus, Cudahy 1959 pp. 139, 161.

51. See also Rick Gelinas "Of Dylan Thomas. A Prophet with a Principle" *Razor's Edge* March 1958 pp. 2, 4.

CHICAGO TRIBUNE

Chicago daily.[52]

13 April 1952   Paul Engle review of *In Country Sleep* p. 5

5 April 1953   Paul Engle review of *Collected Poems* p. 4

28 June 1953   Vincent Starrett review of *Doctor & Devils*

2 May 1954   Paul Engle review of Olson p. 6

---

52. The only notable item we have from the *Chicago Sun-Times* is a review of Brinnin by Nelson Algren on 1 January 1956, "An Intimate Look at Dylan Thomas":

This reviewer's line of goods being prose, I was not intimately acquainted with the product being handled by the poetry trade in the fall of 1951. I felt myself on more solid ground in discussing beer than the avant garde.

My first concern, therefore, in meeting Dylan and Caitlin Thomas was to limit the conversation to the virtues of local brands of malt and hops.

Discoursing quietly yet commandingly—I had at that time a certain nasal quality that was not without its own peculiar charm—I advised my guests of my work with Michelob, Budweiser, Edelweiss and Schlitz.

I would have done better to stick to poetry. Thomas' own studies had been extended to Persian, Icelandic, Manx, Mexican, Frisian, Turkish and Moorish beers. He was a philosopher of beer, a prophet of beer, a John Foster Dulles of beer.

Outclassed, I made one last weak try. "Anyhow," I told him, "I once knew a man named Champaign who drank nothing but beer."

"I knew a man named Beers who drank nothing but champagne," Thomas assured me.

I decided I liked him whatever his trade, and we went forth in search of either beer or champagne. We found both.

I never saw Thomas after that night. But I began listening to his recordings that I had not till then heard. Before he died it was at last borne in upon me that I had been greatly privileged. I had been with a great man, the only great man I had ever known.

I had also been with a babyishly self-indulgent fellow carrying too much weight for his size. He was like a child who has discovered that it can have its own way by threatening a tantrum.

John Malcolm Brinnin has been sharply criticized for proving here that this man, too, was Dylan Thomas.

I do not think Brinnin has betrayed friendship in so doing, nor that his book is less a labor of love for that. I think the job he has done here needed doing, after the paeans and wails, that followed Thomas' death, of those who served him less generously in life than Brinnin.

The book sets the record straight that needed setting. And if the tone is injured, that is because its author got hurt. Thomas spared none but his enemies.

More than anyone, Brinnin made possible Thomas' American readings, though it meant accommodating every whim of a man playing the part of a satyr, whose wife was so overwhelmed by envy and fright that at one moment she cried out, "Is no man in America worthy of me?"

Where Brinnin's book disappointed me was that it offered no insight into what was driving Thomas so terribly. The character of Mrs. Thomas comes through more clearly.

Too clearly.

9 May 1954   Fanny Butcher news column

18 June 1954   Claudia Cassidy review of *Under Milk Wood* p. 54

19 December 1954   A. C. Ames review of *Quite Early* p. 3

5 June 1955   Elder Olson review of *Adventures* pt. 4 p. 7

27 November 1955   Elder Olson review of Brinnin p. 4

13 October 1957   Paul Engle review of *Leftover Life* p. 3

2 February 1958   Vincent Starrett review of *Letters to Vernon Watkins*

3 February 1963   Margaret H. Carpenter review of Emery

6 October 1963   Dan Herr review of *Beach of Falesá*

20 December 1964   William Stafford review of *Choice*

28 February 1965   William Stafford review of Ackerman, Holbrook, and Read

GOLDEN GOOSE

San Francisco.

May 1952   William Kolodney "Norman MacLeod and the Poetry Center" p. 187

September 1953   F.E. [Frederick Eckman] review of *Collected Poems* p. 85

BELOIT POETRY JOURNAL

Beloit College, Wisconsin, quarterly.

Summer 1952   Morris Greenhut review of *In Country Sleep* pp. 28–29

Summer 1954   Wright Booth "On the Death of Dylan Thomas" (poem) p. 17 reprinted in *Garland*

NEW YORK POST

5 April 1953   Paul Engle review of *Collected Poems*

19 December 1954   Paul Engle review of *Quite Early*

5 June 1955   Randall Jarrell[53] review of *Adventures*

20 November 1955   Dawn Powell review of Brinnin

6 October 1957   Dawn Powell review of *Leftover Life*

20 January 1964   Richard Watts Jr. review of *Dylan*

---

53. See also his *Poetry and the Age* New York: Knopf 1953 pp. 7, 8, 155.

24 October 1965 Passages from FitzGibbon

31 October 1965 Anon. review of FitzGibbon

BUFFALO EVENING NEWS

11 April 1953 Charles A. Brady review of *Collected Poems*

21 November 1953 Obituary

 8 May 1954 Charles A. Brady review of *Under Milk Wood* p. 7

11 December 1954 Charles A. Brady review of *Quite Early*

11 December 1963 David Posner review of *Entrances*

CLEVELAND PLAIN DEALER

12 April 1953 Don A. Keister review of *Collected Poems* p. 40d

13 June 1954 Don A. Keister review of *Under Milk Wood* and Olson p. 66d

24 May 1964 Peter Bellamy on a production of "Dylan" p. 1b

 3 January 1965 Abe C. Ravitz review of *Choice* p. 32e

12 November 1967 Abe C. Ravitz review of *Notebooks*

HARTFORD COURANT

12 April 1953 Samuel F. Morse review of *Collected Poems* p. 18

22 November 1953 Samuel F. Morse review of *Doctor & Devils* p. 18

 4 April 1954 Photo of Thomas with Oscar Williams p. 19

19 December 1954 Samuel F. Morse review of *Quite Early* p. 18

22 May 1955 Morse Allen review of *Adventures* p. 19

27 November 1955 Samuel F. Morse review of Brinnin p. 14

HARPER'S MAGAZINE

May 1953 Gilbert Highet, six lines of verse as a review of *Collected Poems* p. 96

July 1955 Marvin Barrett review of *Adventures* p. 89

October 1955 Randall Jarrell review of *Under Milk Wood* p. 96

January 1958 Lloyd Frankenberg "A Refusal to Mourn, Etc" (poem) p. 47 reprinted in *Garland*

August 1962 Caitlin Thomas "Not Quite Posthumous Letter to My Daughter" pp. 27–33

November 1965 Roderick Cook review of FitzGibbon pp. 132–133

WASHINGTON POST

3 May 1953   Announcing poetry reading[54]

20 December 1953   Paul Sampson review of *Doctor & Devils*

12 December 1954   Glendy Dawedeit review of *Quite Early*

7 August 1955   Glendy Dawedeit review of Stanford and *Adventures*

20 November 1955   Glendy Dawedeit review of Brinnin

13 October 1957   Glendy Culligan review of *Leftover Life*

BOSTON HERALD

21 June 1953   E.R. review of *Collected Poems*[55]

9 May 1954   John Finch review of *Under Milk Wood* and Olson

27 November 1955   Robert Taylor review of Brinnin

17 January 1965   George J. Pine review of Ackerman

CANADIAN POETRY MAGAZINE

Toronto quarterly of the Canadian Authors' Association;[56] Arthur S. Bourinot, editor.

Summer 1953   Arthur S. Bourinot review of *Collected Poems* p. 29

Winter 1953–1954   Curt Long "On the Death of Dylan Thomas" (poem) p. 9

February 1956   Alan Brown review of Brinnin pp. 257–258

AMERICAN MERCURY

July 1953   Frank Meyer review *Collected Poems* p. 143 "Thomas is boring in his brilliant emptiness"

January 1958   Harold Lord Varney review of Brinnin pp. 146–147; Nina N. Kann review of *Leftover Life* pp. 147–148

SATURDAY NIGHT

Toronto weekly news and critical magazine.

17 October 1953   Robertson Davies review of *Doctor & Devils* p. 26

26 June 1954   Robertson Davies review of *Under Milk Wood* pp. 24–25

---

54. The *Washington Star* also announced the reading on that day and had reviews by Mary McGrory: Brinnin on 27 November 1956; *Letters to Vernon Watkins* on 29 December 1957; and *Selected Letters* on 28 May 1967.

55. Reviewed by Edward Davison in *The Freeman* 15 June 1953 p. 676.

56. The association's quarterly *Canadian Author and Bookman* Spring 1954 had article "Man Like Lawrence—a New Look at Dylan Thomas" by R. C. Robbins pp. 5–6.

5 February 1955   Robertson Davies review of *Portrait* and *Quite Early* pp. 12–13

January 1965   Dan O'Neill "Letter from Wales" pp. 8–9

THE HARVARD CRIMSON

The newspaper of Harvard College.

4 November 1953   Michael Maccoby review of *Doctor & Devils* pp. 4, 6

29 April 1954   Arthur J. Langguth review of *Under Milk Wood* p. 3

ST. LOUIS POST-DISPATCH

22 November 1953   Richard E. Haswell review of *Doctor & Devils*

9 January 1955   Jack Aldridge review of *Quite Early*

8 June 1955   Webster Schott review of *Adventures*

13 November 1955   Thomas B. Sherman review of Brinnin

20 October 1957   A. Mervyn Davies review of *Leftover Life*

1 December 1957   Alexander M. Buchan review of *Leftover Life*

9 March 1958   Charles Gunther review of *Letters to Vernon Watkins*

9 July 1967   Reed Hynes review of *Selected Letters*

BOOKS ABROAD

University of Oklahoma quarterly.

Autumn 1953   Stanley K. Coffman review of *Collected Poems* p. 436

Autumn 1954   Hugh Corbett review of *Doctor & Devils* p. 438; review of Olson, p. 481

Spring 1955   Harriet Zinnes review of *Under Milk Wood* p. 176

Summer 1955   Harriet Zinnes review of *Quite Early* p. 309

Spring 1956   Harriet Zinnes review of *Adventures* p. 178

Autumn 1959   B. A. Park review of *Letters to Vernon Watkins* p. 417

HIGH FIDELITY

Phonograph technical and review monthly,[57] Great Barrington, Massachusetts.

November–December 1953   Edward T. Wallace "Caedmon's Girls" pp. 46–48

---

57. Similar record reviews include *American Record Guide* August 1964 "Alec Guinness as Dylan" pp. 1143–44; *Records & Recording* November 1958 F.G.B. on the Caedmon recordings p. 41

May 1954   R.H.H. Jr. on Caedmon recordings p. 64

June 1956   J.G. review of "Under Milk Wood" recording p. 71

July 1956   J.G. on Caedmon recordings p. 58

May 1958   J.G. review of Caedmon recordings p. 74

June 1964   O.B. Brummell review of Thomas recordings p. 65

NEW YORK TIMES

See *New York Times Index* for some news items not included here.

10 November 1953   Obituary p. 31

14 November 1953   "Poets Attend Rites" p. 17

22 November 1953   Letter from J.B. [Bonnyman] Jones p. 8

28 April 1954   Orville Prescott review of *Under Milk Wood*

16 May 1954   Brooks Atkinson on "Under Milk Wood" sec. II p. 1

12 November 1954   On *Yale Literary Magazine* special issue p. 23

15 December 1954   Orville Prescott review of *Quite Early* p. 29

26 December 1954   MSS and letters presented to Harvard by Oscar Williams p. 60

23 October 1955   Thomas Lask on "Under Milk Wood" recording

15 November 1955   Orville Prescott review of Brinnin p. 31

22 August 1956   W.A. Darlington on Edinburgh "Under Milk Wood" p. 25

6 October 1957   Emlyn Williams "Studying Dylan Thomas" sec. II p. 3

8 October 1957   Brooks Atkinson on Emlyn Williams p. 41

10 October 1957   Anon. review of *Leftover Life* p. 31

18 August 1958   Mrs. D.J. Thomas obituary p. 19

21 January 1959   MIT production of "Under Milk Wood" reviewed p. 27

30 March 1961   Circle in the Square "Under Milk Wood" p. 25; reviewed, 9 April 1961 sec. II p. 1 and 18 October 1961 p. 48

16 April 1961   C. Greenberg on Jackson Pollock, likens him to Thomas, p. 42; 30 April 1961 letters and Greenberg's reply p. 4

7 November 1963   Charles Poore review of *Not Quite Posthumous*

12 January 1964   Lewis Nichols on "Dylan" p. 63; 20 January 1964   Howard Taubman on "Dylan" p. 18

9 March 1966   Caitlin Thomas sues Douglas Cleverdon for recovery of "Under Milk Wood" MS p. 38; 12 March 1966 Dana Adams Schmidt "Court finds in favor of Cleverdon" p. 22

25 June 1967   Horace Gregory review of *Selected Letters* p. 5

AMERICA

New York Catholic weekly review founded in 1909.

12 December 1953   J. P. Clancy "Dylan Thomas: Promise Clipped" pp. 295–296

21 August 1954   T. P. McDonnell "The Emergence of Dylan Thomas" pp. 500–502

 1 January 1955   H. C. Gardiner "Welsh Chanter's Spell" review of *Quite Early* p. 363

 2 November 1957   J. P. Clancy review of *Leftover Life* pp. 139–140

12 April 1958   Philip Scharper review of *Letters to Vernon Watkins*

 8 January 1966   Edward F. Jost review of FitzGibbon

THE NEW LEADER

14 December 1953   Harvey Curtis Webster on *Doctor & Devils* p. 21

10 May 1954   Anon. review of Olson

 3 January 1955   Granville Hicks review of *Quite Early* pp. 23–24

26 December 1955   Granville Hicks "Dylan Thomas and George Orwell" pp. 16–17; 16 January 1956 letter from Robert Gorham Davis; 23 January 1956 letter from Hicks

 2 December 1957   Sonya Rudikoff review of *Leftover Life* p. 25

27 May 1963   John Simon review of Jack Howell's film p. 31

 6 December 1965   Herbert Leibowitz review of FitzGibbon pp. 24–26

 5 June 1967   George Woodcock review of *Selected Letters* pp. 18–20

MADEMOISELLE

February 1954   John Malcolm Brinnin[58] "Dylan Thomas and his Village" pp. 108–109; Dylan Thomas "Under Milk Wood" pp. 110–122, 144–156; photographs by Rollie McKenna[59]

February 1955   Dylan Thomas "The Vest" pp. 142–143

November 1955   John Malcolm Brinnin "Dylan Thomas' First Week in America" pp. 98–101, 161–172 with photos by Bunny Adler and Ray Shorr

July 1956   "Dylan Thomas on Reading his Poetry: Introduction to a Poetry Reading" pp. 34–37

---

58. See also *Vassar Alumnae Magazine* December 1951 John Malcolm Brinnin "Dylan Thomas in America" (BBC talk) pp. 12–15.

59. See also her photographs in *American Society of Magazine Photographers Picture Annual* 1957 pp. 94–101.

June 1966 "The Poetry Place: Poems by Dylan Thomas," five poems from the Buffalo notebooks edited by Ralph Maud pp. 84–85; "Letters: Dylan Thomas" pp. 99–101, 158–161

ARIZONA QUARTERLY

Winter 1954 George Woodcock "Dylan Thomas and the Welsh Environment" pp. 293–305

Spring 1955 George Woodcock review of *Quite Early* pp. 79–81

Spring 1956 George Woodcock review Brinnin pp. 87–88

Summer 1961 John Nist "Dylan Thomas: 'Perfection of the Work'" pp. 101–106

FILMS IN REVIEW

New York monthly.

March 1954 Robert Downing on *Doctor & Devils* pp. 150–151

January 1964 Alice H. Witham review of *Beach of Falesá* pp. 40–41

THE REPORTER

Fortnightly newsmagazine.

27 April 1954 Mary Ellis Barrett "A Luncheon with Dylan Thomas" pp. 45–48

14 November 1957 Marya Mannes on "Under Milk Wood" (Henry Miller Theatre) pp. 38–40

24 March 1966 Dylan Thomas "Resolutions for 1934" pp. 45–46, extracts from a letter

ORIGIN

Editor: Cid Corman, Boston, Massachusetts.

Spring 1954 (XII) William Carlos Williams "On Measure—Statement for Cid Corman" pp. 337–340: "Dylan Thomas is thrashing around somewhere in the wings but he is Welsh and acknowledges no rule—he cannot be much help to us":[60] Cid Corman "A Note on Dylan Thomas" pp. 256–258:

---

60. Included in his *Selected Essays* New York: Random House 1954 p. 338. See also his *Selected Letters* New York: McDowell, Obolensky 1957 pp. 278, 287–288:

I have found it impossible to go to hear Dylan Thomas while he was here. Just the dreamy look that comes into the eyes of our partial writers and so-called competent critics—who control the publicity columns of the avant garde forums and

It would not be unkind if, instead of the blatant haloings of his overamorous admirers, the equally-blatant blackwashing of so-called scrutinizers, and those one or two, like Kenneth Rexroth, who will use the man's death as lever for an attack on bourgeois society, some straight words are spoken.

Thomas often said more than he meant, but he always meant to be candid. And I can see no reason to treat him with less honesty than was his own intent. The first time I saw him and heard him read it was at Harvard in March of 1950. He had been drinking, although I don't know what else any sensitive man could be expected to do, not being an academic personage, to persist in such a milieu. No other escape was permissible. His face impressed me most, though he was bulkier and less angelic than the Augustus John frontispiece led me to believe. He was under tension undoubtedly. His lips were full as his face was round, fore and aft. A certain grossness. And that was good to see in such a place. His eyes, which slanted sadly at the edges ("as though he were crying" I noted later that day), were piercing and open. He was rude to Jack Sweeney who introduced him, but he had to say something to break into speech and that helped.

He read well. With deliberateness and practised resonance. And sincerely, with relish for what he chose to read. The accent was not, surprisingly, Welsh so much as it was English. And he would find himself tracing the rhythms and inflections with his right hand.

When he was loudly applauded at the end, he seemed genuinely astonished, perhaps because he had forgotten they were there.

I heard him again later that spring at Brandeis (he was still being floated about the country, increasing his audience, but, I suspect, earning very little, since he always gave as many public readings as private). He was this time even more intoxicated; and I heard later that he had drunk at every bar between Boston and Waltham. He had no desire to "perform," but he was pushed onto the stage (and later directed off). I don't tell this as though I were telling some clever gossip, since, in fact, this is not news at all. But I tell it to indicate Thomas's evidently unhappy state of mind and the fact that human sympathy does not actively go very deep in such situations. I noted briefly of him then: "He has the overwhelmed look of an unnecessarily hurt child."

He was, I think, that perpetual child with an ear for ditties and as though completely victimized by that moment when childhood fatefully recognizes, if it refuses to realize, that the cradle will not hold age back. Credit for his lovely childhood expressions, of and for the life of the child, remains a critical affirmation. That was and is his kingdom.

This comment is followed by Corman's verbatim record of Thomas' opening remarks at Brandeis.[61]

---

publications, has been enough for me. They drool at the mouth. And I think I'd like Thomas if I could get him alone. . . .

What they cannot see is that American poems are of an entirely different language and operate under a different compulsion. They are more authoritarian, more Druidic, more romantic—and they are, truly, more colorful. WE CAN'T AND MUST NOT WRITE THAT WAY.

61. Compare "Preface to a Reading" transcribed from a tape recorded at the University of California at Los Angeles in *Canto* (Vol. 1 No. 2) Spring 1960 pp. 11–12.

BLACK MOUNTAIN REVIEW

Black Mountain College, North Carolina; Robert Creeley, editor.

Spring 1954   M.S. [Martin Seymour-Smith] review of *Collected Poems* pp. 57–58

Fall 1954   R.C. [Robert Creeley] "Comment" on previous issue's anti-Thomas review p. 64

COLORADO QUARTERLY

Spring 1954   E. P. Bollier "Love, Death and the Poet—Dylan Thomas" pp. 386–407

Summer 1954   Forest Williams[62] "Dylan: Detour to Laugharne" pp. 94–95

RENASCENCE

Catholic Renascence Society, St.-Mary-in-the-Woods, Indiana.

Spring 1954   Charles F. Knauber "Imagery of Light in Dylan Thomas" pp. 95–96, 116

Autumn 1955   Charles F. Knauber review of *Under Milk Wood* pp. 52–54

Winter 1956   D.R. Howard "Then I Slept" review of *Child's Christmas*, Brinnin, and *Poetry* for November 1955 pp. 91–96

Spring 1957   Sister Mary Julian "Edith Sitwell and Dylan Thomas: Neo-Romantics" pp. 120–126, 131

Summer 1959   Samuel J. Hazo "The Passion of Wilfred Owen" p. 201

Winter 1960   John Logan "Dylan Thomas and the Ark of Art" pp. 59–66

Summer 1954   Sister M. Joselyn "Green and Dying: the Drama of 'Fern Hill'" pp. 219–221

WESTERN HUMANITIES REVIEW

Spring 1954   Ralph Maud review of Olson pp. 165–166

Autumn 1959   Bernice Slote and James E. Miller Jr. "Of Monkeys, Nudes and the Good Grey Poet: Dylan Thomas and Walt Whitman" pp. 339–353[63]

Autumn 1960   Edward A. Bloom[64] "Dylan Thomas' 'Naked Vision'" pp. 389–400

---

62. See also his review of *Selected Letters* in *Rocky Mountain News* 2 July 1967.

63. Included in their *Start with the Sun* (1960); see review by Gertrude M. White in the *Walt Whitman Review* December 1960 pp. 76–78; and Grace D. Yerbury "Of a City Beside a River; Whitman, Eliot, Thomas, Miller" in the issue of September 1964 pp. 67–73.

64. See also his article with Lillian D. Bloom "Dylan Thomas: His Intimations of Mortality" *Boston University Studies in English* Autumn 1960 pp. 138–152.

UNIVERSITY OF CHICAGO ROUND TABLE

18 July 1954 (#849)   Elder Olson,[65] Reuel N. Denny and Alan Simpson "The Poetry of Dylan Thomas" pp. 1–12

ENGLISH JOURNAL[66]

National Council of Teachers of English, Chicago.

September 1954   Anon. review of Olson p. 333

October 1954   David Daiches "The Poetry of Dylan Thomas" pp. 349–356

January 1955   Anon. review of Treece p. 57

February 1955   Anon. review of *Quite Early* p. 117

April 1956   K.W. Hunt review of Brinnin p. 232

January 1957   John T. Muri "The Use of Recordings in High School English Classes" p. 33; March 1957 Patrick D. Hazard on recordings p. 184

March 1958   Laura Jepson review of *Letters to Vernon Watkins* p. 175

May 1958   Anon. review of "Many Voices," a record to be used with *Adventures in Appreciation* New York: Harcourt, Brace 1958 p. 314

March 1962   Anon. review of "Anthology of Twentieth Century English Poetry" (Folkways Record) p. 229

January 1966   M.R. Jones "Wellspring of Dylan" pp. 78–82

December 1966   Jack L. Jenkins "How Green Is Fern Hill?" pp. 1180–82

January 1969   Mary C. Davidow "Journey from Apple Orchard to Swallow Thronged Loft: 'Fern Hill'" pp. 78–81

POETRY DIGEST

Waterbury, Connecticut.

October 1954   Alvin Winestock "In Memory of Dylan Thomas" p. 11

QUARTERLY JOURNAL OF SPEECH

October 1954   Gordon Lebert review of Olson p. 349

December 1966   Don Geiger review of FitzGibbon, Moynihan, and Cox pp. 400–401

---

65. Elder Olson's book on Thomas was reviewed in some magazines which gave no other attention to Thomas, including *New World* (Chicago) 3 September 1954; *Chicago Review* Fall 1954 M.J. Phillips pp. 112–118; *University of Chicago Magazine* November 1954; *U.S. Quarterly Book Review* September 1954; *University of Toronto Quarterly* July 1955; *Perspectives USA* Autumn 1954 p. 173; *Personalist* Spring 1955 pp. 213–214; *Nomad* (Canada) June 1954; *Living Church* 23 May 1954 and 26 September 1954; *The C.E.A. Critic* March 1954.

66. The first three items were reprinted from the sister journal *College English*.

CATHOLIC WORLD

November 1954   Sister Mary Christopher review of Olson pp. 159–160

February 1955   Beverly Boyd review of *Quite Early* pp. 396–397

December 1957   Euphemia Van Rensselaer Wyett on Emlyn Williams p. 228; Barbara LaRosa review of *Leftover Life* p. 238

July 1958   T. P. McDonnell "Who Killed Dylan?" pp. 285–289

January 1962   Sister Claude of Jesus "For Dylan Thomas" (poem) p. 229, reprinted in *Garland*

YALE LITERARY MAGAZINE

November 1954   Editorial comment by W.S.B. [W. S. Byler] p. [2]; Richard Eberhart "Some Memories of Dylan Thomas" pp. 5–6, reprinted in Tedlock; Statement by Marianne Moore p. 6; William Jay Smith "Life, Literature and Dylan" p. 7, reprinted in Tedlock; Babette Deutsch "For Dylan Thomas on the Day of his Death" (poem) p. 8 reprinted in *Garland*; José Garcia Villa "Death and Dylan Thomas" (poem) p. 9 reprinted in *Garland*; Marguerite Harris "Four Poems" pp. 10–12; Winfield Townley Scott "The Death, and Some Dominions of It" pp. 13–14 reprinted in *Casebook*; Kimon Friar "Dylan Thomas and the Poetic Drama" pp. 15–19; E. E. Cummings statement[67] p. 19; Alastair Reid "A First Word" p. 20 reprinted in Tedlock and *Casebook*; William Carlos Williams "Dylan Thomas" pp. 21–22[68]; Isabella Gardner "When a Warlock Dies" (poem) p. 22 reprinted in *Garland*; Joseph Tusiani "For Dylan Thomas on the Day of his Death" (poem) pp. 23–25; Kenneth Rexroth "Lament for Dylan Thomas" (poem) pp. 26–27 reprinted as "Thou Shalt not Kill" in *Garland*[69]; Wallace Fowlie "On the Death of Dylan Thomas" pp. 28–29; Horace Gregory "The Romantic Heritage of Dylan Thomas" pp. 30–34 reprinted in *Casebook*[70]

December 1955   Carl Morse review of Brinnin p. 26

NEWSWEEK

20 December 1954   Anon. review of *Quite Early* p. 86

28 November 1955   Anon. review of Brinnin pp. 18, 120–121

21 October 1957   Anon. review of "A Boy Growing Up" p. 99

28 October 1957   Anon. review of "Under Milk Wood," "A Boy Growing Up," Brinnin, and *Leftover Life* p. 96

---

67. The circumstances of this statement are recorded in Charles Norman *The Magic-Maker: E. E. Cummings* New York: Macmillan, 1958 pp. 347–348

68. Reprinted in his *Selected Essays* New York: Random House 1954 pp. 326–328.

69. After separate publication in a pamphlet (with the author's note) Goad Press, California, 1955.

70. From *Poetry* March 1947; revised for inclusion in his *The Dying Gladiator* New York: Grove Press 1961.

4 November 1963   Anon. review of *Not Quite Posthumous* pp. 105–106

27 January 1964   Anon. review of "Dylan" (N.Y.) pp. 58–59

1 November 1965   Anon. review of FitzGibbon p. 96

27 December 1965   Anon. review of FitzGibbon p. 73

22 May 1967   Jack Kroll review of *Selected Letters* p. 103

APPROACH

Rosemont, Pennsylvania, Spring 1947–Summer 1967; Albert and Helen Fowler, editors.

1954 (No.11)   Joseph Millar "Lullabye for Dylan" (poem) p. 6; Dachine Rainer "Dirge on the Death of Dylan Thomas" pp. 14–15

Winter 1959   Paris Leary "Letter from Oxford" pp. 14–16, 18

Winter 1962   John Nist "No Reason for Mourning; a Reading of the Later Poems of Dylan Thomas" pp. 3–7

AUDIENCE

Cambridge, Massachusetts.

4 February 1955   Ralph Maud "Dylan Thomas' manuscripts in the Houghton Library" pp. 4–6

15 April 1955   Ralph Maud "A Note on Dylan Thomas's Serious Puns" pp. 5–7

10 February 1956   Ralph Maud review of Brinnin pp. 6–8

PAPERS OF THE BIBLIOGRAPHICAL SOCIETY OF AMERICA

1st quarter 1955   William White review of Olson pp. 90–93[71]

1st quarter 1957   Gerald D. McDonald review of Rolph pp. 98–100

4th quarter 1958   William White "Dylan Thomas and A. E. Housman" pp. 309–310

3rd quarter 1966   William White "Dylan Thomas, Mr. Rolph, and 'John O'London's Weekly'" pp. 370–372

---

71. See also in the *Bulletin of Bibliography* September–December 1954 his review of Olson p. 103, and of *Under Milk Wood* p. 104; and in the issue of Winter 1957–1958 his review of Rolph p. 32. In the *American Book Collector* December 1967 he reviewed *Concordance, Notebooks,* and Min Lewis *Laugharne and Dylan Thomas* (1967) pp. 6–7.

TRACE

April 1955   Lawrence Lipton "Some Shop Talk on Poetry and Drama" p. 10; also August 1955 p. 19

August 1956   Martha Millet "The Quick and the Dead" pp. 4, 7

August 1957   James Russell Grant "Poetry and Mind" pp. 3, 6

February 1958   On West Coast Poetry and Jazz Festival "dedicated to" Thomas

February–March 1959   David Clay Jenkins[72] "Dylan Thomas and *Wales* Magazine" pp. 1–8

Summer 1962   Jean Burden "An Experiment in Creativity" pp. 229, 233 (Thomas recordings used in the classroom)

Autumn 1963   David Galloway "The Innocents Abroad" on *Portrait* pp. 257–259

Winter 1964   David Clay Jenkins "Dylan Thomas' *Under Milk Wood*: The American Element" pp. 325–338

THE PROGRESSIVE

October 1955   John M. Muste review of *Quite Early*[73] p. 47

POETRY PUBLIC

Chadron, Nebraska, quarterly.

October 1955–March 1956   L.R.H. [L. R. Holmes] "The Nonsense, Common Sense and Uncommon Sense of Poetry" pp. 1–4

ESQUIRE

December 1955   Dylan Thomas "A Child's Christmas in Wales" pp. 95–98

December 1957   A. T. Baker "The Roistering Legend of Dylan Thomas" pp. 201–209, reprints "Fern Hill" and "Lament"

December 1964   Dylan Thomas "Me and My Bike" pp. 146–149, 218, 221

December 1965   Dylan Thomas "Solace from Swansea" pp. 151, 280, 282–284, a letter to Trevor Hughes January 1933[74]

---

72. See also his "Poetry and Places: Dylan Thomas's Laugharne" *Eleusis of Chi Omega* (Quarterly of the Chi Omega Fraternity, Menashe, Wisconsin) February 1963 pp. 48–58.

73. Michael Harrington reviews this book in *The Catholic Worker* March 1955.

74. From *Selected Letters*. *McCall's* February 1966 has "Love Letters from a Poet to His Wife" pp. 73, 178, which were not included in *Selected Letters*.

WHETSTONE

Philadelphia, Pennsylvania.

Winter–Spring 1956   [Jack Lindeman and Edgar H. Schuster] "Letter from the Editors: A Note on Dylan Thomas" pp. 164–165

THE NATIONAL REVIEW

New York weekly journal of opinion.

11 January 1956   Edward Case review of Brinnin pp. 26–27

18 January 1958   R. Phelps on *Letters to Vernon Watkins* p. 69

11 February 1964   R. Bemis review of *Beach of Falesá* p. 122

THE VILLAGE VOICE

Greenwich Village, New York, weekly.

25 January 1956   Harvey Jacobs "D.T. in New York" (poem) p. 4

10 October 1956   Charles Marowitz on *Under Milk Wood* and photo of White Horse Tavern pp. 7, 10

24 September 1964   Melvin Shestack "The Day Dylan Died" pp. 6–7, 18

QUEEN'S QUARTERLY

Published since 1893 by Queen's University in Kingston, Ontario.

Spring 1956   William F. Blissett "Dylan Thomas: A Reader in Search of a Poet" pp. 45–48

Summer 1957   Clara Lander review of Treece pp. 290–291

Autumn 1958   Clara Lander "With Welsh and Reverent Rook: the Biblical Element in Dylan Thomas" pp. 437–447[75]

Autumn 1964   Derek Stanford "Dylan Thomas; A Literary Post-Mortem" pp. 405–418[76]

MODERN LANGUAGE NOTES

June 1956   Arnold Stein review of Olson pp. 455–57

February 1959   Ralph Maud "Dylan Thomas's First Published Poem" pp. 117–118 on "And death shall have no dominion"

---

75. *Dalhousie Review* Winter 1965–1966 has Thomas Saunders "Religious Elements in the Poetry of Dylan Thomas" pp. 492–497, and Evelyn J. Broy "The Enigma of Dylan Thomas" pp. 499–507.

76. Included in the revised edition (1964) of his book originally published in 1954. See also his "Dylan Thomas: Recollections and Assessment" *The Norseman* November–December 1955 pp. 423–427; and "Dylan Thomas's Animal Faith" *Southwest Review* Summer 1957 pp. 205–212.

December 1961 Elsie Leach "Dylan Thomas' 'Ballad of the Long-legged Bait'" pp. 724–728; Mark Spilka review of James E. Miller et al *Start with the Sun* (1960) pp. 892–96.

MAINSTREAM QUARTERLY

Palatine, Illinois; quarterly journal of poetry.

Spring 1957 Dylan Thomas Memorial Award to Robert S. Sward for "Home-Coming" p. 54

Winter 1958 Second Award to Curtis Zahn for "Experiment with Memory" p. 21

THE UNIVERSITY OF KANSAS CITY REVIEW

In 1963, new title: *The University Review.*

Summer 1957 James E. Miller Jr.[77] "Four Cosmic Poets" pp. 312–320

Summer 1967 Warren French "Two Portraits of the Artist: James Joyce's *Young Man*; Dylan Thomas's *Young Dog*" pp. 261–266

THE AMERICAN IMAGO

A Psychoanalytic Journal.[78]

Summer 1957 Burton S. Glick M.D. "A Brief Analysis of a Short Story" pp. 149–154 discusses "The Followers"

THE FLORIDA REVIEW

Fall 1957 Ruth de Bedts "Dylan Thomas and the Eve of St. Agnes" pp. 50–55

PRAIRIE SCHOONER

University of Nebraska quarterly; Karl Shapiro, editor.

Fall 1957 Mary Owings Miller "Dylan Thomas" (poem) p. 210; Robert Beum "Syllabic Verse in English" pp. 259–275

Spring 1958 Ralph Pomeroy "In Memory of Dylan Thomas" (poem) p. 44 reprinted in *Garland*

---

77. See also his "Whitman and Thomas: the Yawb and the Gab" in *English Institute Essays* 1960 pp. 137–163.

78. *Psychiatric Quarterly* has short anonymous reviews of *Under Milk Wood* in pt. 2 1954; of Brinnin October 1955; and of *Adventures* April 1957. By far the most substantial psychological analysis of Thomas is in a recent article by B.W. Murphy in the *British Journal of Medical Psychology* (Vol. 41) 1968 "Creation and Destruction: notes on Dylan Thomas" pp. 149–167.

Summer 1958   Bernice Slote review of *Letters to Vernon Watkins* pp. 85–86

Spring 1959   Jane Hill review of *Leftover Life* pp. 100–103

Summer 1963   William White[79] "Presenting an Unknown Dylan Thomas Piece" pp. 128–130; Rose Rosberg "A Visit to Laugharne" (poem) p. 258

Spring 1966   Gabriel Gersh review of FitzGibbon pp. 82–83

TAMARACK REVIEW

University of Toronto quarterly.[80]

Autumn 1957   Robert McCormack review of *Leftover Life* p. 91

Spring 1958   Anon. review of *Letters to Vernon Watkins* pp. 109–110

FRESCO

University of Detroit.

1958 (No. 9)   Robert L. Peters "The Uneasy Faith of Dylan Thomas: A Study of the Last Poems" pp. 25–29

PMLA

Publications of the Modern Language Association of America.

June 1961   Ralph Maud "Dylan Thomas' *Collected Poems:* Chronology of Composition" pp. 292–297

September 1963   Donald Tritschler "The Metaphoric Stop of Time in 'A Winter's Tale'" pp. 422–430

December 1964   William T. Moynihan "Dylan Thomas and the 'Biblical Rhythm'" pp. 631–647[81]

CARRELL

Journal of the friends of Miami University Library.

June 1961   Clark Emery[82] "Two-Gunned Gabriel in London" pp. 16–22

---

79. See also his "Unpublished Letters of Dylan Thomas" *Orient/West* September 1962 pp. 63–73; and his "Dylan Thomas and Henry Miller" *International Henry Miller Letter* December 1962 p. 11.

80. *University of Toronto Varsity* March 1955 had a review of *Quite Early* by Peter Grant.

81. See also his "The Auditory Correlative" *Journal of Aesthetics and Art Criticism* September 1958 pp. 93–102; his "Dylan Thomas' 'Hewn Voice'" *Texas Studies in Language and Literature* Autumn 1959 pp. 313–326; and his "Dylan Thomas's Conception of Poetry" *Forum* (Texas) Fall–Winter 1965 pp. 10–16.

82. See *Miami News* 20 January 1963   Fred Shaw "The World of Clark Emery" p. 6B and a review of Emery's book by William C. Doster.

EVERGREEN REVIEW

July–August 1961 (Vol. 5 No. 19)   Jerry Tallmer "The Magic Box" reference to Thomas on p. 117 as follows:

In fifteen years of watching television with erratic regularity, I have seen one moment of drama—apart from politics, investigations, etc.—which still sticks in my head. And it was not pre-packaged as such; it was almost an accident. The week that Dylan Thomas died, Alistair Cooke came on with an impromptu postscript at the conclusion of that Sunday's *Omnibus* program. With his customary urbanity he told us that a great poet had just died and that we would now hear the voice of Dylan Thomas reading, "Do Not Go Gentle Into That Good Night." Mr. Cooke bowed off, and on the screen they showed us a still photo of the poet from the jacket of one of his books. They held it there as that voice which was the voice of Thomas read its poem, and then as it neared the end of the poem they slowly backed the camera away from the photo to make the man seem to draw farther and farther away from *us*, and as it retreated it became smaller and smaller until finally it dwindled into a pinhole of light and then the pinhole winked out into complete darkness and the poem ended. It was—well, it was the way to do it.

TEXAS QUARTERLY

University of Texas, Austin; Harry H. Ransom, editor.

Autumn 1961   John Lehmann "English Letters in the Doldrums?" pp. 58–59, 63; Allan Rodway "A Note on Contemporary English Poetry" pp. 67–68

Winter 1961   Richard Jones "Dylan Thomas Country" pp. 34–42; Richard Jones introduction to "Poetic Manifesto" p. 44; Dylan Thomas, facsimile of MSS "Poetic Manifesto" pp. [45–52]; Vernon Watkins note to "A Painter's Studio" p. 54; Dylan Thomas "A Painter's Studio" pp. 54, 56–57;[83] Vernon Watkins "Swansea" pp. 59–64

Winter 1962   George Barker "Letter to the Poet, Gene Derwood" p. 40

Summer 1966   Bert Trick "The Young Dylan Thomas" (introduced by Bill Read) pp. 36–49

BALL STATE TEACHER'S COLLEGE FORUM

Muncie, Indiana; twice yearly; editor: Thomas Wetmore.

Spring 1963   Melvin Goldstein "A Source for Faulkner's 'Nobel Prize Speech of Acceptance' " ("In My Craft or Sullen Art") pp. 78–80

Autumn 1963   Naomi Christensen "Dylan Thomas and his Doublecross of Death" pp. 49–53

---

83. On p. 57 there is a sketch by Thomas of a figure at a bar. For similar drawings reproduced, see *The Transatlantic Review* Spring 1960 (No. 3) p. 24.

FILM CULTURE

Summer 1963 (No. 29)   Maya Deren, Parker Tyler, Dylan Thomas, and Arthur Miller "Poetry and the Film: A Symposium" pp. 55–63, transcribed from a discussion at Cinema 16 on 28 October 1953

UNION SEMINARY QUARTERLY REVIEW

March 1964   Tom F. Driver[84] review of Kleinman pp. 269–270

ALPHABET

Waterloo, Ontario.

June 1964   Peter Revell "Altarwise by owl-light" pp. 42–61

EMORY UNIVERSITY QUARTERLY

Summer 1964   Frank Manley "The Text of Dylan Thomas' *Under Milk Wood*" pp. 131–144[85]

WISCONSIN STUDIES IN CONTEMPORARY LITERATURE

Autumn 1964   Richard Ohmann "Criticism 1963 (Part II)" review of *Entrances* and Kleinman pp. 282–284

Autumn 1965   Richard Ohmann "Criticism 1964 (Part II)" review of *Druid* and T. H. Jones pp. 379–380

Summer 1967   Ralph Maud review of Moynihan pp. 450–453

CAVALIER

"A Man's Magazine." [86]

September 1964   Anatole Broyard "A Fling with Dylan" pp. 20–22, 33— reminiscences

THE NEW YORK REVIEW OF BOOKS

25 February 1965   John Wain[87] review of Ackerman, Read, and Holbrook pp. 12, 14–15

---

84. He reviewed "A Boy Growing Up" in *Christian Century* 30 October 1957 pp. 1288–89, and "Under Milk Wood" (Henry Miller Theater) 6 November 1957 p. 1324.

85. For a further discussion of this manuscript of the play, see *Yale University Library Gazette* July 1964 p. 54.

86. *Dude*, "A Man's Magazine," reprinted "Just Like Little Dogs" November 1958 pp. 6–8, 62–63.

87. See also his review article on FitzGibbon in *Commentary* April 1966 pp. 89–93.

9 December 1965   Conor Cruise O'Brien "The Dylan Cult" review of Fitz-Gibbon and Holbrook pp. 12; 3 February 1966   Letter from Constantine FitzGibbon and reply from Conor Cruise O'Brien p. 25

3 August 1967   Matthew Hodgart review of *Selected Letters* and *Concordance* pp. 19–22

THOTH

Department of English, Syracuse University.

Winter 1965   Louis K. Greiff "Image and Theme in Dylan Thomas' 'A Winter's Tale' " pp. 35–41

CHOICE

Books for college libraries.

June 1965   Anon. review of *Choice* p. 230

January 1966   Anon. review of FitzGibbon p. 770

April 1966   Anon. review of *Me & My Bike* p. 137

May 1968   Anon. review of *Selected Letters* p. 348

October 1968   Anon. review of Sinclair's *Adventures* p. 982

November 1968   Anon. review of *Notebooks* p. 1134

BUCKNELL REVIEW

March 1966   W. E. Yeomans "Dylan Thomas: The Literal Vision" pp. 103–115

SOCIAL EDUCATION

April 1966 (No. 4)   Arthur W. Brown review of FitzGibbon p. 299

THE UNIVERSITY OF DENVER QUARTERLY

Autumn 1966   Donald J. Cockerill review of *Druid* pp. 154–155

SEVENTEEN

November 1966   Elizabeth Brown (aged 18)[88] review of FitzGibbon p. 22

NATIONAL OBSERVER

15 May 1967   William Kennedy review of *Selected Letters* p. 21

---

88. For a second teen-age point of view, see Karen Crossen "I love you Dylan" *Ingenue* May–June 1959 pp. 59, 74.

NEW MEASURE

Spring 1967   Richard Burns "The Drunkard (in memory of Dylan Thomas)"
pp. 10–15

WALL STREET JOURNAL

8 June 1967   Edmund Fuller review of *Selected Letters*

ENGLISH LANGUAGE NOTES

March 1969   Joseph Anthony Wittreich "Dylan Thomas' Conception of Poetry: A Debt to Blake" pp. 197–200

SECTION V

FOREIGN-LANGUAGE PUBLICATIONS

FRENCH

L. Bonnerot   Review of *Twenty-five Poems* in *Études Anglaises* January 1937 p. 79

Dillon Fitzgibbon (pseud. Constantine FitzGibbon) trans. "The hand that signed the paper" *La Nouvelle Saison* (Vol. 1 No. 3) July 1938

Hélène Bokanowski trans. "The force that through the green fuse," "Light breaks," and "This was the crucifixion on the mountain" (sonnet VIII) *Fontaine* (Alger) (No. 25) November–December 1942 pp. 544–548; trans. with Armand Guibert "In Memory of Ann Jones" *Fontaine* (No. 37–40) 1944 pp. 441–443; trans. "A Winter's Tale" *Le Temps de la Poesie* (No. 3) Paris: GLM 1949 pp. 42–55

Francis Dufau-Labeyrie trans. "Perspective sur la Mer" *L'Arche* August–September 1946; trans. *Portrait de l'artiste en jeune chien* Paris: Éditions de Minuit 1947

R. Las Vergnas "Où va la Littérature anglaise?" *Les Nouvelles Littéraires* 9 January 1947 p. 1—report of interview with Thomas

Suzanne Roussillat "Dylan Thomas" (Thesis) Sorbonne 1947

Georges-Albert Astre "Un Jeune et Grand Poète Anglaise" *Critique* (Vol. 4, No. 20) January 1948 pp. 21–29—a review of *Deaths & Entrances, Selected Writings* and *Portrait;* ed. with introduction *Anthologie de la poésie anglaise contemporaine* Paris: L'Arche 1949—nine Thomas poems trans. by the editor and Armand Guibert, Jean-Jacques Mayoux, Jean Wahl pp. 186–211; trans. "Ears in the turrets hear" *Age Nouveau* (No. 49–50) May 1950 pp. 66–67

Roger Asselineau trans. Three poems in *Diadème* (No. 7) May–June 1948 pp. 51–54; article "Dylan Thomas" in *Études Anglaises* January 1954 pp. 89–100; review of *Quite Early, Adventures,* and *Prospect* in *Études Anglaises* July–September 1956 pp. 272–274

Jean Le Tailleux trans. "The Burning Baby" *Les Lettres Nouvelles* (No. 1) March 1953 pp. 31–37

Claude Legangneux "L'Enfant terrible de la Poésie anglaise contemporaine" *Journal des Poètes* June 1953 p. 3

Michel Habart Review of *Collected Poems* in *Critique* January 1954 pp. 85–87

Dominique Aury Obituary *La Nouvelle Revue Francaise* 1 February 1954 pp. 306–307

René Elvin Review of *Under Milk Wood* in *Les Nouvelles Littéraires* 8 April 1954 and review of Brinnin in issue of 17 May 1956

Armand Robin trans. Several poems in *La Nouvelle Revue Francaise* 1 September 1954 pp. 567–576

Roger Giroux trans. *Under Milk Wood* in three issues of *Les Lettres Nouvelles* (No. 23) January 1955 pp. 1–24, (No. 24) February 1955 pp. 235–249, (No.

25) March 1955 pp. 380–392; trans. "Tom Twp" *Les Lettres Nouvelles* 6 May 1959 pp. 15–20

Jean Markale   "La poésie de Dylan Thomas" *Cahiers du Sud* June 1955 pp. 86–90, trans. (with L.-G. Gros) poems pp. 91–97

Nicole Gauchon   "The Theme of Death and its Literary Expression in the Works of Dylan Thomas" Diplôme d'Études Supérieures, Université de Paris 1956

Jean Simon trans.   *Poèmes Choisis* (with introduction) Paris: Pierre Seghers 1957

A.-R. Tellier   Reviews in *Études Anglaises:* July–September 1958 review of *Leftover Life* pp. 270–271, review of *Letters to Vernon Watkins* pp. 271–272; April–June 1959 review of *Under Milk Wood* (acting version) pp. 180–181; July–September 1961 review of Tedlock pp. 261–262; October–December 1961 review of Sanesi pp. 371–372; July–September 1964 review of Holbrook pp. 296–297; October–December 1965 review of T. H. Jones, *Entrances*, Ackerman pp. 427–429; October–December 1968 review of Read p. 435. Publications de la Faculté des Lettres et Sciences Humaines de L'Université de Clermont, deuxième series, fasc. 18 *La poésie de Dylan Thomas: Thèmes et formes* Paris: Presses Universitaires de France 1963

Fernand Corin   "En Traduisant Dylan Thomas" *Revue des Langues Vivantes*[1] (Vol. XXV, No. 4) 1959 pp. 286–299

Michel Manoll   "Deux Chants de la Mer pour Dylan Thomas" *Mercure de France* August 1961

Jacques Coudol trans.   "A Prospect of the Sea" *Tel Quel* Winter 1961 pp. 69–75

Hélène Bokanowski and Marc Alyn   *Dylan Thomas* ("presentation" of texts, portraits, bibliography etc.) Paris: Pierre Seghers 1963

Cecily Mackworth   "Dylan Thomas et la double vision" *Critique* June 1963 pp. 500–516—review of *Collected Poems*, *Prospect*, *Portrait*, and Bokanowski and Alyn's *Dylan Thomas* (1963)

Monique Nathan trans.   *Un Noël d'enfant au Pays de Galles* Paris: Lettres Modernes 1967

SWEDISH

Artur Lundkvist   "Engelsk Lyrik under Kriget" *Bonniers Litterära Magasin* November 1944 pp. 770–775

---

1. Multilingual magazine published in Brussels; contained a review of Holbrook in English by J. Noel, Summer 1963 pp. 529–535.

John Hayward "Dylan Thomas. Brev fran London" *Bonniers Litterära Magasin* October 1953 pp. 604–607

Gerard De Geer trans. "The Followers" *Aub* July 1954 pp. 600–607 with note by Erik Lindegren

Östen Sjöstrand Review of *Quite Early* in *Stockholms-Tidningen* 13 November 1954

Erik Lindegren & Thorsten Jonsson trans. *Porträtt Av Konstnären Som Valp* Stockholm: Albert Bonniers 1954 (another edition 1963)

Editorial on Brinnin *Bonniers Litterära Magasin* February 1956 pp. 91–94

Harald Åström trans. *Äventyr i skinnbranschen* Stockholm: Raben & Sjögren 1956 with introduction by Folke Isaksson

Lasse Söderberg Review of the translated *Adventures* in *Bonniers Litterära Magasin* February 1957 pp. 170–171

Jan Berg trans. *19 Dikter* Stockholm: Albert Bonniers 1957

Thomas Warburton trans. *Intill Mjölkhagen* Stockholm: Albert Bonniers 1958

DUTCH

Max Schuchart "Moderne Engelse pöezie" *Het Woord* August 1946 pp. 278–283; trans. *Avonturen aan den Lijve* Rotterdam: Ad Donker 1959; trans. *Uitzicht op zee* Rotterdam: Ad Donker 1961

G. Sôtemann Review of *Doctor & Devils* in *Algemeen Handelsblad* 6 June 1953; review of Brinnin in *Algemeen Handelsblad* 20 May 1956

H. Bronkhorst Obituary *De Tijd* 28 November 1953

Moyra Calderott Obituary *Kronick van Kunst en Kultuur* 14 January 1954 pp. 97–100

Henk Tikkemeijer trans. *Gedichten* Amsterdam: De Beuk 1956 (another edition 1962)

Bert Voeten & Conrad Bonifazi "Dylan Thomas" *Wending* pp. 404–419

Eric Van Der Steen Review of *Letters to Vernon Watkins* in *Litterair Paspoort* January 1958 p. 15

Jacques Den Haan Article in *Litterair Paspoort* February 1958; review of Tedlock and Heppenstall in issue of January 1961 pp. 2–4

Hugo Claus trans. *Als Een Jonge Hond* Rotterdam: Ad Donker 1958; trans. *Onder het Milkwoud* Amsterdam: De Bezige Biji 1958

ITALIAN

Giorgio Melchiori trans. "Lie Still, Sleep Becalmed" and "In My Craft or Sullen Art" *Lettere D'Oggi* (Nos. 6–7) March–April 1947 p. [3] with note; "La poesia visionaria di D. Thomas" *Lo Spettatore Italiano* December 1953 pp. 547–557

Eugenio Montale trans. "The force that through the green fuse" in *Quaderno di Traduzioni* Milan: Edizioni della Meridiana 1948

Luigi Berti ed. Photographic facsimile of MS of "In country sleep" with translation by Tommaso Giglio and photographs of Thomas in Italy in *Inventario* Spring 1949 pp. 76–83; review of Brinnin in *Inventario* January–December 1956 pp. 284–289, and also in *La Fiera Letteraria* 14 July 1957 p. 5

A. Livi "Sugli scogli di Rio" *Inventario* Autumn 1949 pp. 154–156

Carlo Izzo ed. *Poesia inglese contempoaranea da Thomas Hardy agli Apocalittica* Modena: Guanda 1950—three poems pp. 448–453 with notes pp. 543–544; review of *Under Milk Wood* in *Gazetta del Popolo* 27 May 1955

Salvatore Rosati "Dylan Thomas Poeta Neoromantico" *Il Mondo* 27 December 1952 p. 6

Roberto Sanesi[2] "Sesso, nascita e morte in Dylan Thomas" *Aut-Aut* November 1953 pp. 529–540; trans. "In the white giant's thigh" *Aut-Aut* September 1954 pp. 406–413; trans. "A Winter's Tale" *Inventario* May–December 1954; trans. with introduction and notes *Poesie di Dylan Thomas* Parma: Ugo Guanda 1954 (reprinted 1962); "Il 'Portrait' e la prose di Dylan Thomas" *Aut-Aut* July 1955 pp. 316–318; "Nell 'intricata immagine di Dylan Thomas" *Inventario* January–December 1956 pp. 42–85; trans. parts of *Doctor & Devils* in *Cinema Nuovo* 15 December 1957 pp. 315–317; trans. *Poesie Giovanili* Milan: Edizioni del Triangolo 1958

Dylan Thomas Milan: Lerici edition 1960—full-length study with bibliography

---

2. As editor of *Poesia e Critica*, Sanesi compiled a special Dylan Thomas issue December 1963 (No. 5) containing the following: R.S. "Premessa" pp. 5–6; Cid Corman "For the Lovers" pp. 8–13 (trans. pp. 14–19); Giovanni Raboni "Omaggio a Dylan Thomas" pp. 20–23; Gilberto Finzi "Una Lunga, Continua Poesia" pp. 24–28; Mariapina Rizzi & Charles Haines "Dialogo Aperto" pp. 29–53; John Wain's review of *Collected Poems* trans. pp. 54–60; Guido Aristarco "A Proposito de 'Il Dottore e i diavoli' " pp. 61–69; Ruggero Jacobbi "Dylan Thomas Drammaturgo" pp. 70–75; Mario Corona "Notizie Sul Giovane Thomas" pp. 76–93;

Vernon Watkins "Research and Reperception" (on "I make this in a warring absence") pp. 94–99 (trans. pp. 100–106); Spartaco Gamberini, note on "I see the boys of summer" pp. 107–116; trans. of Thomas' "Reply to a Questionnaire" pp. 117–119; Roberto Sanesi ed. three early poems and a letter to Ralph Wishart pp. 120–133;

Mario Corona "Bibliografia" pp. 134–181, an extensive checklist, which should be consulted for some items in Italian periodicals in addition to those listed above (see also addenda to the checklist in issue No. 6–7 1965 pp. 272–273).

Trans. "Poesie giovanili" *L'Europa Letteraria* March 1960 pp. 40–42 with a note; trans. "Our Country" *L'Europa Letteraria* June–August 1961 pp. 198–200

Mario Praz "Ricordo di un poeta" *Il Tempo* 11 November 1953

Renato Poggioli "In memoriam di Dylan Thomas" *Letteratura* December 1953 pp. 84–87

Alfredo Rizzardi "Poesie di Dylan Thomas" *Corriere dell'Adda* 6 February 1954 and 20 February 1954

Claudio Gorlier "Dylan Thomas e il cinema" *Rivista di Cinema Italiano* October 1954 pp. 11–17

Lucia Rodocanachi trans. *Ritratto di Giovane Artista* Torino: Guilio Einaudi 1955 (the 1962 edition has translator's name as Maria Rodocanachi); trans. with F. Bossi, C. Izzo, A.Fanio *Prose e Racconti* Torino: Guilio Einaudi 1961

Alfredo Giuliani *Il cuore zoppo con sette versioni da Dylan Thomas* Varese: Editrice Magenta 1955

Ugo Varnai Review of Brinnin in *Communita* June–July 1956 pp. 61–62

Angela Biandioni "Caitlin all'Elba" *Il Mondo* 5 August 1958 p. 9

Mario Lavagetto "Ritorno a Dylan Thomas" *Palatina* (Vol. V) 1961 pp. 45–55

Giorgio Manganelli "Prose e racconti di Dylan Thomas" *L'Illustrazione Italiana* August 1961 pp. 70–71

Vanna Gentili trans. with others *Molto presto di mattina* Torino: Guilio Einaudi 1964; "Il mondo rappreso di Dylan Thomas" *Paragone* (Vol. 202) 1966 pp. 15–41

Ariodante Marianni trans. with Alfredo Giuliani *Dylan Thomas Poesie* Torino: Guilio Einaudi 1965

Giovanna Capone *Drammi per voci: Dylan Thomas, Samuel Becket, Harold Pinter* Bologna; Patron 1967

GERMAN

Kurt Heinrich Hansen trans. "Poem in October" and "Fern Hill" *Merkur* (1948 No. 2) pp. 188–193

Reinhard Paul Becker "Ein neuer Englischer Lyriker" *Die Literatur* 1 January 1952 p. 5; trans. *Tode und Tore* (*Deaths & Entrances*) Heidelberg: F. H. Kerle [1952]

Erich Fried trans. *Unter dem Milchwald* Heidelberg: Drei Brücken 1954 (Rororo edition with additional material 1958); trans. "A Visit to America" and "Crumbs of One Man's Year" *Texte und Zeichen* (No. 2) 1955 pp. 186–196; trans. "I will now read aloud" *Merkur* January 1957 pp. 30–37; trans. *Am Frühen Morgen* Heidelberg: Drei Brücken 1957; trans. *Der Doktor und die Teufels* Frankfurt: S. Fischer 1959; trans. with Enzio von Cramon *Ein Blick aufs Meer* Heidelberg: Drei Brücken 1961; trans. *Eines Kindes Weihnacht in Wales* Heidelberg: Drei Brücken 1966; trans. *Ausgewählte Gedichte* Munich: Carl Hanser 1967

Helmut M. Braem "Dylan Thomas" in Hermann Friedmann & Otto Mann eds. *Christliche Dichter Der Gegenwart* Heidelberg: Wolfgang Rothe 1955 pp. 254–266

Hildegard Pruischütz *Sensualismus als Stilelement in der Modernen Anglo-Walisischen Prosadichtung* Inaugural-Dissertation der Philosophischen Fakultät der Friedrich-Alexander-Universität zu Erlangen 1955

Wolfgang Schmeditz "'. . . als ein Weg des Schicksals, als eine Stimme'" *Salzburger Nachrichten* 4 April 1956, article on Yeats and Thomas

Henning Rischbieter trans. "Fern Hill" and article on *Under Milk Wood Die Volksbühne* September 1957 pp. 33–41

Günter Blöcker "Zu Dylan Thomas 'Unter dem Milchwald'" *Akzente* (Munich) February 1959 pp. 89–95

Dieter Kappus *Die dichterische Entwicklung von Dylan Thomas* Ph.D. dissertation University of Albert-Ludwigs, Freiburg 1960

Johannes Bobrowski "Dylan Thomas" (poem in German) *Merkur* October 1960 p. 947

Horst Oppel Review of Tedlock in *Die Neueren Sprachen*[3] 1961 (Heft 7) pp. 340–341; ed. *Die moderne englische Lyrik: Interpretationen* Berlin: E. Schmidt 1967, on "In My Craft or Sullen Art" and "A Refusal to Mourn" pp. 244–261

Hans Combecher "Interpretationen zu drei Gedichten von Dylan Thomas" *Die Neueren Sprachen* 1962 (Heft 3) pp. 130–142; "Tod und Transzendenz in zwei Gedichten von Dylan Thomas" *Die Neueren Sprachen* December 1963 pp. 554–562

Horst Meller "Zwischen Laugharne und Llaregyb: zur Entstehungsgeschichte von Dylan Thomas' 'Under Milk Wood'" in *Festschrift für Walter Hübner* Berlin: Schmidt 1963 pp. 327–336; "Zum literarischen Hintergrund von Dylan Thomas' *Under Milk Wood*" *Die Neueren Sprachen* February 1966 pp. 49–58 (see *Abstracts of English Studies* November 1966 p. 593)

Roland Hill "Naturgott aus Wales?" *Frankfurter Allgemeine Zeitung* 9 December 1964, discussion involving Kleinman, *Entrances*, and *Druid*

---

3. This bilingual monthly published, in English, C. Barry Hyams & Karl H. Reichert "A Test Lesson on Dylan Thomas's Poem 'The Hand that Signed the Paper'" 1957 (Heft IV) pp. 173–177; and Richard Martin "For the love of man and in praise of God: An evaluation of Dylan Thomas' poem 'This bread I break'" March 1964 pp. 133–136.

Nikolaus Happel "'The force that through the green fuse'" *Die Neueren Sprachen* September 1968 pp. 433-438

DANISH

Jørgen Andersen trans. "Poem in October" *Ord och Bild* (No. 58) 1949 pp. 321-322; trans. with Jørgen Nash *Portraet Af Kunstneren Som Hvalp* Copenhagen: Gyldendal 1955; trans. with others *Rejsen Tilbage* Fredensborg: Arena-Fortatternes 1958

Jørgen Nash trans. "Fern Hill" and "A Refusal to Mourn" *Dialog* (No. 3) 1950, included in anthology *Vredens Sange* Copenhagen: Borgen 1951; trans. "Poem in October" *Dialog* (No. 5) September 1952 pp. 6-7; trans. *Forår i Milk Wood* Copenhagen; Gyldendal 1956

Harald Sverdrup "Møte Med Dylan Thomas" *Vinduet* (Vol. 5 No. 6) 1951 pp. 476-480, report on his visit to Thomas at Oxford July 1948

Erik Thygesen trans. *En Pelshandlers Eventyr* Copenhagen: Steen Hasselbalchs 1965

POLISH

Andrzej Nowicki & Krystyna Tarnowska trans. "Under Milk Wood" in *Dialog* (No. 4) 1954 pp. 49-78

JAPANESE

Masao Nakagiri trans. Several poems in *Shigaku* November 1954 pp. 25-35; further translations and comment in issue of December 1957 pp. 18-23

Ichiro Nishizaki & Nobuko Suto eds. *Quite Early One Morning* Tokyo: Hokuseido 1956—preface and notes in Japanese

Naomi Matsu-ura trans. *Dylan Thomas Shishu* Tokyo: Eureka-sha 1960

Ichiro Ando "Dylan Thomas and His Poetic World" in Japanese with English summary in *Area and Culture Studies* (Tokyo University) (No. 11) 1964 pp. 1-47, 173

NORWEGIAN

Lorentz Eckloff   Review of *Doctor & Devils* in *Dagbladets* 2 February 1955; review of *Portrait, Collected Poems,* and Olson in *Dagbladets* 18 March 1955

Inger Hagerup trans.   *Milk Wood* Oslo: J. W. Cappelen 1956

SPANISH

SPAIN

Esteban Pujals trans. with introduction   *Poemas* Madrid: Ediciones Rialp 1955

Jorge Ferrer-Vidal trans. with introduction   *Poemas Escogidos* Madrid: Agora 1958

M. Manent trans.   Three poems in *La Poesía Inglesa* Barcelona: José Janés 1958

José Alberich   "Una Ojeada a Dylan Thomas" *Arbor* 1958 (Vol. 39) pp. 74–87

PUERTO RICO

Maria Teresa Babin   "Poesia y Muerte di Dylan Thomas" *Asomante* (University of Puerto Rico) July–September 1954 pp. 27–33 with trans. of "Do not go gentle"

MEXICO[4]

Ramón Xirau trans.   Three poems in *Universitidad de Mexico* February 1958 pp. 5–6

Luisa Josefina Hernandez trans.   *El Doctor y Los Demonios* Xalapa, Mexico: Ficción Universidad Veracruzana 1960

Anon. trans.   "A Child's Christmas in Wales" *el cuento* December 1964 pp. 29–34

ARGENTINA

Juan Angel Cotta trans.   *Con distinta piel* Buenos Aires: Jacobo Muchnik Editor 1957; trans. *Retrato del artista cachorro* in same series 1957

---

4. The following appeared in the English language *Mexico City News:* 30 May 1954 Neil Smith review of *Under Milk Wood* and reminiscences p. 2B; 26 December 1954 Irene Nicholson review of *Quite Early;* 19 January 1958   Donald Demarest review of *Letters to Vernon Watkins* p. 8A.

Anibal C. Goñi "El Poeta de Fern Hill" *Sur* (Buenos Aires) July–August 1958 pp. 27–35 with trans. of "Fern Hill" by Félix della Paolera pp. 35–37

Juan Rodolfo Wilcock Review of *Letters to Vernon Watkins* in *Ficción* (Buenos Aires) May–April 1959

Victoria Ocampo & Felix della Paolera trans. *Bajo el Bosque de Leche* Buenos Aires: Editorial Sur 1959

Alejandro Tarnopolsky Review of Brinnin in *Ficción* January–February 1960 pp. 142–143

FINNISH

Aatos Ojala On *Under Milk Wood* in *Kirjallisuudentutkijain Vuosikirirja* (Helsinki) (No. 15) 1956 pp. 139–163

Tuomas Anhava trans. Selection from *Under Milk Wood* in *Parnassus* (Helsinki) (No. 2) 1959 pp. 74–82

Veli Sandell trans. *Taiteilijan Omakuva Penikkavuosilta* Turku: Kustannuslüke Tajo 1963

CZECH

Jiřina Hauková trans. Several poems in *Svetová literatura* (No. 4) 1956; trans. *Zvláště Když Řijnový Vitr* Prague 1958, selected poems with an essay by Josef Skvorecký; trans. "Doktor a běsi" *Svetová literatura* (No. 2) 1960 pp. 26–90

Petr Pujman trans. *Portrét Umělee Jako Štěněte* Prague 1961

YUGOSLAV

Miodrag Pavlovic & Svetozav Brkic eds. *Antologija Savremene Engliske poezije* Belgrade 1957, six poems with discussion pp. 66–73

Branka Petrovich trans. *Pripovetke* Belgrade: Prosveta 1961

Nikico Petrak trans. *Poezija* Zagreb 1964

Anon. trans. *Pod Mleonom Sumon* Belgrade 1964

HUNGARIAN

Ágnes Gergely "Dylan Thomas költészete" *Filológiai Kozlony* January–March 1958 pp. 79–97; trans. *Az iro arckepe kolyokkutya korabol* Budapest: Europa Könyvkiadó 1959

Bányay Geyza trans. *A Mi Erdönk Alján* Budapest 1960

PORTUGUESE

Alfredo Margarido trans. *Retrato do artista quando jovem cão* Lisbon: Edicao Livros do Brasil 1961; "A Paródia do 'Jovem Cão' de Dylan Thomas" *LBL* (Brazil)

INDEX

Index

Abbreviations used in this volume are found in alphabetical order in boldface type.

Abbott, Charles D., 15
Abercwmboi, Shinkins, 61
Aberpennar, Davies (= Pennar Davies), 61, 70, 84
Abertawe, Evan (= John Jennings), 67, 68
Abse, Dannie, 27, 101, 151, 156n, 171
Abstracts of English Studies, 222
Accent, 184–185
Ackerman = John Ackerman *Dylan Thomas: His Life and Work* (1964), 37, 56, 66, 76, 79, 80, 83, 103, 106, 112, 119, 127, 128, 129, 129n, 132, 143, 148, 153, 164, 164n, 182, 184n, 192, 195, 197, 212, 218
Ackroyd, Graham T., 112, 132
Adam, 15n, 45n, 62, 93n, 144–145
Adams, Frederick B., 156n
Adams, J. Donald, 180, 188
Adams, Phoebe, 178, 179
Adams, Robert Martin, 190, 190n
Adelphi, 68, 94–95
Adix, Marjorie, 156, 156n
Adler, Bunny, 200
Adult Education, 162
"Adventure from a Work in Progress, An," 25, 123
"Adventures in the Skin Trade," 25, 135, 145, 154, 193
"Adventures in the Skin Trade" (play by Andrew Sinclair), 79, 106, 131, 142
Adventures = Dylan Thomas *Adventures in the Skin Trade* (1955, and later editions), 25, 26, 40, 101, 102, 105, 112, 113, 115, 116, 117, 119, 120, 127, 127n, 128, 130, 132, 134, 142, 143, 145, 152, 153, 157, 159, 160, 163n, 169, 172, 173, 174, 175, 176, 177, 179, 180, 181, 182,
185, 186, 192, 195, 196, 197, 198, 209n, 217, 219, 223
"After the Fair," 25, 87, 193
"After the funeral," 6, 9, 11, 13, 17, 20, 39, 185
Agate, James, 126, 126n
Agee, James, 180
Age Nouveau, 217
Aiken, Conrad, 168, 168n, 175, 175n, 178
Aivaz, David, 16, 190
Akzente, 222
Alberich, José, 224
Aldington, Richard, 9, 10
Aldridge, Jack, 198
Algemeen Handelsblad, 219
Algren, Nelson, 194n
"All all and all the dry worlds lever," 3, 19
Allen, Charles, 127
Allen, Jane, 88
Allen, Morse, 196
Allen, Walter, 101, 111, 111n, 112, 132, 181
Allott, Kenneth, 17
Allsop, Kenneth, 154, 154n
Alphabet, 212
"Altarwise by owl-light" (= "Sonnets"), 6, 9, 19, 39, 121, 185, 190, 212
Alvarez, A., 92, 122, 157
Alves, W. M. J., 106
Alyn, M., 218
Amateur Stage, 158n
Ambit, 153n
Ambler, Eric, 88
America, 200
American Book Collector, 206n
American Imago, 209
American Mercury, 197

American Record Guide, 198n
American Scholar, 188–189
Ames, A. C., 195
"Amherst Poet, The," 101
Amis, Kingsley, 105, 105n
"Among Those Burned to Death was a Child Aged a Few Hours," 64
"Among Those Killed in the Dawn Raid," 11, 13, 20, 107, 185
Anchor Review, 15n
"And death shall have no dominion," 9, 10, 11, 12, 13, 19, 28, 34, 67n, 87, 87n, 185, 208
Andersen, Jørgen, 223
Anderson, Patrick, 168
Ando, Ichiro, 223
Andrews, Allen, 142
Anglo-Welsh Review, 75–76
Angry Penguins Broadsheet, 141n
Anhava, Tuomas, 225
Anstey, Edgar, 104
"Answers to an Enquiry," 95
Antioch Review, 184n
Ap Gwilym, Dafydd, 82n
Apollo, 152n
Approach, 206
Arbor, 224
Arche, 217
Archer, Thomas, 105
Area & Culture Studies, 223
Argonaut, 172n
Aristarco, Guido, 220n
Arizona Quarterly, 201
Arlott, John, 15, 95, 104, 105
"Armistice Day," 46
Armitage, Gilbert, 121
Armstrong, Martin, 89, 90, 91
Arnold, Lilian, 96
Arrowsmith, William, 190
Artesian, 29n
Arthur, David, 128
"Artists of Wales," 23, 157
Arts in Society, 169n
Aryan Path, 163n
Ashcroft, Peggy, 102
Asomante, 224
Asselineau, Roger, 217
Aston, Alasdair, 163, 163n
Astre, Georges-Albert, 145, 217
Åstrom, Harald, 219
Athenaeum Club, 114n
Atkin, Rev. Leon, 64, 82
Atkins, A. H., 88
Atkinson, Brooks, 199

Atkinson, Frank, 144
Atlantic, 150, 178–179
Atthill, Robin, 148
Atwater, Mary M., 99
Aub, 219
Auden, W. H., 15, 15n, 51, 96, 100, 109, 115, 124, 167, 176
Audience, 206
"August Bank Holiday," 178
Aukland Star, 146
AUMLA, 164n
Aury, Dominique, 217
Ausonia, 159n
Austin, Hugh, 99
Austin, Richard, 163n
Austin, Tony, 65
Aut-Aut, 160n, 220
"Author's Prologue" (= "Prologue"), 18, 33, 90
Avirett, Barbara, 175
Avison, Margaret, 183
Ayrton, Michael, 12, 118, 130, 144, 147

Babin, Maria Teresa, 224
Bailey, H. C., 98
Bain, Bruce, 128
Baistow, Tom, 117
Baker, A. T., 207
Baker, Denys Val, 11, 14, 16, 70
Baldwin, Michael, 161
"Ballad of Salad, A," 46
"Ballad of the Long-legged Bait," 10, 11, 13, 15, 20, 31, 32, 39, 129, 160, 170, 174, 185, 186, 209
Ballard-Thomas, David, 151
Balliett, Whitney, 172
Balloon Site 568 (film), 136
Ball State Teachers College Forum, 211
Band Wagon, 149
Baner, 80
Banister, Elsie M., 118
Banyard, Grace, 122
Baptist Times, 105
Barcynski, Countess, 82, 82n
Barcynski, Count Nicholas, 64
Bard Review, 187
Barker, Eric, 178, 178n
Barker, Frank Granville, 158
Barker, George, 7, 14, 16, 29, 90, 92, 96, 120, 144, 156, 157, 167, 168, 170, 211
Barn, 83–84
Barnes, Djuna, 122, 184
Barnes, William, 33
Baro, Gene, 169, 173, 178

"Baroness Journeys Into Gower, A," 57
Barrett, Christopher, 46, 47
Barrett, Marvin, 179n, 196
Barrett, Mary Ellis, 201
Barrows, John, 97
Barry, Gerald, 47
Bartholomew, R. L., 155
Bartlett, Phyllis, 185, 185n
Bateman, David, 62, 64
Bates, H. E., 10, 97, 122
Bateson, F. W., 159, 159n
Battenbo, J., 56
Baum, Bernard, 168
Bayley = John Bayley *The Romantic Survival* (1957), 29, 158
BBC (= British Broadcasting Corporation), xi, 14, 22, 51, 53, 54, 55, 56, 62, 63, 75, 77, 89–92, 94, 111, 115, 119, 120, 122, 130, 132, 153, 154, 168, 169, 200n
BBC Quarterly, 91n
"Beach of Falesá," 191
Beach of Falesá = Dylan Thomas *The Beach of Falesá* (1963, and later editions), 33, 79, 92, 103, 106, 112, 128, 131, 161, 163n, 172, 173, 175, 177, 182, 187, 192, 195, 201, 208
Beardsley, Monroe C., 189
Beatitude, 35
"Because the pleasure-bird whistles," 11, 20, 61, 121, 123, 126, 170
Becker, Reinhard Paul, 221
Beckett, Samuel, 88, 221
Beeching, Jack, 128
Beedham, Brian, 143
"Before I knocked," 3, 19
"Before we mothernaked fall," 87
Behan, Brendan, 106, 179
Beharrel, Leo, 132
Bell, Adrian, 105
Bell, David, 55
Bell, H. Idris, 71n
Bell, 163n
Bellamy, Peter, 196
Bellerby, Frances, 163
Beloit Poetry Journal, 195
Bemis, R., 208
Benét, William Rose, 176
Bennett, Joseph, 190
Bentall, R. G., 157
Beresford, J. D., 113
Berg, Jan, 219
Berger, John, 128
Bergonzi, Bernard, 92, 105, 150
Berlin, Sven, 120

Berry, Rex, 155n
Berryman, John, 170, 171
Berti, Luigi, 220
Bertram, Anthony, 151
"Best of All," 46, 144
Betjeman, John, 115, 132, 142, 147
Beum, Robert, 209
Bevan, Hugh, 83
Bevington, Helen, 35
Beynon, Bleddyn, 79
Bhartrihari, 162
Biandioni, Angela, 221
Birch, Edwin, 152
Birmingham Gazette, 129n
Birmingham Post, 128, 129n
"Birthday Poem," 107
Bittner, William, 177
Bjerknes, Chris, 36n
Blackburn, Thomas, 32
Blackfriars, 149
Black Mountain Review, 203
Blake, William, 149n, 214
Blakestone, Oswell, 153, 153n
Blast, 149n
Blissett, William F., 208
"Blithe Spirits," 119
Bliven, Naomi, 172
Blöcker, Günter, 222
Bloom, Edward A., 203, 203n
Bloom, Lillian D., 203n
Boatwright, James, 192
Bobrowski, Johannes, 222
Bode, Carl, 122
Bodenheim, Maxwell, 128n
Bodenstein, Beatrice E., 27
Bogan, Louise, 171, 171n, 172
Bokanowski, Hélène, 217, 218
Bollier, E. P., 203
Boltz, C. L., 12
Bonifazi, Conrad, 219
Bonnerot, L., 217
Bonniers Litterära Magasin, 218, 219
Book Collector, 161
Bookman, 97
Book reviews, 68, 68n, 88, 94, 95, 97, 98, 99, 100, 101, 119, 122
Books, 144n
Books Abroad, 198
Books & Bookmen, 160–161
"Books and People," 68
Book Week, 173
Booster, 123
Booth, Wright, 195
Boothby, Robert, 105

Boothroyd, J. B., 153
Borshell, Allan, 156n
Bossi, F., 221
Boston Herald, 197
Boston Transcript, 172n
Boston University Studies in English, 203n
Botteghe Oscure, 150
Botterill, Dennis, 108, 143
Bottomly, Gordon, 108
Bottrall, Ronald, 145
Bourinot, Arthur, 197
Bourne, Mark, 110
Bowden, R. H., 143
Bowen, Alexander, 78
Bowen, Elizabeth, 4, 109, 131
Bowen, Euros, 80, 80n, 83, 84
Box, Leonore, 38, 41
Box, Sidney, 38
Boyd, Beverly, 205
Boyers, Arthur, 154
"Boy Growing Up, A" (stage performance). *See* Williams, Emlyn
Boyle, Kay, 88, 174
Boy's Own Paper, 87, 87n
Bozman, E. F., 116, 144, 144n
Bozman, M. M., 12
Brace, Keith, 129
Bradbury, Malcolm, 113, 114
Bradley, Ernest, 178
Brady, Charles A., 196
Braem, Helmut M., 222
Brahms, Caryl, 106, 158
Brande, Dorothea, 99
Brandt, Bill, 135, 191
Branston, Ursula, 151
Brecon, David, 83
Breit, Harvey, 157, 168, 180, 180n, 181
"Brember," 47
Bridger, John, 118
Bridson, G. D., 168
Brierley, Walter, 88
Brinnin, John Malcolm, 14n, 18, 31, 35, 49n, 173, 176, 179, 180, 193, 194n, 200, 200n. *See also* **Casebook**
Brinnin = John Malcolm Brinnin *Dylan Thomas in America* (1955, and later editions), 26, 55, 63, 69, 75, 79, 82, 91, 101, 102, 102n, 105, 110, 112, 113, 115, 116, 117, 118, 119, 120, 121, 122, 126, 127, 127n, 128, 129, 129n, 132, 133, 134, 134n, 142, 142n, 143, 143n, 145, 146, 146n, 151, 152, 153, 154, 155, 156, 157, 158, 159n, 160, 161, 170, 173, 174, 175, 177, 179, 180, 184, 188n, 189, 191, 192,

194n, 195, 196, 197, 197n, 198, 199, 201, 203, 204, 205, 206, 208, 209n, 219, 220, 221, 225
Britain Today, 145
British Annual of Literature, 141
British Book News, 151–152
British Film Institute, xi, 140
British Journal of Medical Psychology, 209n
British Museum Quarterly, 89n
British Poetry Association, 62n
British Weekly, 155
Brittain, Robert, 164
Brkic, Svetozov, 225
Broadsheet, 69n
Brockway, J. T., 147
Bronkhorst, H., 219
Brooke-Rose, Christine, 30, 152
Brooklyn Eagle, 172n
Brooks, Cleanth, 17
Brooks, Elmer L., 185
Brossard, Chandler, 181
Brown, Alan, 183, 197
Brown, Arthur W., 213
Brown, Elizabeth, 213
Brown, Harry, 182
Browne, Douglas G., 99
Brownlow, Timothy, 149n
Broy, Evelyn J., 208n
Broyard, Anatole, 212
Brummell, O. B., 199
Buchan, Alexander M., 198
Bucknell Review, 213
Bude, John, 98
Buffalo Evening News, 196
Bulletin of Bibliography, 206n
Bullett, Gerald, 96, 156
Bullough, Geoffrey, 10, 128
Bunker, Robert, 188
Burden, Jean, 207
Burdette, Robert Kenley, 38
Burgess, Anthony, 106
Burgess, C. J., 63
Burnaby, Nigel, 98
"Burning Baby, The," 7, 9, 13, 25, 110, 170, 217
Burns, Richard, 214
Burton, Miles, 99
Burton, Phillip, 145
Burton, Richard, 115n, 173
Butcher, Maryvonne, 151
Butcher, Fanny, 195
Butler, Frank A., 189
Butts, Mary, 88

Byler, W. S., 205
Bynner, Witter, 175
Byrde, Richard, 108
Byrne, Barry, 181
Bystander, 131

Caedmon Records, 97, 176, 177, 186, 198, 198n, 199
"'Caesar's Wife' At Swansea," 57
Caetani, Marguerite, 150
Cafyn, Cornelius, 98
Cahiers du Sud, 218
Cahoon, Herbert, 192
Calder-Marshall, Arthur, 93n, 97, 142
Calderott, Moyra, 219
Caldwell, Erskine, 88
"Callous Stars, The," 47
Callow, Philip, 128
Cambon, Glauco, 160, 160n
Cambrian Daily Leader, 49n
Cambrian News, 74n
Cambridge Front, 135
Cambridge Review, 158n, 162n
Camden Journal, 40n
Cameron, Norman, 128, 129
Campbell, Colin, 179
Campbell, James, 161
Campbell, Roy, 90, 119, 126, 144, 169, 192
Canadian Author & Bookman, 197n
Canadian Forum, 183
Canadian Poetry Magazine, 197
Cane, Melville, 176
Canto, 202n
Cap & Gown, 68–69
Capon, Eric, 149n
Capone, Giovanna, 221
"Captain Bigger's Isle," 47
Caravel, 70, 109
Carleton Miscellany, 36n
Carmarthen Journal, 77n
Carolina Quarterly, 102n
Carpenter, Margaret, 195
Carpenter, Maurice, 163, 163n
Carr, John Dickson, 98, 99
Carrell, 210
Carruth, Hayden, 167, 170, 190
Carter, Thomas H., 192
Case, Edward, 208
Casebook = John Malcolm Brinnin *A Casebook on Dylan Thomas* (1960), 14, 14n, 15, 16, 26, 28, 31, 95, 111, 115, 117n, 129, 144, 144n, 145, 147, 154n, 156, 158, 159n, 169, 170, 175, 180, 190, 191, 192, 205

Caseg Broadsheet, 10, 70
Casey, Bill, 185
Cassandra, 153n
Cassidy, Claudia, 195
Cassill, V. R., 184
Catholic Herald, 111
Catholic Worker, 207n
Catholic World, 205
Cavalier, 212
C.E.A. Critic, 204n
Cecil, David, 29
C.E.M.A. (film), 137, 141
"Cento," 47
"Ceremony After a Fire Raid," 12, 13, 20, 39, 141, 154, 184
Chamberlain, Brenda, 10
Chambers, Marlene, 186
Chance, John Newton, 99
Chaneles, Sol, 16
Chanticleer, 35
Chaplin, Charles, 66
Chapman, Max, 153n
Chapman, Robert, 36n
Charvat, William, 17
Chatterji, P. C., 155
Chaturvedi, B. N., 155n
Cherwell, 141n
Chicago Jewish Forum, 178n
Chicago Review, 204n
Chicago Sun-Times, 194n
Chicago Tribune, 194
Chick, Katie, 64
"Children's Hour, or Why the BBC Broke Down," 47
"Child's Christmas in Wales, A," 23, 190, 190n, 207, 224
Child's Christmas = Dylan Thomas *A Child's Christmas in Wales* (1955, and later editions), 26, 174, 180, 203, 218, 222
Choice, 213
Choice = Ralph Maud & Aneirin Talfan Davies eds. *Dylan Thomas' Choice* (1964), 34, 169, 177, 192, 195, 196, 213
Christensen, Naomi, 211
Christian Century, 212n
Christian Science Monitor, 179
Christie, Agatha, 99
Christopher, Sister Mary, 205
Church, Richard, 12, 95, 96, 97, 115, 153
Churchill, R. C., 32
Church Times, 122
Churchward-Tinsley, A. F., 71
Ciardi, John, 176, 177

Cincinnati Times-Star, 179n
Cinema Nuovo, 220
Cine-Technician, 156n
Circus, 150
CIV/n, 35, 36n
Clair, John A., 185
Claire, Pierre, 57
Clancy, J. P., 200
Clare, John, 95
Clark, John W., 35
Clark, Kenneth, 102
Clark, Leonard, 143
Clarke, Austin, 127n
Claude of Jesus, Sister, 205
Claus, Hugo, 219
Cleveland Plain Dealer, 196
Cleverdon, Douglas, xi, 91n, 133, 199
Climax, 36n
Clinton-Baddeley, V. C., 91n
Clurman, Harold, 174
Cobb, Florence, 178
Coblentz, Stanton A., 118, 181, 181n
Cockerill, Donald J., 213
Cocks, David, 142
Coffin, Charles M., 24
Coffman, Stanley K., 198
Cogswell, Fred, 35
Cohen, J. M., 31
Coldoff, David, 180
Cole, G. D. H. & M., 98
Cole, Thomas, 175
Colin, Saul, 158
Collected Poems = Dylan Thomas *Collected Poems* (London 1952, New York 1953, and later editions), 3, 4, 5, 12, 18, 21, 31, 38, 40, 54, 61, 62, 69n, 71n, 76, 90, 91, 95, 96, 101, 102, 103, 104, 110, 111, 113, 114, 117, 119, 121, 128, 133n, 134, 142, 143, 143n, 145, 146, 147, 148, 149n, 151, 152, 152n, 154, 158n, 160, 168, 169, 170, 171, 172, 173, 174, 175, 176, 178, 178n, 180, 181, 183, 184, 186, 188, 190, 191, 192, 194, 195, 196, 197, 197n, 198, 203, 210, 217, 218, 220n, 222, 224
College English, 189, 189n, 190, 204n
Collier, Kay, 153
Collinge, Patricia, 172
Collins, A. S., 14, 18
Collins, Clifford, 147
Collins, Elliobe, 146
Colorado Quarterly, 203
Colour of Saying = Ralph Maud & Aneirin Talfan Davies eds. *The Colour of Saying* (1963), 34, 46n, 50n, 56, 65, 79, 103, 106, 116, 127n, 128, 132, 133, 134, 152, 162
Combecher, Hans, 222
Comfort, Alex, 16, 144, 158
Coming Events in Britain, 116n
Comment, 108
Commentary, 212n
Common, Jack, 152
Commonweal, 181–182
Communita, 221
Compass, 171n
Concordance = Robert Coleman Williams *A Concordance to the Collected Poems of Dylan Thomas* (1967), 40, 206n, 213
Condon, Richard A., 185
Connell, John, 142n
Connolly, Cyril, 15, 111, 114, 115, 115n, 116, 116n, 129, 129n, 130n
Connolly, Thomas E., 185
Connors, Thomas E., 180
Conquest of a Germ (film), 104, 141
Conran, Anthony, 74, 75, 84
Contemporary Poetry & Prose, 110
Contemporary Review, 122
Contemporary Verse, 190
"Conversation About Christmas," 25, 148
Conversation About Christmas (1954), 23
"Conversation of Prayer, The," 13, 20, 34, 108, 176, 185
Cook, Bruce A., 182
Cook, Roderick, 196
Cooke, Alistair, 211
Cooke, Dorian, 193
Coombes, H., 112, 112n
Cooper, Lettice, 143
Cooperman, Stanley, 36
Corbett, Hugh, 198
Corbin, Joan Lee, 178
Corey, Herbert, 98
Corin, Fernand, 218
Corke, Hillary, 156, 156n
Cork Examiner, 127n
Corman, Cid, 184, 201, 202, 220n
Corona, Maria, 220n
Corriere dell'Adda, 221
Cotta, Juan Ange, 224
Coudol, Jacques, 218
Counterpoint, 191n
"Countryman's Return, The," 135
Country Quest, 83
Cour, Ronald, 56, 76n
Cousins, Norman, 176
Coutts, Lorne, 179

Cox, C. B., 162, 162n
Cox = C. B. Cox ed. *Dylan Thomas: A Collection of Critical Essays* (1966), 33, 39, 111, 154n, 162, 169, 189n, 190n, 192
Cox, J. Stevens, 131
Cox, R. G., 134
Craft, Robert, 144n
Craig, Alec, 160
Crampton, Michael, 112
Cranston, Maurice, 113
Crashaw, Richard, 190
Crawford, Iain, 158
Crawley, Alan, 190
Crawshay-Williams, Eliot, 62, 63
Creasey, John, 98
Creeley, Robert, 203
Creft, 76n
Criterion, 59, 97
Critic, 147
Critical Quarterly, 162
Critique, 217, 218
Croft, Freeman Wills, 98, 99
Cronin, Anthony, 159n
Cross, Gustav, 134
Crossen, Karen, 213n
"Crumbs of One Man's Year, The," 23, 90, 222
Cruttwell, Patrick, 190
Cuento, 224
Culligan, Glendy, 197
Cullis, Michael F., 109
Culpan, Norman, 161n
Culpin, Howard, 127
Cummings, David E., 24
Cummings, E. E., 176, 205, 205n
Cummings, Ridgely, 176
Curnow, Allen, 35
Curtis, A. Ross, 76
Curtis, Robert, 98
Cuscaden, R. R., 35

Dagbladets, 224
Daiches, David, 17, 30, 144, 168, 183, 189, 189n, 204
Daily Express, 126
Daily Herald, 142
Daily Mail, 117, 153–154
Daily Mirror, 142n, 153n
Daily Sketch, 142n
Daily Telegraph, 131–132
Daily Worker, 118–119
Dale, James, 106

Dalhousie Review, 208n
Dalton, Moray, 98, 99
Daly, Carroll John, 99
Dane, J. Y., 99
Daniel, Earl, 10
"Dare I?", 96
Darlington, W. A., 132, 199
Davenport, John, 92, 105, 106, 115, 119, 120, 144, 146n, 152, 187n, 191
Davidow, M. C., 204
Davie, Donald, 26, 103, 157
Davie = Donald Davie *Articulate Energy* (1955), 159
Davies, A. Mervyn, 198
Davies, Andrew, 92
Davies, Aneirin Talfan, xi, 22, 23, 33, 66, 71, 71n, 74, 75, 76, 79, 81, 82n, 83, 84, 89n, 102, 106. *See also* **Choice; Colour of Saying; Druid**
Davies, Anthony, 117
Davies, B. J., 78
Davies, D. G., 118
Davies, D. J., 47
Davies, E. D., 63
Davies, Emlyn, 65
Davies, Ernest T., 53
Davies, F., 62
Davies, G. K., 180
Davies, Herbert, 54, 55, 63
Davies, Idris, 61, 75
Davies, Iolo, 48
Davies, M., 63
Davies, M. Bryn, 164, 164n
Davies, Means, 98
Davies, Pennar, 62, 75. *See also* Aberpennar, Davies
Davies, Peter, 116
Davies, Phyllis, 65
Davies, Rhys, 71, 107
Davies, Robertson, 197, 198
Davies, W. H., 7, 90
Davies, Walford D., 38, 103, 159, 162
Davies, Rev. W. Penry, 63
Davis, Robert Gorham, 200
Davison, Edward, 197n
Davy, Colin, 99
Dawedeit, Glendy, 197
Dawn, 69n, 76–77
"Dawn Raid" (= "Among Those Killed"), 20
Dawson, S. W., 159
Day, Douglas, 159n
Deakin, John, 120, 188

"Dearth of Comic Writers, A," 23
"Deaths and Entrances," 10, 11, 13, 30, 39, 129, 182
Deaths & Entrances = Dylan Thomas *Deaths and Entrances* (1946), 12, 20, 54, 60, 61, 71, 88, 90, 96, 101, 104, 108, 110, 111, 113, 114, 117, 119, 127, 127n, 128, 129, 133, 134, 134n, 141, 142, 143, 144, 145, 146, 147, 148, 149n, 155, 176, 183n, 217, 221
de Bedts, Ruth, 209
Decachord, 146n
Decision, 182
"Decline and Fall of Cassius Jones," 47
De Geer, Gerard, 219
de la Mare, Walter, 89, 102
della Paolera, Félix, 225
Delmas, Claude, 145
Delta, 70, 121, 123
Demarest, Donald, 224n
Den Haan, Jacques, 219
Denham, Carl O., 35
Dennis, C. R., 64
Dennis, Nigel, 133
Denny, Reuel N., 204
Dent, Alan, 97, 117
Dent, J. M. & Sons, 4, 5, 8, 9, 12, 17, 18, 21, 22, 23, 25, 26, 27, 28, 29, 33, 34, 37, 38, 39, 40, 41, 58, 70, 109, 144, 144n
Deren, Maya, 212
Derwood, Gene, 211
"Desert Idyll," 46
Desmond, Frankie, 64
De Tijd, 219
Deutsch, Babette, 21, 173, 174, 205
Devas, Nicolette, 39
de Vere White, Terence, 127n
Devlin, Polly, 187n
de Vries, Peter, 133, 167
de Wet, Hugh Olaf, 65
Dhall, A. D., 37
Diadème, 217
Dialog, 223
"Diarists, The," 109n
Dickin, John, 144
Dickins, Anthony, 158
Dickinson, Emily, 101
Dickinson, Patric, 122
Dickson, Carter, 99
Dickson, Grierson, 99
Diers, Richard, 35
Dillon, George, 167

Dissertation Abstracts, 24, 28, 30, 32, 33, 37, 38, 40, 41
Dobrée, Bonamy, 104, 130
Docken, W. P., 40
Dock Leaves, 74–75
"Doctor & Devils" (play), 65, 106, 131, 153, 156, 158
Doctor & Devils = Dylan Thomas *The Doctor and the Devils* (1953, and later editions), 22, 46n, 54, 62, 74, 78, 79, 91, 96, 102, 104, 111, 113, 114, 117, 118, 119, 127, 127n, 128, 130, 131, 143, 145, 146n, 151, 152, 153, 155, 156, 156n, 157, 169, 172, 173, 174, 176, 177, 178, 180, 181, 183, 184, 186, 189, 191, 192, 194, 196, 197, 198, 200, 201, 219, 220, 222, 224, 225
Doctor & Devils and Other Scripts = Dylan Thomas *The Doctor and the Devils and Other Scripts* (1966), 39, 175, 192
Documentary News Letter, 135–140
Dodsworth, Martin, 92
Dolbier, Maurice, 189
Donaghy, Lyle, 95
"Do not go gentle," 12, 18, 20, 24, 34, 92, 115, 125n, 130, 150, 156, 160, 170, 211, 224
Doone, Rupert, 114n
Dos Passos, John, 88
Doster, William C., 210n
Dougherty, Donald, 187
Douglas, Dennis, 133
Douglas-Home, Robin, 127
Dow, A. Warren, 114
Downes, G. S., 63
Downing, Robert, 156n, 201
Downing, Todd, 98, 99
"Do you not father me," 6, 13, 19, 34, 106
Dragon, 69n
Drain, Richard L., 148
Drake, W. R., 118
Dramatics, 191n
Drax, Peter, 99
"Dream of Winter, A," 39, 135
"Dress, The," 5, 6, 25, 108
Drew, Elizabeth, 9, 30
Drew, Philip, 132
Drinkwater, John, 46, 50, 58
Driver, Tom F., 212, 212n
Druid = Aneirin Talfan Davies *Dylan: Druid of the Broken Body* (London 1964; New York 1966), 37, 46n, 56, 66, 71n,

76, 79, 92, 103, 106, 110, 112, 129, 132, 134, 145, 148, 149n, 152, 161, 162, 163n, 164, 164n, 192, 212, 213, 222
D'Souza, Frank, 155n
Dubliner, 149n
Dubois, Arthur E., 171
Duchene, L. F., 113
Dude, 212n
Dudek, Louis, 36n
Dufau-Labeyrie, Francis, 217
Duffy, John, 188
Dugdale, J. S., 37
Duke Chronicle, 193n
Duncan, Margaret, 116
Dunn, Peter, 116, 119
Dupee, F. W., 175
Durband, Alan, 32
Durrell, Lawrence, 21, 123, 126, 157
"Dylan" (play), 65, 76, 106, 114, 131, 189, 190, 196, 199, 206
Dylan = Sidney Michaels *Dylan: A Play* (1964), 37, 76, 79, 103, 116, 195
"Dylan Thomas on Edgar Lee Masters," 191
Dyment, Clifford, 21, 101, 144
Dynevor Secondary School Magazine, 48n
Dyson, A. E., 162n

Eagleton, Terry, 114
"Early One Morning," 89
Earp, T. W., 90
"Ears in the turrets hear," 6, 19, 96, 171, 217
East, Roger, 98
Eberhart, Mignon G., 98, 99
Eberhart, Richard, 12, 105, 175, 180, 205
Eckerson, Olive, 179
Eckloff, Lorentz, 224
Eckman, Frederick, 195
Economist, 161–162
Edel, Leon, 168
Edman, Irwin, 176
Edmead, Frank, 163n
Edmunds, David, 83
Edwards, A. D., 48
Edwards, A. T. G., 61
Edwards, Charman, 100
Edwards, H. L. R., 69
Edwards, J. M., 80n
18 Poems = Dylan Thomas *18 Poems* (1934, and later editions), 3, 4, 5, 10, 15, 19, 27, 51, 52, 58, 59, 68, 89n, 93n, 94,

95, 96, 97, 98, 100, 101, 103, 104, 107, 109, 111, 161, 184
Eldridge, J. S., 72, 73, 136, 138, 140
"Elegy," 21, 27, 34, 156, 156n, 179
Eleusis of Chi Omega, 207n
Elfed, 82, 82n
ELH, 171n
Eliot, T. S., 51, 89n, 97, 100, 102, 190, 203n
Ellman, Richard, 171, 171n
Emery, Clark, 210, 210n
Emery = Clark Emery *The World of Dylan Thomas* (1962), 33, 112, 182, 192, 195, 210n
Emery, M. J., 77
Emmanuel, Pierre, 144
Emory University Quarterly, 212
Empire News, 82–83
Empson, William, x, 111, 112, 119, 120, 129, 147, 159, 162, 167, 174
Encounter, 62, 156–157
"End of the River, The," 87
"Enemies, The," 5, 7, 25, 27, 97, 126
Engle, Paul, 89, 194, 195
English, 147–148
English Association, 5, 18, 147, 147n
"English Festival of Spoken Poetry, The," 23, 90
English Institute Essays, 209n
English Journal, 204
English Language Notes, 214
English Miscellany, 160
English Review, 121
English Studies, 148
English Studies in Africa, 164
Enrico, Harold, 35
Enright, D. J., 105, 105n, 112, 147
Entrances = Ralph Maud *Entrances to Dylan Thomas' Poetry* (1963), 36, 92, 103, 106, 196, 212, 218, 222
Epos, 36n
Eryri, Mab, 77n
"Especially when the October wind," 3, 4, 5, 6, 7, 13, 19, 33, 89, 91, 186
Esquire, 207
Essays in Criticism, 26, 159
Essig, Erhardt H., 185
Esty, Jane, 35
Etheridge, Ken, 91, 145
Études Anglaises, 217, 218
Europa Letteraria, 221
European, 159

European Quarterly, 100, 100n
Evans, Brinley, 63
Evans, B. Ifor, 95, 128, 152
Evans, Caradoc, 64, 82, 151, 152
Evans, Clifford, 63
Evans, D. L., 62
Evans, Edith, 115n
Evans, Emrys, 164
Evans, Gareth Lloyd, 129, 129n
Evans, George Ewart, 4, 70
Evans, Gwynne D., 77n
Evans, Hubert, 64
Evans, Illtud, 149, 151
Evans, J. Alban, 111
Evans, Oliver, 160, 160n
Evans, Rev. David R., 82
Evans, T. F., 162
Evans, T. H., 77n
Evans, W. Lindsey, 76
Eve, Beatrice, 114
Evening News, 142n
Evening Standard, 142
Everett, Barbara, 114
Evergreen Review, 211
Every, George, 16, 134
Everybody's, 83n
Everyman, 87n
Ewart, Gavin, 111, 154, 158
Exe, 149
Experiment, 129n
Experimental Review, 179n
Explicator, 185–186
Explorations, 156n, 183n
"Extraordinary Little Cough," 8, 17, 39, 107, 135

Fallon, Gabriel, 127
Fanio, A., 221
Fantasy, 171
Faulk, Carolyn Sue, 37
Faulkner, William, 211
Faust, Richard L., 28
Fazio, Guiseppe, 187
Felix, Morton N., 180
Fenton, Charles, 193
Ferguson, Suzanne C., 32
Ferling, Lawrence, 191
Ferlinghetti, Lawrence, 191n
"Fern Hill," 9, 13, 20, 27, 28, 34, 39, 97, 116, 129, 147, 148, 162, 174, 185, 186, 203, 204, 207, 221, 222, 223, 225
Ferrer-Vidal, Jorge, 224
Ferris, Paul, 83n

"Festival Exhibition, 1951, The," 23, 90
"Fey, Dollfuss, Vienna," 95
Ficción, 225
Fiddlehead, 35
Fiedler, Leslie, 184
Fielding, James, 119
Fiera Letteraria, 220
"Fight, The," 8, 107, 130
Film Culture, 212
Film Forum, 156
Film News, 156n
"Films, The," 46
Films in Review, 156n, 201
Filológiai Kozlony, 226
Financial Times, 161n
Finch, John, 197
"Find meat on bones," 19, 109
"Fine Beginning, A," 53, 135
Finney, Brian, 159n
Finzi, Gilberto, 220n
Firmage, George. *See* **Garland**
Fisher, Charles, 52n, 53, 60
Fisher, Fanya, 72, 73
Fitt, Mary, 100
Fitts, Dudley, 176, 177
Fitzgerald, William, 167
FitzGibbon, Constantine, 103, 106, 126, 179, 213, 217. *See also* **Selected Letters**
FitzGibbon = Constantine FitzGibbon
The Life of Dylan Thomas (1965), 38, 45n, 46n, 49, 56, 66, 75n, 76, 79, 80, 84, 89n, 92, 103, 106, 110, 111, 112, 113, 116, 119, 120, 122, 126, 127n, 128, 129, 131, 132, 133, 133n, 134n, 142, 142n, 143, 143n, 145, 148, 151, 152, 153, 153n, 154, 155, 161, 161n, 172, 173, 176, 177, 179, 181, 182, 183, 184n 187, 187n, 189, 191, 192, 196, 200, 204, 206, 210, 212n, 213
"Five Early Poems," 169
Fjelde, Rolf, 183n
"Flamboyant All the Way," 119
Fleming, Edward Vandermere, 114, 117
Fleming, William, 154
Fletcher, Raymond, 128
Florida Review, 209
Florida State University Studies, 186n
Flower, Walter, 64
Focus Five, 168n
Focus One, 170n
Foell, Earl W., 179
Folios of New Writing, 53, 135
"Followers, The," 25, 32, 34, 146, 193, 209, 219

Fontaine, 217
Forbes, Diana Fraser, 36n
Forbes-Boyd, Eric, 179
"Force that through the green fuse, The,"
  4, 5, 6, 7, 9, 10, 12, 17, 19, 22, 33, 93,
  125, 185, 217, 220, 223
Ford, Boris, 32
"Forest Picture," 46, 144
Forsythe, Robin, 98
Fortnightly, 122
Forum, 210n
"Foster the light," 6, 13, 19, 93, 110
"Four Lost Souls," 193
Fowkes, Robert A., 82
Fowler, A. D. S., 159
Fowler, Albert & Helen, 206
Fowlie, Wallace, 193, 205
Foyle's, 62, 78, 111
Francis, William, 179n
Frankel, Haskel, 177
Frankenberg, Lloyd, 16, 27, 180, 196
Frankfurter Allgemeine Zeitung, 222
Fraser, G. S., 10, 22, 29, 103, 111, 112,
  124, 150
Fraser = G. S. Fraser *Dylan Thomas*
  (1957), 28, 152
Freedom First, 155n
Freeman, Cecil, 98
Freeman, Kathleen, 63
Freeman, 197n
Freethinker, 153n
Fremantle, Anne, 181
French, Warren, 193, 193n, 209
Fresco, 210
Friar, Kimon, 18, 205
Fried, Erich, 221, 222
Friederich, Willard, 191n
Friend, 163n
From In Memory of Ann Jones (1942), 10
"From love's first fever," 3, 6, 13, 19, 34,
  97, 185
Fry, G. H., 114
Fuller, Edmund, 214
Fuller, Jean Overton, 93n, 118
Fuller, John G., 177
Fuller, Roy, 21, 88
Furbank, P. N., 92
Furioso, 174
Furlong, John, 55
Furlong, Monica, 92
Fuson, Ben W., 192

Galloway, David D., 132, 207
Galsworthy, John, 47, 50, 56

Galsworthy and Gawsworth (1954), 23
Gamberini, Spartaco, 220n
Gandhi, M. K., 94
Gannett, Lewis, 189
Gardiner, H. C., 200
Gardiner, Wrey, 143
Gardner, Erle Stanley, 99, 100
Gardner, Isabella, 169n, 205
Garland = George Firmage ed. *A Garland
  for Dylan Thomas* (1963), 34, 66, 75, 91,
  92, 96, 103, 106, 107, 111, 116, 118, 122,
  124, 129, 144, 145, 146, 147, 150, 151,
  153, 154, 157, 158, 161, 168, 169, 171,
  175, 176, 177, 178, 181, 182, 189, 190,
  192, 193, 195, 196, 205, 209
Garlick, Raymond, 69, 74, 74n, 75, 76, 80,
  101, 103, 145, 149
Garrigue, Jean, 35, 169
Gascoyne, David, 14
Gassner, John, 31
Gauchon, Nicole, 28, 218
Gawsworth, John, 23, 34, 90n
Gazetta del Popolo, 220
Geare, Michael, xi, 111
Geiger, Don, 204
Gelinas, Rick, 193n
Gellert, Roger, 112
"Genius and Madness Akin in World of
  Art," 50
Gentili, Vanna, 221
George, George L., 156n
Gergely, Ágnes, 226
Gersh, Gabriel, 210
Geyza, Bányay, 226
Ghiselin, Brewster, 169, 183, 184
Gibbins, John, 152n
Gibbs, Wolcott, 172
Gibson, Henry, 147
Gibson, Wilfred, 97
Giglio, Tommaso, 220
Gildea, Margo M., 187
Gillett, Eric, 121
Gilliatt, Penelope, 187n
Gingerich, Martin E., 40
Giovannini, G., 185
Giroux, Roger, 217
Giuliani, Alfredo, 221
"Give London a Chance," 154
Glamorgan County Magazine, 74
Glasgow Evening Times, 132n
Glasgow Herald, 131–132
Glassheim, Eliot, 35
Glen Ridge Paper, 179n
Glick, Burton S., 209

Glossop, John, 118
Glover, C. Gordon, 149
Goebel, Gertrude, 187
Golden Goose, 195
Goldring, Douglas, 133
Goldstein, Lawrence, 173
Goldstein, Melvin, 211
Golffing, Francis, 36
Goñi, Anibal C., 225
Goodchild, George, 98
Goodfellow, Dorothy W., 26
Goodland, John, 123
Goodwin, J. C. H., 146
Goodwin, Michael, 152
Gordon, James, 141, 160
Gore, William, 99
Gorell, Lord, 98
Gorlier, Claudio, 221
Gould, Gerald, 3
Goulden, Mark, 93, 104, 111
Gower, Anthony, 71
Gower, 81
Graddon, John, 117, 118
Graecen, Robert, 157, 157n
Graeme, Bruce, 99
Graham, Malcolm, 57
Graham, Rachel, 36n
Graham, Ruby G., 64
Graham, Stephen, 118
Graham, Virginia, 104
Gram, William Porter, 175
Gramophone, 115n
Gransden, K. W., 89n
Grant, James Russell, 207
Grant, Peter, 210n
Granta, 114
Graves, Allen Wallace, 24
Graves, Robert, ix, 26, 159, 159n, 176, 176n, 182
"Greek Play in a Garden," 51, 57, 59
Green, G. F., 17
Green, Harry, 63, 64
Green, Peter, 143
Greenburg, C., 199
Greene, Graham, 102
Greenhut, Morris, 195
Gregg, Cecil Freeman, 99
Gregor, Hugh, 63
Gregory, Horace, 151, 168, 168n, 180, 181, 184, 199, 205, 205n
Greiff, Louis K., 213
Grenander, M. E., 162
Gribble, Leonard R., 98

"Grief ago, A," 4, 6, 12, 17, 19, 106, 109, 115n, 147n
"Grief thief of time," 6, 19, 108
Grierson, Francis D., 98, 99
Griffith, William, 63, 64
Griffiths, Bryn, 78, 79, 83n, 106
Griffiths, Glyn, 83
Griffiths, Hugh, 115n
Griffiths, J. Gwyn, 56
Griffiths, Robert, 174
Griffiths, Teifion, 78
Griffiths, William, 78, 82, 144
Grigson, Geoffrey, ix, 4, 5, 15, 16, 36, 89n, 95, 95n, 97, 98, 103, 112, 113, 119, 120, 125, 129, 144, 144n, 158, 163, 167
Grindea, Miron, 144
Gros, L.-G., 218
Grose, Kenneth, 143n
Gross, Harvey, 37
Grosvenor, Peter, 126
Grubb, Frederick, 38
Guenther, John, 35
Guhl, Thane, 180
Guibert, Armand, 217
Guinness, Alec, 37n, 106, 114, 198n
Gunn, Thom, 158, 158n
Gunther, Charles, 198
Gwynn, G. M., 45
Gwynne, George H., 47n

Habart, Michel, 217
Hackett, Roland, 119
Hacquoil, Francis W., 114
Hadfield, John, 21
Haffenden, Alfred Hy., 95
Hagerup, Inger, 224
Haidukewicz, Robert, 29n
Haines, Charles, 220n
Hale, Lionel, 119
Hales, Madge, 118
"Half of the fellow father," 6
Hall, Alice, 63
Hall, Donald, 17, 142
Hall, W. E., 129
Hallam, Atlantis, 177
Halperen, Max, 21, 186, 186n
Halsband, Robert, 177
Haltrecht, Montague, 116
Hamilton, Alex, 161
Hamilton, Edith, 177
Hamilton, Elaine, 98
Hamilton, Elizabeth, 97
Hamilton, Ian, 92

Hamilton, Peter, 158
Hammerton, H. J., 163n
Hammnett, Nina, 50
"Hand that signed the paper, The," 6, 7, 9, 12, 13, 19, 22, 30, 34, 96, 186, 217, 222
Hanley, James, 153
Hanley, T. E., 31n, 189n
Hansen, Kurt Heinrich, 221
Hanson, Michael, 159n
Happel, Nikolaus, 223
Harding, Joan, 122
Hardwick, Elizabeth, 170, 170n
Hardy, Evelyn A., 36n
Hardy, Thomas, 162
Hare, Kenneth, 114
Harmon, Phil, 146
Harper's Bazaar, 190–191
Harper's Magazine, 196
Harries, Derrick, 64
Harries, Eva M., 63
Harrington, Michael, 207n
Harris, E. Howard, 52, 55, 57n, 59, 60, 62
Harris, Marguerite, 35, 205
Harrisson, Tom, 90
Hartford Connecticut Times, 172
Hartford Courant, 196
Hartley, Anthony, 161n
Harvard Advocate, 179n
Harvard Crimson, 198
Harvey, Norman, 162
Harvill, Olga DeHart, 186
Hassall, Christopher, 89n
Hassan, Ihab H., 185
Haswell, Richard E., 198
Hatwell, Donald, 112
Hauková, Jiřina, 225
Hauser, Marianne, 180
Hawken, Noel, 133n
Hawkes, Terence, 75, 75n, 78, 84, 92, 162, 189
Hawkins, Desmond, 87, 100, 101, 104, 109
Hawley, Clifford, 106
Hay, M. Doriel, 98
Haycraft, Howard, 11
Hayes, Richard, 181, 182
Hayes, Rod, 67n
Hays, H. R., 168
Hayward, John, 14, 27, 219
Hazard, Patrick D., 204
Hazo, Samuel J., 203
Heath-Stubbs, John, 22, 102n, 146n, 150, 151
Hecht, Roger, 187

Heddiw, 71
Hedley, Leslie Woolf, 36n
Helmstetter, Carol Ruth, 41
Henderson, Philip, 145
Hendry, J. F., 9, 10
Henry, W. T., 64
Hentzell, Shirley W., 177
Heppenstall, Rayner, 31n, 87, 95
Heppenstall = Rayner Heppenstall *Four Absentees* (1960), 31, 64, 92, 97, 103, 105, 112, 113, 120, 130, 148, 151, 152, 153, 158, 160, 182, 219
Herald of Wales, 49, 52, 52n, 56–60
"Here in this spring," 4, 6, 19, 60, 171
Hernandez, Luisa Josefina, 224
Heron, Shaun, 155
Herr, Dan, 195
Herring, Robert, 107
"Her tombstone told when she died," 123, 168, 170. *See* "Tombstone told when she died"
Heseltine, Nigel, 61, 69, 69n, 126
Hess, M. Whitcomb, 188
Het Woord, 219
Hewes, Henry, 176, 177
Hewitt, Douglas, 113
Hicks, Granville, 200
Higgins, Brian, 152
Higham, Charles, 134
Higham, David, 102
Highet, Gilbert, 188, 188n, 196
High Fidelity, 198, 199
HIKA, 171n
Hill, Jane, 210
Hill, Roland, 222
"His Repertoire," 45, 144
"His Requiem," 61
Hitchcock, George, 183
Hobson, Harold, 115
Hodgart, Matthew, 213
Hodge, Alan, 109
Hoffman, Frederick J., 12
Hoffman, John, 118
Hogan, William, 191
Hogue, Caroline, 180
Holborn, Lord, 105n
Holbrook, David, ix, 32, 103, 157, 162, 162n, 163
Holbrook = David Holbrook *Llareggub Revisited* (1962), published in U.S. as *Dylan Thomas and Poetic Dissociation* (1964), 32, 65, 75, 76, 78, 92, 103, 105, 112, 113, 114, 116, 118, 119, 122, 129,

Holbrook *(Continued)*
132, 143, 148, 149, 151, 152, 154, 155, 159, 163, 169, 188, 195, 212, 213, 218, 218n
"Hold hard, these ancient minutes," 6, 13, 19, 34, 60, 109, 171
Holdridge, Barbara, 189
Holdsworth, John, 112
"Holiday Memory," 23, 90, 187
Holland, Julian, 154
Holloway, David, 117
Holloway, John, 32, 159
Holmes, John, 172n
Holmes, L. R., 207
Holmes-Coleman, Emily, 153n
Holpfner, T. C., 179n
Holroyd, Stuart, 29, 118
Holt, Gavin, 99
"Holy Six, The," 7, 25, 110
"Holy Spring," 13, 20, 129, 184
Holzhauer, Jean, 182
"Homage to Dylan Thomas" (memorial), 103, 114n, 115, 115n, 172
Hood, John, 129
Hope-Wallace, Philip, 113
Hopkins, Bill, 97
Hopkins, Gerard Manley, 30, 33, 70, 180
Hopkins, Kenneth, 141, 160
Horan, Robert, 171
Horder, John, 113
Horizon, 10, 129–130
Hornick, Lita R., 30
Horowitz, Iona, 193n
"Horse's Ha, The," 25, 109
House, Jack, 132n
Housman, A. E., 206
Houston, Donald, 64
Howard, D. R., 185, 203
Howe, Conrad, 110
Howells, Jack, 48, 56, 65, 66, 78, 82, 200
"How shall my animal," 6, 9, 13, 20, 97, 170
"How soon the servant sun," 19, 106, 186
"How to Be a Poet," 23, 25, 150, 178
"How to Begin a Story," 23, 90
Huddlestone, Linden, 135, 145
Hudson Review, 190
Huff, William, 24
Hugh-Jones, Stephen, 112, 113
Hughes, Joan, 65
Hughes, Raymond, 64
Hughes, Richard, 8, 52, 53, 90, 115
Hughes, Ted, 112, 162

Hughes, Trevor, 51, 68, 87n, 109, 109n, 114, 207
Hull, Richard, 99
Humboldt, Charles, 182
Hume, David, 99
Humphrey, Linton, 48
Humphreys, David, 149n
Humphries, Rolfe, 174
"Hunchback in the Park, The," 10, 11, 17, 20, 108, 185, 186
Hunt, Albert, 112
Hunt, K. W., 204
Hunter, Alan, 105
Hurston, Norah, 88
Hutchens, John K., 189
Hutchings, Reginald, 108
Hutchinson, Pearse, 127
Hyams, C. Barry, 222n
Hynes, Reed, 198
Hynes, Sam, 181, 185, 189

"I am Going to Read Aloud," 158, 222
Icarus, 149n
"I dreamed my genesis," 3, 13, 19, 34
"Idyll of Unforgetfulness," 46
Ifan, Wil, 63
"I fellowed sleep," 3, 19, 34
"If I were tickled by the rub of love," 6, 19, 95, 95n, 186
"'If my head hurt a hair's foot'," 6, 13, 20, 125, 170
"I have longed to move away," 6, 9, 19, 96, 159n, 180
"I, in my intricate image," 6, 12, 19, 34, 69, 96
Illustrated London News, 155–156
Illustrazione Italiana, 221
"I make this in a warring absence," 6, 13, 20, 69, 121, 123, 170, 220n
Imprint, 149n
"In Borrowed Plumes," 46
"Incarnate devil," 6, 10, 19, 94, 171
"In Country Heaven," 131, 133, 150
"In country sleep," 16, 18, 21, 130, 162, 178, 220
In Country Sleep = Dylan Thomas *In Country Sleep* (1952), 18, 21, 168, 172, 173, 174, 176, 180, 191, 192, 194, 195
Indian Review, 155n
"Individual and Collective," 97
"In Dreams," 46
Ingenue, 213n
Ingot, 156

"In Memory of Ann Jones," 5, 10, 18, 107, 124, 145, 170, 217
"In my Craft or Sullen Art," 13, 20, 34, 39, 108, 149, 185, 211, 220, 222
"Insults," 147
"International Eisteddfod, The," 23
International Henry Miller Letter, 210n
"Interview with Dylan Thomas," 193
"In the beginning," 3, 19, 34
"In the Direction of the Beginning," 25, 69, 70, 170
"In the Garden," 47, 47n
"In the white giant's thigh," 18, 21, 102, 150, 178, 185, 186, 220
"Into her Lying Down Head," 9, 11, 20, 107, 182
"Introduction to a Poetry Reading," 200
Inventario, 220
Ireland of the Welcomes, 127n
Iremonger, Valentin, 127n
Irish Press, 127
Irish Times, 127n
Isaksson, Folke, 219
"I see the boys of summer," 5, 12, 19, 95, 220n
Isis, 141–142
"I, the first named," 123
"It is the sinners' dust-tongued bell," 4, 6, 13, 20, 121, 170
Izzo, Carlo, 220, 221

"Jack of Christ," 64
Jackson, Sara, 96
Jacobbi, Ruggero, 220n
Jacobs, Harvey, 208
James, David Lloyd, 149
James, Dwynwen, 78
James, H. E., 57
James, J. D., 35, 36n, 142
James, L. W., 62
Jameson, R. D., 95
Janes, Alfred, 52, 55, 63, 64, 68, 76n, 81, 131, 145
Janeway, Elizabeth, 180
"January 1939," 121, 123, 170
Janus, 108–109
"Jarley's," 47
Jarrell, Randall, 188, 195, 195n, 196
Jeffares, A. Norman, 163
Jeffrey, Sydney, 110
Jeffreys, David L. R., 82
Jeffreys, F. V., 56
Jellett, H., 99

Jenkins, David Clay, 28, 71n, 207, 207n
Jenkins, Gwyn Oliver, 149
Jenkins, Islwyn, 75
Jenkins, Jack L., 204
Jennings, Elizabeth, 27, 92, 105, 156n
Jennings, John, 67, 68, 68n
Jensen, Owen, 146n
Jepson, Laura, 204
Jo, Sue-Jin M., 40
John, Augustus, 5, 12, 18, 52, 53, 54, 92, 102, 115, 115n, 116, 130, 144, 202
John, Gwen, 55
John, J. R., 56
John O'London's Weekly, 96–97, 206
Johns, H. W., 63
Johnson, Geoffrey, 117, 164
Johnson, Pamela Hansford, 68n, 93, 93n, 111, 114, 121, 127, 144, 144n, 160, 161
Johnson, S. F., 185
Jolas, Eugene, 110
Jones, Benjamin W., 28
Jones, Blanche, 63
Jones, Bobi, 76
Jones, Daniel, 22, 29, 29n, 46n, 48, 54, 55, 60, 74, 156
Jones, David, 83n, 151, 151n
Jones, D. Glynne, 63
Jones, Dylan, 48
Jones, E. E. Duncan, 128
Jones, Evan, 154n
Jones, Gareth A., 66
Jones, Glyn, 16, 41, 64, 65, 71, 75, 95, 144, 151
Jones, Gwyn, 9, 27, 29, 61, 61n, 63, 71, 95, 108
Jones, Ieuan Lloyd, 63
Jones, I. M., 63
Jones, J. A., 31, 159. *See* **Ackerman**
Jones, Jack Raymond, 79, 164
Jones, J. Bonnyman, 199
Jones, J. C. Griffith, 63
Jones, J. Gareth, 63
Jones, J. Idris, 71, 76
Jones, John Morris, 80n
Jones, M. R., 204
Jones, Mrs. E., 65
Jones, Noel A., 141
Jones, Owen R., 61
Jones, Phyllis M., 9
Jones, Richard, 65, 211
Jones, Robert C., 185
Jones, S. Beryl, 71
Jones, Siriol Hugh, 187n

Jones, Stanley, 69, 132
Jones, T. Gwynn, 61
Jones, T. H., 35, 36n, 84
Jones, T. H. = T. H. Jones *Dylan Thomas* (1963), 36, 65, 76, 103, 114, 118, 122, 212, 218
Jones, T. James, 35, 41
Jonsson, Thorsten, 219
Joost, Nicholas, 181
Joselyn, Sister M., 203
Josephson, Mimi, 62n, 64, 74, 96
Joshi, Umashankar, 169
Jost, Edward F., 200
Journal des Poètes, 217
Journal of Aesthetics & Art Criticism, 210n
Journal of the Welsh Bibliographical Society, 71n
Joyce, James, 16, 209
Julian, Sister Mary, 203
"Just Like Little Dogs," 8, 70, 212n

Kafka, Franz, 88
Kaiser, Georg, 88
Kann, Nina N., 197
Kappus, Dieter, 222
Kavanagh, Patrick, 88
Kaye-Smith, Sheila, 147n
Kazin, Alfred, 179, 179n
Keats, John, 35, 209
Keene, Mary, 72, 73
Keister, Don A., 196
Kelly, Francis, 116
Kemmis, Agnes, 120
Kendrake, Carleton, 98
Kenmare, Dallas, 118
Kennedy, Maurice, 127n
Kennedy, Milward, 100
Kennedy, William, 213
Kent, Patrick, 126n
Kenyon Review, 170–171
Keown, Eric, 153
Kerr, Walter, 189, 189n
Kiely, Benedict, 127
Killick, Capt. W. R. J., 54, 72, 73, 74, 74n
King, C. Daly, 88
King, Francis, 133
Kington, Miles, 115n
Kirchwey, Freda, 173
Kirjallisuudentutkijain Vuosikirirja, 225
Kirkup, James, 101
Kleinman, H. H., 17
Kleinman = H. H. Kleinman *The Religious Sonnets of Dylan Thomas* (1964),

37, 103, 106, 116, 129n, 148, 160, 168n, 169, 182, 190, 192, 212, 222
Knauber, Charles F., 203
Kneiger, Bernard, 185, 186, 190
Knight, Kathleen Moore, 99
Knox, E. V., 131
Koegler, Horst, 158
Kolodney, William, 195
Kolokon, 163n
Korg, Jacob, 174, 184, 184n
Korg = Jacob Korg *Dylan Thomas* (1965), 38
Korn, Albert Ralph, 181n
Kristol, Irving, 156
Kroll, Jack, 206
Kronick van Kunst en Kultuur, 219
Kultur, 159n
Kunitz, Stanley J., 11, 26, 181

Laetsch, W. M., 176
Laing, R. D., 157
Lambert, Elizabeth, 34
Lambert, J. W., 114, 115
Lambert, Rose & Dudley, 98
"Lament," 18, 21, 150, 160, 170, 207
Landels, D. H., 100
Lander, Clara, 183, 208
Landfall, 35
Landor, Walter Savage, 57
Lane, Rose Wilder, 88
Lane-Jones, Morris, 70
Langbaum, Robert, 188
Lange, Irma, 177
Langguth, Arthur J., 198
Larkin, Philip, 112, 184
LaRosa, Barbara, 205
Lask, Thomas, 199
Lassaw, Ibran, 131
"Last night I dived my beggar arm," 15, 125, 126
"Laugharne," 23, 62
Laughlin, James, xi, 12, 17, 168n, 170
Laurentia, Sister M., 185
Lavagetto, Mario, 221
Lawrence, D. H., x, 197n
Laws, Frederick, 117
LBL, 226
Leach, Elsie, 209
Leary, Paris, 206
Leavis, F. R., ix, 122, 134
Lebert, Gordon, 204
Le Brun, P., 162
Lee, Lawrence L., 112

Lee, W. B., 180
Leech, Geoffrey, 163
Leeming, Glenda, 128
Leftover Life = Caitlin Thomas *Leftover Life to Kill* (1957), 28, 36n, 75, 82, 101, 103, 105, 112, 113, 114, 115, 117, 118, 120, 126n, 127, 127n, 128, 131, 132, 134, 142, 143, 149, 153, 155, 157, 158, 159, 160, 161, 172, 173, 174, 175, 176, 177, 179, 180, 182, 187, 187n, 191, 192, 195, 197, 198, 199, 200, 205, 210, 218
Legangneux, Claude, 217
Leggett, Barbara, 180
Lehmann, John, 3, 90, 95, 97, 128, 133, 135, 144, 157, 157n, 158, 184, 211
Lehmann, Rosamond, 104
Leibowitz, Herbert, 200
Leighton, Florence, 98
Leitch, David, 116
"Lemon, The," 25, 107
Lentricchia, Frank, 169
Lerner, L. D., 157
Lester, Susan, 116n
Le Tailleux, Jean, 217
Letteratura, 221
Letterature Moderne, 162n
Lettere D'Oggi, 220
"Letters: Dylan Thomas," 201
Letters from England, 164
"Letters to Oswell Blakestone," 153n
Letters to the Editor, 67, 68, 125, 150
Letters to Vernon Watkins = Vernon Watkins ed. *Letters to Vernon Watkins* (1957), 28, 55, 64, 75, 79, 82, 92, 101, 103, 105, 111, 113, 114n, 115, 117n, 120, 121, 127, 128, 129, 130, 132, 133, 143, 152, 153, 158, 159n, 160, 169, 172, 173, 174, 175, 177, 178n, 179, 180, 189, 191, 192, 195, 197n, 198, 200, 204, 208, 210, 218, 219, 224n, 225
Lettres Nouvelles, 217, 218
Levertov, Denise, 181
Levitt, John, 112
Levy, Dennis, 114
Levy, Mervyn, 15, 54, 55, 70, 76n, 83, 97
Lewis, Alun, 10, 70, 152
Lewis, C. Day, 9, 15, 35, 88, 89, 91, 94, 107, 124
Lewis, E. Glyn, 71
Lewis, Graham, 119
Lewis, Haydn, 80, 80n, 83
Lewis, Ivor, 70
Lewis, Min, 40, 65, 77n, 83, 206n

Lewis, Naomi, 120
Lewis, Saunders, 7, 66, 75, 149
Lewis, Stanley, 40, 83
Lewis, Wyndham, 115n
Library Journal, 192
Library Review, 161
Lieberson, Goddard, 37n
Liebert, Herman W., 169n
"Lie Still, Sleep Becalmed," 13, 20, 108, 220
Life & Letters Today, 107–108
"Life-belt," 46
Light & Dark, 122
"Light breaks where no sun shines," 3, 4, 5, 6, 9, 16, 19, 89, 89n, 185, 217
Lilly, Jean, 98
Lindegren, Erik, 219
Lindeman, Jack, 176, 208
Lindon, J. A., 96
Lindsay, Jack, 119, 124, 141, 154, 154n, 182
Lindsay, Phillip, 24, 144
Lindsay, Vera, 114n
Lipman, Beata, 65
Lipton, Lawrence, 146, 207
List, George N., 88
Listener, 3, 50n, 59, 89–92
Literary Digest, 90n
Literary Half-yearly, 164
Literary Repository, 131
Literary Review, 168n
Literatur, 221
Littarair Paspoort, 219
Litvinoff, Emanuel, 144, 150
Liverpool Daily Post, 110
Livi, A., 220
Living Age, 9n
Living Church, 204n
Llafar, 82n
Llanelly Star, 77–78
"Llareggub (A Piece for Radio Perhaps)," 150
Llewellyn, John, 65
Lloyd, L. C., 104
Lockwood Library, Buffalo, xi, 15, 92, 169, 201
Loesch, Katherine Taylor, 32
Logan, John, 181, 203
London Calling, 91n, 190n
"Londoner, The," 39
London Forum, 146n
London Magazine, 157–158
London Mercury, 97, 109, 109n

London Quarterly & Holborn Review, 152n
London Review, 159n
London Welshman, 78
Lones, D. E. J., 63
Long, Curt, 197
Longcore, Chris, 162
Lord, Graham, 127
Los Angeles Times, 63n, 179n
Lougee, David, 169
"Love in the Asylum," 11, 13, 20, 125, 186
Loveland, Kenneth, 79
"Love me, not as the dreaming nurses," 93
Lowell, Robert, 170, 171n, 184
Lucifer, 159
Lundkvist, Artur, 218
Lutyens, Elisabeth, 144
Luzi, Mario, 144
Lynd, Robert, 7

Macaulay, Rose, 147
McAuley, James, 134
McBeth, George, 116
McBrien, William A., 30
McCall's, 207n
Maccoby, Michael, 198
McCord, Howard L., 162
McCormack, Robert, 210
MacDiarmid, Hugh, 124, 134n, 144
McDonald, Gerald, D., 192, 206
McDonnell, A. G., 68
McDonnell, T. P., 200, 205
MacDougal, Allan Ross, 115
McEachran, F., 22
McGrath, John, 77
McGrath, Thomas, 182
MacGregor-Hastie, Roy, 159, 159n
McGrory, Mary, 197n
McInery, E. F., 46
McKenna, Rollie, 37, 200, 200n
MacKenzie, John K., 187
Mackworth, Cecily, 218
McLaren, Floris, 190
MacLaren-Ross, J., 91, 158, 158n
McLaughlin, J., 119
MacLeod, Alison, 118, 119
MacLeod, Norman, 195
MacLeod, Runia Sheila, 93n, 108, 144
Maclure, Marshall, 183
Maclure, Millar, 183, 183n
MacManus, Francis, 127
McNeese Review, 163n
MacNeice, Louis, 5, 74, 83, 87, 102, 112, 114n, 115n, 156, 156n, 157, 164, 180

Macpherson, Donald, 98
McQueen, D. C., 47
MacVicar, Angus, 98
McWhinnie, Donald, 30
McWilliams, Carey, 173
Maddocks, Melvin, 179
Mademoiselle, 200–201
Madoc, Perry, 97
Madtes, Richard E., 177
Mainstream, 182
Mainstream Quarterly, 209
Mair, John, 109
Mairet, Philip, 87
Mais, S. P. B., 145
Mallalieu, H. B., 88, 167
Malody, Bonnie May, 36n
Manchester Exhibition, 64, 83, 113
Manchester Guardian, 113
Manchester Guardian Weekly, 113–114
Mandarà, Emmanuele, 159n
Mandel, Oscar, 175
Mander, John, 112
Mandrake, 154
Manent, M., 224
Manganelli, Giorgio, 221
Mankowitz, Wolf, 134, 144, 147
Manley, Frank, 212
Mann, Klaus, 182
Mannes, Marya, 201
Manning, Hugo, 144
Manoll, Michel, 193, 218
"Map of Love, The," 5, 7, 25, 34, 69
Map of Love = Dylan Thomas *The Map of Love* (1939), 5, 6, 20, 53, 60, 61, 70, 71, 88, 89, 101, 104, 107, 109, 110, 111, 113, 117, 123, 124, 126, 127, 129, 161
March, Richard, 125
Margarido, Alfredo, 226
Marianni, Ariodante, 221
Markale, Jean, 218
Marlowe, Christopher, 35
Marowitz, Charles, 208
Marquand, John P., 88
"Marriage of a Virgin, The" (= "On the Marriage of a Virgin")
Marriott, R. B., 144
Marsh, Edward, 89, 89n
Marsh, Ngaio, 99
Marshall, John, 154
Marshall, Margaret, 173, 174
Marshall, Percy, 39
Martin, Arthur, 141
Martin, David, 127
Martin, Harold C., 190n

Martin, J. H., 103
Martin, Richard, 222n
Martz, Louis L., 183
Mason, A. E. W., 98
Mason, W. H., 32
Masses & Mainstream, 182–183
Masson, André, 69
Masters, Edgar Lee, 191, 191n
Matchett, William, 36n
Mathews, Elkin, 24
Mathias, Roland, 75
Matsu-ura, Naomi, 223
Maud, Ralph, 30, 39, 76, 148, 159, 159n, 174, 185, 191, 201, 203, 206, 208, 210, 212. *See* **Choice; Colour of Saying; Entrances; Notebooks**
Maura, Sister M., 188, 189
Mayer, Stanley D., 171
Mayhead, Robin, 134
Maynard, Theodore, 174
Mayo, E. L., 35
Mayoux, Jean-Jacques, 217
"Me and My Bike," 207
Me & My Bike = Dylan Thomas *Me and My Bike* (1965), 38, 41, 112, 175, 179, 213
Meanjin, 154
Mearns, David C., 169
Melbourne Age, 133
Melbourne Herald, 133n
Melchiori, Giorgio, 220
Melchiori = Giorgio Melchiori *The Tightrope Walkers* (1956), 27, 157
Meller, Horst, 222
Mellors, W. H., 134
"Memories of Christmas," 23, 34, 70, 89
Memphis Commercial Appeal, 179n
Menai, Huw, 61, 62, 63, 64, 70, 91
Mercer, Vivian, 174
Merchant, W. Moelwyn, 70
Mercure de France, 218
Merkur, 221, 222
Merlin, Milton, 63n, 179n
Merton, Thomas, 193, 193n
Merwin, W. S., 145
Methodist Magazine, 163n
Methodist Recorder, 163n
Mewis, Leslie E., 68
Mexico City News, 224n
Meyer, Frank, 197
Meyer, Gerard Previn, 176
Meyerhoff, Hans, 176
Miami Herald-Leader, 186n
Miami News, 210n

Michael, D. Parry, 84
Michaels, Sidney, 189. *See* **Dylan;** "Dylan"
Micheline, Jack, 36n
Michie, James, 157
Michigan's Voices, 35
Michinton, J., 130
Miles, Hamish, 97
Miles, Josephine, 18
Millar, Joseph, 206
Millay, Edna St. Vincent, 101, 183
Miller, Arthur, 176, 212
Miller, Henry, 123, 210n
Miller, James E., 31, 203, 203n, 209, 209n
Miller, J. Hillis, 40, 184n
Miller, Joseph J., 31
Miller, Lee, 187
Miller, Mary Owings, 209
Millet, Martha, 207
Mills, Clark, 175
Mills, Ralph J., 37, 38, 185, 185n
Milton, John, 90
Minattur, Joseph, 155n
Ministry of Information, 70
"Minor Poets of Old Swansea," 57
"Minor Poets of Swansea," 57
Minton, John, 119
Miscellany = Dylan Thomas *Miscellany: Poems Stories Broadcasts* (1963), 33, 114, 116, 141n
Miscellany Two (1966), 39
"Missing," 46
"Mr. William Shakespeare," 46
Mitchison, Lois, 92
Mizener, Arthur, 171, 174
Modern Language Notes, 208–209
Modern Language Review, 129n
"Modern Poet of Gower, A," 57
"Modern Poetry," 46
Modern Review, 155n
Moffat, Ivan, 136
Mohan, Jag, 155
Mondo, 220, 221
Monroe, Harriet, 167
Montague, Gene, 184, 186
Montague, John, 193
Montale, Eugenio, 220
Montgomerie, William, 94
Month, 74n
Monthly Film Bulletin, 140–141
Montieth, Lionel, 146
Moody, J. N., 182
Moody, John, 115n
Moore, Geoffrey, 171, 171n

Moore, Harry T., 33, 123
Moore, Henry, 115
Moore, John, 128
Moore, Marianne, 168n, 176, 205
Moore, Nicholas, 123, 125, 143
Moose, Roy C., 102n
Moraes, Dom, 155n
Morehouse, Marion, 18, 21
Morgan, Douglas V., 62
Morgan, Frederick, 190
Morgan, Gerald, 41, 84
Morgan, Harold, 58
Morgan, John, 110
Morgan, Mary, 127
Morgan, Telynog Em, 36n
Morgan, T. J. W., 114
Morgan, W. D., 48
Morgan, Winifred, 80n
Morgan, W. John, 152
Morgannwg, 75n
Morley, F. V., 88
Morley, John Royston, 108
"Morning in Wales," 181
Morning Post, 98–100
Morrell, R. M., 36n
Morse, B. J., 69n
Morse, Carl, 205
Morse, Samuel French, 196
Mortimer, Penelope, 115
Morton, Guy, 100
Morton, Richard, 148
Moss, Howard, 31, 171, 172
Moss, Stanley, 34, 176
Moult, Thomas, 7, 97
"Mouse and the Woman, The," 5, 7, 13, 25, 34, 110
Moynihan, William T., 33, 181, 185, 210, 210n
Moynihan = William T. Moynihan *The Craft and Art of Dylan Thomas* (1966), 39, 66, 81, 92, 103, 106, 128, 131, 132n, 133, 148, 184n, 204, 212
Muecke, D. C., 154
Muir, Alexander, 142n
Muir, Augustus, 98
Muir, Edwin, 7, 89n, 100n, 102, 109, 119, 145, 191
Mumbles Press, 66–67
Murdy = Louise Baughan Murdy *Sound and Sense in Dylan Thomas's Poetry* (1966), 39, 103
Murdy, T. L. B., 33
Muri, John T., 204
Murphy, B. W., 209

Murphy, Gwendolen, 7
Murray, Elizabeth, 159n
Murray, George, 154
Murry, John Middleton, 94
Muste, John M., 207
Mutiny, 35
"My hero bares his nerves," 3, 6, 19
"My world is pyramid," 19, 95

Nairn, Ian, 120
Nakagiri, Masao, 223
Narceja, 35
Nash, Jørgen, 223
Nathan, Monique, 218
Nation, 173–174
National & English Review, 121
National Book League, 15, 64, 144n
National Library of Wales Journal, ix, xi
National Museum of Wales, 131
National Observer, 213
National Review, 208
Nault, Clifford A., 190
Naumann, Anthony, 36n
Neame, Alan, 159
"Nellie Wallace's Mimicry," 50
Nemerov, Howard, 171
Neuburg, Victor, 62, 93, 93n, 94, 108
Neueren Sprachen, 222, 222n, 223
Neuville, H. Richmond, 38, 186
New Directions, 6, 9, 11, 12, 18, 21, 22, 23, 25, 26, 27, 28, 29, 34, 39, 40
New Directions in Poetry & Prose, 70, 121, 167, 170
New English Review, 146n
New English Weekly, 87–88
New Haven Journal-Courier, 179n
New Leader, 200
New Masses, 182
New Measure, 214
New Mexico Quarterly, 188
New Poems = Dylan Thomas *New Poems* (1943), 11, 168, 170, 171, 174, 175, 176, 180, 183, 184
New Quarterly of Poetry, 187
New Republic, 141n, 175–176
New Road, 125
News Chronicle, 117
New Society, 161n
News of the World, 74n, 82
Newsreel, 156n
New Statesman, 111–112
New Stories, 97
Newsweek, 205–206
New Towns for Old (film), 136, 140

New Ventures, 36n
New Verse, 95–96, 97, 167
New World, 204n
New World Writing, 193, 193n
New Yorker, 171–172
New York Herald Tribune, 189
New York Herald Tribune Book Review, 173
New York Herald Tribune Magazine, 189
New York Post, 195–196
New York Review of Books, 212–213
New York Times, 199
New York Times Book Review, 180–181
New York Times Magazine, 181
New Zealand Herald, 146n
New Zealand Listener, 36n, 146n
New Zealand Truth, 146n
Nichols, Lewis, 199
Nicholson, Geoffrey, 117
Nicholson, Irene, 224n
Nicholson, Norman, 10, 122
"Nightmare, The," 47n
Nimbus, 159n
Nimrod, 125n
Nine, 150
Nineteenth Century & After, 152
Nishizaki, Ichiro, 223
Nist, John, 35, 201, 206
Noel, J., 218n
Nomad, 204n
"No man believes," 94
Norbury, James, 115
Norman, Charles, 205n
No Room at the Inn (film), 104, 141, 189
Norris, Leslie, 147
Norseman, 208n
Northern Echo, 113n
North Wales Times, 80n
Notebooks = Ralph Maud ed. *The Notebooks of Dylan Thomas* (1967, in London 1968 with the title *Poet in the Making*), 40, 65, 76, 84, 103, 121, 153, 162, 177, 181, 187, 196, 201, 206n, 213
Notes & Queries, 162
"Notes on the Art of Poetry" (= "Poetic Manifesto")
"Not from this anger," 20, 167
Not Quite Posthumous = Caitlin Thomas *Not Quite Posthumous Letters to My Daughter* (1963), 28n, 92, 103, 106, 112, 143, 173, 177, 181, 182, 189, 192, 199, 206
Nouvelle Revue Francaise, 217
Nouvelle Saison, 217

Nouvelles Littéraires, 217
Novick, Donald, 30
"Now," 4, 19, 59
Now, 150n
Nowicki, Andrzej, 223
Nowottny = Winifred Nowottny *The Language Poets Use* (1962), 33, 148
Nye, Robert, 65, 128, 129, 132n, 143
Nyren, Dorothy, 192

Oakes, Philip, 152
Oakley, Robin, 110
Oboler, Eli M., 192
Oborn, G. N., 108
O'Brien, Conor Cruise, 213
O'Brien, E. D., 156
O'Brien, Edward J., 3, 97
O'Brien, Flann, 88
Observer, 119–121
Ocampo, Victoria, 225
Occident, 193
Ochshorn, Myron, 188
O'Connor, Philip, 78, 78n, 157
O'Duffy, Eimar, 98
"O Fickle Sea," 47
O'Halloran, Michael, 79
O'Hara, James D., 29
Ohmann, Richard, 190, 190n, 212
Ojala, Aatos, 225
"Old Garbo," 8, 107
Oliver, Edith, 172
Olson, Elder, 169, 195, 204
Olson = Elder Olson *The Poetry of Dylan Thomas* (1954), 24, 95, 102, 105, 111, 118, 151, 157, 159, 160, 169, 173, 174, 175, 177, 179, 181, 182, 183, 184, 189, 191, 194, 196, 197, 198, 200, 203, 204, 204n, 205, 206, 206n, 208, 224
"O make me a mask," 11, 20, 107, 167, 182
"On a Wedding Anniversary," 10, 11, 20, 125
"Once below a time," 11, 12, 13, 20, 107
"Once it was the colour of saying," 6, 20, 39, 69
O'Neill, Dan, 198
"One Warm Saturday," 8, 13
"On no work of words," 20, 69
"On Poetry," 23, 156
"On Reading One's Own Poems," 23
"On the Marriage of a Virgin," 10, 11, 13, 20, 108, 144, 164, 185, 186
Oppel, Horst, 222
Orage, A. R., 87, 94

"Orchards, The," 4, 5, 7, 13, 25, 97, 170
Ord Och Bild, 223
Orient/West, 210n
Origin, 201–202
Origo, Iris, 150
Orlovitz, Gil, 36n
Ormerod, David, 148, 186
Ormond, John (= John Ormond Thomas)
"Orpheus," 46
Orton, I. R., 35
Orwell, Charles, 146
Orwell, George, 200
Osbiston, Alan, 137, 138
Osborn, E. B., 98
O'Sullivan, Maurice, 37
Ottaway, Robert, 142n
"Our Country," 23, 70, 140, 221
Our Country (film), 104, 138, 139, 140, 141
"Our eunuch dreams," 3, 19, 95
Our Time, 141
"Out of the Pit," 87
"Out of the sighs," 3, 9, 19, 145
Outposts, 146–147
"Over Sir John's hill," 18, 21, 39, 101, 148, 150, 162, 190
Owen, B. Evan, 122, 145, 146
Owen, Daniel, 78
Owen, Gaynor, 41
Owen, Wilfred, 23, 203
Oxford Mail, 145
Oxford Times, 145n

Pachter, Henry M., 176
Pack, Robert, 35
"Painter's Studio, A," 65, 211
Palatina, 221
Palestine Post, 133
Palmer, Herbert, 122
Palmer, Stuart, 99
Pan, 35
Panter-Downes, Mollie, 172
Pape, Mark, 177
"Paper and Sticks," 12, 20, 123
Papers of the Bibliographical Society of America, 206
Paragone, 221
Park, B. A., 198
Parker, Derek, 96
Parker, Dorothy, 88
Parker, Kathleen B., 30
Parnassus, 225
Parrott, Ian, 64
Parry, John, 144
Parry, Thomas, 71n

Parsons, I. M., 104
Partisan Review, 170
Parton Bookshop, 3, 4, 107, 118
Partridge, Colin John, 84
Patmore, Derek, 144
"Patricia, Edith, and Arnold," 8, 124
Patrick, Q., 98
Pavey, L. A., 97
Pavlovic, Miodrag, 225
"Peaches, The," 8, 13, 107, 135
Peake, Mervyn, 156
Peden, William, 177
Peel, J. H. B., 143n, 180
P.E.N., 21, 27, 124, 156n
Penguin New Writing, 135
Penrose, Roland, 149
People, 126
People's World, 118n, 119n
Perkins, Mrs. Bertie, 51, 57n, 59
Perrine, Laurence, 186
Perrott, Roy, 113
Personalist, 204n
Perspective, 184n
Perspectives USA, 204n
Peschmann, Hermann, 17, 88, 148
Peters, Robert L., 210
Peterson, Mrs. Emerson W., 179
Petrak, Nikico, 225
Petrovich, Branka, 225
Pettigrew, Lawrence, 64
Petts, John, 10, 89
Pfeiffer, Eric A., 146
Phail, Ian Sinclair, 89n
Phelps, G. H., 14
Phelps, R., 208
Phelps, Robert, 184
Philbrick, Charles, 173
Phillips, A. L., 133n
Phillips, Arthur, 154
Phillips, B. F., 62
Phillips, James, 63
Phillips, M. J., 204n
Phillips, Robert S., 163n
Phillips, W. A. P., 133
Phillips, William, 170n
Philmore, R., 98, 99
Picasso, Pablo, 117, 149, 149n
Pickrel, Paul, 183
Picture Post, 148–149
Pierpont Morgan Library, 156n
Pihodna, Joe, 189
Pike, Stephen, 118
Pine, George J., 197
Pinter, Harold, 221

Pinto, Vivian De Sola, 18
Pitman, Robert, 126
Pitter, Ruth, 95, 97
Plaid Cymru, 69
Plan, 160
Plays & Players, 158
"Plea for Intellectual Revolution, A," 68
PMLA, 210
Pocock, Robert, 144
"Poem (for Caitlin)," 69, 121, 123
"Poem for Sunday," 94
"Poem in October," 13, 14, 17, 20, 21, 34, 96, 129, 168, 221, 223
"Poem in the Ninth Month," 170
"Poem on his Birthday," 18, 21, 39, 146, 169, 178
"Poems for a Poem," 107
Poems in Sequence (proposed book), 109
Poesia e Critica, 220n
Poesie Giovanili, trans. Roberto Sanesi (1958), 220
"Poet, 1935," 58
"Poetic Licence," 90
"Poetic Manifesto," 34, 211
Poet in the Making. See **Notebooks**
Poetry, 167–169, 203, 205n
Poetry & Audience, 156n, 159n
"Poetry and the Film: A Symposium," 212
Poetry & Poverty, 151
Poetry & the People, 141
Poetry Book Magazine, 36n, 75n, 187n
Poetry Commonwealth, 157n
Poetry Digest, 204
Poetry (London), 125, 147, 158
Poetry London-New York, 125, 126
"Poetry Place: Poems by Dylan Thomas," 201
Poetry Public, 207
Poetry Quarterly, 143
Poetry Review, 114, 117
Poetry Society, 28, 117
Poetry Wales, 84
Poets of Reality = J. Hillis Miller *Poets of Reality* (1966), 40, 184n
"Poets of Swansea, The," 56, 57, 59
Poggioli, Renato, 221
Points, 109
"Poison or Grapes," 171
Polemic, 15, 125, 143–144
Politics & Letters, 147
Pollock, Jackson, 199
Pomeroy, Ralph, 92, 209
Pool, Phoebe, 12

Poore, Charles, 199
Popkin, Henry, 191
Porter, Bern, 123
Porter, Katherine Anne, 180
Porteus, Hugh Gordon, 88, 101, 105
Portis, Charles, 139
Portrait = Dylan Thomas *Portrait of the Artist as a Young Dog* (1940, and later editions), 8, 16, 26, 53, 60, 61, 79, 88, 96, 101, 104, 107, 109, 111, 113, 116, 118, 119, 122, 128, 130, 131, 132, 133, 134, 163n, 171, 172, 173, 174, 175, 179, 179n, 180, 181, 198, 207, 209, 217, 218, 219, 221, 223, 224, 225, 226
Posner, David, 196
Potocki, Count, 126, 126n
Potter, Stephen, 133
Pottersman, Arthur, 142
Potts, Paul, 92, 92n, 101, 105, 128, 133, 141, 143
Pound, Ezra, 8, 51, 115
Pound, Reginald, 91
Powell, Anthony, 133, 153
Powell, Charles, 113, 119
Powell, Dawn, 195
Powell, D. H. I., 55
Powell, Ivor, 159
Powys, T. F., 32, 91, 111n, 112, 112n
Prairie Schooner, 209–210
Pratt, Annis V., 38, 39
Praz, Mario, 160, 221
Preece, Peter, 75
"Preface to a Reading," 202
Prescott, Orville, 199
Press, John, 26, 30, 116, 153
Preston, Hayter, 93
Preston, Raymond, 91
Price, Cecil, 76, 145
Price, R. G. G., 153, 153n
Price, W. I., 177
Pringle, J. M. D., 134
Pritchett, V. S., 131
Private Eye, 115n
Privett, Katherine Jo, 182
"Process in the weather of the heart, A," 5, 13, 19, 93
Programme, 106
Progressive, 207
Prokosch, Frederic, 88
"Prologue" (= "Author's Prologue"), 131, 169n, 178
"Prologue to an Adventure," 7, 25, 53, 69, 123
Promenade, 84n

Prose & Verse, 50n
"Prose Introduction to *An Exhibition of Work by Mervyn Levy*," 15, 54
Prospect, 146
"Prospect of the Sea, A," 7, 9, 13, 25, 39, 53, 107, 218
Prospect = Dylan Thomas *A Prospect of the Sea* (1955), 25, 46n, 55, 66, 75, 79, 91, 101, 102, 105, 110, 112, 115, 119, 120, 121, 122, 127n, 128, 132, 134, 142, 143, 143n, 145, 151, 152, 154, 157, 160, 161n, 183, 190n, 217, 218, 219, 222
Providence Journal, 172–173
Pruischutz, Hildegard, 222
Pryce-Jones, Alan, 173, 189
Prys-Jones, A. G., 61, 62, 63, 74, 75, 78, 79, 151
Psychiatric Quarterly, 209n
Pudney, John, 97, 149, 149n
Pugh, Charles, 63
Pujals, Esteban, 224
Pujman, Petr, 225
Punch, 153
Punshon, E. R., 98
Purdom, C. B., 91
Purdum, Richard, 36n
Purpose, 68, 109

Quaderno di Traduzioni, 220
Quarterly Journal of Speech, 204
Quarterly of Films, Radio & Television, 91n
Queen, Ellery, 98
Queen's Quarterly, 208
Quennell, Peter, 154, 154n
"Questionnaire: the Cost of Letters," 130, 130n
Quicksilver, 35, 36n
Quigly, Isabel, 105
Quinn, Kerker, 173, 184
Quinn, Patrick F., 181
"Quite Early One Morning," 23, 39, 70, 181
Quite Early = Dylan Thomas *Quite Early One Morning* (1954), 22, 23, 26, 46n, 55, 57n, 63, 63n, 75, 76, 78, 79, 80n, 81, 89n, 102, 105, 110, 111, 113, 115, 118, 119, 121, 128, 142, 143, 145, 149, 149n, 151, 152, 155, 156, 157, 163n, 169, 172, 173, 174, 177, 178, 180, 181, 184, 186, 186n, 187n, 189, 190, 191, 192, 195, 196, 197, 198, 199, 200, 201, 204, 205, 207, 207n, 210n, 217, 219, 221, 222, 223, 224n

Raboni, Giovanni, 220n
Radice, Sheila, 88

Radio Times, 89n, 91n. 92n
Rago, Henry, 167
Rahv, Philip, 170n
Raine, Kathleen, 76, 111, 125n, 146n
Rainer, Dachine, 181, 206
Raj, Shankar, 155
Ralph the Books (= Ralph Wishart), 65
Rand, Charles C., 177
Rann, 150–151
Ransom, Harry H., 211
Ransom, John Crowe, 170, 171, 171n
Raskin, Ellen, 26
Rathkey, W. A., 62
Raven, Etienne, 63
Raven, Simon, 106
Ravitz, Abe C., 196
Rawson, Claude, 33, 162
Ray, Danny, 64
Ray, Paul C., 162
Raymond, David, 78, 127
Raymond, John, 112
Razor's Edge, 193n
Rea, J., 190
Read, Bill, 31, 106, 161, 177, 211
Read = Bill Read *The Days of Dylan Thomas* (1964), 37, 45n, 49n, 66, 76, 79, 103, 106, 112, 116, 177, 195, 212, 218
Read, Herbert, ix, 61, 123, 156, 156n, 170
Reader's Guide = William York Tindall *A Reader's Guide to Dylan Thomas* (1962), 33, 92. *See also* **Tindall**
Readers News, 71n
"Real Christ and the False, The," 68
Ream, Donald C., 187
Reavey, George, 111
Rebecca's Daughters = Dylan Thomas *Rebecca's Daughters* (1965), 38, 41, 66, 76, 116, 132, 143, 161, 179, 192
"Recent Novels," 88
Recorded Sound, 163
Recordings, 112, 120, 130, 163, 198, 199, 204, 207
Records & Recordings, 198n
Reddington, Alphonsus, 41
Redmond, Patrick, 127
Rees, Alwyn D., 76
Rees, Cadman, 83
Rees, Caleb, 64
Rees, David, 71, 103, 106
Rees, Goronwy, 102
Rees, Ioan Bowen, 76
Rees, Leslie, 55, 144
Rees, Richard, 94, 158
"Refusal to Mourn, A," 9, 12, 13, 14, 17,

20, 27, 39, 129, 147, 175, 185, 190n, 222, 223

Rego, Paula, 91

Reichert, Karl H., 222

Reid, Alastair, 205

Reid, Katherine, 79

Reifer, May, 28

"Reminiscences of Childhood," 23, 34, 54, 60, 89, 156

Renascence, 203

Reoch, Ernest, 142n

"Replies to an Enquiry," 23, 220n

Reporter, 201

"Request to an Obliging Poet", 46

"Request to Leda," 11, 129

"Resolutions for 1934," 201

Resor, Robert, 188

"Return Journey," 23, 32, 34, 54, 57n, 104, 131, 187n

Revell, Peter, 212

Review of English Literature, 163

Review of Reviews, 145

Revue des Langues Vivantes, 218, 218n

Rexroth, Kenneth, 16, 187, 188, 193, 202, 205, 205n

Reynolds, Reginald, 129

Reynolds News, 127

Rhode, John, 98, 99

Rhys, Aneurin, 117, 143

Rhys, Ernest, 70

Rhys, Keidrych, 11, 53, 56, 61, 69, 69n, 70, 77n, 78, 103, 106, 108, 113, 126n, 141

Rice, L. L., 188

Rice, Philip Blair, 170

Richards, Ceri, 55, 115n, 125, 125n

Richards, Tom H., 61

Richardson, Kathleen Valmai, 118

Richardson, Maurice, 120

Richart, Bette, 182

Richmond, Lee J., 186

Rickey, Mary Ellen, 185

Ricks, Christopher, 116

Ridler, Anne, 9, 17

Riggs, Thomas, 174

Right Review, 126

Rimbaud, Arthur, 160

Rischbiter, Henning, 222

Ritchey, John, 179

Rivista di Cinema Italiano, 221

Rizzardi, Alfredo, 221

Rizzi, Mariapina, 220n

Roach, Helen, 163n

Road, Alan, 56, 121

Robb, Crawford, 156

Robbins, R. C., 197n

Roberts, Bechhofer, 98

Roberts, C. Benson, 63, 112

Roberts, Denys Kilham, 3, 4, 5

Roberts, Duncan, 101

Roberts, Enid, 65

Roberts, G. L., 76

Roberts, Glyn, 61

Roberts, Lynette, 55

Roberts, Michael, 4, 17, 97, 109, 167

Roberts, Peter, 158

Roberts, Sally, 79

Robie, Rurton A., 192

Robins, Natalie S., 36n

Robinson, Theodore R., 164

Roche, Arthur Somers, 99

Rocky Mountain News, 203n

Rocky Mountain Review, 183, 184

Rodgers, W. R., 90, 91, 116, 150, 160

Roditi, Edouard 168, 168n

Rodman, Selden, 12, 16

Rodocanachi, Lucia (Maria), 221

Rodway, Allan, 211

Roethke, Theodore, 156, 168n, 176, 185n

Rogers, Timothy, 148

Rolo, Charles J., 178, 179

Rolph = J. Alexander Rolph *Dylan Thomas: A Bibliography* (1956), 3n, 4, 5, 6, 8, 9, 10, 11, 17, 18, 22, 27, 91, 101, 103, 110, 113, 115, 118, 132, 160, 161, 206, 206n

Rolph, John, xi, 113, 206

"Romantic Isle, The," 89n

Roose-Evans, James, 40

Rosati, Salvatore, 220

Rosberg, Rose, 210

Rose, W. K., 115n

Rosenberg, James L., 177, 191

Rosenberger, Francis C., 175

Rosenfeld, Paul, 173

Rosenthal, M. L., 31, 174, 177

Roskolenko, Harry, 178, 178n

Ross, Alan, 101, 145, 158

Ross, Ethel, 46n, 64, 81

Rothberg, Winterset (pseud.), 168

Roughton, Roger, 110

Roussillat, Suzanne, 15, 145, 217

Routley, Eric, 155

Rowe, Dilys, 54, 60, 70

Rowland, Richard, 91n

Rowlands, Sheila, 75, 77

Roy, Ian, 149n

Royal Festival Hall, 132
Rubenstein, J. S., 182
Rudikoff, Sonya, 200
Rundall, Jeremy, 116
Russell, Francis, 179
Russell, Peter, 150
Ryan, Patrick, 153

Sachs, Arieh, 164
Sackville-West, Edward, 163n
Sackville-West, V., 119
"Saint about to fall, A," 6, 13, 20, 125
St. Louis Post-Dispatch, 198
St. Martin's Review. 117n
Salt, Sydney, 94
Salter, William, 111, 112
Salt Lake Tribune, 179n
Salzburger Nachrichter, 222
Sampson, George, 32
Sampson, Paul, 197
Samuel, Evan, 71
Samuel, Graham, 65
Samuel, Viscount, 147n
Sanborn, Ruth Barr, 100
Sandell, Veli, 225
Sanders, Charles, 30
Sanesi, Roberto, 220, 220n, 221
Sanesi = Roberto Sanesi *Dylan Thomas* (1960), 103, 218, 220
San Francisco Chronicle, 191
Sansom, William, 157n
Santa Barbara News-Press, 172n
Saroyan, William, 160, 160n
Saturday Evening Post, 160n
Saturday Night, 197–198
Saturday Review, 176–177
Saul, Patrick, 163
Saunders, Thomas, 208n
Savage, D. S., 126, 141n, 167, 176
Savage, Henry, 92
Sayers, Dorothy L., 99
Scannell, Vernon, 95, 151
Scarfe, Francis, 10, 70, 129, 134
Scharper, Philip, 200
Schevill, James, 191
Schimanski, Stefan, 16
Schlauch, Margaret, 27
Schmeditz, Wolfgang, 222
Schmidt, Dana Adams, 199
Schmidt, Kenneth J., 180
Schoeck, R. J., 188
Schoff, Gretchen Holstein, 40
Scholes, Robert, 36n
"School for Witches, The," 7, 25, 110, 170

School Librarian, 161n
"School Memories," 46
Schott, Webster, 198
Schuchart, Max, 219
Schuster, Edgar H., 208
Schwartz, Delmore, 176, 180
Scotland, 100n
Scotsman, 132n
Scott, Caroline, 160
Scott, Eleanor M., 173
Scott, Hardiman, 146
Scott, Nathan A., 38
Scott, Sutherland, 99
Scott, Tom, 91, 158
Scott, Winfield Townley, 172, 173, 176, 177, 205
Scottish Bookman, 106
Scott-James, R. A., 109
Scriven, R. C., 152, 153
Scrutiny, 76, 134, 144, 157
Scudamore, W. K., 114
Seager, Allan, 185n
Searle, Humphrey, 153n
Searle, Ronald, 150
Seattle Post Intelligencer, 179
"Second Best, The," 87
"Seed-at-zero, The," 4, 19
Selected Letters = Constantine FitzGibbon ed. *Selected Letters of Dylan Thomas* (1966, 1967), 39, 66, 92, 103, 106, 112, 116, 120, 121, 122, 125n, 128, 131, 132n, 133, 153, 153n, 161, 162, 172, 173, 176, 177, 179, 181, 187, 197n, 198, 199, 200, 203n, 206, 207n, 213, 214
Selected Writings = Dylan Thomas *Selected Writings of Dylan Thomas* (1946), 12, 13, 168, 171, 172, 173, 174, 175, 176, 180, 184, 186, 187, 188, 217
Semmler, Clement, 134
Sennet, 159n
Sennish, Robert Brady, 28
Sergeant, Howard, 88, 122, 146, 148, 163, 163n
Seven, 9n, 123–124
"Seven Letters to Oscar Williams," 193
Seventeen, 213
Sewanee Review, 184
Sewell, Elizabeth, 26n
Seymour, William Kean, 28, 117n, 118, 122, 160
Seymour-Smith, Martin, 203
"Shall gods be said to thump the clouds," 4, 19

Shapiro, Karl, 31, 95, 156, 167, 169, 169n, 176, 209
Sharp, Willoughby, 98
Shaw, Fred, 210n
Shawe-Taylor, Desmond, 163n
Shenandoah, 192–193
Shephard, Peter, 64
Shepherd, T. B., 152n
Sherek, Henry, 92n
Sheridan, Mary, 120
Sherman, Thomas B., 198
Shershow, John C., 33
Shestack, Melvin, 208
Shetland Times, 113n
Shiel, M. P., 24
Shields, Robert W., 177
Shigaku, 223
Shimanski, Stefan, 184n
Shivpuri, Jagdish, 155
Shorr, Ray, 200
"Should lanterns shine," 6, 19, 96
Shrapnel, Norman, 113
Shulman, Milton, 142
Shuttleworth, Martin, 111
Siddha, 155n
Sidney, Sir Philip, 23
Siegel, Eli, 35, 173
Sier, Arthur G., 141
Sieveking, Lance, 115n
Sillen, Samuel, 182
Simbolica, 178n
Simon, Jean, 218
Simon, John, 190, 190n, 200
Simpson, Alan, 204
"Sincerest Form of Flattery, The," 47
Sinclair, Andrew, 40, 40n, 213. *See* "Adventures in the Skin Trade" (play)
Sinclair, T. A., 102
Singer, Burns, 101, 103
Singh, Manjeet Lal, 155
Sinha, Krishna N., 155
"Sir Philip Sidney," 23
Sitwell, Edith, ix, 3, 27, 29, 90, 96, 102, 107, 109, 114, 114n, 115, 116, 116n, 120, 141, 144, 147, 154, 169, 173, 178, 189, 203
Sitwell, Osbert, 102
Sjöstrand, Osten, 219
Skelton, Robin, 27, 37
Skvorecký, Josef, 225
Slater, Humphrey, 143
Slater, Montagu, 21

Slevin, Gerard, 151
Slivka, David, 131
Slocombe, Marie, 163
Slote, Bernice, 31, 203, 203n, 210
Smart, P. E., 46, 46n
Smith, A. J., 32, 162, 162n
Smith, Harrison, 177
Smith, Janet Adam, 3
Smith, John, 28
Smith, Neil, 224n
Smith, Peter Duval, 161n
Smith, Ray, 192
Smith, R. G., 155
Smith, Stevie, 112, 145
Smith, Timothy d'Arch, 161
Smith, Vivian, 134
Smith, William Jay, 205
Smithies, Alan, 142
Smythyman, Kenrick, 141n
Snell, Gordon, 142
Social Education, 213
Socialist Call, 178
Socialist Leader, 128n
Söderberg, Lasse, 219
"Solace from Swansea," 207
Solomon, I. L., 177
"Song of the Mischievous Dog, The," 28, 45, 144
Sonnets, 13, 19, 37, 107, 110, 185, 186, 217
Sôtemann, G., 219
Souster, Raymond, 36n
Soutar, William, 94
South Atlantic Quarterly, 168n
Southeby's, 103
Southern Review, 170n
Southern Review (Australia), 164
South Wales Argus, 79
South Wales Daily (or *Evening*) *Post*, 49–56, 57n, 58, 59, 60, 81
South Wales Echo, 80
South Wales Sunday News, 67n
South Wales Voice, 80n
Southwest Review, 208n
Spacks, Patricia Meyer, 185
Spark, Muriel, 172
"Speaking Personally," 153
Spectator, 104–106
Spencer, Bernard, 96
Spender, Stephen, 14, 27, 87, 89n, 95, 102, 102n, 104, 111, 118, 120, 124, 129, 130, 133, 134, 144, 145, 153, 156, 156n, 157, 180
Spettatore Italiano, 220

Speyser, Patricia E., 31
Sphinx, 114n
Spilka, Mark, 209
"Spire cranes, The," 6, 13, 20, 69, 124, 167
Spirit, 188
"Spoon River Anthology," 191
Spread Eagle, 46n
Sprigg, C. St. John, 98
Spurling, Hilary, 106
Squire, J. C., 109, 109n
Srigley, Michael, 149n
Stafford, William, 169, 195
Stage, 158n
Stand, 35
Stanford, Derek, 102, 111, 132, 160, 208, 208n
Stanford = Derek Stanford *Dylan Thomas: A Literary Study* (1954), 24, 75, 91, 102, 112, 119, 146, 152, 155, 157, 160, 174, 192, 197, 208n
Stanier, Maida, 145
Stanners, H. H., 100
Star, 142n
Starr, S. T., 114
Starrett, Vincent, 194, 195
Stauffer, Donald A., 15
Stauffer, Robert E., 175
Stearns, Marshall W., 184, 184n, 185
Stefanile, Felix, 35
Stein, Arnold, 208
Stein, Gertrude, 8
Steiner, George, 171
Stephens, James, 90, 156
Stephens, J. Oliver, 82
Stephens, Meic, 79, 84
Stephens, Peter J., 187, 187n
Stephens, S. Martin, 48
Stevens, Elizabeth G., 28
Stevens, Wallace, 168n, 171, 176
Stevens, W. F., 62
Stevenson, Robert Louis, 33
Stewart, J. I. M., 157
Stewart, Sarah, 180
Stewart, S. S., 143n
Stock, Noel, 154
Stockholms-Tidningen, 219
Stocking, D. M., 191
Stonesifer, R. J., 185
Stonier, G. W., 111
"Story, A," 23, 25, 91, 191
Stout, Rex, 99
Strand, 147

Stravinsky, Igor, 24, 64, 115, 144, 144n
Street, James, 100
Strickhausen, Harry, 169
Strong, L. A. G., 9
Student Forward, 149n
Summers, John, 76
Sun, 142
Sunday At Home, 153n
Sunday Express, 126–127
Sunday Graphic, 126n
Sunday Referee, 3, 4, 93–94, 104, 107, 108, 111, 144
Sunday Telegraph, 133
Sunday Times, 96, 114–116, 117
Sunday Times Magazine, 116–117
Sur, 225
Surrealists, 123, 162, 168, 175
Suss, Irving D., 182
Suto, Nobuko, 223
Sverdrup, Harald, 223
Svetová literatura, 225
Swain, Barbara, 193n
Swan, Maurice, 172n
Swan, 46n
"Swansea and the Arts," 54
Swansea & West Wales Guardian, 67–68
Swansea Grammar School Magazine, 45–49, 50, 53, 144
Swansea Public Library, xi, 46n, 55, 82n
Sward, Robert S., 209
Sweeney, John L., 9, 12, 176, 192, 202
Swenson, May, 191n
Swift, Jonathan, 162
Swinburne, A., 174
Swingler, Randall, 87
Swinnerton, Frank, 119
Sydney Bulletin, 134n
Sydney Morning Herald, 134
Symons, Julian, 88, 107, 121, 153, 167, 170, 170n, 171, 171n
Symons, W. T., 109
Synge, John, 92

Tablet, 151
Taggart, Joseph, 142n
Taig, Thomas, 76
Talbot, Norman, 164
Talisman, 191
Tallant, Mildred C., 178
Tallmer, Jerry, 211
Tamarack Review, 210
Tambimuttu, M. J., 10, 125, 125n, 126, 158

Taormina Prize, 62
Tarnopolsky, Alejandro, 225
Tarnowska, Krystyna, 223
Tate, Allen, 29, 168n
Tatler, 131
Tattersall, Malcolm H., 118
Taubman, Howard, 199
"Taverns in General," 88
Taylor, Donald, 22, 137
Taylor, Geoffrey, 101
Taylor, John Russell, 92
Taylor, Phoebe Atwood, 98, 99
Taylor, Robert, 197
Teacher, 164
Tedlock = E. W. Tedlock ed. *Dylan Thomas: The Legend and the Poet* (1960), 15, 31, 56, 64, 71, 75, 78, 80, 88, 92, 97, 101, 103, 105, 112, 114, 116, 118, 119, 120, 127, 128, 129, 132, 142, 143, 144, 144n, 145, 145n, 148, 155, 156, 156n, 157, 160, 161, 162n, 168n, 169, 171, 176, 184, 187n, 190, 205, 218, 219, 220
Tellier, A. -R., 218
Tellier = A.-R. Tellier *La poésie de Dylan Thomas: Thèmes et formes* (1963), 129n, 148, 218
"Telling the Truth to the Public," 67
Tel Quel, 218
Temple, Ruth Z., 40
Tempo, 221
Temps de la Poesie, 217
Tenby Observer, 79
"Terrible Tale of Tom Tipplewhite, The," 47
Terry, Arthur, 151
Texas Quarterly, 211, 211n
Texas Studies in Language & Literature, 210n
Texas University, 64, 131
Texte und Zeichen, 222
"That sanity be kept," 93
"That the sum sanity might add to nought," 67
Thayer, Lee, 100
Theatre Arts, 191
Theatre World, 158
"Then was my neophyte," 6, 13, 19, 109, 110
Theology, 163n
"There was a Saviour," 10, 11, 13, 20, 33, 34, 129
These Are the Men (film), 104, 137, 141

"This bread I break," 6, 13, 19, 60, 87, 102, 163, 222n
This is Colour (film), 135
"This Side of the Truth," 13, 20, 108, 175, 180
"This was the crucifixion on the mountain," 110, 217
Thomas, Beb Bowen, 78
Thomas, Caitlin, 5, 18, 26, 29n, 64, 69, 72, 77, 77n, 112, 116, 120, 121, 123, 126, 126n, 127, 133, 160, 179, 187, 187n, 194n, 196, 199, 207n, 221. *See also* **Leftover Life; Not Quite Posthumous**
Thomas, D. J., 45, 48, 58, 60, 65, 77, 180
Thomas, D. S., 118
Thomas, Edward, 7, 97, 122
Thomas, Edward M., 79
Thomas, Florence (Mrs. D. J.), 64, 77, 77n, 81, 83, 83n, 199
Thomas, Gilbert, 118, 163n
Thomas, Gwyn, 62, 65, 151
Thomas, H. W. V., 46
Thomas, Johnny, 83
Thomas, John Ormond, 22, 54, 55, 149
Thomas, Leslie, 142n
Thomas, Llewellyn, 53, 64
Thomas, R. George, 63, 69n, 75, 148
Thomas, Rosemary, 188
Thomas, R. S., 34, 97
Thomas, Stuart, 102
Thomas, S. Vaughan. *See* Vaughan-Thomas, A. Spencer
Thomas, T. K., 155
Thomas, W. D., 29, 71
Thomas, Wynford Vaughan, 50n, 53, 91n, 92, 102
Thompson, Dunstan, 175, 182
Thompson, Francis, 119
Thompson, John, 35
Thompson, Kent E., 38, 57n, 76
Thompson, Tracy, 35
Thomson, David Cleghorn, 106
Thomson, George Malcolm, 142
Thornton, Alan, 76
Thoth, 213
Thought, 155
"Three Nursery Rhymes," 46
"Three Poems," 23
Three Weird Sisters (film), 104, 141
Thwaite, Anthony, 29, 105, 158
Thygesen, Erik, 223
Tikkemeijer, Henk, 219
Tillotson, Geoffrey, 104

[258] *Index*

Tillyard, E. M. W., 103
Time, 186–187
Time & Tide, 96, 100–101
Times, 81, 130–131, 193
Times Bookshop, 65, 131
Times Educational Supplement, 155
Times Literary Supplement, 101–103
Times of India, 155n
Tindall, William York, 15, 188, 188n
Tindall (= **Reader's Guide**), 92, 103, 112, 160, 192
Tinsley, A. F., 70, 71
"Today, this insect," 6, 13, 19, 109, 185, 186
Todd, Ruthven, 70, 87, 88, 92, 157, 169
Todd, William B., 161
Toksvig, Signe, 88
Tomalin, Nicholas, 116
"Tombstone told when she died, The," 6, 20, 123, 124, 168, 170, 185
Tomlinson, Charles, 105
"Tom Twp," 218
Toohy, Elizabeth, 174
Toosey, C. B., 118
"To Others than You," 9, 11, 20, 123, 174
"To the Spring-spirit," 46
Toulson, Shirley, 164
Town, 115n
Toynbee, Philip, 119, 120, 121
Trace, 207
"Tragedy of Swansea's Comic Genius," 57
Tramp, 178
Transactions of the Honorable Society of Cymmrodorion, 71n
Transatlantic Review, 211n
Transformation Three, 184n
Transition, 110
"Tree, The," 5, 25, 94
Treece, Henry, 9, 10, 14, 16, 75, 87, 88, 114, 123, 124, 125, 125n, 146, 174, 178, 184n
Treece = Henry Treece *Dylan Thomas 'Dog Among the Fairies'* (1949, 1956), 14, 16, 27, 54, 61, 74, 75, 88, 90, 101, 103, 111, 114, 118, 134, 141, 142, 143, 146, 157n, 160, 168, 180, 183, 189, 191, 204, 208
Tremayne, Sydney, 142
Trewin, J. C., 91n, 92, 156
Tribune, 127–128
"Tributes to Hugh MacDiarmid," 124
Trick, A. E., 51, 67, 67n, 68, 83, 83n, 89n, 93, 211

Trinity College Dublin Magazine, 149n
"Triolet," 46
Tripp, John, 106
Tritschler, Donald, xi, 210
Troop, Robert, 116
"True Story, The," 25, 126, 193
Truss, Seldon, 100
Truth, 152–153
"Tub, The," 47
Tucker, Martin, 40
Turco, Lewis, 175
Turner, Josiah, 149n
Turner, W. J., 104
Turner, W. Price, 143
Tusiani, Joseph, 205
Tutuola, Amos, 119
"Twelve," 67
Twentieth Century, 152
Twentieth Century (Australia), 154n
Twentieth Century Literature, 193n
Twentieth Century Verse, 121
Twenty-five Poems = Dylan Thomas *Twenty-five Poems* (1936), 4, 6, 19, 52, 58, 59, 60, 61, 68, 69, 87, 95, 96, 100n, 101, 104, 107, 108, 109, 110, 111, 113, 113n, 114, 117, 118, 119, 121, 122, 141, 153n, 167, 217
"Twenty-four years," 6, 9, 10, 13, 20, 107, 186
Twenty-six Poems (1950), 17
Twenty Years = Dylan Thomas *Twenty Years A-Growing* (1964), 37, 39, 46n, 79, 103, 127n, 128, 129, 132, 148, 152, 161
Two Cities, 123
"Two Decorations," 47
Two Epigrams of Fealty (1954), 23
"Two Images," 47
"Two Poems Towards a Poem," 110
Two Tales (1968), 41
Tyler, Froom, 55, 56
Tyler, Harmon, 187
Tyler, Parker, 123, 169, 171, 171n, 212
Tynan, Kenneth, 120, 120n, 178

"Under Milk Wood" (play), ix, 35, 48, 55, 62, 63, 64, 65, 66, 75, 77, 79, 80, 83, 91, 92, 101, 111, 112, 113, 115, 117, 119, 120, 122, 127, 130, 131, 132, 133, 148, 151, 152, 153, 155, 158, 162, 172, 174, 176, 177, 181, 182, 187, 189, 190, 191, 199, 200, 201, 205, 212
Under Milk Wood = Dylan Thomas *Under Milk Wood* (1954, and later editions), 22, 28, 29, 37, 39, 41, 46n, 55, 63, 66, 75,

76, 78, 82, 91, 92, 97, 101, 102, 103, 105, 110, 111, 112, 113, 115, 117, 118, 119, 121, 127n, 128, 129n, 130, 134, 142, 142n, 143, 143n, 145, 151, 152, 154, 155, 157, 158, 159, 163n, 164, 169, 172, 173, 174, 175, 177, 178, 179, 180, 183, 184, 191, 191n, 192, 195, 196, 197, 198, 199, 203, 206n, 207, 208, 209n, 212, 212n, 217, 218, 219, 220, 221, 222, 223, 224, 224n, 225

Unicorn, 162
Union Seminary Quarterly Review, 212
U.S. Quarterly Book Review, 204n
Universitidad de Mexico, 224
University of Chicago Magazine, 204n
University of Chicago Round Table, 204
University of Denver Quarterly, 213
University of Kansas City Review, 209
University of Toronto Quarterly, 204n
University of Toronto Varsity, 210n
University of Wales Review, 76
"Unluckily for a Death," 11, 20. 107
Untermeyer, Louis, 10, 26, 177n, 183
Urquhart, Fred, 88

Valk, Gordon, 99
Vallins, G. H., 31
Vancouver Province, 190n
Van den Bergh, T. E., 118
Vanderbilt, Gloria, 177
Van Der Steen, Eric, 219
Van Dine, S. S., 99
Van Doran, Mark, 18
Van O'Connor, William, 168, 168n
Vanson, Frederick, 163n
Varnai, Ugo, 221
Varnbury, Robert, 114
Varney, Harold Lord, 197
Vassar Alumnae Magazine, 200n
Vassar Chronicle, 193n
Vassar Miscellany News, 193n
Vaughan, Richard, 62
Vaughan-Thomas, A. I., 180
Vaughan-Thomas, A. Spencer, 46n, 52, 57
Vendler, Helen Hennessy, 183
Venture, 35
Vergnas, Raymond Las, 144, 217
Verschoyle, Derek, 104
"Verse of James Chapman Woods," 57
Vesey, Paul, 36n
"Vest, The," 25, 126, 200
Vice Versa, 182
Victor, Roydon, 97
Views, 35
Villa, José Garcia, 150, 205

Village Voice, 208
Vinduet, 223
Virginia Quarterly Review, 174–175
"Vision and Prayer," 13, 14, 18, 20, 129, 145, 184, 186
"Visitor, The," 4, 5, 6, 25, 34, 97
"Visit to America, A," 22, 23, 39, 91, 186, 188, 221
"Visit to Grandpa's, A," 8, 14, 27, 39, 88, 135
Voeten, Bert, 219
Vogel, Joseph F., 32
Vogue, 187, 187n, 188
Voice of Scotland, 124
Voices, 175
Volksbühne, 222
von Cramon, Enzio, 222
von Hutten, Baroness, 99

Wade, Henry, 99
Wade, Rosalind, 118
Wahl, Jean, 145, 217
Wain, John, x, 120, 154, 154n, 157, 184, 212, 212n, 220n
Wake, 168
Wales, 8, 53, 60, 61, 69–71, 101, 107, 113, 121, 124, 127, 207
"Wales and the Artist," 23
Wales—Green Mountain, Black Mountain (film), 141
Wall, Bernard, 142
Wallace, Edward T., 198
Wallace, Nellie, 50, 92
Wall Street Journal, 214
"Walter de la Mare as a Prose Writer," 14, 23
Walters, Raymond, 177
Walt Whitman Review, 203n
Wanning, Andrews, 170, 170n
Warburton, Thomas, 219
"War Can't Produce Poetry," 14
Ward, A. J., 46, 47
Warner, Thomas, 53, 60
Warren, C. Henry, 122
Warren, Robert Penn, 17, 168n
Washington Post, 197
Washington Star, 197n
"Was there a time," 19, 60, 87
"Watchers, The," 45
Watkins, Vernon, 21, 26, 27, 54, 56, 56n, 76, 76n, 90, 102, 106, 107, 120, 130, 150, 156, 157, 163, 169, 179, 192, 193, 211, 220n. *See also* **Letters to Vernon Watkins**

Watson, Boris, 102
Watson, Peter, 129
Watson, Wilfred, 35, 75
Watts, Richard, 195
Way, Brian, 69n, 76, 105, 162
Weales, Gerald, 193
Weatherby, W. J., 114
Weatherhead, Benet, 151
Webb, Hari, 84, 84n
Webb, Phyllis, 36
Webster, Harvey Curtis, 200
Webster, Margaret, 191
Wedman, Les, 190n
Weekend Telegraph, 133
Weekly Mail, 62n
Weekly Post, 156n
Weeks, Edward, 178
Wells, Henry W., 189
Wells, H. G., 88
Welsh Anvil, 76
Welsh Gazette, 54n, 72–74
Welshman, 77
"Welshman as Poet," 178
Welsh Nation, 69
Welsh Nationalist, 69
Welsh Outlook, 83n
"Welsh Poets," 23
Welsh Review, 71, 71n
Welsh Secondary Schools Review, 84
"We lying by seasand," 4, 5, 20, 69, 147, 167
Wending, 219
Werry, Richard R., 189
Wesleyan Poets, 35
West, Anthony, 11, 172
West, Geoffrey, 97
West, Paul, 148
West, Ray B., 183
Western Express, 67n
Western Humanities Review, 203
Western Mail, ix, 61–66, 79, 81
Western Review, 184
Wetmore, Thomas, 211
Weymouth, Anthony, 98
Whaley, F. J., 99
Wharton, Gordon, 160
Wheatley, Dennis, 99
Wheelock, John Hall, 188
"When all my five and country senses see," 6, 7, 13, 20, 167, 186
"When I Woke," 11, 20, 123, 144, 174
"When, like a running grave," 3, 6, 12, 19
"When once the twilight locks," 5, 13, 19, 95

"Where once the waters of your face," 4, 5, 6, 19, 93
"Where Tawe Flows," 8, 39
Whetstone, 208
Whitaker, Frank, 96n
White, Eric Walter, 144n
White, Gertrude M., 203
White, William, 206, 206n, 210, 210n
Whitehead, Frank, 18
Whitman, Walt, 31, 203, 203n, 209n
Whittemore, Reed, 183
Whittington-Egan, Richard, 160, 161
"Who Do You Wish Was With Us?", 8, 39
"Why east wind chills," 6, 19, 87
Wickes, George, 123
Wiggin, Maurice, 126
Wilcock, Juan Rodolfo, 225
Wilcox, Ella Wheeler, 46
Wilder, Amos N., 21
Wilder, Thornton, 176
"Wilfred Owen," 23
Wilke, John, 162
Wilkins, Eithne, 103
Williams, A. R., 74
Williams, Charles, 107
Williams, Emlyn (= "A Boy Growing Up"), 55, 63, 70, 102, 112, 115, 130, 158, 177, 182, 187, 191, 199, 205, 212n
Williams, Forest, 203, 203n
Williams, Griffith, 66, 79, 145
Williams, Gwyn, 151
Williams, Islwyn, 65
Williams, Ivy, 64
Williams, J. D., 49, 50, 51, 52, 52n, 58
Williams, J. Morgan, 49, 64
Williams, J. Morris, 49
Williams, John Ellis, 75
Williams, John Stuart, 84
Williams, J. Roberts, 82
Williams, M. G., 82n
Williams, Michael, 71
Williams, Miles Vaughan, 141
Williams, Morys, 64
Williams, Mrs. G., 81
Williams, Oscar, 9, 9n, 10, 11, 12, 14, 18, 24, 28, 34, 168, 183, 193, 196, 199
Williams, Raymond, 92, 147, 162
Williams, Rhydwen, 82n
Williams, Robert Coleman, 40. *See* **Concordance**
Williams, Tennessee, 176
Williams, T. H., 66
Williams, T. H. Parry, 80n

Williams, Tom, 64
Williams, Trevor, 142
Williams, William Carlos, 88, 168n, 184, 201, 201n, 202n, 205, 205n
Williams, W. T., 96n
Willingham, John R., 192
Wills, Cecil M., 100
Willy, Margaret, 96, 147
Wilson, Eve, 118
Wind & the Rain, 146
"Winding Film, A," 168
Winestock, Alvin, 204
"Winter's Tale, A," 13, 20, 129n, 168, 210, 213, 217, 220
Wisconsin Studies in Contemporary Literature, 212
Wishart, Ralph, 64, 65, 144, 220n
Witham, Alice H., 201
Witter, Jere, 191
Wittreich, Joseph Anthony, 214
Wollman, Maurice, 15, 30
"Woman Speaks, The," 94
Wood, Frederick T., 148
Wood, J. N., 177
Woodcock, George, 151, 151n, 200, 201
Woods, James Chapman, 57, 59
Woodthorpe, R. C., 98
Woolf, Cecil, 161
World I Breathe = Dylan Thomas *The World I Breathe* (1939), 5, 168, 170, 170n, 171, 171n, 172, 172n, 173, 174, 175, 176
World Review, 145–146
Worthing, Beatrice M., 79
Wright, David, 22, 101, 104, 145
Writer's Markets & Methods, 179n
Wyett, Euphemia Van Rensselaer, 205

Xirau, Ramón, 224

Yale Literary Magazine, 199, 205
Yale Poetry Review, 183n
Yale Review, 183
Yale University Library Gazette, 212n
Yates, Andrew, 64
Y Cymro, 66n, 80n
Y Ddinas, 78
Y Drych, 82
Yeats, W. B., 37, 46, 87, 222
Yellowjacket, 126
Yeomans, W. E., 213
Yerbury, Grace D., 203
Y Genhinen, 82
Yorkshire Evening Press, 143n
Yorkshire Observer, 143n
Yorkshire Post, 143
Young, Kenneth, 132, 157
"Your breath was shed," 15, 125, 126, 126n
"Youth Calls to Age," 57
Yr Einion, 76
Yr Enfys, 82
Y Traethodydd, 80n
Y Tyst, 80n

Zabel, Morton Dawen, 167
Zahn, Curtis, 209
Zandvoort, R. W., 148
Zebra, 149n
Zigerell, James, 186
Ziman, Anna P., 27
Ziman, H. D., 132
Zinnes, Harriet, 198
Zuideme, I., 118